Tetrazzini in the title role of *Lucia di Lammermoor*

Luisa Tetrazzini
the Florentine Nightingale

Charles Neilson Gattey

Published in Great Britain by
SCOLAR PRESS
Gower House
Croft Road
Aldershot
Hants GU11 3HR
England

British Library Cataloguing in Publication Data

Gattey, Charles Neilson
    Luisa Tetrazzini: Florentine Nightingale
    I. Title 782.1092

ISBN 1 85928 010 2

Phototypeset by Intype, London. Printed in Great Britain at the
University Press, Cambridge

In memory of my mother

Contents

List of Plates

Frontispiece: Tetrazzini as Lucia di Lammermoor
(courtesy of William R. Moran)

(between pages 112 and 113)

1 Tetrazzini as Violetta
   (courtesy of the Covent Garden Archive)
2 Tetrazzini as Rosina
   (courtesy of Martin Breese)
3 Tetrazzini as Lakmé
   (courtesy of the EMI archive)
4 Marriage Certificate
   (courtesy of James Gray)
5 Marriage to Vernati
   (courtesy of William R. Moran)
6 American Concert Tour Poster
7 United Kingdom Concert Tour Poster
   (courtesy of Peter Dempsey)
8 Tetrazzini's arrival at Hayes
   (courtesy of the EMI archive)

(between pages 272 and 273)

9   Caricatures of Caruso and Tetrazzini
    (courtesy of the EMI archive)
10 Studio photograph of Tetrazzini, 1907
    (courtesy of the Covent Garden Archive)
11 Tetrazzini in her dressing-room with Campanini
    (courtesy of the Covent Garden Archive)

Preface and
Acknowledgements

When I wrote a chapter on Tetrazzini in my book, *Queens of Song*, published in 1979, I was surprised to find that there was no biography of her in print. Her memoirs, *My Life of Song*, had been 'ghosted' by Fred Gaisberg who said later that an Italian middle class upbringing made her careful not to reveal anything that might harm one's public image. I have given talks in the Royal Opera House to the Friends of Covent Garden, always the most discerning of audiences, and when I spoke about Tetrazzini, illustrating my remarks by playing selections from her recordings, the prolonged applause after each item proved to me that today's opera-goers can still react as enthusiastically to a great coloratura blessed with a wonderful sense of joy in the act of singing as did that 1907 audience when, unheralded by any prior publicity, Tetrazzini made her triumphant Covent Garden début and was hailed by a major critic as having 'the voice of the century'.

It was following my talk that I began to work in earnest on writing this biography – and I must admit had I then known what a long and arduous undertaking that would prove to be I might never have attempted it. The critic John Pitts Sanborn wrote in 1912: 'The true history of a diva, could it ever be written, would make curious and engrossing reading'. He doubted whether any was more mysterious than Tetrazzini. 'An oyster she is and will probably remain so.' I found that even her entries in reference books were often inaccurate. I ended by visiting the Cimitero Monumentale in Milan only to search in vain for her mausoleum. Someone else's stood on the site. The lease for the ground had expired, and her remains were surreptitiously moved to a neglected plot in the cemetery for the poor.

On learning this from me, Peter Dempsey the tenor wrote back that he had shown my letter to Joseph Higgins, who runs the 'Tetrazzini Circle' at the University of Aston, and who now shared his dismay at what had happened. Peter Dempsey also sent me a rare poster in perfect condition of the diva – 'as a token that I appreciate your continuing efforts to redeem from oblivion the memory of one of the most glorious vocal artists the world has ever seen'.

There are many to thank for assistance in gathering vital information. In Milan I was much indebted to the late John Gualiani who knew many people connected with Tetrazzini and from whom I learnt much when we met and in correspondence later, also to Giorgio Cavallari to whom I was introduced when working in the Biblioteca Livia Simoni at the Museo Teatrale alla Scala by its Director, Professor Giampiero Tintori, thanks to whose good offices I had several conversations over the telephone with Mary Casalini Costa. When young Mary Casalini Costa had spent the summer holidays in Salsamaggiore with her grandmother and aunt, respectively cook and companion to Eva Tetrazzini Campanini with whom Luisa often stayed and about whose private life Signora Costa learnt much. In Milan I was accompanied by Rosemary Moritt whose fluent Italian proved indispensable and who tirelessly spent days with me in libraries seeking data in books unavailable elsewhere, and poring through newspapers on microfilm. Then in Lugano I visited Tetrazzini's retreat, *Il Paradiso*, now a convent.

In Florence to my disappointment I faced a complete lack of interest in Luisa Tetrazzini – Joseph Higgins of the 'Circle Tetrazzini' had a similar experience – and I was in despair when James Gray (fortunately domiciled there and a master of research) obtained for me copies of her birth and marriage certificates and photocopies of reviews, some kindly given for me by Alessandro Scalaberni, Tetrazzini's grand nephew through marriage, now living and working as a furrier in Florence.

In the United States I was based at the Long Island home of my sister and brother-in-law, Patricia and John, whose encouragement and help were invaluable. Robert Tuggle, Director of the Metropolitan Archives, and his assistant, John Pennino, showed me all they had relating to Tetrazzini's original contract with the Met. Mr Tuggle (like John F. Cone had earlier) urged me to look at the Robinson Locke scrapbooks of newspaper cuttings in the Billy Rose Library at the Lincoln Center which I found to be a treasure house for the researcher, supplementing what I had already received on microfiche from the libraries of the *San Francisco Chronicle* and the *Examiner*. In the New York Public Library's Musical Section there are files of Tetrazzini cuttings earlier inspected by me when researching for my *Queens of Song*.

Andrew Farkas, Director of Libraries at the University of North Florida and co-author of a biography of Caruso, and W. R. Moran, who apart from being a distinguished discographer, has a monumental knowledge of singers' careers, read a draft of my script whilst I was in America and made constructive criticisms, pointing out in particular times during Tetrazzini's career calling for further research. It was then that I joined forces with Thomas G. Kaufman to prepare the Chronology and this enabled me to fill in the gaps in question. More about this will be found in the introduction to the Chronology itself, for which I could not have had a more knowledgeable collaborator. Tom sent me from America reels of microfilmed theatrical journals providing facts about Tetrazzini's seasons in Russia that I needed.

Ruth Edge, in charge of the EMI Archives at Hayes, allowed me complete access to all the Tetrazzini correspondence, confidential reports, details of contracts and protracted negotiations both with the Gramophone Company and with the Victor Talking Machine Company in America, and most of what I disclose in my chapters dealing with these matters has never been published before. Ruth Edge also produced the original recordings sheets and other information that I needed for preparing the Discography. She and her staff were eager to help and most co-operative both on my visits and in responding to my letters and phone calls afterwards. When working on the Discography I was often guided by Alan Kelly's earlier research at Hayes and his explanations in correspondence.

Mary Jane Phillips Matz, the distinguished Verdian scholar, and W. R. Moran deserve my especial thanks for bringing to my notice the truth regarding Tetrazzini's début in Buenos Aires whilst Dr Eduardo Arnosi of that city generously shared with me the fruits of his investigations into her career in Argentina.

My sources for details of Tetrazzini's career in Mexico were written in Spanish and for expert translations I relied on a friend, George Crawshay, and his wife, and also on Michael Young's skill at swiftly extracting only what was important from puffs and reviews covering Tetrazzini's three seasons in Mexico City and masked in long-winded hyperbole. For similar assistance with the German language, my thanks are due to Doris Couper and Kensington Davison – with Italian, Paul Chand and John Davies – and with Russian, April Fitzlyon.

Francesca Franchi, the Covent Garden Archivist, gave me access to all the programmes covering Tetrazzini's performances there and the press cuttings relative to them.

Richard Bebb, with his encyclopaedic knowledge of opera houses and singers backed by a unique library and a fascinating collection of memorabilia, often solved problems for me – and apart from his expert contribution to the Discography provided most of the material for the chapter on Tetrazzini's historic broadcast in 1925.

Whenever Giorgio Bazelli, the Roumanian tenor, has been mentioned in other books, such references described him as Tetrazzini's husband and as having died before she married Pietro Vernati in 1926. On enquiring at the Academia de Musica in Bucharest I was told that in 1920 he settled in Craiova in western Roumania where with his 'wife', Eugenia Bazelli, a well-known pianist and singing teacher, he presided over a literary salon and died there in 1953, and she six years later. Coming from such an authority I might have accepted this as correct had I not then been introduced in London to Dan Mustata who came from Craiova and who most kindly arranged with his sister-in-law, Daniela Constantin, still living there to research further. She discovered that Eugenia was not Bazelli's wife but his sister! Ms Constantin went to the trouble of advertising in the local paper to which there was one response only, coming from an old lady who claimed to have known them both intimately and who said that after the Second World War he lived in France and later moved to Switzerland, dying there and not in Craiova, leaving two children now living in France whose mother the old lady believed to have been Luisa. She told Ms Constantin that she used to have photographs of the children but lost them 'in strange circumstances'. My informant added that she seemed to have an excellent memory and was very fond of the Bazellis. So far I have not succeeded in tracing these descendants.

Dr Eduardo Arnosi of Buenos Aires wrote to me that he knew the Argentinian baritone, the late Renato Cesari, whose grandfather was Pietro Cesari and whose grandmother it was rumoured could have been Luisa Tetrazzini. However, I have found no evidence to support such a supposition.

Mrs Pauline Forster and Mrs Gloria Parkes, granddaughters of Luisa Tetrazzini's 'black sheep' brother mentioned in Chapter 1, visited me and told me about him but although they said that besides playing in brass bands he composed and also transposed music for the BBC and Sir Thomas Beecham, my research has produced no evidence of this so far. They gave me a photocopy of a studio photograph of him taken in uniform at Torquay.

The selections from Tetrazzini's recordings mentioned in my opening paragraph came from the collection of John Freestone who helped me in other ways. He heard her singing in concert in 1931 when she was very much past her prime, but found that there was enough of her voice left to show what a superb instrument it must have been. He felt sure that as a coloratura she had 'a brilliance and a dynamic range which were unequalled by any of her contemporaries'.

I should also like to express gratitude to the following people who gave me their time, answered my letters, searched their memories, files, archives, or in other ways assisted me:

Bruno Amaduci of Lugano; Lucia Antonucci, British Embassy, Rome; Norma Armstrong, Head of Information Services, Edinburgh Music Library; Rosemary Ashbee, Savoy Hotel, Archivist; Michael Aspinall,

Rome; Rusty Balah, Music Department, Los Angeles Public Library; Professor Nicolae Beloiu, *Academia de Muzica Bucuresti*, Bucharest; Mavis Hammond Brake, National Sound Archives, British Library; Patricia Breedon, Local Studies Dept., Birmingham Library Services; Julian Budden; Rodolfo Celletti; Cheltenham Public Library; Chicago Public Library, Music Information Center; F. A. Clarke, Cultural Service Division, Central Library, Doncaster; Richard Colvig, Oakland Public Library; Robert Commanday, San Francisco; John F. Cone; M. E. Corbett, Central Library, Halifax; Richard Cowley, Instituto Cultural Anglo-Uruguayo, Montevideo; Ms Louise Croll, British Consulate, Florence; Ms D. Dyer, Community Leisure Dept., Central Library, Bristol; Martin Esslin; Natalia Ezdina, State Central Theatre Library, Moscow; Natalija Yefimovra, *Filipchenko*, Ukranian Theatre and Music Museum, Kiev; Ian Gardhouse; Barbara R. Geisler, Librarian, San Francisco Performing Arts Library and Museum; Elaine Gilleran, History Dept., Wells Fargo Bank, San Francisco; Keith Hardwick; Michael Henstock; Joseph Higgins, Tetrazzini Circle Music Group, University of Aston; Paula Howard, Librarian, Dublin Public Library; Ken Jagger, EMI Classics Historical Productions Co-Ordinator; Felicity Jones, Music Librarian, Belfast Public Libraries; J. B. Jones, Local Studies Librarian, Central Library, Cardiff; Mrs Agatha Pfeiffer Kalkanis, Chief Music and Performing Arts Dept., Detroit Public Library; Irmhild Karkhoff, Arts Assistant for Eastern Germany, British Council, Berlin; Dr Ferenc Kerényi, Director, *Magyar Szinházi Intézet*, Budapest; Dr Heinz Lanzke, Director, *Die Deutsche Bibliothek, Deutsches Musikarchiv*, Gärtnerstrasse, Berlin; Marie Lewis, Eastbourne Public Library; Vivian Liff; S. Linton, Information Services, Central Library, Sheffield; Karen Lovejoy, Chicago Public Library; Larry Lustig; Carlo Marinelli, Rome; E. Masi, British Vice Consul, Florence; A. Mendez, Biblioteca Montevideo; Rodney Milnes, Editor, *Opera*, Ministero de Educion y Justicia, Secretaria de Cultura, Biblioteca Nacional, Buenos Aires; Mrs N. L. Monks, Blackburn Central Library; Jerrold Northrop Moore; Paul Morby, New York Public Library, Music, Newspaper and Special Collections Divisions; Christopher Norton-Welsh, Vienna; François L. Nouvion; Yarka Odvarko, Librarian *San Francisco Examiner*; Kathleen O'Connor, National Archives, Pacific Sierra Region, San Bruno, California; Annegret Ogden, Reference Library, Bancroft Library, University of Berkeley; Dr Jaromír Paclt, Prague; M. J. Parker, Central Library, Middlesborough; Biblioteca Palatina di Parma, Sezione Musica; Giorgio Piombi, Civico Museo Bibliografico Musicale, Bologna; Colin Price, Central Library, Leeds; Katarzyna Raczkowska, Librarian, Biblioteca Narodowa, Warsaw; Dr. Jŏachim Reiber, Gesellschaft der Musikfreunde in Wien; John Rosseli; Rutgers University Library; *San Francisco Chronicle* Archives; *San Francisco Examiner* Archives; San Francisco Public Library Newspaper Division; San Francisco Public Library

Special Collections Division; San Francisco Public Library Theater Division; Victoria San Vicente, Directora del Archivo Historica Centrale, Mexico City; Margaret Sharp, Central Library, Edinburgh; Sheffield Central Library, Local Studies Section; Janet Smith, Principal Archives Officer, Liverpool Record Office; Taňa Součková, National Theatre Archives, Prague; Martin Thacker, Music Librarian, Central Library, Manchester; Mariam Tsuladze, Rustaveli, Theatre Institute, Tbilisi, Georgia; Richard Warren Jr., Curator, Historical Sound Recordings, Yale University Library; Nóra Wellmann, Archives, Magyar Àllami Operaház, Budapest; Mena Williams, District Central Library, Preston; Mrs Sibylle Zemitis, Reference Librarian, California State Library, Sacramento; Julio Oscar Zolezzi, Secretaria de Cultura, Biblioteca Nacional, Buenos Aires.

This being the first biography of Luisa Tetrazzini and my having included so much hitherto unknown about her before, which I was at first reluctant to cut (the typed script originally totalled some 180,000 words) that might have made it an expensive book to sell in these difficult times. Working closely with John Steane, author of *The Grand Tradition*, through careful cutting and condensation I reduced it to its present length. It proved in the end a most happy partnership with eventually my even wanting to cut passages that he thought might remain!

Professor Stanley Henig read the script on behalf of the Historic Singers Trust and they have made a grant to Tom Kaufman and myself towards the cost of research in completing the Chronology, which we much appreciate.

Finally my thanks are due to Ellen Keeling, Rachel Lynch and others at Scolar Press for the care taken over the production of this book.

CNG

1 The 'Florentine Nightingale' Flies Off

Luisa Tetrazzini – or the 'Florentine Nightingale' as some called her – was born in apartments on the ground and first floors of a large block of dwellings at 3 Via dei Renai, Florence, on 29 June 1871, the youngest of the three daughters of a military tailor, Emilio Tetrazzini, and his wife Giovanna (née Bianchi). The baby was christened 'Luigia Giuseppa Assunta Maria Pierina'. There were also two brothers – Rodolfo, who possessed a good tenor voice, but who made no professional use of it and worked as an operatic agent and manager, and Aristo who was disowned by his parents when, as a student, he became involved with Anarchists and fled to London to avoid arrest. There he changed his surname to Biancoli and spent the rest of his life playing in brass bands, composing and transposing music. He married an English woman, Minnie Ransom, and the youngest of their five children, Olga, born in 1901, became Luisa's favourite niece. She had a fine voice which her famous aunt wanted to have trained in Milan but Minnie refused to let her go. When in London Luisa would sometimes visit them in their Clerkenwell Road home.[1]

Eva, the eldest of the Tetrazzini sisters, born in Milan in March 1862, was the first to take up singing as a career and to make her name known internationally.

The second sister, Elvira, also a soprano, was the least talented. Born in 1867, she married Vittorio Martucci, nephew of the composer, Giuseppe Martucci, and musical director of Fonodisc in Milan for whom during 1906–7 she recorded some eighteen arias and songs, having in 1904 already made discs for Columbia also in Milan – published in their 'Black and Silver' label collections (details are given in the Discography). On these her voice comes over as shrill and wobbly. Failing to make much impact as a professional singer, she later became a singing teacher in that city.

The youngest, whose first name was 'Luigia', soon became known as

1

'Luisa' instead. According to her reminiscences 'ghosted' in 1921 by Fred Gaisberg, from the age of three she sang at every opportunity, even in class and was punished for doing so. When older she was made to help in the home by sweeping and scrubbing, and to render this less tedious she says she performed scenes from operas assuming in turn the various characters, much to her parents' amusement.

Luisa claimed that she inherited her father's tailoring skills and that her first public success was to win the main prize for the costume she made and wore as Napoleon at a ball. Years later she was to design two gowns, one patterned with the iridescent form of a peacock and the other with tropical fish which she wore when giving concerts.[2]

A major problem when researching to write this book was the considerable number of factual errors in *My Life of Song*. Some of these were undoubtedly due to the true facts becoming a blur after many years, but others can doubtless be ascribed to a selective memory. In a few cases Luisa's version will be repeated, followed if possible by the likely truth as supported by documentary evidence. She states that during the four years Eva studied singing at the Istituto Musicale under Ceccherini and practised roles at home, she learnt them, too, and determined to become an opera singer. Having overcome parental opposition she says that she applied for admission shortly after her tenth birthday, but since in her book she gives her age as only 16 at the time of her Pagliano début whereas it was really 19, it is possible that the earlier event was also three years later.

According to Luisa, on being interviewed by the principal she astonished him by choosing Margherita's prison cell aria from Arrigo Boito's *Mefisto-fele* as her test piece – and he commented that nobody had ever before attempted to sing it when seeking admission but only on completion of their training. After listening to this exhibition of her talents, however, he told her teacher he agreed with him that she was a 'natural' with an impeccable ear who would not need to go through the drudgery of placing the voice and ironing out imperfections of register, so he put her in the second year class under Ceccherini who soon regarded her as the most outstanding of his pupils.[3] She had a remarkably accurate memory and was never to forget her roles, most of which were drummed into her by répétiteurs in her youth.

As Luisa studied, the success of her eldest sister spurred her on. Eva made a promising début in 1882 as Marguerite in Gounod's *Faust* at the Teatro Nicolini in Florence and was also admired for her Alice in *Roberto il diavolo* three years later. In 1885 she sang Aida and also Valentina in *Gli Ugonotti* at the Carlo Felici in Genoa and the following year other roles in South America.

Luisa alleges that one day a parcel was delivered for Eva, which contained a copy of the score of Verdi's new opera *Otello* that a friend of hers assisting Verdi had borrowed so that Eva might study the role of Desdemona ahead of any other soprano and hopefully become the most proficient in the part at auditions.[4] A few mornings later, young Luisa thought it would please her maestro at the Conservatoire if he were allowed to see the score. So she wrapped it up when Eva was out and took it to him. He grew more and more excited as he pored over the work until at last he went off to an out-of-the-way practice room where there was a piano and started to play. Soon Luisa was singing Desdemona. At first she kept her voice low, but later was so carried away that her tones grew louder and reached the Principal who, coming to investigate and finding the door locked, rapped on it.

The score was hurriedly replaced by another before the professor was admitted. He peered suspiciously at the music. This was certainly not what he had heard. He demanded an explanation so had to be let in on the secret. 'Yes, it's unquestionably by Verdi,' he declared, according to Luisa's account. Then late that afternoon on returning home, she says she found Eva distraught through assuming the music had been stolen. However, despite having thus gained an advantage over other competitors for the role of Desdemona, Eva was not to sing it at *Otello*'s triumphant world première at La Scala on 5 February 1887. Romilda Pantaleoni was chosen instead.

Guilio Ricordi published the score of the opera and the firm's archives in Milan tell a different story – that a copy was sent to Eva for study when they learnt that Italo Campanini had engaged her to sing Desdemona at *Otello's* American première on April 16 1888 with his brother Cleofonte conducting. She received much praise from the critics and in particular for the purity and sweetness of the pianissimo with which she approached the high 'A' at the conclusion of Desdemona's prayer. Two years later she married Cleofonte, destined to become one of the greatest of conductors.

It was in early June 1890 that Eva sang for the first time at Covent Garden. Bernard Shaw, in his guise as 'Corno di Bassetto', the *Star*'s music critic, wrote of her Leonora in *Il Trovatore* that 'with her tip-tilted nose, her pretty mouth, her ecstatic eyes, her delicately gushing style, and the intense gratitude of her curtsey whenever she brought down the house, she did very well'. But as Valentina in *Gli Ugonotti*, he found that her Italian tremolo and stage hysteria were so intensified that but few of her notes had any definite pitch, whilst her acting was 'monotonously lachrymose throughout'. When she sang in the manner of a light soprano and so steadied her voice for a moment, everybody was pleased, but when she tried to be 'dramatic' the charm vanished. 'And yet you cannot get these Italian ladies to believe this.'[5]

P. G. Hurst wrote in *The Age of Jean de Reszke* that it has been related, probably with more malice than truth, that the audience hurriedly left the auditorium during the last act of *Gli Ugonotti* when Eva and a tenor of a singularly unattractive appearance were singing the duet. Vibrato was loathed by English audiences and Eva never again sang at Covent Garden.

In October that year Luisa herself was to make her own début, later colourfully and inaccurately described by her in *My Life of Song*.[6] She claims that the Tetrazzinis were regular patrons of the Teatro Pagliano in Florence and that one day its manager told her brother, Rodolfo, that he and the family ought not to miss the performance on Sunday evening of Meyerbeer's *L' Africana* as a promising new soprano would be coming to Florence to sing the role of Inez. Consequently a box was booked. Luisa asserts that she herself had learnt the part and longed to sing it on the stage. Then on the night, before the overture was due to begin, the conductor announced that as the soprano had withdrawn because of illness the performance would have to be cancelled. Whereupon Luisa jumped up onto her seat and cried that she was capable of playing the role. The conductor rejected her offer. However many present having heard her sing, urged him to change his mind which he did – providing she rehearsed first, so the opening was postponed a few days.

On 21 October with Rosa Caligaris-Marti singing the other soprano role of Selika and Emilio Usiglio conducting, Luisa gave such a polished performance that she won an ovation.

Such is the account given by Luisa in *My Life of Song* but apart from really being aged 19, she was not living at home but in two rooms high up in the Pagliano building, for a year earlier on 14 October 1889 she had married its manager in the *Casa Communale* at the Palazzo Vecchio. Her father had died and on the marriage certificate she is described as 'casalinga' – housewife – and her husband's full names as 'Giuseppe Santino Alberto Scalaberni' aged 35. He had been active in Florence for many years and was the younger son of Luigi Scalaberni, a well-known impresario.[7]

As for the début in *L' Africana*, a different story was told by a pupil of Luisa's to Millie Robbins of the *San Francisco Chronicle* in 1968. The American soprano and coach to Mario Lanza, Luisa Franceschi Runge, studied and lived with Tetrazzini in Milan during the 1930s.[8] According to Mme Runge, the old lady had confided to her how, as a young bride, she would go into the theatre and sit for hours watching rehearsals from the gallery. The conductors often came up to the little apartment to rest or have a dish of pasta.

In her newspaper report, Millie Robbins wrote that Mme Runge recalled how Tetrazzini said that one day a conductor arrived distraught because a soprano had been taken ill. The future diva offered to take her place. The sceptical maestro played a few arias on her rickety piano, and to his complete amazement she knew them all. He immediately put her into rehearsal and the following night she sang and received an ovation. Seeing the handwriting on the wall, her husband literally locked up his young wife. But in proper melodramatic fashion she escaped by tying sheets together and ran away.

As a result of that success at the Pagliano, Luisa was engaged by Emilio Usiglio to sing with his new company at the Argentina, then the largest theatre in Rome, and she performed brilliantly again as Inez on 26 December 1890.[9] She alleges in *My Life of Song* that the soprano singing Selika went extremely flat during the sextette scene, dragging the others down with her, which left Luisa with the task of supporting the whole fabric of the music. After the unaccompanied part, the orchestra failed to take up the accompaniment again. When Usiglio demanded why, they replied that the Selika had fallen nearly a tone, leaving them stranded.

The conductor was not taking any chances, so before the curtain rose on the first night, he arranged that when Selika went off key he would signal to Luisa to sing sharp and this would pull the others up. The audience included the King and Queen of Italy. Luisa claims that, moved no doubt by the importance of the occasion, instead of ending on E as the score required, she found herself suddenly reaching a note a full octave higher, the E in alt. It was so clear, she wrote, that even those outside in the street heard it.[10]

On 28 February 1891 Luisa was given the title role in *Mirella*, the Italian version of Gounod's *Mireille*, and the last opera in the season at the Argentina. The critics praised in particular her rendering of the waltz song, *Oh, d'amor messaggera*.[11]

As a result of Luisa's achievement, Queen Margherita invited her to sing in Italian the *Liebestod* from Wagner's *Tristan und Isolde* at a command performance on 2 March 1891. It was the Queen's favourite opera and she sent her own singing master to rehearse Luisa, who proved such a success that according to *My Life of Song* Margherita predicted a distinguished career for her.[12]

The new discovery then joined the opera buffa company of Pietro Cesari at Rome's Teatro Nazionale and appeared first with him on 29 March playing Vittoria in Carlo Pedrotti's *Tutti in maschera* (based on Goldoni's comedy *L'impresario della Smirne*).[13] *La Riforma* reported that an enthusiastic audience applauded Cesari and Luisa Tetrazzini Scalaberni, 'a versatile artist of rare ability'. Luisa's next role was as Tersicone in Usiglio's *Le nozze in prigione* of which the plot revolved round her marriage in prison to the character taken by Cesari. Realising her potential he coached her assiduously and there were packed houses for five more evenings. She also sang at a concert held before the Queen in aid of those injured in rioting.[14]

In June Cesari's company moved to the Teatro Nicolini in Florence. The

Gazzetta Musicale di Milano for the 24th of the month in its half-yearly report from that city declared:

> The most attractive novelties were the performances of Signora Tetrazzini Scalaberni in the comic operas *Tutti in maschera* and *Crispino e la Comare* for which kind of music she is the most perfect exponent thanks to her refreshingly lively voice, alert and attractive personality, and flair for comedy. She has the youthful daring to succeed in whatever roles she attempts.

The report ends that Tetrazzini Scalaberni was said to have been engaged to sing at the Real in Madrid for the winter season. But she never sang there. In fact careful searching through the columns of Italy's operatic periodicals – the *Gazzetta, Cosmoramo Pittorico, Rassegna Melodrammatica, Mondo Artistico*, and *Rivista Teatrale Melodrammatica* – have revealed no mention of her singing anywhere else after Florence until the sensational events of the summer of the following year. The agencies representing artists would publish in these papers lists of their clients showing the theatres where they were performing or the addresses where they could be contacted if resting. Up to the third week of October, Luisa's address is given as her home in Florence; then from the next week onwards she is no longer included.

Cesari – Maestro and Lover

Meanwhile Pietro Cesari was enjoying one success after another. He is not mentioned in *My Life of Song* nor does any other book deal with the major role he played in Luisa's life for the next fourteen years – neither is any reference made to Scalaberni's being her husband. Cesari was an artist of considerable talent. Born at Pordenone of working-class parents in 1849 and 22 years older than Luisa, he was a violinist and librettist for operettas as well as a singer with a voice that ranged between baritone and bass.[15] After his début at the Dal Verme in Milan in 1874 with great success in Lecocq' *Giroflé-Girofla* he went on to perform in the leading opera houses of Italy and also those of Vienna and Barcelona. Handsome, with mobile features, excelling in comedy parts but never overacting, he was popular both with the public and the critics who never gave him a bad review.

Up to 1881 Cesari had won acclaim for his singing in baritone roles. He then successfully added bass ones to his repertoire and at the Manzoni in Milan in April that year received the coveted operatic award of a laurel crown. Three years later in Valparaiso, he appeared in his first serious role as Rodolfo in *La Sonnambula*, proving again his remarkable versatility. Back in Milan he became both performer and impresario for several seasons at the Dal Verme where he employed the 20 year old Toscanini as conductor.

In 1891, before his season at the Nazionale in Rome with Luisa, Cesari continuing to pursue this dual role with distinction, presented and sang in three operas at the Regio of Turin. After the May performances in Florence, he went on to do the same elsewhere in the autumn but the parts one might have expected Luisa to have taken were sung instead by another soprano. On 20 January the following year he was hailed as the finest *basso comico* of the day when he created Il Pedone in the première of Catalani's *La Wally* at La Scala. Then after his performance as Figaro in *Il Barbiere di Siviglia* at the Filodrammatici of Milan on 17 April the critics united in hailing him as the ideal artist for such a character. There followed more praise for his Lord Cockburn in *Fra Diavolo* on 5 May.

One can only speculate as to what was happening to Luisa in the meantime. Can it be that her husband, jealous of her close association with Cesari, had, as already mentioned in Luisa Franceschi Runge's account, 'literally locked up his young wife'?

In *My Life of Song*[16] Luisa Tetrazzini claimed that when her season in Rome ended she was offered £280 a month to go to Buenos Aires as the prima donna of 'the chief opera house' in Argentina, which was seven times as much as she had been paid in the Italian capital and fourteen times what she had received in Florence. Her parents, she wrote, were reluctant to let her go, so a chaperon was engaged to accompany her on the ship from Genoa. Her mother wept bitterly as they parted and said 'I shall be here to meet you when you return at the end of the season.' But three years were to pass before they saw each other again.

Luisa describes the voyage from Genoa to Buenos Aires as being for the main part enjoyable and uneventful. She claimed that she used to dress as 'a minstrel and sing Neapolitan airs to entertain the other passengers' and that when not doing this she used to dance about the decks or explore 'the old vessel from stem to stern' and listen for hours to 'old salts' spinning yarns. Although after she recovered from early sea-sickness Luisa enjoyed the novelty of the passage on the small steamer, she admits that she never became fond of travelling by sea.

So much for Luisa's account, which differs widely from the truth. She was not accompanied by a chaperon but by Pietro Cesari. Verdi, writing to Giulio Ricordi from Montecatini in the summer of 1892, refers to Emilio Usiglio's recommendation of 'la Tetrazzini, not the one who sings Desdemona so well, but the other one who, they say, ran off to America with the bass Cesari. Will she come back? Are they staying there?'[17]

As to be told later, Fred Gaisberg of the Gramophone Company was closely associated with Luisa Tetrazzini from the time she started recording for the company in 1907. In the autumn of 1920 she asked him for help, as her English was so poor, in the writing of her life story and promised him part of the royalties. He states in his diary that he felt as she related 'the various episodes of her crowded career that she was only showing the façade to the gaze of the world'.

After Tetrazzini's death in 1940, Fred Gaisberg published six years later his own autobiography in which he wrote that a journalist friend had suggested he ought to include some sensational stories about prima donnas. 'One international artist whose memoirs had already appeared omitted this saucy episode in which she played the role of misleading lady.' It occurred on

> a gala night at the end of a brilliant opera season. During a supper party in her apartment, the prima donna succeeded in making her husband drink so much that he fell fast asleep. Whereupon she and her lover, a handsome basso, stretched him out on the floor, surrounded him with flowers taken from the bouquets she had received that evening. Then, like Tosca, after bumping off Scarpia, she placed a lighted candle at each end of him and a crucifix on his chest before eloping together.

According to Gaisberg, 'the betrayed husband caught up with the lovers at Buenos Aires and accepted a monetary consolation of some size to resign his claim on the lady'.[18]

Not only are neither Scalaberni nor Cesari mentioned anywhere in *My Life of Song*, but, according to Tetrazzini, she triumphed there on arrival at her début gaining a powerful friend in the President of the Republic, Luiz Saenz Peña. We shall now learn what really happened.

2 In South America

Buenos Aires was the most cosmopolitan city in South America. Those descended from the conquistadores were Spanish speaking, while the middle and lower classes were overwhelmingly Italian, immigrants from the depressed parts of their mother country whose favourite form of entertainment was opera, especially that of the lighter kind. As a result every spring touring companies recruited in Milan or Naples came to give seasons in several theatres. The newspapers with the largest circulations were in Spanish – *La Prensa*, the most important in South America, *La Nación*, esteemed for its literary quality, and the *Diario*, the chief evening paper. For the Italians as well as for the French and English colonies there were dailies in their own languages such as the *Buenos Aires Herald* and *The Standard*.

As Fred Gaisberg wrote in *Music on Record*, the roaring nineties were the days when

> money dripped from the pampas grass of Argentina, the rubber of the Amazon, and the nitrates of Chile, and the fortunes of many Italian artists were built up from their engagements in those countries during that period.

Prima donnas were loaded with gifts and jewels, their dressing-rooms filled with flowers, and on gala nights the students would unharness the horses and pull their favourite's carriage to her hotel. The principal theatres were the Opera on the Calle Corrientos and the Politeama Argentino, a former circus splendidly converted by its owner the Florentine impresario Cesare Ciacchi.

It was at the Politeama that in 1886 Eva Tetrazzini had sung with some success as Marguerite in *Faust*, Rachel in *L'Ebrea*, Leonora in *La Favorita*, and the title role in *La Gioconda*. She had then crossed the River Plate to sing these parts in Montevideo's Teatro Cibils where on 17 July the President of Uruguay, General Santos, had been as enchanted with her Rachel as Luis Saenz Peña, the Argentinian President, was to become with Luisa's Lucia. Eva had returned to the Politeama in 1889 to perform with a company that had as its main attraction Adelina Patti – now aged 46 but still brilliant in her great roles – and also included Pietro Cesari with whom Luisa Tetrazzini had now eloped.

Ciacchi's rival was Angelo Ferrari, at one time impresario at La Scala, who ever since 1868 had brought out companies headed by singers such as Battistini and Tamagno. There was also another manager, although not in the same league: Raffaele Tomba, who presented seasons of light opera at the San Martin, a second-rate theatre on the Calle Esmeralda, since 4 July 1889, when his company made its début before a crowded house with a performance of Maggi's *La Fornarina*. There were luxurious sets and costumes, it was well sung and produced and received clamorous ovations. Then, in the middle of the same month, an event occurred which shocked the staid and respectable members of society: a number of rich rakes made off with the most attractive chorus girls and installed them in their ranches outside the city. Tomba could not carry on without them, so he was forced to negotiate with the representatives of the abductors and a compromise was reached. The girls were allowed to perform nightly for the period of their contracts and some even permitted to attend rehearsals.

Mariano G. Bosch wrote in his *Historia del Teatro en Buenos Aires*[1]:

> The Tomba girls had been seduced in a very elegant manner, and it was arranged for carriages with men in livery and matched pairs of horses to take the girls to and from the San Martin. Each girl had her own carriage and the coachman was ordered to treat the occupant as if she owned the vehicle. It was natural that this uncustomary splendour, without precedent in the annals of the Italian opera in Europe, produced the desired effect and reconciled the girls to their fates.

The desertion of the chorines and second sopranos, many of whom settled permanently in Buenes Aires, had a demoralizing effect on the others in the troupe until what had begun as a successful season ended abruptly after three months. 'From the rise of the curtain last night,' *El Diario* reported on 5 October,

> it was felt that a general feeling of cold contempt and suspicion pervaded the audience as they watched the artists whose life in Buenos Aires had become a continuous feast of Balthasar. Without proper rehearsals, the pieces had been butchered. The artists appeared to do only what they wanted.

At the end of the second act of *Fra Diavolo*, when the audience were preparing to enjoy having refreshments during the interval, all the lights were suddenly extinguished. The cast had decided that they were not going on with the performance as they did not want to be late for a party.

> From all parts came shouts and threats against Commendatore Tomba. Chairs were seized and hurled onto the stage, and the disturbance assumed such grave

proportions that it was necessary to call a platoon of soldiers to clear the theatre.

In 1891 the old San Martin was destroyed by fire and its owners the Ghigliani Brothers rebuilt it. Then, the following year, Tomba returned with a newly recruited troupe including Luisa Tetrazzini and Pietro Cesari. On Saturday night 30 June Raffaele Tomba and his opera company opened the season at the cool and attractive auditorium with Cesari being acclaimed by a full house for his performance in Auber's *Fra Diavolo*. Next evening the demand was so great to hear Offenbach's *Orphée* that the box office had to be closed and the *Standard* congratulated the 'energetic impresario on the success of his troupe'. Crowds were turned away from performances of Mascagni's *Cavalleria Rusticana*, Usiglio's light opera of the same title based on Goldoni's *Le Donne Curiose*, and Offenbach's *La Belle Hélène*, but before Luisa Tetrazzini-Scalaberni could make her début, husband Alberto arrived in a rage from Italy determined to take her back with him. She refused to go, so he went to law for restoration of his conjugal rights and she pleaded for a legal separation. The affair became the talk of Buenos Aires. On Tuesday 23 August the case opened and next day the *Standard* reported: 'Before the judge could put on his specs she eloped with Cesari and is now *non est inventus*. Can all this be a clever advertisement? It rather looks like it.' Mariano G. Bosch wrote in his *Historia del Teatro de Buenos Aires* that Scalaberni 'screamed like a demon' and rushed to seek the assistance of the Italian Consul. They searched the town for days trying to find the fugitives, assisted by another Italian, a 24 year old army lieutenant Luigi Genazzini, well-known for his terrible temper, and rumoured to be also in love with Luisa.

> He was *persona non grata* in his own country, so on the pretext of carrying out a mission to purchase horses, the Italian government had sent him to Buenos Aires. . . . At last they discovered the turtle doves and Scalaberni carried his wife to the local courts.

The couple had been concealed by their lawyer Don Mariano Ozabál in the Hotel Giobo (which impresario Ciacchi had once taken over for the sole use of Sarah Bernhardt).

With Cesari now back at the San Martin, Tomba made capital out of the publicity aroused by presenting him on 19 September in Cagnoni's *Papa Martin*. Announcing this the previous day, the *Standard* commented: 'This is Signor Cesari's *cheval de bataille*, and the popular singer may be sure of receiving an ovation' – which he did.

On Friday 23 September Luisa and her husband appeared in court before Judge Mendez Paz who, as Bosch puts it, 'in order to escape the verbal torrents which assailed him from all sides decided to resolve the difficulties by asking the parties to have a reconciliation,' but Luisa would not hear of it. According to *La Nación* next day, she declared

> that her resolution is unbreakable, that she has adopted her position after long meditation, that the reasons are so many and so serious that, in respect for the judge, she has refrained from giving them in detail, and concluded by declaring that if the choice were offered to return to her husband, or go to prison she would take the latter course and would without the slightest hesitation row as a galley slave for twenty years. After this decisive statement, the judge turned to Sr Scalaberni asking him 'And what do you say to all of this?'
> 'I? That I want nothing more than my wife.'
> 'Then that is my verdict,' replied Mendez Paz.

But Luisa protested vociferously that nothing would make her live again with her husband. According to the report in next day's *Standard*, 'The latter, on hearing this, said "All right" and declared he would not take her to Europe, even if she asked him. The Judge sighed and dismissed them.'[2] Then Scalaberni returned on his own to Florence where he was to die many years later on 3 June 1905, still separated from Luisa.

A few hours after the case ended, Cesari played the lead in a new opera by Alberto Franchetti about Columbus which proved a success, thanks to his brilliant performance.

A fortnight later, the same paper for Saturday 8 October predicted 'an awful crush at the San Martin tonight and tomorrow night as Mme Tetrazzini who has afforded the public so much food for gossip lately makes her début in *Crispino e la Comare* as Annetta'. Four years earlier Adelina Patti had sung that role to Pietro Cesari's Crispino at the Politeama Argentino. How would the newcomer compare with the great diva, the cognoscenti wondered.

The *Standard* reported on 11 October:

> La Tetrazzini has a fine, well-schooled voice and is a capital actress. She delighted us with several sustained high Ds and an E. The enthusiasm she aroused ought to be set off against all the legal worry she has lately gone through.

La Prensa praised 'the delicious touches of humour with which she enlivened her rendering of *Io non sono più l'Annetta*'. There followed mounting praise for new additions to her repertoire – as a cheeky vivandière in the title role of Donizetti's *La Figlia del Reggimento* with Cesari playing the protective Sergeant with more passion than the part required – as Micaela to Mme Paoli-Bonazzo's Carmen and Cesari's Escamillo when *La Nación* for 4 November found that she sang 'with perfect legato' – as Gilda in *Rigoletto* when the *Standard* reported that she was 'frantically applauded' after *Caro nome* – and as Lucia when according to *La Prensa* in the Mad Scene it was impossible, like with Patti, for most to tell which were her notes and which were those of the accompanying flute.

Tomba moved his company for the month of December to the Teatro Olimpo in Rosario where Tetrazzini won more plaudits from packed audiences as Annetta, Maria and Micaela, followed by two new roles, those of Corallina in Usiglio's opera buffo *Le Donne Curiose* and of Amina in Bellini's *La Sonnambula* when the customers clamoured for an encore of the popular rondo finale and she obliged. Then after returning to the San Martin in early February, Tomba announced that their spring and summer seasons would be spent in São Paulo and Rio de Janeiro. Meanwhile the Italian impresario Angelo Ferrari had arrived with Cleofonte Campanini as conductor and with singers headed by Luisa's elder sister Eva. They occupied the more prestigious Teatro de la Opéra where Eva was well received in *L'Africana, Lohengrin, Mefistofele* and *Cavalleria Rusticana*. The sisters had not met since the elopement, so it would have been interesting to learn what Eva had to say, but the Tetrazzinis never discussed family problems with others.

In the second week of February it was the capital's turn to hear Tetrazzini as Amina and Corallina. The *Standard* reported how impressed audiences were with her versatility. 'She and Cesari carry everything before them.' A week later readers were told that the short season had ended the previous evening. At the end of the performance, Cesari had vastly entertained the audience with a witty speech and a song composed for the occasion. Then on the 23rd the same paper revealed:

> The favourite actors, Cesari and Tetrazzini, have again mysteriously vanished from the public gaze. When the Tomba company embarked on board the *Bearn* for Brazil, the two leading artists were not to be found. It appears the dogs of law are after the interesting pair for the costs of the legal separation from her husband which created such a stir here some months ago.

According to the researches of Professor Eduardo Arnosi of Buenos Aires, Tetrazzini escaped from there disguised as a sailor on board the *Bearn*.[3] Presumably Cesari would have adopted some similar disguise.

Luisa in *My Life of Song* gives quite a different reason for her escape. Placing the event later in her career, she wrote that her impresario had a rival powerful in government circles who had made her a very tempting offer which she had rejected. Determined to force her to sing for him, he threatened to prevent her from leaving the country. So she disguised herself in the rig of a pilot's boy.

> We were well away in a tiny open boat when what my impresario feared happened. Suddenly there was shouting through megaphones ashore and government officials came aboard the steamer to tell the captain that Signora Tetrazzini could not be allowed to leave the country. A vigilant search followed, but I was not to be found.[4]

The officials, satisfied that she had missed the ship, went ashore and it proceeded on its way until outside Argentinian waters. Meanwhile, the choppy sea was becoming dangerously rough and the captain of the passenger ship told her horrified impresario that it was too dangerous to risk picking up a boat in such conditions and he must signal to her to return to the shore. The impresario argued with the captain, but it was only after 'a handsome bribe' had been paid that he agreed to stop the ship and rescue her.

Opening at the Teatro San José in São Paulo on 1 March, Tetrazzini and Cesari sang in the same operas as at the San Martin except for *Le Donne Curiose* which was replaced by Donizetti's *Linda di Chamounix* in which (for the first time) she played the title role and he the buffo Marquis de Boisfleury. Travelling on to Rio de Janeiro's Teatro Lyrico Fluminense in the third week of June they repeated this programme and she added the parts of Zerlina in Auber's *Fra Diavolo* and of Violetta in *La Traviata* to her repertoire. Cesari appeared as Lord Cockburn and Germont respectively. The reception she won from press and public in Verdi's tragic work was tremendous. The stage was completely covered with floral tributes.

On 22 November 1893 the *Standard* reported: 'The Tombas are coming back to the San Martin at the end of the month. All the dudes in town are happy.' And the lawyers, too, for having made a great deal of money. Tetrazzini and Cesari had paid them their outstanding bills. The new season opened on the 30th with Cesari in *Giroflé-Girofla* playing to a full house that found his powerful voice 'as fresh as ever'. Luisa's reappearance was delayed, however. According to gossip, the evening that this should have occurred she failed to go to the San Martin and the performance had to be cancelled. This was because she had been in bed with Cesari and had lost all sense of time. The management pretended that she had been taken ill. Professor Eduardo Arnosi writes: 'It is told that a man was needed always at her disposal in the camerinos [dressing-rooms] because frequently she needed coitus, for singing the following act in an opera, as others need to smoke.[5]

The 'Editor's Table' in the *Standard* informed readers on Wednesday 20 December 1893:

> The habitués of the San Martin will learn with delight that Cesari, the brilliant baritone, will appear tonight in his crack opera *Fra Diavolo*. Every theatre-goer here will recollect Cesari's inimitable acting and superb singing in the role of the bandit's accomplice, particularly in the dressing room scene (*Grazie al Cielo*). We have heard Cesari go through the score six times running in answer to the encores of the audience.... Mme Tetrazzini is not sufficiently well to sing just yet.

At last on 5 January 1894 a packed house assembled to welcome back

Luisa in the title role of *Lucia di Lammermoor*. 'The audience cheered her all through and recalled her five times for her Mad Scene,' wrote the *Standard*. *La Prensa* was impressed with her 'bravely delivered and faultlessly executed staccati' and *La Nación* with 'the ease and agility of her chromatic scales'. Of her *Linda di Chamounix* on the 15th, the *Standard* pointed out that many believed her singing of *O luce di quest' anima* reminiscent of Patti's, while *La Prensa* found that this opera semiseria with alternating scenes of comedy, romance and pathos enabled her to demonstrate that she was developing as an actress. *La Nación* called her 'a charmer with a most persuasive style'.[6] Nine evenings later her Maria in *La Figlia del Reggimento* was 'enthusiastically applauded, particularly at the end after she sang the waltz from *Mireille*'.[7]

When on February 12 Luisa sang Amina, a Brazilian millionaire in a stage box kept throwing bouquets at her throughout the performance.[8] Captivated during the season in Rio de Janeiro, he had come specially to Buenos Aires to hear her again. It may have been this admirer who gave her the magnificent diamond she now owned which had belonged to the unfortunate Don Pedro, once Emperor of Brazil. *La Nación* was impressed by the agility and speed with which she had executed the coda to the Act I cabaletta, *Sovra il sen*, and the accuracy with which she sped through the most intricate of coloratura.[9]

The 72 year old President of Argentina, Dr Luis Saenz Peña, a former judge of the Supreme Court and a most worthy man, had been an infrequent visitor to the theatre but *Lucia di Lammermoor* was his favourite opera and the eulogistic reviews of Tetrazzini's performances attracted him, too, to the San Martin. He was so taken with her sparkling stage presence and the way that she threw off the fioriture with increasing brilliance and aplomb that he never missed any of her subsequent performances. According to *My Life of Song*[10] to celebrate her 50th appearance he arranged for a gala to be held in her honour which three former Presidents attended, and on the night he sent her a gift of a magnificent diamond star which she pinned to her gown, and later during the second interval went in person to thank him. He took her into his box, then led her forward and presented her to the spectators, who hailed her with cries of 'Viva Tetrazzini!' She wrote that his nightly visits to the opera became the talk of the town.

On 6 March, the *Standard* forecast that Luisa would surpass her sister, Eva, as an operatic star. Despite standing room being allowed, people were being turned away every time she appeared. That evening, she sang Rosina in *Il Barbiere di Siviglia* for the first time and the same paper reported how she had triumphed in the role, receiving an ovation after the Lesson Scene. 'It was great,' agreed the Editor, but why, fair and gifted warbler, did you insist on gilding the purest musical gold extant? Was the marvellously florid score not florid enough for you, without taxing your grand voice by adding your *fioritura?* Nevertheless, you are a splendid Rosina.[11]

Tetrazzini's friendship with President Luis Saenz Peña led to her being approached by the mother and the wife of a young naval lieutenant sentenced to a long term of imprisonment after the wrecking of his ship. For nine years the two women had been trying to have the case reopened and had written several times to the President without receiving any reply. Would Tetrazzini use her influence to obtain the man's release?

Tetrazzini says she told her visitors that it was unlikely the President would interfere just to please her, but she would visit the prisoner, which she did. She was so appalled by his appearance and state of mind that on leaving she went straight to the President's palace and asked to see him though she had not made an appointment.

Peña saw her. She began by saying she had come to ask a favour. He asked her not to do so. It was already granted. As he had signed the warrant admitting her to the prison, it was not surprising that he should have deduced the reason for her visit. He had therefore done something which would please her – better than immediate release – for a release would still carry the stigma of the original verdict. He had ordered an immediate retrial and before that took place he could tell her the outcome. The man would be found innocent, for Peña had studied carefully the papers in the case and it was clear that there had been a miscarriage of justice.[12]

On Friday 16 March 1894 the Tomba company gave a gala performance at the San Martin as the benefit night for Tetrazzini. She had chosen *Lucia* for the occasion. Next day the *Standard*'s Editor wrote that it had reminded him of one of Patti's gala nights at the Politeama theatre. Hundreds had been refused admission. *La Prensa* called her an operatic acrobat without a rival in her ability to manage endless trills and runs.[13]

Then on Sunday 1 April, the eve of President Peña's birthday, he was present at the San Martin to hear her sing in the title role of *Linda di Chamounix* when crowds tried to force their way in. At the end from his box he proclaimed Tetrazzini 'The Nightingale of the Rio de la Plata'. The public had already started to call her '*la niña mimada de Buenos Aires*' – 'the beloved baby'.[14]

Three days later the season closed with a gala performance of *Il Barbiere di Siviglia* with Luisa as Rosina and the *Standard* next morning prophesied: 'In a few years, Mme Tetrazzini will be a star of the first magnitude.'

From April to early May 1894, Luisa sang at the Nuevo Politeama in Montevideo with Pietro Cesari in major roles opposite her. She described as one of her happiest memories the first time she crossed the River Plate to sing at Montevideo on its hill occupying a small peninsula jutting out just where the estuary merges into the Atlantic. After the fashion of a scene in medieval Venice small boats gaily decorated came out to meet her. 'A carriage richly upholstered with roses awaited me while tiny bombs exploded as if my arrival was being heralded by artillery.'[15] In the town itself the fresh breeze coming up the streets leading to the pleasant Plaza Independencia day and night, made her reluctant to leave for a season in Mendoza and glad to return for further performances in July.

Meanwhile in Italy sister Eva was gaining plaudits with husband Cleofonte Campanini conducting, first at the San Carlo on 10 March for her Alice Ford in Verdi's new opera *Falstaff*, then at the Pagliano in Puccini's *Manon Lescaut* on 8 May when she had to sing seven encores and was rewarded with 30 curtain calls.

In August the press in Buenos Aires announced that the *Gran Compania Lirica Italiana* directed by Señor Beccario y Ca which had been enjoying spectacular success in Montevideo would soon be starting a season at the San Martin with no fewer than three sopranos, four tenors, three baritones and two basses, as well as 50 instrumentalists conducted by Nicola Guerra.[16] They opened on 1 September, then three days later Luisa sang in her favourite opera, *Lucia*[17] and the thunder of welcome back from the audience when she first appeared was loud and long enough to stop the orchestra. On the 8th praising her Rosina the *Standard* commented: 'It seems astonishing that at a fourth of the cost you can today hear as fine music at the San Martin as at the Opéra.'

Bellini's *I Puritani* had not been heard in Buenos Aires since Patti's time and Tetrazzini had promised to sing Elvira when she had thoroughly studied that gruelling coloratura role. After several postponements, the event took place on 9 October. The *Puritani* Mad Scene is an exercise in portamento requiring the voice to be perfectly placed. *La Nación*'s critic wrote that Tetrazzini proved herself thoroughly accomplished in this, thus making music and words tell simultaneously. 'Mme Tetrazzini sang divinely', began the Standard's account. 'Last night was truly magnificent. Cesari, too, was acclaimed for his Riccardo. He is the same full baritone as ever, and his voice is the same as it was in 1883.'[18]

On Friday 19 October President Saenz Peña brought with him for a performance of *Lucia* several of his ministers and, reported the *Standard*, applauded her 'most energetically at every opportunity'. He had presented her with a magnificent basket of flowers and she had responded by kissing a bloom and handing it to him.[19]

Tetrazzini sang the title role in Meyerbeer's *Dinorah* for the first time in her career on 15 November and delighted the audience with her rendering of the Shadow Song. Four days after this her benefit performance proved a brilliant occasion with the applause once more led by the President.[20]

On 5 November, the *Standard* had told its readers: 'Buenos Aires's beloved baby proposes to visit the States shortly.' Tetrazzini, however, did not then do so: this was not to occur for some years yet. Instead she went to sing at the Olimpo in Rosario and was to have opened as Lucia on Saturday 7 December,[21] but must have been taken ill for the *Standard* stated on the 11th:

> We are glad to announce that Mme Tetrazzini is now completely out of danger. She has been about a fortnight laid up and underwent several operations but thanks to the skill of Dr Dozzelli she is herself again and will soon be able to start on her tour through the provinces.

Three days later the paper revealed that she had made her postponed appearance at the Olimpo to 'an ovation'. However, there was bad news just before Christmas when eight cases of cholera in Rosario brought business to a standstill, although Tetrazzini gallantly carried on. By the New Year, no more cases were reported and on 11 January 1895 the *Standard* disclosed that she had pocketed the by no means small sum of $20,000 during her singing in Rosario.

Argentina was then rife with unrest and threats of revolution. Tetrazzini's friend and admirer President Luis Saenz Peña's policy had been to try and run the republic for the common good, whereas the Senators and Deputies were mostly only in politics to further themselves. He scrupulously refused to use patronage to buy votes for his reforms. Through his attempting to keep the country solvent, taxes had been increased and the people were becoming rebellious. In fact, there was an insurrection not far from Buenos Aires in the New Year and on 21 January 1895 Peña announced his resignation. The *Standard* next day reported that he had been popular in all foreign circles and they regretted his departure. After a little over two years of wear and tear that might well have crushed a younger man, he had decided to hand over the burden and his term of office was served out by the Vice President, Dr José Uriburu, whose nephew was to become sensationally involved with Tetrazzini later in San Francisco. She wrote in *My Life of Song* that when in 1898 Peña was taken ill and died, 'some of the more irreverent writers, speaking of how my voice had dragged him from his usual haunts to the theatre declared that he had died of his love for Tetrazzini'.[22]

Touring in out of the way places

Tetrazzini decided that January 1895 was not a propitious time to return
to Buenos Aires so she suggested to her fellow artists that they might
embark on a provincial tour of out of the way places which, if all Argentin-
ians loved opera, ought to prove a lucrative undertaking. But this received
a negative reaction. An aged baritone told her that these projects always
lost money. Once he and some others had set out on such an adventure
but before long business was so bad that they had to pawn their costumes
to buy food and accommodation. The tenor and he had to walk 150 miles
back to Buenos Aires, singing in the streets for sustenance on the way.
The others present supported the baritone with depressing accounts of
disastrous tours. But Luisa had made up her mind and told them she was
going to take a small company round the hinterland. Who would come
with her?

The first to volunteer was an impulsive instrumentalist and soon Luisa
had also recruited some of the younger performers, but older, wiser heads
were firmly shaken in dissent. According to her account in *My Life of
Song*,[23] she, the youngest of the party, took charge, making herself responsible for all receipts and payments. She failed to mention that the troupe
was called the Cesari Tetrazzini Company, so Cesari must have
accompanied and supported her. She claimed that from first to last on this
tour not only were all expenses met out of the takings but she was left
with enough profit to share out equally among the participants.

News of Luisa's success had spread widely, for when they reached Salta
Orientale where *Lucia di Lammermoor* was performed on 2 May 1895,
the Governor, paying her a rare courtesy, instead of merely coming to the
station to welcome them, travelled by an earlier train in their direction
and met them half-way. At Salta itself, it seemed that the entire population
packed the station – people had climbed the telegraph poles to get a better
view. A red carpet stretched along the platform and bouquets were pressed
upon her from all sides. Church bells pealed. Luisa later learnt that the
authorities had argued that this would attract people into the town from
the outlying districts, which would bring business to the shops and money
to the coffers of the churches.

Singing to save a cemetery

At Tucumán,[24] the Governor called to ask if Luisa would visit a small
town a short distance away by rail where its inhabitants were anxious to
consult her, so accompanied by some fellow singers she went there and
was met at the station by a group of leading citizens who then revealed

that they needed her help urgently in order to build a high wall round their cemetery and thus keep out the hyenas that were desecrating the graves. Would she sing in the town to raise the money for this purpose? She agreed but there was no building where such an event could take place. Somewhat rashly, she thought, they promised to erect a theatre within five days which they guaranteed would be packed out. It seemed impossible but following the lead of a man from Boston who owned the largest sawmill in the area and supplied the timber and the nails, other residents responded by providing the rest of the required materials and the Teatro Luisa Tetrazzini was built on a suitable site in the courtyard behind the house of a leading supporter. The railroad company rose to the occasion and put on two special trains to take the opera company and others from Tucumàn to the small township.

The evening performance proved a sombre affair for the whole audience together with the singers and the instrumentalists were dressed in deep mourning. Luisa sang Gounod's *Ave Maria* and Pinsuti's *Libro Sacro*, before appearing in the title role of *Lucia di Lammermoor*. All the company's expenses she herself paid and the total takings of 5000 Argentinian dollars were handed over to the cemetery wall fund. After the opera had ended Tetrazzini was presented with a commemorative gold medal bearing her name in diamonds and rubies.

Following this episode, Luisa sang in the Teatro Olimpo of Rosario during the rest of May, and then at the Teatro Rivera Indarte of Córdoba for a month from mid-June where she was first heard in the role of Marguerite in Gounod's *Faust*.

However, things did not always go smoothly. The orchestra became envious of the large sums Tetrazzini was now earning and demanded double pay. She refused, so in one town – she does not give its name – they went on strike. Going before the curtain she told the audience the position and that this meant the performance would have to be cancelled and their money refunded.

A man in the gallery shouted down asking whether the conductor and the other artists were willing to perform, and when told that they were he pointed at the piano and a violin in the orchestra pit. There must be two members of the audience who could play these instruments and would volunteer to do so. Several hands flew up. 'Then on with the show and hang the strikers!' the fellow shouted, to approving cheers.

So the singers sang the opera as best they could, and far from the performance proving unsatisfactory, they received more applause that night than when the orchestra accompanied them. During the course of the evening the Governor who was present had sent for the municipal band which was awaiting Luisa at the stage door and, playing snatches from the opera, they escorted her through the crowded streets. The people cheered and the church bells were rung.

After such a demonstration the orchestra quickly changed their minds. Next day they relented, sent her an apology, were forgiven and she had no more trouble with them.

Return to Buenos Aires

Meanwhile, despite the political turmoil, opera continued to prosper in Buenos Aires, where Tetrazzini was much missed. The Ghigliani brothers accordingly offered her generous terms to return. She duly accepted and joined their company at the San Martin in mid-August 1895 after provincial wanderings during which, reported the *Standard* for the 13th of that month, she had harvested 'a considerable collection of jewellery' from admirers. Ignoring all safety regulations, people stood in the aisles to hear her again in familiar roles and also for the first time as Philine in Thomas's *Mignon* when the brio, precision and brilliant tone of her rendering of the polacco won yet another ovation – as also did her mischievous Lady Harriet in Flotow's *Martha* on 18 October.

Another impresario, Ciacchi, was holding a season of opera at the Politeama and when he had to vacate it his company combined with that of the Ghiglianis to give six performances by subscription at the invitingly attractive Teatro Nacional in the Calle Florida where the well-heeled and the sophisticated congregated. This opened on 11 October with *Il Barbiere* which was attended by a capacity audience 'in an excessively critical spirit' according to *Le Nación* of 12 October. Whilst Fernando de Lucia's Count Almaviva gained 'thunderous applause', Luisa as Rosina was frowned upon for 'stylistic contradictions, the use of ornament in the first statement of the principal theme of her aria, and the long top notes scattered profusely throughout'.[25] Her admirers, however, rallied to her support with the result that extra performances of the opera had to be given.

Once the season had ended, Luisa returned to Italy after an absence of nearly four years. In Milan she had an emotional reunion with her widowed mother and her sister Elvira.

3 Singing with Caruso

After the spectacular triumphs in South America, Luisa's career in Europe advanced steadily across the continent from Lisbon to St Petersburg. In February 1896 she sang her popular roles of Lucia and Rosina in Lisbon and then Marguerite in Gounod's *Faust*, following which she sang the first two parts at the San Carlo, Naples, where a jealous soprano who had arranged for the claque to crow during the Lesson Scene in *Il Barbiere di Siviglia* was thwarted, not by the recruitment of a counter-claque (which was the usual practice) but by Tetrazzini's brilliance. The hirelings who came to crow cheered instead.[1]

In May and June Luisa joined a company in Warsaw, where in addition to her usual roles she was heard in two new ones – Nedda in *Pagliacci* and the Queen in *Gli Ugonotti* accompanied in all of them by the great baritone Antonio Scotti. Returning to Italy in August she toured with Pietro Cesari and sang as Lucia and Rosina at the Teatro Malibran in Venice. From there they went to his birthplace, Pordenone, to sing in early September and where the tiny town was en fête during their stay. Next, by popular request, they staged *Lucia* with Cesari as Ashton at Treviso's Teatro Garibaldi and Udine's Teatro Minerva. The autumn brought engagements at the Real in Madrid where she added a new role to her repertoire – that of Ofelia in Ambroise Thomas's *Amleto*.

Début in St Petersburg

Apart from the 1896 summer season in Warsaw, Luisa's career had been confined to Latin countries. Then in December came the opportunity for the Florentine Nightingale to try out her wings in St Petersburg when she and Pietro Cesari joined impresario Antonio Ughetti's visiting Italian company in the *Grande Salle du Conservatoire* there. Two of the greatest singers of that epoch now sang with her and gave her every encouragement – the tenor Angelo Masini and that elegant charmer of a baritone, ever generous, bright and merry, Mattia Battistini. After a propitious début as Oscar in *Un Ballo in Maschera*, Luisa won further praise for her tender Adina in *L'Elisir d'Amore* with Cesari cleverly comic as the quack Dulcamara; her Bertha opposite the *tenore di forza* Tamagno in Meyerbeer's *Il Profeta*, her Gilda in *Rigoletto*; and her Queen Margherita di Valois in *Gli Ugonotti* when she audaciously wore a double crown. Finally, after a moving performance as Lucia, she was regarded as the finest new soprano since Adelina Patti.

According to Tetrazzini's *My Life of Song* her success had infuriated a star soprano 'whose name I advisedly suppress' and who tried – unsuccessfully – to destroy the reputation of the newcomer. It is impossible to identify who this might have been as Tetrazzini's account is confusing, no doubt intentionally so. She acknowledges the help of Battistini and Masini in turning what was intended as a trap into a triumph.[2]

Luisa stayed on in St Petersburg for the Lent season, enjoying acclaim as Leila in *I Pescatori di Perle*, Tamara in Anton Rubinstein's *Il Demone* and Micaela in *Carmen*. She also appeared for the only time in her career in the première of an opera, *Lenora*, by Jules Capri. The critics were disappointed that her role as Molli provided no opportunities for coloratura display. The public nevertheless liked the total ensemble and further performances were well supported.

Tetrazzini now went back to Madrid's Principe Alfonso, opening on 2 May 1897 with Amina, then followed by a new role, that of Catherine in Bizet's *La Jolie Fille de Perth* (sung in Italian), Lucia, and Margherita di Valois. But she had to give up singing in late May because, according to Rodolfo Celleti's entry for her in *Le Grandi Voci*, her voice declined 'gravely'. Fortunately this proved only temporary and she had fully recovered by 6 October when she sang Rosina at the Teatro Dal Verme in Milan, then Lucia in both Turin and Trieste. In December she travelled with Cesari all the way to Odessa to take part in the Winter Season at its Teatro Municipale with spectacular success.

Returning to Italy in the spring of 1898, Tetrazzini sang Lucia in Bologna before sailing from Genoa to Buenos Aires to join impresario Amalia Ferrari's *Gran Compania Lirica Italiana* at the Teatro de la Opera and to open in the same role on 24 May with Giuseppe Borgatti as Edgardo. Next day the *Standard* wrote: 'The place was crammed despite the most unfavourable state of the elements.' Three years had passed since Luisa's last season in the city and she was received

> without recognition but the coldness disappeared after her first solo, and the famous rondo in the Mad Scene won such applause as is seldom heard in the Opera House.

During her absence Tetrazzini had become 'a great artist' and her voice 'as clear and resonant as ever in the upper notes' had improved considerably in the lower register.

The last performance of *Lucia* took place on 29 June when, according to the *Standard*, during the Mad Scene

> some youthful scion in the gallery allowed himself the most unbecoming jest of disturbing the breathless listening audience by imitating Señorita Tetrazzini as she sang her difficult staccati with her accustomed blameless security.

On 7 June 1898 Luisa had played Mathilde for the first time that season with Eugenio Giraldoni in the title role of *Guglielmo Tell*.

> The lion of the night was Tamagno who sang the part of Arnoldo to perfection and was obliged to repeat his aria of vengeance . . . Señorita Tetrazzini looked and sang charmingly and it is a pity that in this opera she has so little to show what an excellent 'soprano leggero' she is.

Despite this she produced 'with her velvet voice of admirable pureness, especially in the duet with Arnoldo, a fascinating effect upon her audience.'[3]

When *Guglielmo Tell* was performed for the third time on 20 June the *Standard* thought it might be considered to have been 'a great musical treat but we almost believe that Tamagno's powerful voice is entirely too strong to accompany Señorita Tetrazzini'.[4]

Return to St Petersburg

From August to mid-November 1898 Tetrazzini and Cesari toured, performing in La Plata, Montevideo, Córdoba and Rosario before returning to Milan in late November where, after resting at their home in the Via Abramo Lincoln, they set out for St Petersburg to take part in the Winter Season in the *Grande Salle du Conservatoire*. Here, on 2 January 1899, Tetrazzini sang Gilda with Angelo Masini as the Duke and Mattia Battistini as Rigoletto. The audience refused to allow the performance to continue until she had repeated *Caro nome* and next day the critic Ivan Ivanoff praised her 'golden voice's astonishing agility'. She also had to sing again *Saper vorreste* as the page Oscar in *Un Ballo in Maschera* nine evenings later.

When on January 30 Sigrid Arnoldson sang Mimi to Caruso's Rodolfo in *La Bohème*, Tetrazzini was cast as Musetta. The review in the *Novoe Vremia* found that she acted most engagingly and sang 'with perfect legato and portamento and exemplary carrying over of phrases'. It was the first time she had appeared with Caruso who on 22 February played Edgardo to her Lucia. One reviewer accused Donizetti of lacking melody but this was a common criticism in some Russian musical circles where it was felt that Italian opera's popularity was stifling the young Russian school, and was therefore an enemy to be fought. Regarding Tetrazzini's performance the critics vied with one another in their praise.

'Already in the first aria', declared the *Petersburgskiia Vedomosti*,

> one could not have asked for anything better than her coloratura which was shown off with full brilliance in the very difficult Mad Scene (the echoes with the flute demonstrated the singer's amazingly pure intonation). In the aria accompanying this scene everything was irreproachable – the scales and trills, and all those kinds of vocal tricks which Italian composers often try to substitute for lack of melody and dramatic effect. Besides this, the dreaminess and fine susceptibility of the heroine were made to stand out by this first class artist, who also showed great warmth in the duet with Caruso. That recently invited artist, who had a success in *La Bohème*, this time, too, showed off the beauty of his soft, lyrical tenor, which all the same had little scope in *Lucia*.

The applause after the Mad Scene made the police outside fear a bomb had exploded.

There was a similar reaction next night after her rousing *Io son Titania* when Tetrazzini sang Philine with Arnoldson as Mignon. Then on the 26th St Petersburg witnessed her Rosina for the first time with Battistini as Figaro, Masini as Almaviva and Cesari as her guardian Dr Bartolo. He was heartily applauded for his rendering of the buffo aria. *A un dottore della mia sorte*. *Il Barbiere* was repeated on 11 March for her *serata d'onore* when it seemed the Lesson Scene would never end and when it did Luisa endeared herself to the old guard by singing the Russian song *Solovei*, as Patti once had some thirty years earlier. Lastly, Luisa was cast as Ofelia in *Amleto* and lauded for her Mad Scene.

Winter and Lent 1900 Russian Seasons

Russian food did not appeal to Luisa who longed for spaghetti and regretted not having brought a large supply with her as Verdi had when he came to direct the première of his *La Forza del Destino*. So she was no doubt glad on that account to return to Italy, in early May to sing in Rovigo, Treviso, Livorno, Fermo, Turin and Rome – and feast on pasta before regaining St Petersburg to take part in the Winter Season in the *Grande Salle du Conservatoire* from 1 January to the end of February, and then during March at the Bolshoi in Moscow. In both cities she sang with Caruso again in *Un Ballo in Maschera* and *Lucia* – and in the former also once more as Musetta in *La Bohème*. They became firm friends and his headaches would vanish when her fingers massaged his forehead. He enjoyed her imitations of aristocrats who threatened to shoot themselves unless their charmer yielded. At the fashionable Restaurant Cuba the best table was always reserved for her. Once at a party in the palace at Tsarskoe-Selo when the Grand Duke Vladimir asked her to sing *Funiculi, funiculà*, the Tsar himself joined in.

Caruso's son, Enrico, has written:

> When his partner's voice did not carry as well as his, he would hold back in the duets so as not to overpower or overshadow her – unless it was Melba or Tetrazzini. He was less careful of Melba, because he resented her dislike of him as an Italian, and of Tetrazzini, because she came close to overshadowing him![5]

After Tetrazzini had sung Dinorah and (for the first time in Italy) Elvira at the Adriano in Rome, 'Sebetius' – Amilcare Lauria – wrote in *Le Cronache Musicali Illustrate*, 1 May 1900: 'Her spontaneity, her vocal facility, her musical intelligence and intuition, her dramatic understanding of every scene, are remarkable in every opera that she sings.' Regarding her Elvira, he added:

> The part seems written for her . . . In the *polacca*, in the Mad Scene, she aroused the usual enthusiasm and in order to satisfy her admirers she had to sing the whole of her role twice over. Such artists are rare indeed and to see them appreciated gives us reason to hope that good taste is not yet completely extinguished in our Italian audiences.

Next, indefatigable as ever, Tetrazzini went in May to Warsaw for the second time and there gathered further réclame at the Teatr Wielki for her Dinorah, Rosina and Ofelia.[6]

Luisa's brother, Rodolfo Tetrazzini, was then running an operatic agency in Milan and managing the Teatro Apollo in Lugano where in April 1898 he had engaged Amalia Ferrari's company to present a season of operettas and *opere buffe*. As a result of Rodolfo's association with the Apollo, his sister and Cesari spent the summers of 1899 and 1900 at the Hotel Walter in Lugano.[7]

Luisa's success in the spring of 1900 at the Teatr Wielki led to her returning in October to sing further roles from her repertoire.[8]

Triumphs in Tiflis, Kharkov and Kiev

Then early in 1901 she travelled with Cesari to Georgia where she opened in late March at the Imperial Theatre of Tbilisi (Tiflis) as Lucia followed by Rosina. The correspondent of the *Rassegna Melodrammatica* reported on 2 April that her impact on audiences had been sensational. On the 7th his account described her third triumph, this time in *Dinorah*. She went on to sing four more of her roles to mounting admiration. Students with flaming torches pulled her conveyance to her hotel after every performance. Male admirers sent her jewels but were no doubt kept in check by Cesari.

From Tbilisi Luisa went to Kharkov to sing under the baton of the Italian conductor Esposito who later told the Milan musicologist, John Gualiani, that never in the 35 years spent in that country had he witnessed such enthusiasm as when she sang Rosina there.

The next reports came from Kiev where in May the diva was heard in six of her great roles. A report dated 7 May shows her to have had the same effect there as in Kharkov: 'After her performance in *La Sonnambula* there were scenes of frenzied adulation in and outside the building never witnessed in this city before.'

Tetrazzini then travelled to Lugano to give a concert to raise the money for building a hospital before appearing in a number of performances at the *Teatro Apollo* as Lucia with Cesari as Ashton. The doyen of critics, Béha, confessed: 'Luisa Tetrazzini made the chords of my heart vibrate that I thought had become immune to emotion years ago.' It needed D'Annunzio, he believed, to express adequately in a poem the effect she had on one.

On 25 October back at the Adriano in Rome, Tetrazzini sang Rosina with such success that six more performances were given due to public demand.

Winter 1902 St Petersburg season

Then in January 1902 she and her familiar Cesari returned to St Petersburg where as well as Rosina she sang Elvira, Gilda, Micaela, Musetta, Oscar, Isabella (in Meyerbeer's *Roberto il Diavolo*), Rosina, Matilde (in *Guglielmo Tell*), the title role in *Martha*, and Margherita di Valois. Critics in the years to come were to express astonishment how Luisa, with so little training in her youth, became so accomplished a soprano. During the first fourteen years of her career she went everywhere with Cesari so she must have learnt a great deal through him.

The *Rassegna Melodrammatica* for 7 March 1902 published a tribute to Pietro Cesari stating that he had contributed brilliantly to the season's success:

This renowned *basso comico* is still one of the few singers who conforms to the tradition of a rapidly disappearing school. Few singers possess his knowledge of singing. He can truly be considered a master of expression and of good taste. If he sings something sentimental, he does it with artistry that few others can match. His fun-loving temperament has made him a superb *basso comico*, but many opera goers will know with what dramatic power he can attack a serious role, as for example in Donizetti's *Linda di Chamounix* or Cagnoni's *Papa Martin*. In St Petersburg during the past season, he has sung in *Werther, Il Barbiere*, Laertes in *Mignon*, two roles in *La Bohème*, and Sulpizio in *La Figlia del Reggimento*.

Tetrazzini and Cesari next travelled south to take part for the second time in the Lent and Spring Season at the Imperial Theatre of Tiflis. It was a series of triumphs for her, judging from the reports that were published in the *Rassegna*. Cesari sang with her in four operas and was well liked.

In May the couple travelled to Berlin where the critics were harder to please and where Luisa sang to a German audience for the first time. She had been engaged by Angelo Neumann to join his company assembled for the Verdi Festival at Kaiser Wilhelm II's opera house in the Königsplatz, familiarly known as Kroll's after the former owner. The event opened on Sunday 4 May with *Un Ballo in Maschera*. The *Berliner Lokalanzeiger* wrote next day that Neumann had wanted to keep faithful to the composer's style and spirit and had certainly achieved this. 'Much beauty was discovered by the astonished listeners – much never before fully appreciated in Berlin.' Luisa Tetrazzini as the page sang 'clearly and with ease'. The *Deutsche Blatt*'s verdict was that the performance was 'entirely exemplary'.

On the following Sunday *Rigoletto* was presented with Mario Sammarco in the title role. The *Lokalanzeiger* for 13 May found the performance disappointing.

> Gilda sung by Tetrazzini was missing in heart and soul, but she gained admiration for using her voice like a virtuoso plays a musical instrument. The applause did not reach its height until the tender duet between father and daughter when the audience clamoured for an encore. As the scenery was already being changed, Signor Sammarco brought Signorina Tetrazzini before the curtain where the duet was repeated. That, however, was not in good form.

The third and last role sung by Luisa in Berlin was Violetta. The same critic wrote on 21 May that in addition to her fine singing her acting was 'well thought out and one observed some moving touches, but they lacked subtlety so did not grip one'. However, she completely deserved the enthusiastic applause awarded her.

The Kaiser's Emerald

Kaiser Wilhelm II had attended the performances of all three operas and like President Peña of Argentina was enchanted by Tetrazzini's vocal magic. After the final curtain fell on *La Traviata*, she was summoned to his box where he presented her with an emerald set in platinum ring made by the court jeweller which she was to call 'my token of hope' and to wear on every first night for the rest of her life.

The opera company then travelled to Prague where Tetrazzini was heard as Oscar and Violetta at the *Neues Deutsches Theater*. Critic Dr Richard Batka, reviewing *Un Ballo in Maschera* in *Bohemia* for 1 June 1902 wrote:

After Press reports from Berlin, everyone was very excited about Signora Tetraz-zini. The most important critics had described her as phenomenally brilliant, others judged her as just good, while some were unimpressed. I take the middle road and gladly report how lightly her bright voice soared. Furthermore, the lady, exhausted from the long journey was clearly not in full possession of her normal powers.

Regarding Tetrazzini's Violetta, Dr Batka wrote in *Bohemia* for 3 June:

Signora Tetrazzini has greatly exceeded our expectations. She has a sharp, ringing tone with a considerable flute-like sound and provided many happy moments during the performance. Many judge her greater than Melba. . . . Enough to say that she is excellent and was an outstanding success.

After spending the rest of that summer in Lugano, Luisa sang for the first time at Genoa's Politeama in October, her roles being Lucia and Rosina with Cesari as Bartolo. According to the *Rassegna Melodrammat-ica* for 28 October 1902 she was rapturously received by 'all the great and the good of the city'. Then for the first time since June 1891 she returned to the Teatro Nicolini in Florence to sing Rosina on 17 November. *La Nazione* wrote next day that people filled every vacant space they could find to hear the singer 'who so happily took her first steps among us, steps that led to greatness'. She did not belie her fame and had achieved the previous evening 'one of those successes adding to the glory of the lyric stage'. To demonstrate how versatile she could be to her fellow Florentinians she sang Elvira followed by Amina – and the same critic wrote that she 'transported her audiences with her angelic voice and her outstanding art'.

The year ended with performances in Bucharest. 'Claymoor' in the 'High Life Notebook' of *L'Indépendance Roumaine* praised the 'impressively original manner' in which Tetrazzini portrayed Violetta's death scene in *La Traviata*, while Hunding in the *Epoca* wrote after her successes as Lucia and as Rosina that so perfect had been both her singing and her acting that 'it would be difficult to say in what scene she shone the most'. Cesari also had his share of the commendations and was described as Tetrazzini's husband.

Last St Petersburg Season

The *Rassegna Melodrammatica* in June had revealed that Tetrazzini, taking advantage of her popularity in St Petersburg demanded substantially higher fees from the impresario planning the next Winter Season at the *Grande Salle du Conservatoire* before she would agree to take part. Her terms having been accepted she opened as Musetta to Arnoldson's Mimi on 23 January 1903. Then at last she was given a role that she longed to sing there – that of Violetta in *La Traviata* with Angelo Masini as Alfredo, and achieved one of her greatest successes. The next night she played another part for the first time in Russia, that of Leila in *I Pescatori di Perle* when ovations rewarded her singing of the arie *Siccome un dì* and *Brahma, gran Dio*. There followed on 1 February her sparkling Philine to Arnoldson's Mignon, and a fortnight later Cesari, too, was acclaimed for his Bartolo to her coquettish Rosina and Masini's elegant Almaviva.

In its issue for 22 March the *Rassegna Melodrammatica* carried a long report from its correspondent in the Russian capital.

> A prominent topic of conversation here is the latest operatic triumph of Luisa Tetrazzini. Nevertheless this merely confirms what others have already known who have been present when she has sung other roles and have come away extolling her. Now she has surpassed herself as Juliet in Gounod's opera – a superb creation. . . . Every performance in the vast auditorium could have been filled many times over by the people besieging the box office. Even the most sophisticated in taste have gone wild with enthusiasm. Words fail me to describe adequately the scene and the effect this veritable Queen of Song has on all who listen to her. As previously reported, she has already appeared as Violetta in no less than eight performances of *La Traviata* made necessary by the unprecedented flood of requests from the public to be given the opportunity of hearing her in that role. So great has been her success that she has given a Command Performance in the Imperial Theatre before the Czar himself. And now this fascinating artist has ended her engagements here as Juliet, a part which she invested with astonishing passion revealing yet another aspect of her artistry. The management begged her to remain for further performances but as a result of her triumph in Bucharest last autumn the Roumanian impresario Jean Feder had already engaged her on excellent terms to sing in a concert tour of that country in April. She left for Bucharest yesterday.

And so ended Luisa Tetrazzini's last season in Russia.

Return to the Teatro Pagliano, renamed the 'Verdi' in 1901

Luisa's estranged husband Alberto Scalaberni's health was failing and the Teatro Verdi was now being managed by her brother Rodolfo. It was there, of course, where she had made her début in 1890 and he arranged for her to return to its stage as Rosina on 5 May 1903, followed by Lucia a week later with Ernesto Colli as Edgardo. The critic of the *Fieramosca* wrote of her Lucia:

> It was as if some magical power enabled her to manifest such perfection that those present who had heard Patti and other divas in their youth declared that this their very own Florentine nightingale surpassed them all.

There were eleven performances in all of the two operas. Finally, a gala in Luisa's honour was held on 23 May. The programme consisted of the first three acts of *Lucia* and the last one of *La Sonnambula*. As all who wished to be present could not be squeezed into the auditorium, an 'overflow' gala took place next night when the same programme was repeated.

So many were the floral tributes that a large stand was erected stretching across the back of the stage on which they were displayed in rows. The *Fieramosca* described the effect as that of a horticultural exhibition.

E. M. Forster in his novel *Where Angels Fear to Tread* makes his most insular character describe a performance of *Lucia di Lammermoor* which is based on one that took place in May in the Teatro Pagliano in which Tetrazzini played the title role. Forster wrote that he and E. J. Dent attended this and thought her 'splendid' but never imagined that she would become internationally famous. When she did, he toyed with the idea of writing to her as he believed her to be an 'amiable lady as well as a great artist'. However, he decided against it as he had described her as being 'ugly and stout'.[9]

Luisa's old friend the great tenor, Angelo Masini, was giving a 'farewell' opera season at a theatre in Faenza, near his home town of Forli, and had invited her to take part, so she now went there and on 6 June and for seven further performances sang Leila to his Nadir in *I Pescatori di Perle*. *Il Ravennate*'s review is typical of what the critics wrote. 'Tetrazzini magnificently brings Leila to life.... She never overacts and avoids all melodramatic gesturing.'

On 17 June Luisa sang Violetta to Masini's Alfredo and repeated the success achieved in St Petersburg the previous year.

4 At the Teatro Arbeu

It was in the autumn of the year 1903 that the period of Tetrazzini's greatest success began with her engagement by the impresario Ettore Drog to sing at the Teatro Arbeu in Mexico City. Mexico, then the largest capital in the world, was being busily modernized and adorned with monuments and statues by President Portifirio Diaz. Aged 73, he was to become as great an admirer of Tetrazzini as Peña had been in Buenos Aires.

The company included Giorgio Polacco as conductor and Giulio Rossi, nine years older than Luisa, who was within a year to cause the end of her long partnership and love affair with Cesari. Originally a tenor, Rossi became ill after falling into the river in winter, and his voice changed to a deep bass. He had sung with Luisa in *Gli Ugonotti* and *Il Demone* in St Petersburg in 1897, and after making his début in Parma in 1886 had also sung with Adelina Patti in South America. He had come to the Teatro Arbeu from La Scala where in April that year he was cast as Amfortas in *Parsifal*.[1]

On 22 October Luisa made her Mexican début in *Lucia di Lammermoor* with Ernesto Colli as Edgardo. The critic of *El Imparcial* devoted three columns in praise of her singing.[2] He said she had 'a nest of nightingales in her throat'. *El Popular*[3] wrote of 'a religious and solemn silence in the auditorium whenever she sang as no one wished to miss a single note'. It praised her 'scintillating vocalism and melting legato'. Tickets sold on the black market at many times their face value for the second performance on Sunday the 25th and on the 29th for Luisa's first Rosina in *Il Barbiere* with Colli as Almaviva, Guillermo Caruson as Figaro, Cesari as Bartolo and Rossi as Basilio. There were the usual rave reviews. Tetrazzini was 'the ideal Rosina, as brilliant an actress as she was a singer', Cesari 'a superb comedian', and Rossi with his 'powerful and well managed voice was loudly applauded for his rendering of the *Calunnia* aria'.[4]

A slight indisposition caused the postponement of Luisa's first Violetta from 5 November to the following evening. *El Imparcial*[5] found her *Ah,*

33

fors' è lui 'tellingly phrased, beautiful in tone, bringing the character to life through felicitous vocal colour'. Colli was 'a most passionate Alfredo'. On Sunday 8 November at the matinée, President Diaz himself and his young wife Carmen led the applause after the Mad Scene when Tetrazzini sang Lucia for the third time and it was twenty minutes before she could continue.[6] For her Oscar in *Un Ballo in Maschera* on the 15th[7] and for her Elvira in *I Puritani* on the 19th[8] the reviews were as ecstatic as ever.

On 28 November Luisa appeared as Margherita di Valois in *Gli Ugonotti*[9] with Valentina sung by the Argentinian soprano Amalia De Roma, who sounded breathless and insecure. All the critics admired Luisa's performance but were scathing about De Roma's. This brought to a head the jealous resentment of Tetrazzini's success among De Roma and her friends who now spread rumours that Luisa was Drog's pet and that he was promoting her at the expense of the Argentinian who in consequence had not been given the recognition she deserved and whose performances were of genuine artistic merit only to be appreciated by connoisseurs and not what they described as 'the over-publicized antics and exaggerated posturing of a certain other singer catering for vulgar tastes'. The management's response was to attribute all this to jealousy and to claim that De Roma's lack of success was due to her laziness and failure to take pains with her singing. But the cabal against Luisa remained active.

Although Luisa had been living with Cesari for ten years now, this did not prevent her from having other affairs. On every Sunday in November bullfights were held in the Plaza Mexico opening on the 1st when the Spanish matador Antonio Montes was the attraction. Then on the 15th a toreador from Córdoba, known as *Bebé chico y Machaquito*, starred when Luisa was present. She became friendly with him and came again to encourage him on the following Sunday when he was injured and taken to a hospital. She was his first visitor. On the 22nd this was reported in *El Imparcial*[10] which commented: 'Let us hope Montes does not hear of it, otherwise next Sunday he'll expect similar favours from the lady as compensation.'

This started a whispering campaign among De Roma's supporters. It was alleged that Tetrazzini had done far more than visit Machaquito. A week later the same paper published a letter to its editor from impresario Ettore Drog, which read:

> Through your columns we wish to appeal to the gentlemanly instincts of newspaper editors, urging them to stop an unworthy campaign which for reasons we do not want to make public is being waged by certain journals against that distinguished lady, Luisa Tetrazzini. As she has refused to have recourse to the courts we would wish that editors would be polite enough to stop this campaign which at bottom has no other motive than curiosity. . . . [11]

For her part, Tetrazzini was interviewed by *The Mexican Herald* which reported her as saying:

> I have been perfectly well treated by the Mexican press, but one incident on this visit has upset me. This is the absurd rumour that I embraced one of the bullfighters who was wounded last Sunday.

Tetrazzini need not have worried. In her admirers' eyes as a singing goddess she could do no wrong, and when she sang Gilda on 1 December with 'extraordinary delicacy' there was 'a standing ovation after her sublime *Caro nome*' according to *El Imparcial*.[12]

For her benefit, on the evening of 8 December, Luisa sang Amina in *La Sonnambula*[13]. President Diaz who had heard her sing all her roles during the season was there and *The Mexican Herald* claimed that the brilliance of her final *rondo* sent him and the audience 'into a delirium of enthusiasm never before known in the city'. Many gifts were presented to her, including a silver amphora embossed with Cupids from rival Amalia De Roma, and an Empire style silver dressing-table set in a case of white leather decorated with wide moiré ribbon in the Spanish national colours from the matador Machaquito.

The critics went on indulging in hyperbole when describing their reactions to Luisa's performances. On 19 December *Dinorah* was presented with her in the title role for conductor Polacco's benefit.[14] Four days later the Drog company left for Guadalajara, the second largest city in the country, where in its lavishly beautiful Teatro Degollado – half the size again of Covent Garden Opera House – full audiences acclaimed Luisa's art.[15] They then gave four performances in Puebla, a stronghold of snobs proud of their Spanish descent. Puebla's tumbledown theatre was in sharp contrast with the Teatro Degollado; it had been raining for several days when the Drog company arrived and the roof over the stage was beginning to leak. When Luisa suggested cancelling the opening performance on account of this, the manager was horrified. It would break his heart to refund the money as the theatre was on the brink of bankruptcy and it was the first time for years that every seat had been sold. The backstage staff, too, pleaded with her not to deprive them of their pay, so she reluctantly agreed to appear.[16]

Unfortunately there was torrential rain on the first night, and although pails had to be set in strategic spots to collect the water coming through the roof, some of it splashed over on to the boards which were still very wet despite mopping up operations. To avoid spoiling the fine white gown worn as Lucia, Tetrazzini gathered up its train and held it high over her arm as she stood singing in the few dry areas. Unaware of the real reason for her doing this, a sour-faced old dowager, seated in a box slightly lower than the level of the stage and unable to see its condition, was outraged by such apparent immodesty, and after glaring at the *prima donna* turned her chair round and sat with her back to the stage.

This was more than Luisa could bear. The water had seeped through the soles of her shoes and her gown, despite her efforts, was in a sorry state, so when an opportune moment occurred she made her way as near as possible to the disapproving dragon and sang in Spanish to Donizetti's music:

> Madam, you are shocked, very shocked I know it, yes I do. But do you know the stage is soaking wet and our dresses all are spoiling, yet just to please you I am ready to let my dress drag through the wet and be completely ruined if you, dear madam, will promise to buy me a lovely new one.

Those in the audience who realised what was going on laughed, which so infuriated the occupant of the box that at the end of the act she flung her fur wrap across her shoulders and swept out.

It proved the first time ever in the history of that opera house that people were turned away for five nights running. According to *El Imparcial* Tetrazzini had received $30,000 for the season in Mexico City, having been paid $680 a performance plus the proceeds from her benefit – an all-time record. Thanks to the furore she had created, Drog himself had collected in all some $170,000 at the box office.[17]

Lerner's Contract Offer

An American theatrical manager, Isidore Lerner, had approached Tetrazzini offering her a contract to sing under his direction for a period of six months in the United States. She was to receive $500 for each performance. Luisa signed this on condition that Lerner arranged her entry into the country as well as sending her the railroad tickets and money for the journey. He promised to visit her in Havana on 25 February to settle these details.

El Imparcial for Wednesday 13 January reported that the opera company had left by rail on that Monday morning for Vera Cruz with the exception of Tetrazzini who set off in the evening cocooned in a luxurious *carro salón* provided by the management. They would be sailing for Cuba mid-day aboard the steamer *Francia*.[18]

Tetrazzini opened the season at the Teatro Nacional in Havana on 30 January with her Lucia and went on to sing most of the roles she had performed at the Teatro Arbeu. In addition she sang Mimi in *La Bohème* for the first time on 3 March with Ernesto Colli as Rodolfo.

The next day J. E. Triay wrote in the *Diario de la Marina*:

> The music of *La Bohème* is, of course, to speak plainly, within the broad ambit

of the modernist school. The public listens to it with delight and claps it enthusiastically. I will say little about its interpretation. Sra Tetrazzini made a real sacrifice to perform the part of Mimi, in which the other Tetrazzini, Eva, rose to such heights when I saw her scarcely three years ago at the Royal in Madrid.

Later Enrique Fontanills in the same paper reported that there would be a repeat performance of *La Bohème* 'on Sunday matinée, but with Tetrazzini replaced by Jacobi, an artist who had been unfairly ignored throughout the season'. He added that the audience would also hear 'the brilliant diva sing the waltz from *Dinorah* in homage to maestro Polacco and that afternoon will be for her benefit'.

The impression one gets from these two reports is that Tetrazzini was unhappy in the role of Mimi. She never performed it again on the stage, but she was to sing the Act I love duet with Amedeo Bassi at the reception following her second marriage years later. The season in Havana ended on the above mentioned Sunday but in the evening, with her as Marguerite in the Italian version of Gounod's *Faust*. For the rest of the month and most of April the company toured Cuba performing at the Teatro Otero in Cardenas and at theatres in Cienfuegos and Santiago. Lerner had failed to meet her in Havana as promised, so she decided to go to New York in search of him. First she and the others performed at the Teatro Albisu in Havana opening on 23 April with *La Sonnambula* followed by *Lucia di Lammermoor* in both of which Giulio Rossi sang with her. Then three nights later he played Mephistopheles to her Marguerite.

Break with Cesari

On 10 May *El Imparcial* quoted in full a report[19] that had just appeared in the Havana newspaper *El Mundo* about Luisa's having eloped with Rossi.

> For 14 years she has lived with the 52 year old singer Pietro Cesari as if she were his wife, and according to him he has patiently put up with all the trouble caused by her affairs with other men. One evening he found in her dressing-room a letter from Rossi in which he attacked Cesari and urged her to leave him. Cesari pocketed this and now treated her so offensively that unable to find it she guessed what had happened. Remembering that he had threatened to shoot her if she deceived him again, the lady decided to flee.

After the performance of *Faust* on 29 April Tetrazzini had returned to the house where Pietro lived with her, No. 3 Calle de Zulueta, and in the middle of supper, pretending not to feel well, she had gone out onto the patio and then made for Rossi's lodgings in the nearby Calle de Empedrado, taking with her 300 pesos and Cesari's revolver. The lovers had then left the town and the country. Immediately Cesari discovered he had been duped he rushed to the police station, where at 3 am on 30 April, according to the evening edition of the *Diario de la Marina* of Havana, he demanded to put his complaint before the duty court. There the prompter Luis Uberti described how during the previous evening he had noticed the fugitives whispering to each other with meaningful looks as though they were urgently plotting something.

What upset Cesari most was that Luisa had taken the 300 pesos with her, because he told the court that, having lived together for so many years as man and wife, he considered himself entitled to half their joint earnings and that had always been the arrangement between them. In fact as Tetrazzini earned far more than Cesari he had done extremely well during their long partnership. In return, being 22 years older than she, he had played the role of a protector and father figure as well as a lover.

Years later when Lerner was suing Tetrazzini the *Philadelphia Inquirer* for 14 April 1910 quoted her as saying that his failure to meet her in Havana forced her to sing there in a third class opera house to raise the money to reach New York where she failed to find him. As a result she led a hand to mouth existence for months. 'It was the hardest time of my life,' she told the interviewer.

A talent scout employed by Heinrich Conried, general manager of the Metropolitan, had heard Tetrazzini singing at the Teatro Arbeu and had sent him a highly favourable report. This was the accompanist and conductor Gaetano Merola. Learning about this, she swept one morning into Conried's office and told him that she had enough offers of singing engagements to last her for years. 'Why don't you engage me?' she suggested, according to the account that was to appear later in the *New York World* for 29 December 1907. 'How much do you want?' he asked. She named a sum for performances scarcely one-fifth of which he was paying the Met's star coloratura, Marcella Sembrich – and Conried accepted with such alacrity that Luisa realized she had made a mistake. She now proved herself an astute negotiator and demanded the right to choose the roles in her repertoire she would be asked to sing. This alarmed Conried because it would lead to a contest for the accolades of critics and public between her and Sembrich, who was thirteen years older. The newcomer also wanted the management to contribute towards the cost of her costumes and her travelling. Conried had assumed at the start that she would agree without any demur to his terms, being only too grateful for the privilege of performing at so great an opera house. He pursued delaying tactics which irritated her and when she received an offer from Ettore Drog to rejoin his company in Mexico City for the autumn season she accepted it.

Flawed Contract

This brought matters to a head with Conried and a contract was prepared and signed on 10 September 1904 before Tetrazzini left for Mexico, whereby she committed herself to sing for the Metropolitan for three years as from November 1905. Still uneasy as to whether the terms would lead to trouble with Sembrich, Conried deliberately failed to bind the contract by depositing a guarantee with Tetrazzini's bankers. (See Discography for details of her first records made on 8 September that year at the studios of the Universal Talking Machine Company of New York.)

Meanwhile, Pietro Cesari abandoned hopes of a reconciliation with Luisa. He eventually went to Spain where he continued his career. Later, aged 73, he collapsed and died on 24 October 1922, at the Milan Railway Station while going to take a train to sing the roles of Don Bartolo and Don Pasquale at Casalmonferrat.

The Havana affair does not appear to have harmed Tetrazzini's popularity in Mexico City. In the majority, opera-goers were interested only in her voice and not in her private life. Many blamed Cesari for expecting to go on sharing Tetrazzini's earnings. Others pointed out that Patti, so admired when she sang in Mexico, had lived in adultery with the tenor Nicolini, having left her husband the Marquis de Caux who had refused to divorce her – while Nicolini himself had abandoned his wife and five children. That kind of private life had not deterred the Mexican President from presenting Patti with a solid gold crown at the end of the season in 1889.

In fact both impresario Ettore Drog and opera-goers were relieved that Tetrazzini was back for, with the intention of increasing his profits, he had engaged third-rate singers with the exception of Luisa, soprano Livia Berlendi, tenors Giorgio Bazelli and Carlo Cartica, and bass Giulio Rossi.

Enter Giorgio Bazelli

Bazelli,[20] who had come from Milan, was to play a major role in Tetrazzini's life up to the 1914–18 war. Born in Craiova, Rumania, in 1868, and originally an engineer, he later took up singing as a profession and made his début in the title role of Gounod's *Faust* in 1900 at Bologna. He went on to sing at La Scala and other important opera houses in Italy and Austria. In the autumn of 1904 he joined Ettore Drog's company at the Teatro Arbeu in Mexico City.

The season there opened on 27 September with *Aida*. The title role was taken by Angela Penchi, a fading prima donna who should have retired, for her voice had become harsh and badly worn with the result that even

the distinguished and elegant audience hissed her and the other artists
at the end of the first act. Misfortune pursued the company until 2 October
when Bizet's *Les pêcheurs de perles* was given in Italian with Tetrazzini
as Leila. Her first Lucia of the season followed on the 9th, and although
her own singing gave unfailing pleasure *El Imparcial*[21] was scathing about
Carlo Cartica's Edgardo and Giuseppe La Puma's Enrico.

And so the season continued with Tetrazzini, soprano Livia Berlendi
and Bazelli alone being praised. On 12 October Bazelli appeared as
Wilhelm Meister with Berlendi in the title role of Thomas's *Mignon* and
with Tetrazzini as Philine, acclaimed for her rendering of the polonaise.
Then on the 22nd she sang Amina to Bazelli's Elvino and the next night
Gilda to his Duke. Audiences had been dwindling whenever the other two
tenors Cartica and Frosini sang so Drog cast Bazelli in their roles instead.
This meant that he was being asked to sing almost every night, too great
a burden for him to endure for long, so Drog cabled Ernesto Colli who
had been so successful the previous season to ask if he would rejoin the
company. Fortunately, he was free and agreed to do so.

In the meantime, Bazelli and Tetrazzini sang the title roles on 3 November in Gounod's *Romeo e Giulietta* – 'delicately interpreted' by them
according to *El Imparcial* – on the 10th the couple appeared again in
Mignon with Berlendi and on the 12th they and Rossi enjoyed an enormous success in *Lakmé*. After returning, Colli had given a pedestrian
performance as Alfredo with Tetrazzini as Violetta in *La Traviata* on 17
November. Then six days later, to Drog's discomfiture, he gave the worst
performance of his career, as Canio in *Pagliacci*. This put new heart into
the tenor Frosini, who then took over the role of Canio owing to Colli's
'indisposition' on the 15th. This he did with such feeling and brilliance
that the audience could not believe he was the same tenor they had booed
earlier in the season.

On 20 November Tetrazzini sang Margherita to Bazelli's Faust and
Rossi's Mephistopheles, and on the 26th Rosina for her benefit. This
proved yet another triumph for her, with President Diaz leading the
applause after the Lesson Scene. Nevertheless the *Subsecretaria de Instruction Publica*, which administered the Government's subsidy to the Teatro
Arbeu, was dissatisfied with the way Drog was running the company and
its mounting losses, so it withdrew its concession, bringing the season to
an abrupt close.[22] The principal artists led by Tetrazzini and Bazelli held an
emergency meeting and decided to become financially responsible for
taking over another theatre, the Circo Orrin. They opened to a full house
with *Il Barbiere di Siviglia* on 29 November. *Faust* was presented for
Bazelli's benefit on 6 December, and a miscellaneous programme ending
with Tetrazzini's singing of the Shadow Song from *Dinorah* was put on
for conductor Polacco's benefit next night. Then for the matinée of the

8th Tetrazzini appeared in *Lucia*. This proved to be one of the most momentous occasions in her life, thanks to the presence of 'Doc' Leahy from San Francisco's Tivoli.

Enter 'Doc' Leahy

It has been claimed that no American theatre did more to popularize opera than the Tivoli[23] which Joseph Kreling originated in 1875 as a beer garden in his former residence, a high-busted house on the north side of Sutter Street where the customers sat at tables, drank beer and listened to a ten-piece orchestra and Tyrolean singers. When a fire destroyed the building four years later Kreling built a theatre on Eddy Street which he called the Tivoli Opera House. This never closed for 26 years, save when it was being rebuilt in 1904. Here for four months annually lovers of grand opera listened mostly to works by French and Italian composers, and for the remaining eight months to light opera by Gilbert and Sullivan, Offenbach, Lecoq and von Suppé.

The Krelings had various business interests, including a furniture company where one William H. Leahy, known later as 'Doc' Leahy, was first employed as an upholsterer. He then married Joe's daughter, took over the Tivoli's management in 1893, and later became a successful impresario on the West Coast thanks to his enterprise and flair for spotting musical talent.

In 1904 Leahy, run down through overwork, was ordered by his doctor to take a complete rest, so went off with his friend, Italian editor Ettore Patrizi, to Mexico City, where they were met in the early afternoon of 8 December by Polacco. Explaining that he had to rush away to conduct a performance of *Lucia di Lammermoor*, Polacco mentioned that the mediocre company boasted a coloratura soprano who was proving an enormous attraction and was admired by President Diaz himself.[24] Leahy's interest was immediately aroused and he and Patrizi attended the matinée. The curtain rose to tatty scenery. At least Polacco was a superb conductor who drew the most out of his second-rate orchestra. Then a woman, rather plump but of a pleasing personality, appeared. She completely held the audience's attention and when she sang Leahy was immediately deeply impressed and turning to Patrizi, without knowing it, he repeated what the Buenos Aires critics had said: 'She could become a second Patti.' Then, as the curtain fell at the end of the first act, with his mind already made up, he went in search of Tetrazzini. Entering her dressing-room, he introduced himself and offered her twice what she was then being paid if she came as soon as possible to sing for him at the Tivoli. To have agreed at once would have meant leaving her fellow artists in the lurch, for there was no one among them capable of taking her place. Leahy argued with her but she would not give way. If he wanted her, he must engage the others, too. He yielded.

'Doc' Leahy stayed on to hear Tetrazzini give fine performances in *I Pescatori di Perle* on 10 December and next day in *Rigoletto*. He then decided that Gilda was the part in which she must make her début at the Tivoli. After that he saw her as Violetta on the 15th, and on the following day he returned whilst she and the others travelled to the Teatro la Paz in San Luis Potosi for a short season.[25] Here in this then wealthy silver-producing city she impressed ostentatiously attired audiences with her virtuosity, before going on to the Teatro Degollado in Guadalajara for a few performances.

In an article headed 'by Luisa Tetrazzini' in the Christmas Day issue of the *San Francisco Chronicle* in 1921 soon after the publication of her reminiscences, she gave a vivid account of her journey from Mexico City to San Francisco. Unfortunately, like so much she related about her life, it is inaccurate about the date of her début. The account goes:

> It was in the early summer of 1905 and just at that important moment the Rio Grande river burst its banks in the midst of terrific rain storms, flooding a vast stretch of country. One valley section became not merely a lake but the Salton sea, as it was called, where mile after mile the water surged and eddied. Already we had started, and our route carried us straight into that Salton sea.... On every hand was the mass of waters, muddy, cruel, full of floating debris dashing up against the cars as the engine dragged us ahead slower and more slowly still. Presently the waters began to creep up the car steps as we got in deeper. Soon they were seeping in snake-like streams down the car aisle to where we sat terrified.... We had to get up on the seats as the current streamed past us. Soon the engine stopped stock still. The waters had put its fires out, and we were stalled helpless.... Then came long, piercing whistles. A high, giant engine, whose fires the waters of Salton could not reach, had been sent by Mr Leahy to our rescue.

One wonders if anyone reading this in the San Francisco Chronicle in 1921 had attended Tetrazzini's début at the Tivoli on 11 January 1905 and might have written to the Editor pointing out that it did not occur in June. Whoever penned this graphic invention in her name possibly consulted first the article in the June 1907 issue of the *National Geographical Society's Journal* entitled 'The New Enclosed Sea'. It may be, of course, that the real journey took place in early January and as the weather then was certainly appalling, Tetrazzini's 'ghost' writer yielded to temptation and changed the month to add colour to the event.

The rest of the article, however, is accurate. It continues:

> The opera costumes of the entire company did not arrive with us; many of the chorus did not even have their stage shoes. Additional members of the chorus and orchestra had been recruited locally. Consequently opera costumes for

many had to be routed out of the Tivoli theater storage by Mr Leahy and rehearsals held feverishly by Mr Polacco up to twenty minutes to eight that evening. This I heard later, for I had been hurried at once to a hotel to rest up for the performance.

Yet another version of Luisa's journey from Mexico City to San Francisco is given by André Benoist in his memoirs.[26] He wrote that having accepted Leahy's offer to sing at the Tivoli she was faced with a problem. She had 'an ironclad contract' with the management at the Teatro Arbeu.

> She shrewdly figured that, although a rear entrance, here was an open door to the United States and fame and fortune. But how to get out of the country where penalties for breach of contract were very heavy? Consequently she set about to circumvent the law.

According to Benoist, disguised in a man's clothes, wearing 'a boyish wig' and a false moustache, she boarded a steamer unrecognised. Then, once in her cabin, she heard a commotion on deck and learnt from the steward that the police were searching for a lady who was escaping from the law. Not knowing what better to do, she ran to the men's lavatory and stood alongside other men. As a result when the police looked through the doorway all they saw was her back, and as a result she avoided detection.

Benoist was not to meet Tetrazzini and become her accompanist until five years later and his book was published in 1938. Anecdotes are inclined to become embroidered in the retelling and this one probably has its origins in Tetrazzini's escape from Buenos Aires to avoid paying the legal expenses incurred in the dispute with her first husband, Scalaberni (or even how she managed to get away from Havana after breaking with Cesari). She was also on two other occasions to resort to similar devices to outwit lawyers, as we shall learn later.

5 The Tivoli – and Lawsuits

Samuel Dickson was a journalist who published three books about San Francisco, retelling stories about its past which he had previously broadcast on a weekly radio programme beginning in 1943. In *The Streets of San Francisco*[1] he related how, though many years had passed since the evening on 11 January 1905 when he heard Tetrazzini first sing at the Tivoli, he could still feel 'the exuberance and spellbinding excitement that flowed from her before she uttered even one note'. Then after she had sung *Caro nome* in the first act there was a moment of absolute silence before the whole audience rose and applauded.

> The orchestra men jumped up and cheered. Men stood on the seats of their chairs and threw their hats in the air – women tore flowers from their dresses and threw them on the stage.

And when the pandemonium had ceased, Tetrazzini responded by singing *Caro nome* again.

Giorgio Bazelli sang the Duke of Mantua, Arturo Romboli Rigoletto, and Polacco conducted on that memorable occasion at the old Tivoli. Ashton Stevens, the music critic of the *San Francisco Examiner*[2] wrote similarly that after *Caro nome* 'the crowd was hers'. The gallery full of Italians shouted compliments in their native tongue.

> The family circle desported itself in anything but a dignified way – it was a crescent of swinging arms. And the downstairs sat back in its upholstery and banged away palm on palm, man and woman alike. Twice did Tetrazzini sing that song.

But what established beyond all doubt her greatness was her singing in the second act, wrote Stevens. 'Then a star blazed'.

Next day the *San Francisco Chronicle* commented that it was not surprising that Heinrich Conried had contracted with Tetrazzini for her to sing the Sembrich and Melba roles with the Metropolitan company. After her performance at the Tivoli there was every reason 'to think that at some near-by day Melba and Sembrich may be signed to sing Tetrazzini roles'.

Tetrazzini's success was even more remarkable for she had caught a cold when travelling from Mexico. This now worsened but nevertheless she insisted in singing Rosina as advertised on Friday the 13th with Bazelli as Almaviva, La Puma as Figaro, and Rossi as Basilio. After she had sung the *Carnival of Venice* and the Proch variations in the Lesson Scene, reported the *San Francisco Bulletin* on the morrow, the audience 'stood up and screamed, screamed, screamed, until, cold or no cold, she had to cast the golden notes again'.

Such professional valiance, however commendable, was unwise for the following day she became so ill that her doctor forbade her to leave her bedroom and the evening performance of *Rigoletto* had to be cancelled. It was touch and go as to whether she would recover to sing Lucia on the following Tuesday but she managed it. 'All the beauty and bells and the brightness have returned to Signora Tetrazzini's voice,' declared the *Chronicle* on the Wednesday. It had been 'a tremendous triumph', and after the Mad Scene 'the house went wild with enthusiasm'.

Josephine Hart Phelps, critic of *The Argonaut*, opened her review:

> Tetrazzini, the big little soprano, seems to fix her preference on the operas of the older school. . . . Only a high pure soprano like hers can scale such airy ladders of sound sending from each silver rung a spray of liquid pearls. Her voice is almost altogether made up of white notes and in effect her singing is as effortless as the flow of a running brook. It is odd to see how little she opens her mouth. Yet the tones come forth pure sterling silver, unalloyed by a single vocal blur resulting from misplaced effort. The real climax comes in the flute solo, which displayed not only the purity of Tetrazzini's voice, but the ease and brilliancy with which she duplicated all the chromatic flights of the flute.[3]

Tetrazzini dressed 'expensively' and her fingers were 'loaded with jewels'. She was altogether splendid in the yellow gown that matched her hair, although it was plain to see that her heart was not wrapped up in dress. 'Else would she abjure the too numerous petticoats that prevent Lucia's white lace dressing-gown from clinging statuesquely, and likewise would she know by instinct that all those fidgety little flounces cut down her already diminutive height.'

Lucia was repeated for seven more performances, so great was the popular demand.

On 19 January Tetrazzini sang Violetta with Colli as Alfredo and Arturo Romboli as Germont, and next day the *Chronicle* found that she performed the role to perfection, seizing every opportunity 'for accentuating all her graces'. She was heard again in *La Traviata* four times.

On 24 January Luisa sang Marguerite to Bazelli's *Faust* in the Italian version of Gounod's opera. Giulio Rossi appeared as Mephistopheles –

the same role he had played in May the previous year in Havana when she had deserted Cesari and eloped with him. Rossi had now been supplanted in her affections by Bazelli who, much on his mettle that night, put his whole heart into his acting and singing. The *San Francisco Chronicle's* critic thought his interpretation of the character was 'full of fire and yet poetic' and that he deserved 'all sorts of honors'. Mephistopheles could not have been acted with more malevolence than Rossi had. The tension between the two men upset Tetrazzini and she gave a lacklustre performance. The *Chronicle* regretted that 'she did not recall the brilliant Patti as many expected she would'. There were only two more performances – on the 28th (a matinée) and the 31st. After that she rarely played Marguerite again.

In its review dated 25 January, the *San Francisco Bulletin* wrote that if there were a fault, it was that of the role and not in Tetrazzini 'for she is a lyric singer above all and cannot have the epic quality of Melba'. Melba was on a concert tour of the West Coast and sang at the Alhambra Theater in San Francisco on 7 and 11 February – the same days on which Tetrazzini was singing Lucia at the Tivoli. In the Australian's programme was the Mad Scene from Donizetti's opera and also *Ah, fors' è lui* and *Sempre libera* from *La Traviata*. The rivals enjoyed full houses and the critics carefully avoided offending either in their reviews.

On 9 February Tetrazzini played Leila in *I Pescatori di Perle* at its first performance in San Francisco. She was supported by Bazelli as Nadir. The *Chronicle* next day considered that the part had 'brought out new beauties in her voice, showing unexpected volume and much dramatic fervor'.

The season was originally supposed to end on 4 February, but proved so successful that it was extended for a fortnight. Even then the public clamoured for more, and unexpected news enabled 'Doc' Leahy to keep the company on for another two weeks. They were due to start a season at the opera house in Havana, but a cablegram arrived from its director stating that their opening must be postponed for a fortnight owing to 'a complication with a dramatic company' playing there. Thanks to this, Tetrazzini sang Elvira in *I Puritani* on the 14th. The next day, the *Chronicle* declared her voice in the role to have been 'tenfold bigger' than in any other. 'It soared way up to E absolutely true and clear.' Then on the 24th she was asked to take over at short notice from Fannie Francesca the role of Philine in Thomas's *Mignon*. According to the *Chronicle*: 'Her success was electric. She never sang better than last evening.'

Josephine Hart Phelps in *The Argonaut*[4] commented that Tetrazzini, in the 'florid music' of *I Pescatori di Perle* and *I Puritani*, had demonstrated the brilliancy of her singing. The 'ear noted with pleasure the freshness and purity of her voice and the ease of her execution'. One would do better, however, 'to keep ears open and eyes shut'. In the first opera it was fatal to look at her costume.

> Leila is a Hindoo maiden and Tetrazzini has conscientiously supplied her with a pair of chocolate-colored arms, a sooty neck, and a dusky complexion that doesn't match and shines stickily with the compound of which it is made. 'Away with such realism!' say I.

Samuel Dickson wrote that on the Saturday night of the first week when Tetrazzini sang at the Tivoli he dined with his grandmother at the Marie Antoinette apartment house on Van Ness Avenue, between Pine and Bush Streets. Suddenly they heard 'an exquisite voice coming through the wall' singing an Italian street song with 'an equally beautiful tenor voice'. It was Tetrazzini adding her voice to that of Caruso as she played his gramophone records in the room next door. As a result for the rest of the season at the Tivoli, Dickson went every day to his grandmother's house. 'She wasn't misled, she didn't for a moment believe it was a newly developed devotion for her on my part! I came to hear Tetrazzini and Grandma knew it.'

According to Dickson, Tetrazzini sang all the time from grand opera to folk songs. Day after day, Dickson claimed, he would lie on the floor, his ear pressed to the wall.

> As thrilling as her singing was her laughter. She would sing and go into long peals of the happiest laughter. She would chatter to herself in Italian very fast and begin laughing or singing again. Sometimes grandma would shake her head. People who talked to themselves were not quite right in their minds.

When it was dinnertime, Samuel would wait until he heard Tetrazzini's door open and close, then he would dash out so as to reach the elevator at the same time as her. They went down together evening after evening while she grinned at him and his grandmother, but they never spoke.

Downstairs in the restaurant used by the residents, Tetrazzini sat at the next table. Unlike most sopranos who eat little before singing, Tetrazzini always ordered the same thing – a monster portion of tagliarini and a generous quart of red wine. Dickson watched her wind as much as she could round her fork and plunge it into her wide, laughing mouth, pausing only to wash the food down with a glassful of wine at a time. The meal over, Luisa went off to the Tivoli where her young admirer would follow to listen to her. He wrote that she sang as if each one of her notes was delighting her. 'She played with them as a child might play with the bubbles that dance from a clay soap-pipe.'

The final week of Tetrazzini's first season at the Tivoli provided an opportunity for 'Doc' Leahy to make as much money as he could by presenting her in a different role every night. On Tuesday 21 February she sang Leila; on the 23rd Elvira; on the 24th Philine; and on the Saturday matinée Lucia. She proved indefatigable. Lastly at Polacco's benefit concert on the Sunday afternoon she sang *Io son Titania*, followed in the evening by appearing as Violetta, Gilda and Lucia in one act from each of the operas in question. The *Chronicle* next morning reported that there were 'wild demonstrations' throughout from admirers with whom at the end she played 'battledore and shuttlecock with flowers, while somebody presented her with an Angora cat over the footlights'.

After such hectic activity Tetrazzini remained behind to rest in San Francisco whilst Polacco and the others went on to Havana. In any case after her unhappy experiences there with Cesari she never wanted to sing in Cuba again. Giulio Rossi left, too. Between then and 1919 he sang at various times at the Metropolitan in New York. His affair with Tetrazzini having ended, Bazelli replaced him. She now planned to form once more her own company in which he would sing the leading tenor roles and negotiations were begun for a short summer season in Mexico.

A devout Catholic, Luisa found worshipping in church more congenial if she could do so with song. This was possibly why on the first two Sundays in March, when attending Mass in the Church of Nuestra Señora de Guadalupe, she sang on the 5th the Bach-Gounod *Ave Maria* and on the 12th that by Arrilaga plus Reyer's *O Salutaris Hostia* at Benediction.

On 6 April the Metropolitan's touring company opened at the Grand Opera House with Marcella Sembrich and Enrico Caruso singing Gilda and the Duke in *Rigoletto*, the same opera in which Tetrazzini had made her brilliant début at the *Tivoli*. As in the case of Melba's concert at the Alhambra, the San Francisco papers tactfully avoided offending either lady. Each was superb. 'One must not compare great artists and personal preferences and personality must be the measuring stick,' wrote the *Examiner*. Sembrich had been singing major roles at the *Grand Théâtre du Conservatoire* in St Petersburg when Tetrazzini first sang there in 1897 and they were on friendly terms. Luisa had, of course, sung a number of times with Caruso there as already mentioned.

When on 10 April Sembrich sang Lucia with Caruso as Edgardo, Tetrazzini and Bazelli were seated in the front row and the *Chronicle* next day wrote that Sembrich recognised the other soprano across the footlights and gave her 'a special bow'. In return, 'Tetrazzini waved her handkerchief and rose just enough to make acknowledgement'.

Tetrazzini must have told Caruso that she was soon to set out on an operatic tour of Mexico. It so happened that the 27 year old Italian baritone Domenico Viglione Borghese was in San Francisco at the time, then employed as a salesman by a millionaire miller. He had made a brilliant début as the Herald in *Lohengrin* at Lodi in 1899 but had suddenly given up singing as a career in the hope of making a fortune in California. He happened to sing at a private party where Caruso was present and so impressed him that on learning shortly afterwards that Tetrazzini lacked a baritone he recommended that she should engage Viglione Borghese. She invited him to call on her at the Palace Hotel. He was reluctant to give up lucrative employment but happily a compromise was reached when his employer granted him three months' leave.

Victim of fraud?

Then there was an unexpected hitch. Tetrazzini suddenly discovered that she had been defrauded of a considerable sum of money. In *My Life of Song*[5] she wrote that when in Mexico a man was introduced to her who claimed to have met her in Buenos Aires. She does not give his name but it was Julio Zeigner Uriburu, known by his intimates as 'Lullo', a nephew of the President of Argentina who succeeded Saenz Peña. She describes Uriburu as a 'tall, handsome, magnetic man, middle-aged, and with plenty of assurance' who told her that for a time he had been the Argentine consul in Mexico City. One day he offered to save her money.

> He said that, as he was still connected with the Government, he could have my earnings transferred from Mexico to Italy, or to whoever I chose, without my having to lose so much on the exchange and in postages (sic). I looked at him sharply as the terrible thought occurred – was he trying to rob me? But as his blue eyes looked so honest I felt he must be the soul of honour. Nevertheless I did not agree to his proposal.

Later other members of the opera company (according to Tetrazzini) were approached by the man in the same way, and they used his services. She heard subsequently that the sums in question were all safely received in Italy. There came a time when she wanted to pay her dressmaker for work done, and being very busy she trusted Uriburu to send the money. However, her dressmaker failed to acknowledge receipt of the sums sent, so she asked her 'Adonis-like' agent whether there had been any hitch. He assured her blandly that the transaction had gone through. But her suspicions were not so easily allayed, so she wrote to the dressmaker who at last replied that she had not received any payment. Tetrazzini says that, alarmed by this news, she went straight to a solicitor.

> The police were called, and they soon identified the former consul as an associate of a gang of expert criminals. They also discovered that for a time, hoping to be entrusted with some more of my money, he had made it a daily practice to call for my foreign mail so as to prevent my hearing from my dressmaker. The police were very soon on his track, and not long afterwards he was arrested. They found him in a fashionable restaurant entertaining a well-dressed woman in lavish fashion . . . all at my expense. In the courts the ex-consul told an amazing tale. He . . . solemnly announced that he had found me in London, where I was then an unknown singer. Having discovered that I

was a musical genius ... he had decided to spend all his savings in order to bring me to the front. . . .

And the reason why he had taken this 27,000 francs, he said, was that I, now successful, had forgotten completely my obligations to him. . . . He had asked me to repay him only a little of the money that he had expended in raising me to my pedestal, but that I had haughtily refused. It was then that the idea had entered his mind to recover the money by subterfuge. My astonishment at his audacious tale may be readily imagined. No credence whatever was given to his story by the judge, who sentenced him to – if I remember rightly – seven months' imprisonment. The 27,000 francs were not recovered for me.

That is Tetrazzini's account of what happened. The San Francisco newspapers of that year give a lively, and here and there different, version of the affair. The *Call* for Thursday 20 April 1905[6] reported how that Monday she had received startling news from Milan demanding payment of debts believed settled.

In the sumptuous apartment of Madame Tetrazzini at the Marie Antoinette all was confusion and excitement last night as she began to realize that all her hard work here had gone for naught and was taken with a violent attack of hysterics. Her immediate friends tried to assuage her grief. They were only partly successful, however, for early in the evening she succumbed to the strain and was put to bed. She denied herself to all visitors. The nurse sent down word to all callers that Madame Tetrazzini was too ill to see anyone. Signor Bazelli, a friend, who sang with her, consented to speak to her and told the following story . . .

'When Madame Tetrazzini wanted to send money away, Uriburu would pretend to transmit it through the Swiss-American Bank to the parties for whom it was intended. He would show her a fake duplicate draft which he represented to her was a draft issued by the bank in regular form.

'He would tell her at the same time that he had forwarded the original to Europe for the parties to whom she desired the money sent. He must have taken these bank drafts secretly away from the bank and then filled them out himself. . . . We all thought Uriburu was rich. He made magnificent presents to all of us connected with the company. He gave me this fine gold watch and chain and these handsome gold trinkets attached to it.'

Bazelli went on to tell the reporter that Tetrazzini and he had signed contracts to start singing in opera in Mexico that coming week. They were about to leave the previous night when this sensation was sprung on them. There was no truth in the report of a love affair between Tetrazzini and 'Lullo' Uriburu. That was ridiculous. He only acted as her financial agent. Bazelli did not know now when they would be able to go to Mexico. Tetrazzini had to remain and see the affair straightened out. It might cause them to lose their coming engagements.

According to the *Call*, when searched after his arrest, Uriburu had $455 in gold coins on his person. Interviewed later, he said:

I met Tetrazzini ten years ago in Argentina. Two years ago we came together in the City of Mexico and our friendship increased. The singer confided with me in nearly all of her affairs and I attended to many of her financial matters, particularly in Europe.

He claimed to have handled over 50,000 francs for her. There had never been any trouble until the last few transactions.

> I came to San Francisco about February 1 of this year. I came as a friend of the woman. She had preceded me by several weeks, but upon my arrival I continued to handle her affairs and delivered the last 4000 francs I am accused of embezzling to a local broker with a request that it be sent to Milan. Three days ago I was informed that the money had not reached its destination.

Uriburu ended his story by saying it might be that his broker had absconded with the money. He would be making inquiries.

> However it is probable that the friendship this songbird has bestowed upon me for several years may be on the wane to the profit of someone else and that this charge may have grown out of jealousy.

Owing to a misunderstanding regarding the time of the hearing Tetrazzini failed to appear in Police Judge Conlan's court at 10 a.m. on 20 April 1905 to testify against Julio Zeigner Uriburu, so the case was adjourned until next morning. According to the *Evening Post* for 22 April she swept in wearing 'a gorgeous tea gown' of black net 'en train' with three heavy flounces on the long skirt, huge diamond earrings and a large black picture hat trimmed with white silk. At the calling of the case, Uriburu's attorney asked for a postponement in order that certain information he had called for might be received which would enable him to cross examine Signorina Tetrazzini more closely than if forced to do so after only two days preparing the defence.

Attorney A. Heyneman, special counsel for the plaintiff, opposed a long postponement, as his client was due in Mexico City to sing in opera, but he would consent to a short one until Monday.

When the case was resumed on 27 April Bazelli gave evidence. He told the Judge that he had heard Uriburu say that he had deposited the money in question with the Swiss American Bank but when Tetrazzini became suspicious and wanted to be taken there to verify his statement, he took her instead to the Anglo Californian Bank, and the witness followed them. What took place inside the director's office he knew only from Tetrazzini's statement, and this was not allowed in evidence. He had overheard Uriburu also tell Tetrazzini that he had given the money in trust to one Mugnos, apparently a non-existent person.[7]

Proceedings were adjourned until the following morning. It was expected that the case would go on for two weeks until the defence received certain documents from Mexico by which Uriburu claimed he could show that he not only had a contract with Tetrazzini but that he had advanced money to supply her needs.

Next morning Attilio Chappari, teller of the Swiss American Bank, testified that Uriburu had not sent any money through the bank to Tetrazzini's foreign creditors and also that the handwriting on the alleged receipts and checks which Uriburu had shown Tetrazzini was not that of himself nor anyone else connected with the bank.[8] A detective testified that the defendant had admitted in the presence of his superior officer that he had written and signed the checks himself. The case was adjourned for another two weeks. These adjournments went on while Uriburu's lawyers pleaded for more time on the grounds that obtaining the documents already mentioned from Mexico was taking longer than expected. His bonds were originally fixed at $8000 which Uriburu was unable to arrange. Then a fortnight later the amount was reduced to $1000 or $500 cash, and on 23 May the prisoner was released as the cash had been deposited by a student friend who wrote to his family in the Argentine for the necessary funds.

On 26 July the *Call* carried a couple of paragraphs beginning:

> While the flute-voiced Tetrazzini, erstwhile of the Tivoli, is winning press puffs and floral offerings in Mexico her former private secretary ... continues to engage the occasional attention of Judge Conlan ... and yesterday after many hearings the case was submitted.

Thereupon the Judge raised the defendant's bail to $1000 cash and, unable to find the extra amount, he went back to prison.

Touring with Viglione Borghese

The case was not to be tried until late September after Tetrazzini's return from that Mexican tour on which she had set out in May. Viglione Borghese in his reminiscences, *Due Ore Di Buon Umore*, describes his experiences on this tour in which he was to sing with her in the title role of *Rigoletto*, as Ashton in *Lucia di Lammermoor*, and as Germont in *La Traviata* with Bazelli in the tenor leads. The first stop in the express train south from San Francisco was at Chihuahua. He had omitted to reserve a sleeping compartment, but the guard belonged to the Odd-Fellows and on noticing that the baritone bore their badge in his buttonhole, he made a special point of looking after him and when it grew dark led him to a luxuriously furnished private cabin where he left him with his good wishes.

'Later,' Viglione Borghese writes,

> I was awakened by Luisa's high-pitched shrieks and subsequently learnt that I had been sleeping in her cabin which she had previously booked and paid for. And what did I mean by it? Naturally I had to pretend to know nothing so as not to compromise the man who had done me a favour. This involuntary prank

was certainly responsible for the coldness which from then onwards existed between me and Tetrazzini.

That Tetrazzini should have been upset by this incident is not surprising for had knowledge of it reached Uriburu's lawyers at the time that would have enabled them to portray her as a fickle Delilah.

The company opened at the *Teatro de los Heroes* on 4 May with *Lucia di Lammermoor*; Bazelli sang Edgardo and Viglione Borghese, Ashton. The latter wrote that Tetrazzini in the title role sent the audience into 'a delirium'. He pays tribute to her voice, range, facility, scales. 'I still have them in my ears, and any disagreement cannot affect the utmost respect and admiration I have always had for her.' There followed performances of *La Traviata, Rigoletto, Faust* and *La Sonnambula* with Bazelli and him in the leading tenor and baritone roles. *Rivista Teatrale Melodrammatica* for 1 June 1905 quotes from a letter of hers postmark 'Chihuahua' disclosing that she had no secretary or assistants and handled all the affairs of the company on her own.

They sang next in El Paso, Gomez Palacio, Durango, Torreon, Monterrey, Saltillo, and San Luis Potosi. According to Viglione Borghese, they had much to endure – 'a terrible cyclone' and floods that prevented them from performing.

In late June news reached Tetrazzini that she was a widow, for on the 23rd of that month Alberto Scalaberni had died in Florence – on the death certificate he is described as 'the husband of Luisa Tetrazzini'.

When the tour finished, Viglione Borghese did not go back to work as a miller's salesman but resumed his operatic career. Much that has been published in books of reference regarding this part of it is incorrect. *Le Grandi Voci* says that after his spell with Tetrazzini, he then toured South America (in fact, it was the Caribbean) while the *New Grove* says that the pair did so later in 1905–6. Leo Riemens claims that they next sang together in the West Indies and Venezuela. Actually, Viglione Borghese joined the Sconamiglio Company in Ponce, Porto Rico, in April 1906 and went on in May to Caracas. Aida Gonzaga, a sort of a junior Tetrazzini, was the coloratura for both places.

Back at the Tivoli

On 23 August 1905 the San Francisco press published details of the coming six months' season of grand opera that would open at the Tivoli starting on Monday night, 11 September. Tetrazzini headed the list of the prima donnas. The *Evening Post* announced 'This will positively be her last season at this theater as she begins a three years' contract with the

Conried company at the Metropolitan Opera House, New York, next November.'

But there was more legal trouble for the diva. On Friday 8 September 1905 the *Evening Post* reported that opera-goers would not know whether they would be able to hear her in *Rigoletto* at the Tivoli on the 12th until Judge De Haven decided a case against her in the Circuit Court. On the 7th Sidney M. Ehrmann representing the Conried Metropolitan Company of New York had appeared before Judge Morrow requesting an injunction to prevent her singing in San Francisco. He had issued a temporary restraining order and on the 11th the matter would be decided.

The complaint cited that on 10 September of the previous year Tetrazzini had signed a three year contract whereby she engaged herself to sing exclusively for Conried as from 8 November 1905 and for forty performances including outside concerts during the following five months and at a fee of 1500 francs a performance. She was committed to sing eight times a month or once to three times a week but never twice in succession. Another clause gave the management the right to renew the contract for the year 1906–07 at a fee of 1800 francs per performance and for the year 1907–08 at 2000 francs per performance by notifying the artist before February 15 of each year. Whilst under contract she could sing nowhere else in the United States or Canada. It also stated that only Conried could act as her agent in those countries.

Tetrazzini in her reply pointed out that this contract left her free to sing at the Tivoli until 7 November and that she had been given to understand that she was free to act on her own behalf until the Metropolitan engagement actually began. The document had been written in French which she alleged she could not then read and that she signed it on the representation that it was drawn in accordance with her verbal agreement with the impresario.

The *Evening Post* commented that if Tetrazzini lost her case, she might not sing for Conried nevertheless, but would go to Europe, South America and Mexico until 1908 when the contract expired. 'If she does sing for Conried, San Francisco will certainly go into mourning for the loss of one of the most delightful sopranos that has ever visited this coast.'

On the Monday 11 September the lawyers representing Conried failed to appear in court before Judge De Haven who postponed the hearing until 2 p.m. in spite of Tetrazzini's lawyer Heyneman's protest that the case was an urgent one. In the afternoon, news came that the plaintiffs had changed their tactics. They were going to file a petition in the Circuit Court begging permission to amend the first bill of complaint. In its new form[9] this now stated that the Conried opera company was likely to give a season in San Francisco in the coming year and if so Tetrazzini's singing at the Tivoli would cause the company irreparable damage. The prices at that opera house were less than one half of those that Conried charged, and it was claimed that the fact people had heard her singing at cheaper rates would reduce the New York manager's sale of tickets.

Reporting this, the *Evening Post* suggested: 'The Circuit Court would draw a record crowd it is believed if the singer were permitted to sing her response in recitative!'

Ignoring such a threat of damages being claimed against her, Tetrazzini opened the autumn season at the Tivoli in *Rigoletto* on the 12th. Next day the critic of the *Chronicle* told its readers:

> She has cast her spell upon San Francisco again so completely that even the discreet and diplomatic Polacco was bewitched last night into giving a public opinion of her which he has never before done for any other artist. Her singing as Gilda was nothing less than divine. Always he says she is note perfect, her pitch is absolute and no score is ever out a measure for her. . . . The world's acknowledged greatest coloratura singers have been and gone since Tetrazzini made her first appearance at the Tivoli last spring, and all the beauty of their voices is freely and fully acknowledged, but there is a charm about Tetrazzini's singing that none of the others owns. It grips at one's heart with a quality that one does not look for in a coloratura voice. Small blame to Conried that he involved the law to keep Tetrazzini from singing in this city, wanting to have her for an Eastern sensation.
>
> There is one thing more that must be said in praise of Tetrazzini's voice and that is that it has grown in volume since she first appeared in this city. . . . Bazelli whose voice is always agreeable sang the Duke with fine spirit. But he needs to take warning as he is dangerously near the fatal fat line which is almost twenty pounds too much.

It was not until 19 September that the Uriburu case came to trial and then only on the first of the two embezzling charges. After the jury was sworn in, Charles Peery, Uriburu's attorney, insisted on the plaintiff being present. Tetrazzini's attorney, Ferral, then maintained that this was impossible as she was preparing to sing in the title role of *Lucia* at the Tivoli that evening.[10] Next morning she attended the court in the role of plaintiff. She gave her evidence in Italian and when questioned by the defence agreed that Uriburu had always been kind to her. But he had never been more than a good friend and 'there was no affection – not on my part at any rate'.

Attorney Peery in his closing argument[11] compared his client to Don José, the 'easy mark' in Bizet's opera and said that Tetrazzini was a real life Carmen. Bazelli, Uriburu's successor in her affections, was Escamillo. It was the story of Carmen, all but the dagger scene. Whether this version was to end tragically was for the jury to decide. Peery castigated Tetrazzini for fickleness. He called her 'the siren who lured this young man from his home' and 'that false and vindictive woman'. Dazzled by her, Uriburu had left everything to follow her, only to be cast aside for another.

The plaintiff's attorney was equally hard upon Uriburu. 'He calls himself a diplomat', Ferral sneered. 'Why, the man never earned an honest dollar in his life.'

It took the jury five hours deliberation to reach a verdict. According to next day's *Call*: 'The discarded secretary did not seem to be much interested in his fate. The look of tired disgust that has been on his face since his arrest did not change during the five hour wait.' The verdict was 'Not guilty'. He was then taken back to prison to await trial on the second charge of the same nature. The result was unexpected, but Uriburu's attorneys had made much of his story that he had entrusted the money to a third party who had then vanished with it, that and the fact that he belonged to a distinguished Argentinian family, only spoke Spanish, and had been so long in prison probably persuaded the jury to give him the benefit of the doubt and acquit him. Tetrazzini wrote incorrectly in *My Life of Song* that he was sentenced to seven months' imprisonment.

The previous evening a packed Tivoli had heard the plaintiff for the first time that season as Lucia. Rising to the occasion, she gave no signs of inner anxiety at the prospect of having to give evidence next morning in court. The critic of the *Chronicle* wrote that she had proved 'anew and beyond cavil her clear title to the queenship of coloratura'.

On 24 September Tetrazzini won more admiration for her Violetta[12] but of Bazelli as Alfredo the reviewer wrote: 'His voice is on the verge of getting fat, as well as his figure.'

Il Barbiere was presented for the first time that season on 3 October when, according to the *Chronicle*: 'Tetrazzini as Rosina flirted with her audience as well as with Count Almaviva.' This role was played by Bazelli with Adamo Gregoretti as Figaro. Her handling of the Lesson Scene was rewarded with a standing ovation.

La Sonnambula came into the repertoire on 10 October. The *Evening Post* wrote:

Tetrazzini seemed to sing better than she has ever sung before at the Tivoli. This statement probably reads like a critical platitude, for the same remark has been made after each of her appearances this season. But for some unknown reason the part of Amina seems to be more adapted, both from the acting and the singing point of view, to Tetrazzini's abilities than even her wonderfully successful roles in *Lucia*, *Rigoletto*, *La Traviata* and *Il Barbiere di Siviglia*. Tetrazzini both sang and acted Amina in a manner that set the audience wild with enthusiasm. . . .

The truth of the matter is that there is no other voice in the world – as far as operatic impresarios or musical critics can tell – that can be compared in many respects to the Tetrazzini voice. The bird-like quality of the notes, the freshness of the tones, the powers of endurance of the voice, are all sought for in vain among the great artists who have lately made their appearance in this city. Even Melba, who has the most wonderfully cold voice that the world has known, would now have a difficult task in establishing her superiority to Tetrazzini. . . .

Tetrazzini sang the Mad Scene from *Lucia* last season at the Tivoli on the same night that Melba sang the same music, which had been transposed, at the Alhambra. There were many at that time who thought it sacrilege to compare the great Australian prima donna who had been for so many years regarded as the greatest prima donna in the world with the humble Tetrazzini. But now things are different, and if Tetrazzini will only set her face resolutely against encores she will soon be reckoned among the greatest ones of the musical earth, even by prejudiced Easterners. The abominably provincial encores produce a weariness which does not belong to the top notes of the Tetrazzini voice. This weariness was noticeable in one or two places towards the close of the opera.

Tetrazzini shines as an actress as well as the greatest of the coloratura artists. Her comedy is excellent. Those who recall the acting of Sembrich in the light Italian operas will remember that the Sembrich squint interfered materially with the Sembrich comedy. Tetrazzini has no squint and looked last night like a beautiful big doll. Her acting, both in 'The Barber' and in 'La Sonnambula' revealed histrionic powers which few thought that she possessed. Take her altogether and it must be confessed that Tetrazzini is a revelation.

The weak spots of what was a splendid production were those of all the operas in which Giorgio Bazelli and Rosina Lucchini appeared. In this opera he played Elvino and she Lisa:

Bazelli's lower and middle registers need sandpapering and seem to be going from bad to worse; Lucchini should be seen and not heard. Unfortunately Lucchini's voice has a tremolo that is always with us. This tremolo, vibrato or whatever you may be pleased to call it, rings out unmistakably in the concerted measures and irritates the audience. Bazelli redeemed himself occasionally with his high notes. If ever a tenor who makes pretentions requires redemption it is Bazelli, who is growing more and more fat and who is becoming more and more scant of breath. Let us have Tetrazzini occasionally with another tenor and thereby give both Bazelli and the audience a much needed rest.

The other critics thought the same about Bazelli. It was generally known that he and Tetrazzini were living together, and certainly eating together from the way he was putting on weight. After that season in San Francisco, he gradually gave up singing professionally and assumed the role of her manager.

On 1 November,[13] six weeks after having been acquitted on the first embezzling charge brought against him by Tetrazzini, Uriburu was brought from jail to be tried on the second charge before Judge Lawler. This time 'Lullo' looked cheerful, confident that he would again be found not guilty. The report next day in the *Call* stated that he was in the witness box for most of the afternoon and that his testimony was in keeping with that he gave at the former trial.

Attorney Charles Peery, who succeeded in clearing him of the first charge, in his plea to the jury derided the diva. He condemned her without reserve. He also spoke caustically of Bazelli. The plaintiff's attorney, Ferral, left nothing to prove the charge against Uriburu.

It took longer than before, six hours this time, for the jury to reach a verdict – once more of 'Not guilty'.

The name of Uriburu (spelt differently) also occurs in an extraordinary story related by Elsa Maxwell in her book of reminiscences, *I Married The World*, published in 1954.[14] This is so different in every way that one wonders if, after half a century, memory has played her false and if the facts were embellished for the sake of effect. Elsa Maxwell wrote that when she was 'an adolescent girl in San Francisco at the turn of the century', her father became one of the first members of the Bohemian Club. This was where visiting celebrities were welcomed, and he entertained most of them in his small flat. Elsa claimed that the most volatile personality she met there was Luisa Tetrazzini:

> the greatest of all coloraturas and a figure flamboyant enough to attract attention in a city with a full quota of people studying to be characters.

According to Elsa, Luisa had a simple outlook on life, holding 'all indoor and outdoor records for collecting love affairs'. Hardly had they been introduced than she wanted to know to whom Elsa was engaged to be married and was horrified when the other admitted that she had no sweethearts. '*Sensa l'amore, ecco la morte,*' she cried, wagging a disapproving finger at her. It was not necessary to know Italian to grasp that Tetrazzini was convinced that without love one might as well be dead. A Señor 'Urriburro' was proof of her resolve to remain alive.

Elsa learnt that Luisa had met Urriburro, the President of Peru's nephew, in Italy and had quickly made up her mind that 'her husband of the moment was an intolerable encumbrance'. Conveniently forgetting her many singing engagements, she had eloped to San Francisco with her lover, hoping to be safely beyond the reach of her spouse, but much to her vexation he had pursued them and had challenged Urriburro to a duel. The 'spouse' could not have been Alberto Scalaberni as he had died in Florence that June.

A site near Oakland was chosen for this affair of honour timed to take place at dawn and with pistols at twenty paces. At eight o'clock that morning the quayside at San Francisco was crowded with sightseers ready to acclaim the victor, but neither man came ashore when the ferry docked. Three further boats discharged their passengers without either duellist appearing. Could it be that both had killed each other?

A pack of reporters set off across the bay to investigate. They returned some hours later with the news that they had found no trace of either man nor any signs of bloodshed. The disappointed sensation-seekers dispersed and Elsa made for Tetrazzini's hotel where she discovered her 'in near hysterics, although not with grief'. There sat husband and lover playing cards and drinking toast after toast to each other's health, whilst Luisa denounced them as far too cowardly to fight over a matter of honour, but they ignored her and when Elsa left they were about to pass out.

The worst blow to Tetrazzini's pride came a week later, when Señor Urriburro asked the husband to be his guest in Lima and off they sailed, leaving the furious soprano on her own. She had not intended to sing in opera during her visit, but now 'accepted singing engagements for want of something better to do'.

Nowhere does Elsa Maxwell give the husband's name in her story. She wrote that Tetrazzini never saw him or Señor Urriburro again. Although she spells the latter's surname slightly different he is clearly the same person as the one tried for embezzlement. In reality 'Lullo' Uriburu was the nephew of a former President of the Argentine and not of Peru – and it was 13 years earlier that Tetrazzini had eloped from Italy with Pietro Cesari to Buenos Aires, pursued by her husband Alberto Scalaberni, from whom she then became legally separated. One might have thought that the duel fiasco which, according to Elsa Maxwell, became the talk of San Francisco, would have been mentioned in some newspaper or in other reminiscences. Much research has failed to find this so it is impossible to say from what ingredients she concocted her story. She has been accused of readily exploiting verisimilitude and presenting the unverifiable as facts.

In the last fortnight of the autumn season at the Tivoli Tetrazzini also sang in *Dinorah* with Bazelli as Corentin and for her farewell on 7 November there were excerpts from *Rigoletto*, *La Traviata* and *Dinorah* ending with the *Lucia* Mad Scene. 'Doc' Leahy claimed that some 10,000 people failed to obtain tickets. Thus ended her first two seasons at the Tivoli. It has incorrectly been stated that she also sang Leonora in *Il Trovatore* but it was in fact Oliva Petrella who did so for all performances of that opera.

Compañia de Opera Italiana 'Lucia Tetrazzini'

Tetrazzini was not the kind of person to give way to Conried's threats. She felt that after her triumph at the Tivoli her services were worth $1000 a night. She had no intention of singing for him even at the Metropolitan for a quarter of that amount which would only rise to $500 when the third season was reached. She had planned in the last week of April to take a troupe of artists back to the Teatro Arbeu, but owing to the Uriburu lawsuit this had been abandoned. Using the same Mexican manager to organise the project for her, the *Compañia de Opera Italiana 'Lucia Tetrazzini'*[15] was formed with herself advertised as the sole *estrella*, Esther Adaberto as soprano dramatica, as contraltos Guerrina Fabbri and Amalia Belloni, as tenors Giorgio Bazelli and Carlo Barrera, as baritones Gaetano Rebonato and Rogerio Astillero, and as basses Augusto Dadó and Natale Cervi.

The whole company arrived on 27 November in Mexico City where the management had been busy with advance publicity, describing all the artists as the 'finest' in the world who had been acclaimed by the 'finest' critics for performances in the 'finest' cities in the world. All this attracted a full house for the first night when *Il Trovatore* was presented. However, the audience was bitterly disappointed and the critics scathing in their reviews. Scenery and costumes were of the tattiest, the production amateurish. Only Esther Adaberto sang well as Leonora. Baritone Rebonato as the young Count di Luna had a voice 'as rough as a worn out wooden rattle' whilst tenor Barrera as Manrico was hissed as soon as he started singing his serenade 'in a grating voice and with a tremolo that made the window panes shiver'. Experienced opera lovers told one another he was the worst Manrico they had ever heard. Depressed and humiliated, Barrera left the company and Mexico shortly afterwards.

On Sunday 3 December Tetrazzini gave a superb performance as Gilda but both Bazelli as the Duke and Astillero as Rigoletto sang badly. After the performance the former lost his voice completely, leaving the company without a tenor. The manager, Ysunza, cabled urgently to Milan in search of a tenor of calibre willing to travel to Mexico and join the company but no one suitable was interested. It was useless, he declared, to try and find a tenor in Mexico where all men wanted to star not as opera singers but as bullfighters.[16]

In spite of these disasters, the public clamoured for Tetrazzini. So on Wednesday the 5th, instead of a performance of *Lucia* taking place, those who had booked were refunded their money and invited instead to be Tetrazzini's guests while she sang the three acts of the opera without any tenor. It proved an astonishing *tour de force* that gained an ovation for her.[17]

Fortunately Bazelli recovered his voice sooner than expected and was able to sing with Luisa on the 8th in *Lucia*; followed on the 10th by his playing Almaviva to her Rosina; then two days later he was cast as Alfredo to her Violetta with Rebonato as Germont. But when Tetrazzini was not singing the theatre was never more than half full. Actually until Tetrazzini's triumphant first season in 1903, business had always been bad at the Arbeu which was regarded as having a jinx on it.

On 20 December both Esther Adaberto and Dadó went down with influenza and Tetrazzini and the Mexican singer José Torres Ovando took over at the last moment the roles of Marguerite and Mephistopheles in *Faust*. The company was becoming increasingly demoralized, especially as audiences were packing the far more elegant and modern Teatro del Renacimiento.

During that December in 1905 Tetrazzini was forced to spend more and more of her own money to keep the opera company going, so manager Ysunza had to announce that owing to unsurmountable difficulties the season would end on Sunday 28th when Tetrazzini would sing the last act of *Lucia* and the second of *Dinorah*. All season ticket holders would be refunded what was due to them owing to the curtailment of the programme.

It was a sad end to Tetrazzini's three seasons in Mexico City. The first had been a succession of triumphs and financially rewarding, the second less so, and the third a disaster. The general opinion was that apart from herself, Esther Adaberto and Giorgio Bazelli, the other singers had little talent and did not seem to understand what they were uttering. The 1905 winter season at the teatro Arbeu was regarded as the worst in its history.[18]

Tetrazzini felt sorry for her fellow artists and considered part of the blame due to poor direction and insufficient rehearsing. She paid the fares of those who wanted to leave the country, and formed a small troupe from some she considered had potential and gallantly took them touring in the Mexican hinterland. This meant postponing a projected return to Milan to visit her relatives.

In *My Life of Song*[19], without as usual giving any dates or names, she wrote of her experiences doing this. Takings were divided between her and the theatre owners and the money received was shared out equally among the artists. Not only was travelling arduous and the conditions in the dilapidated buildings where operas were presented dire, but the owners and managers were incompetent and often dishonest. There was no prior publicity, no mention of the furore she had created in South America and in Mexico City. In addition, when at the end of one week, thanks to word-of-mouth recommendation, they played to a full house, Tetrazzini found that her own manager had decamped with the company's share of the box office takings.

Tetrazzini then succeeded in engaging a manager conversant with all the tricks employed to falsify the accounts and who was skilled at counting how many people were in the audience. At one theatre he noticed that there was a big discrepancy between his calculations and the numbers shown on the box office returns. He was given the books of unsold and complimentary tickets to check as well as the torn halves of those taken from the public on admittance and they appeared to verify the accuracy of the figures. Still dissatisfied, he engaged a private detective who soon discovered that there was another book of tickets which were sold to the public. Money taken for the sale of these was omitted from the records. The tickets differed only slightly in appearance from the authorized ones but the doorkeeper knew and had instructions to keep the halves taken from the public separately. The detective found a box stated to be empty was full of them.

The police were informed and arrests made. To Tetrazzini's astonishment the whole scheme had been masterminded by the son of the local Chief of Police with whom the business negotiations for booking the theatre had been conducted.

Tetrazzini was annoyed to find that in towns where there were, at the most, a daily and a weekly newspaper, sometimes as many as seventy persons demanded complimentary tickets, claiming to be opera critics for minor periodicals scattered all over the world. In Morelia there was unexpected trouble from the Catholic Church. All seemed well on arrival. The Archbishop had sent his fine carriage to convey her to the hotel where she was told that neither *La Traviata* or *Il Barbiere* must be presented as the heroine of the former was a courtesan, while in the latter Almaviva disguised himself as a priest. Then on the Sunday before the opening she learnt a Jesuit priest had preached a sermon warning the public against the corrupting effects of opera. 'If you go once, you will go a second time. If a second time, then a third, and thus you will run a grave risk of forgetting your God', he declared. Consequently the first night saw the auditorium only half filled and entirely by men apart from a few American and English women. For the second and third performances attendances fell to barely a quarter of capacity. Then the theatre was closed, it being Sunday, so Tetrazzini sent the priest a strongly-worded letter stressing that never throughout her career had any objections been raised against performing these two operas by the Church to which she was proud to belong. His attack was having a serious effect upon the livelihood of members of her company whose families might soon be starving. Far from being a questionable pastime opera was an elevating one as the Church everywhere else had recognised – no girls in tights; no vulgar language. If he persisted in his opposition, she would be obliged to appeal to the Pope's representative in Mexico on behalf of the families in her employment.

The Jesuit proved reasonable and apologized. According to Tetrazzini's account, he went further and issued a statement praising her company with the result that next evening there was a queue outside the theatre and they played to full houses for the rest of their visit. She adds that so as not to offend religious susceptibilities they took 'a few liberties' with some operas. She changed the title of *Dinorah* to *The Pardon of the Virgin* and advertised it as 'a Biblical Opera'.

Another Mexican town where Tetrazzini sang was at Queretaro where the Emperor Maximilien had been executed by a firing-squad in 1867.

Return to Milan

Then in the spring of 1906 Luisa travelled back to Milan where, on 29 June, she celebrated her 35th birthday, a time of life when a soprano sometimes starts to worry about how much longer her voice can remain at its peak. Tetrazzini's had in fact improved. Referring to how little her voice was affected by the passage of the years, Herbert Caesari was to write in *The Alchemy of Voice*:

> Tetrazzini used to say 'I sing from the bottom of my throat'. She knew. The singer should always be conscious of, and live with, the vibrating principle within the larynx and with the tonal sensations accruing therefrom. That was an essential teaching of the old Italian school curriculum.[20]

6 In a Despotic Diva's Absence

It is thanks to those pioneers of recording the human voice, Fred and William Gaisberg of the Gramophone and Typewriter Company, that we can still listen today to some of the greatest prima donnas of the past such as Adelina Patti, Melba and Tetrazzini.[1] It was Kenneth Muir, the manager of the Milan branch of that company, who started the negotiations that were to lead to the latter's becoming one of their most successful recording artists. On 31 January 1906,[2] he wrote to Theo B. Birnbaum, managing director of the parent company in London, to say that he had just learnt that she was returning to Milan from America and that her relations wished to enter into negotiations with him for a contract. Describing her as 'the most important Italian *soprano leggero* of the day', he had not 'the slightest doubt' that Alfred Michaëlis, his predecessor, who had left to take charge of a new firm, Fonotipia, would do his utmost to secure her services for them, so prompt action was necessary. Muir recommended offering her 'ten per cent per annum at a thousand francs a piece for three years'. She was worth this and more. He would like the matter to receive the Board's urgent consideration.

It would be 'a very bad business for them to let Michaëlis get hold of this artiste who is infinitely better than Barrientos and Regina Pacini, who are at present his two best sopranos'. Moreover, Muir stressed, Tetrazzini would be 'most valuable' for them as they needed a *soprano leggero* to make records to include in their 'Celebrity' catalogue. He added in a postscript to this letter that Tetrazzini had 'an immense success in St Petersburg and should be a highly important artiste for that market'.

Permission was given by the Board in London for Muir to start negotiations with Tetrazzini which he did when she reached Milan, and on 20 June he cabled London: 'Tetrazzini refuses royalty agreement – would accept ten records, twenty thousand francs three years exclusivity'.

Birnbaum at first rejected Tetrazzini's terms. In the meantime Carlo

Sabajno, the Italian branch's artistic director, had been listening to the records made by her in New York on 8 September, 1904. These had just been obtained from there. Muir's deputy wrote back to London on 22 June reporting this and saying that although the recording quality was extremely bad, Sabajno had found the singing was 'very fine'. Consequently they were of the opinion that she could make 'splendid records' with their system.

On the same day that this letter was written, one was sent from the director of the Deutsche Grammophon-Aktiengesellshaft of Berlin to the Gramophone and Typewriter Company office in London stating that he had noticed, in the Spanish Zonophone catalogue of the Universal Talking Machine Company, five records by Luisa Tetrazzini.

> This is an artiste who is exceedingly popular in Russia and if at all possible I should be very glad to get these records to put in the Zonophone catalogue in Russia. Please let me know if this is possible.'

Probably this further indication of interest influenced Birnbaum after all into authorizing Muir to offer Tetrazzini a contract on her terms, and he arranged for Carlo Sabajno to visit her. This distinguished musician had received his musical training at the Royal Conservatoire there under the composer Catalani. At the beginning of his career, Sabajno was assistant conductor to Toscanini and later principal conductor at many European opera houses, including the Dal Verme of Milan, as well as becoming a friend of Leoncavallo, Mascagni, Puccini and Giordano.

Jerrold Northrop Moore, quoting from Gaisberg's unpublished diaries,[3] tells how Carlo Sabajno, having made an appointment to see her one morning, called at her apartment in Milan only to be informed by the maid that she had not finished dressing. Getting impatient at being kept waiting 'like a lackey', he made some remark to that effect to the woman and left, slamming the door after him. Gaisberg continues that he once asked her why she would never sing with Sabajno as conductor and she replied that she had sworn to get her own back. 'This trait of never forgetting or forgiving was most pronounced in the lady,' Gaisberg comments.

On hearing of Sabajno's departure, Tetrazzini told Giorgio Bazelli, now living with her and managing her business, to 'phone him and there was a heated exchange of words, resulting in the breakdown of all negotiations. It was a clash of three strong personalities. Fred Gaisberg wrote about Sabajno in his diary:

> He had a keen intelligence, and it was as well to know in dealing with him that every move had a motive. One of his business axioms was that every man could be reached through some woman.

Colleagues were well aware of this, and years later another recording expert, Edmund Pearse, was to write to Fred:

> Maestro Sabajno and his love affairs would be worth a book in itself – and be a bestseller – if one dared to write all we know, though everybody would think it fiction.[4]

Tetrazzini was supposed to have sung Violetta to Bazelli's Alfredo in *La Traviata* at the Teatro Carlo Felice in Genoa on 22 January the following year, but for some reason she did not and Rosina Storchio appeared in the role instead.

In the early summer of 1907, Luisa came to sing for the last time in Buenos Aires, in the first opera season to be given at the Teatro Coliseo that had opened as a circus the previous year. She was heard in *Lucia di Lammermoor* (with Zenatello), *La Sonnambula*, *La Traviata*, *Rigoletto*, *Il Barbiere di Siviglia*, *L'Elisir d'Amore*, and *Dinorah* from 21 May to 25 July. On 4 and 8 August she sang Lucia and Rosina at the Teatro Urquiza in Montevideo. Then moving to the Teatro Olimpo in Rosario for the rest of the month she gave performances of each of these operas again plus one of *La Traviata* and one of *Rigoletto*. It was the occasion of the 200th anniversary of the founding of the city and after the final curtain had fallen almost the whole population accompanied the artists to the central station where an express train waited to take them to Buenos Aires. On the platform, Tetrazzini, tenor Carlo Dani, and baritone Pasquale Amato were forced by the crowd blocking the track to sing arias for nearly an hour before they were allowed to board the waiting train. Juan Aletta de Sylvas described the event in an article: 'Artistic Rosario in the last 50 years' published in the *Libro de Rosario* in 1925. As the train left, Luisa leaned out of a window and sang, waving farewell to her admirers.

From Buenos Aires, the company went north to Brazil and after giving one performance of *La Traviata* at the Politeama in São Paulo they moved on to the Lyrico in Rio de Janeiro for a *Rigoletto* on 11 September and another *Traviata* on the 14th. Then Luisa sailed for Genoa and thence to her apartment in Milan where a letter awaited her destined to change significantly the course of her life.

*   *   *

In 1907 46 year old Nellie Melba's voice showed no signs of ageing. Her superiority at Covent Garden nevertheless led to ill-feeling. Rivals were sometimes prevented from singing there and such powers even extended over the Press. Northcliffe dismissed the Daily Mail's music critic for disparaging her Juliette. Nevertheless, another journalist risked being banned from the opera house for writing that Melba showed her love for

Romeo by raising one arm and used both arms only to depict intense emotion.[5] She had also alienated its principal conductor for Italian opera, Cleofonte Campanini, on account of the contemptuous way in which she had disregarded his musical authority. It must also have annoyed both him and his wife, Eva Tetrazzini, that she had not been invited back to sing since 1890. By now it was too late for through overtaxing her voice she had been forced to retire[6] leaving him free to concentrate on urging Harry Higgins to employ Luisa at Covent Garden. In 1907 Luisa was thirty-six, nine years younger than Melba, and Cleofonte believed that she might well be the one capable of ousting the arrogant Anglo-Saxon.

On 2 January that year Melba made her début at Oscar Hammerstein's new Manhattan Opera House, then in late March she fell ill with bronchial pneumonia. Despite this she recovered sufficiently to sing in Covent Garden's summer season. But she afterwards felt so debilitated that she went for a long holiday in Australia with the intention of not returning until the following spring.

Covent Garden Offer

Here was Cleofonte Campanini's opportunity, and he urged Harry Higgins, Chairman of the Grand Opera Syndicate, to engage Luisa Tetrazzini for the autumn season. Though Higgins had never heard her sing, he had received excellent reports of her work, so he wrote inviting her to sing the role of Violetta for ten performances at a fee of £120 a time.

Before doing this, he took the precaution of discussing the matter with Melba and wrote afterwards to Percy Pitt, Covent Garden's musical director:

> I have just had a long talk with Melba, who is in a very good temper and quite reasonable. We shall have no trouble about Tetrazzini as far as she is concerned. Their voices are so different that there is no reason for them not to like each other.[7]

£120 was paltry pay compared with what Tetrazzini had received in South America, but to sing at the Garden was her highest ambition and she accepted without hesitation.[8]

A few weeks later came a totally unexpected change of plan in a further communication from Higgins. The engagement was not now to be for the regular season but for the late autumn, starting in November. Opera was actually in trouble at Covent Garden. The Italian school was under a cloud and amongst the more fashionable composers were Wagner, Saint-Saëns and Gounod. The Wagnerian fare offered to the public at the beginning of the year was poorly received at the box office. Then Caruso had returned to play Rodolfo to Melba's Mimi, but even this had not attracted full houses. As a result, Higgins wrote yet again to Tetrazzini that, because the outlook for the autumn was so bleak, he would like to postpone her début until the summer season in the New Year.[9] Having already made provisional plans for that time, Luisa refused to change, so Higgins suggested cancelling her engagement and offered £300 for breaking the original contract. She has recorded that this response infuriated her and that the small amount of compensation proposed proved to her that the Garden management knew nothing about the quality of her voice and the high fees normally paid to her. So the ruffled soprano replied that Higgins's monetary terms had not attracted her to the idea of singing there, and hinted that twice as much would have been demanded to sing elsewhere in England. Her purpose in consenting to come was to prove to London audiences and critics that Italian opera was not moribund as an art form and, like most *prime donne*, not believing in false modesty, she added that her wish was to demonstrate that 'Italy could still produce a soprano able to fill the difficult roles created by the great composers.'[10] Whatever sum Higgins offered, the letter ended, it would be rejected, and should Covent Garden not honour her contract, legal proceedings would follow. The board of directors met, considered this ultimatum – and surrendered. It was arranged that Tetrazzini should make her début as Violetta with Fernando Carpi as Alfredo and Mario Sammarco as Germont père. Ettore Panizza was to conduct.

The soprano's reactions may have been influenced by a visit to a fortune-teller. One aspect of Tetrazzini's character that provided constant copy for the Press was her superstitious beliefs. At the start of her career in South America, before the curtain rose on the first night of *Lucia* in Buenos Aires, the small dagger she carried had fallen onto the stage and had stuck upright in a floorboard. Following her triumph in the part, she came to regard the incident as a lucky omen and from then on before first nights would drop the dagger three times from her forehead. If it stuck in the wood every time, it meant a great success, twice – proportionately less so, but if the knife caught only once or not at all then she became worried. However, as the dagger was always very sharp and her aim expert the augury was invariably auspicious.

In *My Life of Song* (1921) Tetrazzini described how, not long before her Covent Garden début, she visited 'a palmist'.[11] No one, she claimed, knew of her projected visit and she disguised herself in borrowed clothing from a servant. 'I put a tattered shawl over my hair, and I wore a pair of blue cracked spectacles.' The seeress's retreat in a low quarter of Milan looked forbidding and once inside, Tetrazzini says that she found herself comparing it with the assassin's den in *Rigoletto*. The old white-haired woman with 'a croaky voice' used 'a greasy pack of cards' for her prognosticating. Whatever the visitor did would be immensely successful. In New York she would create a great sensation and go from there all over America, continuing to be acclaimed. But before that the disguised diva would receive an offer to go to London. When that came, she must accept it irrespective of her first impression and the attractiveness or otherwise of the proposal. When she had done so, another offer would come which she must refuse, for great things awaited her in the English capital. Her name would be on every lip, crowds would throng to where she was.

'But if as you say, I am a business woman,' Tetrazzini claims she broke in, 'why should crowds come to see a business woman?'

'You have very good business ability, but you aren't a business woman,' the other replied. 'You are in a profession and I believe you are a singer. If so, you must continue to sing, for you are destined to be one of the great singers of the century.'

Tetrazzini ends this account by insisting that she did not reveal her true identity to the fortune-teller, but on leaving presented her with fifty francs which delighted the crone who exclaimed: 'I knew you weren't a poor woman though you're dressed like one. Please write and tell me if what I've foretold comes true.'

7 Covent Garden's 'Voice of the Century'

In the last week of October 1907, after a tiresome journey, Luisa Tetrazzini reached Charing Cross railway station and was taken in a horse cab to the Hotel Cecil. On the way she looked out at the Embankment but could see no River Thames, just a few points of light. 'Before I had been in London for twenty-four hours, I had swallowed more fog than during all the rest of my life,' she claimed later in her book. When she told a visitor this, he laughed and said it was merely a moderate haze. She must wait until she saw the real thing, a genuine London pea-souper.[1]

Next morning when driven to Covent Garden, Tetrazzini says that she wondered 'if a people who would allow their chief opera house to be planted on the edge of a vegetable market could be really musical'. She knew that she had a friend in the conductor Ettore Panizza, born in Buenos Aires in 1875, who had heard her sing there and was a great admirer. Mario Sammarco, who was cast as Giorgio Germont to her Violetta in the opening performance, was also to sing Rigoletto to her Gilda later in the month, which roles they had played together in Odessa and Buenos Aires in 1898 and in Berlin in 1902.

At the first rehearsal she succeeded in impressing the orchestra and when they reached the end of the first act every one of them spontaneously put down their instruments and applauded her, while Higgins rushed over to grasp her hand and clearly meant it as he uttered the clichéd compliment: 'Your singing is nothing short of marvellous.'[2]

But the British press remained uninterested in the newcomer. The sole reference to her approaching appearance in *Traviata* consisted of four lines at the bottom of a column in the *Daily Graphic*. And at Covent Garden Luisa was not even allotted the star's dressing-room. It must have exasperated her to find it locked with MELBA inscribed large on the door and beneath this the command 'SILENCE! SILENCE!', bidding all who passed to do so on tiptoe. It would have been useless to even ask to look inside, for Nellie kept the only key and she was still in Australia – which was just as well in view of what was about to happen.[3]

Tetrazzini once confessed that, when beginning her career as Inez, not for a moment did fear of failure occur to her, but later, after further successes, she became aware of the hazards of her profession when one is faced with having to retain a hard-won reputation. Then, following her seasons in Buenos Aires, first night nerves no longer affected her, and she thought this was for good. But sitting in her hotel on the Saturday afternoon of 2 November waiting to go to Covent Garden for the opening, she almost panicked and fled from London.[4]

To make matters worse, when Luisa peered through a peephole just before the rise of the curtain, there appeared to be very few people in the auditorium. The general manager Neil Forsyth tried to reassure her by pretending it was an illusion caused by fog having drifted into the building and that the house was full. But in reality, though Saturday normally attracted most business, only the first few rows of the stalls were filled and few of the occupants had paid for their seats. In fact, the takings totalled only £120, the same amount as her salary.

Tetrazzini remained apprehensive until the end of the first act, when the small audience, led by London Italians in the gallery, shouted such acclamations that she knew the laurels longed for were within her grasp.

We have it on the authority of Fred Gaisberg that Harry Higgins told him, when he heard the first note of *E strano* and then the brilliant cadenza with those clear ringing attacks on the Cs – a real *leggiero-spinto* with breadth and purity of tone such as he had dreamed of all his life – he ran and telephoned all the papers in Fleet Street that had failed to send critics and urged them to race down reporters to the Garden to listen to this sensational singer. Opera enthusiasts during the interval phoned friends to spread the news, and as a result those who prided themselves on being present on red-letter first nights hurried to Covent Garden to listen to what remained of the performance.[5]

Victorious Violetta

At the end, Luisa was called twenty times before the curtain and delighted her audience by the friendly, uninhibited way in which she behaved, throwing kisses to all and sundry and winking at the men who stood in the previously empty boxes. They found it decidedly refreshing after Melba.

On the Monday, E. A. Baugham in the *Daily News* predicted that the new star would prove 'the greatest attraction Covent Garden has ever had'. He continued:

The quality of tone produced by Tetrazzini ravishes the senses. It is soft and golden and yet has none of the impersonal and chilling perfection of the ordinary light soprano. The most difficult technical problems are executed with the ease which marks a virtuoso's playing of a cadenza in a concerto. Every note is perfect, and the singer's command of her resources so complete that there is no sense of a difficulty being overcome. The voice has dramatic edge, too, when required, and it was noteworthy that Mme Tetrazzini dominated the noisy finales of Verdi's *Traviata*.

Above all, the main impression of her Violetta was not musical alone. I have never seen the pathos of Verdi's heroine realized with such grip and sincerity. In the big scene with Giorgio Germont most sopranos who can sing '*Ah, fors' è lui*' with dazzling effect are not very great actresses. Mme Tetrazzini who, to be sure, had the advantage of playing with Signor Sammarco, gave the scene a new life. Both by use of her voice and by facial expression she vividly conveyed the reality of Violetta's sacrifice, and many of us were impressed for the first time by the fact that Verdi had written dramatic music after all.

In the last act, this great artist did not have recourse to the physical gasping by which the majority of sopranos express the agony of the dying woman, but held the audience spellbound by the simple pathos of her singing and the subtle expressiveness of her acting. It was most beautiful in its restraint. That Mme Tetrazzini made such effect was due solely to her art. In physique, she is scarcely more fitted to the part of Violetta than is Mme Melba. I do not think I am exaggerating when I say that Mme Tetrazzini has the voice of the century and stands out from even the great Italian singers we know in respect of powers of acting with her voice.

When we read the accounts of the celebrated singers of the coloratura school, we wonder how they made such deep impressions on their audiences, and we are forced to the conclusion that singers were judged much as we judge the violin playing of a Kubelik. Mme Tetrazzini explains the mystery. Every bar of the music was sung with feeling, expression and dramatic appropriateness. She phrased according to the meaning of the words, and not merely from the point of view of absolute musical display. A run as she executes it becomes expressive, a high note seems a natural dramatic climax. Indeed she even gave an example of this on her own account. At the end of *Ah, fors' è lui* she introduced a little upward trill which wonderfully expressed the hysterical feeling of Violetta. Such singing gives one a new idea of the capability of the human voice.

The *Daily Mail* critic claimed it to be a curious trait of London audiences that they would never believe in the greatness of an artist unless they had heard her for themselves. Mme Tetrazzini who on Saturday night had made one of those rare sensations which herald the appearance of a new diva had already achieved something like fame in South America.

> But she came to us with no flourish of trumpets, a singer to all intents and purposes unknown. Today all London will be hailing the advent of a new operatic star – one of those commanding figures which sweep across the musical horizon once, perhaps, in a generation.

Tetrazzini brought to the old Verdi opera:

> a human tenderness and a pathos few of us realised that it possessed. She has the magic gift of 'tears in the voice' and is withal a consummate actress. . . .

Her rendering of the familiar aria *Ah, fors' è lui* and the wonderful ease and nonchalance with which she trills upon E in alt completely astonished the audience. . . . Probably since Patti first sang in the past there has not been so great an ovation. . . . There were actual tears among the audience, too, on Saturday night when she sang '*Dite alla giovine*' lifted out of its customary vocal display into a song of renunciation, heart-rending in its emotional intensity. Never in late years have we seen *La Traviata* acted as Tetrazzini played it on Saturday night; rarely, if ever, have we heard Verdi's music so exquisitely sung.

The *Daily Telegraph*'s reviewer had feared that the old art of the *bel canto* was practically lost.

Then suddenly there appears to delight us all, one who still retains it and such a one is Mme Tetrazzini who not only possesses a voice of very beautiful, clear bell-like quality and wide range, but uses it with consummate skill and art while its unusually flexible nature enables the singer to execute the most exacting runs and roulades of the early Verdi with perfect ease. Moreover, Mme Tetrazzini has an emotional power in the voice that is of the rarest among sopranos of the brilliant school, and for once in a way the duet between the wretched Violetta and her lover's father – *Dite alla giovine* – was made entirely convincing by the poignancy and intensity of expression, and *Ah, fors' è lui* was sung with notable brilliancy and ease. Indeed, it was the remarkable manner in which the singer used the colour of her voice to express the varying emotions of the part, in which, in fact, she literally acted with her voice, that lent her interpretation the real distinction that undoubtedly it possessed.

'Nothing succeeds like success,' commented the *Daily Telegraph* of Luisa's second performance as Violetta on 7 November 1907, the Thursday following her début.

The Tetrazzini boom has eclipsed even the excitement attendant on *The Christian* [the drama by Hall Caine]. The public commenced to form on the stairs of the unreserved parts of the theatre before noon. . . . The folk arriving about four – priding themselves on their early bird instincts – were amazed to find their chances of obtaining admission hopeless.

P. G. Hurst recalled, in *The Golden Age Recorded*, that when he went to book a seat he found a queue 'stretching from the Opera House to the Strand'. He failed to obtain one until the following summer.

Tetrazzini was now besieged in the Hotel Cecil not only by reporters but also by agents of firms selling everything from face creams to cures for sore throats who offered to pay her handsomely if she signed testimonials in praise of their products. There were also professional beggars with hard-luck stories, and cranks of all kinds. She described later these experiences.[6] One journalist told her that the English loved Cinderella stories. Wasn't it true that she had once tried in vain to get employment in the chorus at Covent Garden? To which her reply was that she had never been reduced to doing that, having played leading roles from the start. But the man was unimpressed. That wouldn't go down well with his readers. They would consider it boasting.

Tetrazzini was suffering from a cold when she appeared on 15 November as Lucia for the first time at Covent Garden, with Fernando Carpi as Edgardo and Giuseppe de Luca as Enrico. She captivated a packed audience and most of the critics with the brilliance of her singing. The one dissentient was Walter Bernhard who in the *Musical Opinion* for December 1907 wrote that he had heard the new *prima donna* in her favourite role and had read about her till his head was 'almost dizzy with superlatives', but he himself had to confess that he was 'a bit disappointed'. He did not care for the D in alt at the end of *Regnava nel silenzio*. Although sustained with power and firmness, the note appeared to his ears 'a trifle hard in tone'. However, it had aroused such prolonged applause that the rest of the air had to be omitted. This omission might have been intentional, but this was not his impression. Neither could he be enthusiastic over the sustained E_b. It was wonderful but did not appeal to him musically.

Bernhard conceded that he was nevertheless 'greatly delighted by what might be termed the broad features of Tetrazzini's art'. Numerous as were the passages for vocal display set down by Donizetti, it might be said without exaggeration that the singer doubled them; and the good taste and finish of these interpolations afforded him extreme satisfaction. The soft scales of either variety, the delicate shakes and the high staccato notes were all admirable. The time-honoured Mad Scene naturally called forth Tetrazzini's powers and if he did not add a series of laudatory epithets after the style of nine out of ten of the notices of the occasion running through the columns of the press, it was because he did not believe that anyone would be the wiser. Instead, Bernhard made a few more criticisms:

> At the end of the first part of the tremendous solo, a scene took place which might well cause an (artistic) wolf to shed tears. On the other hand, it is spoken of by my learned critics as if it were something rather grand – something illustrating the high artistic spirit prevailing among us. At the last note of the cadenza (before, mind, it had ended) noisy applause stopped the progress of the opera altogether. Lucia had perforce to recover her wits and smile her thanks. After quite a prolonged interval, order was restored and the cadenza was *repeated*! Again, for the same reason insanity had to be dispensed with. Finally, the noisy element having to some extent tired itself out, the rest of the long *scena* came to its appointed end.

Bernhard regarded the extravagant language prevailing in the press as in excess of the occasion:

> We are told of a final shake on E_b in alt! What was the other note of the shake and on what note did the singer end? A representative of the ever delightful *Daily Mail* tells us that the audience were treated on 16 November to a

sustained final high F. I am afraid that I do not believe that any soprano of these latter days – by which is meant the last century – to have been able to *sustain* the said note; anyway, I never heard one. But that is not quite the point. The composition being in the key of E♭, the ending on F by the vocalist would seem to present difficulties.

But the general public were not interested in such musical niceties and they went on flocking to Covent Garden. *The Graphic* for 23 November reported that the congestion in Floral Street outside the Opera House was becoming 'a positive nuisance' and that

> such was the competition among Tetrazzini-ites for the honour of being first in the field that there seemed to be every possibility that, before long, they would be taking their breakfast there, as well as their lunch, tea and dinner.

That evening, Saturday, Tetrazzini first sang Gilda in *Rigoletto* at Covent Garden with Mario Sammarco in the title role and John McCormack as the Duke of Mantua. Some critics thought she was in appearance, at the age of 36, unconvincing as a young girl but all used superlatives to describe her singing. Walter Bernhard admired her more in this role than as Lucia. She was to sing Gilda 23 times in all at Covent Garden – more than any other soprano. Melba performed the same role 19 times at Covent Garden.

S. H. Strong in the *Musical Standard*[7] found it disconcerting that the rest of the cast suffered from Tetrazzini's brilliant performance owing to the fact that the average opera audience did not represent 'a very high degree of vocal culture'. For instance, Sammarco's 'excellent art' did not receive the attention it merited when he sang and acted splendidly the passage commencing *Pari siamo, io ho la lingua*. The house was waiting with noisy impatience for its 'star', and as the passage occurs just before Gilda's entrance, it suffered accordingly from the audience's behaviour.

> The familiar *Caro nome* was sung by Mme Tetrazzini with intensity of expression and great virtuosity. She rippled through the two brilliant runs with consummate ease and although an attempt was made to proceed with the opera the house became delirious and after a pandemonium of applause, extorted a repetition. Finally, at the close of the number, the singer instead of the usual trill in E natural, sustained an E in alt, as clear as a bell and with perfect ease. In the third act again she rose to a great height in interpretative art with Signor Sammarco, and both their singing and acting in the closing *scena* and duet were vivid and convincing. Here again Tetrazzini took an unusual note at the close; this time it was E flat in alt, and it had the effect of electrifying the audience. Signor Sammarco's Rigoletto is one of the finest things he has given us.
>
> Mr John McCormack as the Duke came through the crisis better than I expected, although it would be foolish to pretend that he is anywhere near perfection. His stage action is stilted and self-conscious but that is a small matter and experience will in all probability mend that. . . .

It particularly concerned Tetrazzini that McCormack was most unconvincing as an actor when making love on the stage. Consequently during love duets calling for passionate embraces she would whisper in his ear: 'Hold me tighter. Look as though you mean what you say.' There grew up between them a sincere musical understanding and friendship in which each admired the other's artistry. His voice went so well with hers and they sang more and more often together, and she always led him forward to share her curtain-calls – such altruism, rare in a *prima donna*, all who sang opposite her were to experience and appreciate.

Tetrazzini, McCormack and Sammarco were to be called 'The Triumvirate' because of the frequency with which they appeared together in England and the United States. The last named's baritone, high in range, reaching g' with ease, was mellow throughout its compass and completely under control.

Appraised by Muir

Having heard of Tetrazzini's triumph at Covent Garden, Kenneth Muir wrote to Birnbaum on 6 November[8] that this proved what he had maintained over a year previously, that she was the best light soprano of the day. He believed her to be 'the most likely to step into Melba's shoes to whom she is undoubtedly superior.' But

> in character she is capricious and wayward and if you wish to succeed in obtaining her you must pamper her like a spoiled child by sending her gifts, boxes for theatres, paying her compliments and little personal attentions; in a word you must appeal to the woman in her nature.

Muir goes on:

> She is extremely dissolute in her private life and much affected by flattery and champagne. She is besides a bright, clever woman and rather apt to treat everybody in an independent and off-hand fashion. It was through her having allowed her secretary to telephone in an offensive fashion to the Maestro [Carlo Sabajno] that she drew from him a sarcastic and well-deserved reply, which resulted in her eventually not signing her contract or singing for us, although subsequently she showed plainly that she regretted it and wanted to sing for us. I remember at the time that London agreed to a 20,000 francs contract for ten pieces entirely on my word, but not without searchings of heart as her name was then entirely unknown in England. . . . Now that she has made such a big success at Covent Garden I may repeat that I think there is no risk in securing her even for a big sum. She has a beautiful pure recording voice and as a vocalist is far ahead of Melba.

Tetrazzini had in fact already been visited at the Hotel Cecil on the morning of Monday 4 November, following her triumphant début at Covent Garden on the previous Saturday night. The Gramophone Company's sales manager, Sydney Dixon, had to take his place in the long queue asking to see her. After a very long wait, he was shown into the new star's presence. As she spoke hardly any English the negotiations had to be conducted through Giorgio Bazelli acting as her manager. She demanded 25,000 francs down and 2.50 francs royalty on every record sold. This was the kind of contract which the Gramophone Company always avoided on principle, regarding it as preposterous to suppose they could pay cash *and* a royalty. Dixon withdrew to consult the head office. After much deliberation, Birnbaum wrote to Calvin G. Child, director of Victor Talking Company's Recording Laboratory at Camden, New Jersey, suggesting a joint agreement with Tetrazzini. Would they guarantee Tetrazzini a $1,000 advance royalty if the Gramophone Company did likewise?

But Victor were not interested and cabled back: 'Think most inadvisable establish such precedent as Tetrazzini demands. Must decline participating.'[9]

The Gramophone Company were upset by this reply for while they also considered Tetrazzini's demands to be exorbitant, her appearances were creating an enormous sensation and if they did not sign a contract with her she would probably turn to Fonotipia or Pathé.

However, a situation had arisen in New York that was to cause Victor to change their minds. Oscar Hammerstein I, fascinated by opera, had in 1906 erected on West 34th Street the Manhattan Opera House and had engaged Cleofonte Campanini as artistic director. It was Melba who proved the trump card in the operatic game of poker Oscar then played against the Metropolitan in New York. He had a hard fight persuading her to agree to sing for him, but, apart from the fat fee offered of $3,000 a night, there was the alluring prospect of becoming an undisputed, absolute Queen of Song at the Manhattan, which she had not been at the Metropolitan, so she accepted.[10]

For years, the older opera house had been without a competitor and it looked as if the new venture would fail, for business at the Manhattan had been disastrous since its opening on 3 December 1906. But for Melba's début on 2 January 1907 in *La Traviata*, thanks to Hammerstein's masterly promotion methods, every seat was sold. She received a tremendous ovation at the end, and on following Melba nights, audiences at the Metropolitan shrank to disastrously small numbers. She sang fifteen times for Oscar instead of the originally agreed ten. When her season ended she returned to England where she fell seriously ill with bronchial pneumonia which, as mentioned in the last chapter, so weakened her that she went to recuperate in Australia. This meant that she was not available to sing for Oscar during his second season at the Manhattan. He had already made a tentative bid to engage Luisa Tetrazzini for his opening season while she was at the Tivoli in San Francisco, but did not pursue the matter once Melba had yielded. It was the impresario's son, Arthur, who now suggested to his father that Covent Garden's 'Voice of the Century' so described by the *Daily News*, might successfully replace that of the Australian siren's.

Engaged for the Manhattan

On 30 November Pietro Brignoli sailed on the *Mauretania* with instructions to try and persuade Tetrazzini to sing at the Manhattan.[11] He was an expert linguist whom Oscar had employed in deals with foreign artists. On arrival in London, Brignoli found no seats available for that night at Covent Garden and was driven into buying a ticket from a tout in order to get admittance for her next performance. He was enormously impressed and hurried round to Tetrazzini's dressing-room afterwards to discuss the matter. She was interested but would not be available until January. Brignoli cabled the Hammersteins and was told to offer her a contract commencing at $1,000 a night, rising in stages for further performances to $1,500.[12] Tetrazzini signed. However, in *My Life of Song*, she alleged that she was handed a blank sheet of paper and told to write on it the amount wanted for each performance. She goes on that she put down $2,500 which was agreed.[13] This is probably one of the many exaggerations appearing throughout her book. She also claimed that was the highest amount ever paid to a prima donna, which is incorrect as Oscar had paid Melba $3,000 a performance.

It has already been mentioned in Chapter 4 – *At the Teatro Arbeu* (page 39) and Chapter 5 (page 45) how Heinrich Conried, manager of the Metropolitan, had contracted for Tetrazzini's services in September 1904 for three years with effect from November 1905 and how this had resulted in an inconclusive law suit in the September of that year, when he had tried to prevent her from singing for 'Doc' Leahy at the Tivoli in San Francisco. Now when Conried heard of the deal with Hammerstein, he applied to the courts for an injunction to prevent her from singing at the Manhattan. Her lawyers successfully maintained, however, that he had failed to bind the agreement by not depositing with her banker the minimum sum demanded by her as a guarantee. His meanness in money matters was well-known. He paid members of the chorus only $15 a week. She would have been unhappy working for him in any case as his declared aim was to secure excellence of ensemble rather than brilliance of individual performances. But as we shall see he was to resume his legal battle with her later. So great was the public demand to hear Tetrazzini at Covent Garden that Harry Higgins, though compelled to close the autumn opera season there on Saturday 30 November, arranged to hold four concerts on 3, 7, 10 and 12 December in the opera house. S. H. Strong wrote on 14 December in the

Musical Standard that for the opening concert he was seated near enough to the stage to be well within the sphere of Tetrazzini's 'charming personality' and found that 'the ability to observe her quite easily considerably increased the pleasure derived from hearing her sing and that alone is infinite'. Her voice 'almost bewilders the senses, its beauty is simply amazing, her singing grips and holds me breathless'. She was forced by the unending applause to repeat her opening number, the waltz song from *Roméo et Juliette*. Among other items in her programme were the polacca from *Mignon*, Tosti's *Serenata* and a Neapolitan folk song sung 'with a sense of character and of humour which were exquisite'.

Unaware of the fact that English audiences then expected every soprano of stature to include *Home, Sweet Home* in her programme, Tetrazzini omitted it from her first concert, and was consequently warned by *The Graphic*: 'If she imagines she can retain her hold upon the affection of the British public without it, it is to be that she is doomed to disappointment.' Her daring would lead 'to disastrous results'.

The Times wrote on 9 December regarding the second concert two days earlier:

> The Mad Scene from *Lucia* was interrupted by so much applause that a good many of the hearers thought the singer was obliging with an encore when she was only finishing the song. In this, and in the *Air des Clochettes* from *Lakmé*, the agility and certainty of the *fioriture*, and the power of the high E came up to expectations. The crowd for this occasion was unprecedented, probably the most immense audience ever assembled at Covent Garden, for the space usually filled by the orchestra had been boarded over, and there were in all 25 rows of stalls, while the removal of so many boxes gave room for a far greater number in open balconies so contrived.

The Victor Talking Machine Company of Camden, New Jersey, had refused to enter into a joint venture with the Gramophone Company of London to market Tetrazzini's recordings but this had not deterred the latter from continuing negotiations with her. Then when the news broke that she had signed a contract with Oscar Hammerstein to sing at the Manhattan Opera House, Victor changed their mind, realizing that this would lead to a large demand for her records in the United States, and agreed to a partnership.[14]

Gramophone Company Contract Terms

It was only after a month of fretting and consultation that the Gramophone Company finally settled terms with Tetrazzini, a contract being signed on 11 December 1907. The basic terms were that they would pay her 12,500 francs (£1,000) at the beginning of every six months for the two years run of the contract. This was to be in advance of royalties. A royalty payment of five francs was to be paid on each record sold up to the first 10,000 records, after which the royalty was to be 2.50 francs.

Nine days later, Tetrazzini first visited the Gramophone Company's City Road studios. Sydney Dixon, who was present, described later in the company's magazine *The Voice*[15] his recollections of that occasion. The staff, he wrote, were accustomed to celebrities passing in and out and as a rule went on with their work, but when she arrived all discipline went by the board. It was some time before she could struggle through the crowd into the lift and be taken to the recording theatre.

The first record Tetrazzini made was of her singing *Caro nome* followed by *Io son Titania* and the third and last that day the Bell Song from Delibes's *Lakmé*. Percy Pitt was at the piano and Fred Gaisberg supervised the proceedings.[16] They found that she was no great musician but had an impeccable ear. Most of her roles had been hammered into her during the early part of her career and she had never forgotten them. Like Patti's, her voice had the body of a lyric soprano with the range and flexibility of a *leggiero*. News had spread that she was in the neighbourhood. Sydney Dixon well remembered being in the party that drove back to the Savoy Hotel:

> So great was the Tetrazzini boom in London at that time that all down the City Road across Finsbury Square, and even down Moorgate Street, a crowd of busy City folk had gathered, and Madame, standing up in the open car, kissed hands to them.

An editorial in the *Musical Times* for December 1907 asserted that Tetrazzini's striking success at Covent Garden in *La Traviata* and *Lucia* proved that bel canto was not as dead as many of the younger generation of opera-goers had supposed. Nothing in art that was alive with true human feeling could die and this was undoubtedly true in the case of bel canto that to all appearances would be again the vitalizing factor in opera.

> Some critics had derided performances of the old Italian masterpieces as 'concerts in costume', and such mistresses of *agilita* as Jenny Lind and Patti have been disparaged as mere vocal gymnasts; but their triumphs have demonstrated, as Madame Tetrazzini's are doing, that even *fioriture* are more than decorative – that they have an essential place in the dramatic scheme of which they are part.

In the same issue, a critic added further praise. A still greater success had been achieved by her *Lucia* on 15 November, when her rendering of the Mad Scene had aroused 'an extraordinary demonstration of enthusiastic appreciation'. It was

> her command of tone-colour quite as much as the perfection of her vocalization which so distinguished her performance, and one must go back to the time

when Madame Adelina Patti was in her prime, to find such perfect renderings of old Italian opera numbers.

The Spectator in December published a discerning article on the Tetrazzini phenomenon entitled '*The Re-emergence of the Prima Donna.*' 'C.L.G.' wrote that the autumn season had been remarkable for an event of quite exceptional interest in the annals of opera – the advent of a star of the first magnitude who had created a real *furore* in the old-fashioned Italian operas of the early and mid-Victorian epoch. Since 1881 when, unheralded and unpuffed, Patti sang for the first time in London, there had only been two of these immediate conquests of the public – by Christine Nilsson in 1867 and by Emma Albani in 1872, for Melba's sovereignty was hardly established in her first season in 1888. Tetrazzini's achievement was quite as remarkable as that of any of her predecessors and for a variety of reasons. To begin with, the mere fact that she had been singing for at least a dozen years was scarcely a point in her favour but rather the reverse since one was prone to believe that first-rate singers were bound to gravitate to England without delay, and *per contra* that their absence was a sign of inferiority or at any rate of incapacity to please Anglo-Saxon taste.

The newcomer, however, had had to overcome a still more serious obstacle in her choice of roles for, instead of electing to be heard in the more modern or fashionable works, she had deliberately challenged attention in a type of opera which for the past dozen years had been steadily dropping out of the Covent Garden repertory and which indeed had come to be regarded as dead beyond the possibility of resuscitation. It was not merely that the growing popularity of Wagner threatened to relegate *Traviata* and *Trovatore* to the dustbin, but that Verdi himself had eclipsed the product of his middle period by the far nobler and more distinguished works of his old age.

To revive and lend new lustre to these faded scores, to crowd Covent Garden in the autumn season and send up the prices of the stalls to a premium of more than a hundred per cent – all this was 'clear evidence of an exceptional equipment, of something much more than a beautiful voice and a flexible larynx'. Madame Tetrazzini, so far as sheer beauty of timbre was concerned, need not fear comparison with any living singer. Though her voice was not of exceptional volume, it had 'remarkable carrying power even in its *sotto voce* tones'. She sang with 'delightful and effortless ease', never attempting more than she could perform. She had, in short, 'precisely the endowment and the technique which rendered the most tired vocal frippery not merely endurable but engaging'. She was, moreover, as her performance in the last act of *Traviata* showed, 'an excellent actress on somewhat conventional lines'. Small wonder, then, that the old guard of opera-goers, who had been sorely depressed by what they would call 'the tyranny of Wagner' should hail the newcomer's triumph as convincing proof of the abiding vitality of the old Italian operas.

> The lesson of Mme Tetrazzini's success, however, is not quite so simple as all this. . . . We must remember again that a generation of opera goers has grown up in the last twenty years, many of whom have actually never heard *Traviata* and to whom in consequence its ingenuous morbidity has all the attraction of the unfamiliar. It is the simultaneous existence of the faithful old guard who have never been converted to Wagner together with enlightened modernists who are not altogether immune from reactionary tendencies and of newcomers who have grown up during the Wagner régime and have never heard the old operas before that constitute the opportunity of a great singer like Tetrazzini and when allowance is made for exaggeration and for réclame, her triumphs have been great and genuine enough to acquire a definite significance.

8 Oscar Hammerstein's 'Star of Stars'

Immediately before Christmas 1907 Tetrazzini left London for Paris, spent five days shopping, found three dressmakers who agreed to make within a week gowns for the chief roles she would be playing in New York – and in the meantime she visited her sister Elvira in Milan. She then returned to Paris for fittings which took three days causing her to have to rush to Le Havre to board the French steamer *La Lorraine*.

Across the Atlantic Oscar Hammerstein was impatiently awaiting Luisa's arrival. His publicity agent, Billy Guard, had already adroitly aroused among the public an intense interest in her with the result that every seat for her performances during the first three weeks had been sold. Supported by his staff, he was there to welcome her when the ship docked on 11 January.[1] The *Evening Sun* described her 'as more American than foreign in appearance, wearing a long zibeline cloak, a fox skin boa and a big black hat with plumes'. She greeted her other sister, Mme Eva Campanini, with 'a long, passionate explosive kiss, thrice repeated, with ten encores later for the benefit of the photographers'.

Then Mary Garden, Hammerstein's other star songbird, presented Tetrazzini with a bouquet of orchids. Slim as a boy she was a complete contrast to the newcomer. The two became friends, and Mary agreed to interview Tetrazzini for the *World* before her Manhattan début. Mary Garden wrote:[2]

> It is very unusual for one prima donna to interview another. The most important thing one feels on meeting Mme Tetrazzini is her personality. Photographs fail to show that. There is something present when she is near which has a sort of electric force. That is the way I should put it. She has magnetism, a great deal of it. . . . She is gracious and utterly lacking in the little finicky things which so many great sopranos have.

In her suite at the Hotel Knickerbocker the reporters gathered to inspect the new sensation. Algernon St John-Brenon in the *New York Telegraph* described the singer as having light brown eyes, soft golden hair and a fair complexion. 'Altogether a refreshing personality.' She made no reference to her earlier career in Argentina and pretended instead that it was in Rio de Janeiro that she had made her début, in a leading part as Violetta in *La Traviata*. He reports her as adding:

> It was on that occasion that I was first acclaimed a star. One night after the opera was over, a physician who had been in the audience came on to the stage and sending his name to the dressing-room asked to be allowed to see me. When he came in, he told me he wanted to feel my pulse and did so, saying it was because he thought I might be suffering from consumption like Violetta. He was quite amazed at finding me a perfectly healthy woman. Of course I was in a highly nervous condition in consequence of the strain of the acting. Then he began to talk about the death scene. 'Of course,' he said, 'you have studied the way people die of consumption in hospital?' I said I had not and shuddered.

On the same day, 12 January, the *New York Times* published an account of an interview with Oscar Hammerstein during which he revealed that he had already received $25,000 in mail orders alone for Tetrazzini's first performance. Since the capacity of the Manhattan was $11,500 he had been obliged to return thousands of dollars. In fact, so effective was Billy Guard's publicity campaign that most of the celebrated 400 wealthy leaders of society, who normally patronized the Metropolitan, forsook it and bought boxes or stalls for the Florentine Nightingale's début – something that not even Melba had achieved the previous year.

Three days later Tetrazzini sang Violetta in *La Traviata* before a highly critical New York audience and with brother-in-law Campanini conducting. Alfredo was sung by Amedeo Bassi who owned several palazzo homes in and around Florence and became a firm friend – in 1926 he was to be a witness at the marriage ceremony there when she wed her 'toy boy' second husband Pietro Vernati. Giorgio Germont was played by Mario Ancona, once a business man and now a *bon viveur* baritone and a frequenter of elegant restaurants. Irving Kolodin wrote in *The Metropolitan Opera, 1883–1966* how depressed the management there were when they learnt that New York society had joined the populace in flocking to the rival opera house.[3] The 'Diamond Horseshoe' that evening was deserted and robbed of its refulgence, whilst at the Manhattan in contrast:

> No one could remember . . . when a line of standees began to form at half past one in the afternoon, and patience finally exceeded bounds when the doors opened at seven o'clock. The line dissolved into a milling throng at the box office, the attending police wielded sticks, some standees were nursing bruised ribs as well as sore feet when the day ended [and] it was estimated that two thousand more persons than the house could hold were turned away.

Hammerstein had tried to keep tickets from the touts but seats changed hands at $25 and more each. Hawkers did a huge trade selling postcard photographs of the Florentine Nightingale to those who had already commenced to crowd the lobby at four o'clock in the afternoon. Soon after the doors opened at seven the auditorium was packed.

> Tetrazzini is a novelty. The Society people have a new idol. The musicians have something to argue about. Wagnerians are slightly doleful. 'This will put back the advancement of modern opera ten years,' said one,

commented the *New York Telegraph* while Richard Aldrich in the *New York Times* wrote that in the first act, Tetrazzini threw a kiss to the audience as she entered.

> She was apt to acknowledge with a wink or a wave people she could recognize in the audience, and to join the audience in applause for another performer. . . . Much that she does cannot meet with serious approval.

And Pitts Sanborn described her costume as 'an instrument of percussion'.

But Tetrazzini's tactics were always to win over the customers first and then the critics. When many years later she was interviewed by a reporter from the *Daily Express*, he wrote that she told him:

> You may have the voice of an angel and have it trained by a maestro who is a demi-god, but unless you are gifted with a personality which gives equal pleasure to your audience, you will never become popular or famous. Naturally I have always taken care to put personality into my work.

Although Aldrich disapproved of Tetrazzini's showmanship, he admitted that the applause at the end of the first act was 'such as that rarely given to artists who thoroughly established their right through their achievements to the highest place in the role of great artists'. Her reception was 'almost unparalleled in New York's operatic history.'

According to Reginald de Koven in *The World*, 'the spectators, unwilling to commit themselves too soon, greeted their first sight of her with only faint applause'. As a result for once her confidence became affected and she did not sing the *Libiamo* in full voice. People began to look disappointed, but their attitude completely changed when she started the *Ah, fors' è lui*, now singing with complete assurance, admirable facility and emotional power. Her top C at the end she 'swelled and diminished . . . with evenness and precision' as, to tumultuous applause, she bent down gracefully to unhook a flounce of her dress which had apparently caught on a nail on the stage. When this continued to happen at other performances, not only in New York, but elsewhere, it became obvious that it was a trick. Sometimes she would drop a flower instead and recover it whilst singing the high note.[4]

'The *Sempre libera* was brilliant,' wrote the *New York Press*, the upper tones being of extraordinary volume, the scales delivered with fluency and fire, the final E flat above high C produced with so great an ease and freedom that persons possessed of the sense of absolute pitch almost doubted their senses.

The *New York Press*, commenting on this *tour de force*, added that as she sang 'that magnificent note', Tetrazzini bent to gather up the long train of her gown and strolled into the wings 'all the while holding onto that phenomenal E flat until she disappeared from view'. This gained for her a thunderous ovation.[5]

Reginald de Koven related in his review how, after the first act, Tetrazzini was called back before the curtain a dozen times. Women in the boxes tossed their violets to her. Blowing more kisses to all parts of the house and radiating delight, she nodded her thanks.

> Those nearest the stage heard her rippling laughter. She was as happy as a child. She caught up the flowers which lay around her. She snatched her handkerchief from her bodice and waved a response that would have done credit to a Chautauqua miss.

In the last act she 'preserved the illusion and pathos of the scene in spite of her unconsumptive figure'.

De Koven ended by adjudging Tetrazzini as 'a sensation with her vocal pyrotechnics, dramatic warmth and artistry' who unlike most coloraturas sang the role 'not for mere vocal display but for musical significance'.

Henry Edward Krehbiel in the *New York Daily Tribune* agreed. The secret of Tetrazzini's triumph lay in

> the combination of beautiful singing as such and acting. Not acting in the sense of attitude, motion and facial expression, although these were all admirable, but in the dramatic feeling which imbued the singing – the dramatic color which shifted with kaleidoscopic swiftness from phrase to phrase, filling it with the blood of the play.

Krehbiel, who was music critic of the *Tribune* from 1880 to 1923, had one criticism. Tetrazzini's voice was 'weak and pallid in its lower register'. But it had 'a dozen shades nevertheless, and as it soared upwards it took on strength and glitter, though it lost in emotional force as it gained in sensual charm'.

W. J. Henderson, then the critic of the *Sun*, declared that although Tetrazzini was aged 37, 'the perfectly unworn condition and youthful timbre' of her voice together with 'the splendid richness in its upper range' were what pleased him most. Her coloratura justified much that had been written about her. She sang staccato with consummate ease, though not with the approved method of breathing.

> Her method is merely to check the flow between tones instead of lightly

attacking each note separately. But the effect which she produces, that of detached notes rather than of strict staccato is charming.

Her shake, less praiseworthy, was neither clear nor steady. Her worst shortcoming was 'her extraordinary emission of her lower medium notes'. They were all sung with 'a pinched glottis and with a color so pallid and a tremolo so pronounced that they were often not a bad imitation of the wailing of a cross infant'. Her cantabile was uneven in tone quality,

> the breaks between her medium and upper notes coming out most unpleasantly and her tricks of phrasing in short spasmodic groups with breath taken capriciously and without consideration of either text or music were serious blots upon her delivery. For example, in beginning *Ah, fors' è lui* she deliberately made a phrase after the U, and taking a leisurely breath introduced the I as if it belonged to the next word!

The continued employment of

> cold color in cantabile quite removed the possibility of pathos from *Non sapete* while a pitiless description of her infantile delivery of *Dite alla giovine* would read like cruelty.

On the other hand he liked her *Ah, se ciò è ver* in the Act I duet where Violetta replies to Alfredo's *Un dì, felice*. 'Here the staccato effect and some crisply executed diminutions in short phrase were excellent.'

In Henderson's opinion, it was altogether probable that Tetrazzini would have 'a larger measure of real success when she sings the embroidered Mad Scene of *Lucia*'. Greater recommendation from the public than it accorded her the previous night the soprano could hardly expect.

Desmond Shawe-Taylor on Henderson's Strictures

Regarding Henderson's stricture about Tetrazzini's singing her lower medium notes with a tremolo, Desmond Shawe-Taylor[6] has suggested that it may have been produced by first night nerves since one reads of no further complaints on this score, and it is hardly to be discerned in the many records she made during those years, both in England and America. The question of the 'infantile' or excessively white colour of those lower (or lower-middle) notes, Shawe-Taylor thought must be left to the judgement of the individual listener. His own feeling was that the difference of colour between this part of her voice and the rich and powerful upper register did exist, but was neither so marked nor so disagreeable as Henderson alleged. In support of this view, Shawe-Taylor cites Tosti's song *Aprile*, often regarded as among the best, though not the most characteristic of her records.

> In this song there is nothing brilliant, only a tender lyrical melody lying entirely

(but for a single high B flat towards the end) within the octave from F to F of the treble stave; yet the quality is throughout peculiarly delicate and limpid.

Shawe-Taylor finds it strange, too, in view of complaints such as Henderson's, that Tetrazzini should have sung Tosti's *La Serenata* not in the key of F, which is almost universal for sopranos, but in E flat 'in which key, she lends the song an irresistibly seductive and relaxed charm'.

Desmond Shawe-Taylor draws attention to a still odder fact – that both Tetrazzini's HMV and Victor recordings of *Una voce poco fa* are sung not in the standard soprano key of F, but in the original mezzo-soprano key of E. 'Why', he adds 'should a soprano strong at the top and relatively weak below, choose these unconventionally low pitches?'

John McCormack often accompanied Tetrazzini and was a discerning judge of singers. He told his biographer, L. A. G. Strong, that the middle of her voice was 'white and breathy', probably from overwork as a young singer.

> But above E flat she was superb. Her chromatic scales upward and downward were marvels of clearness and her trill was a trill indeed. She could get an amazing amount of *larmes dans la voix*, far more than I ever heard from any other coloratura soprano.

Desmond Shawe-Taylor comments that what McCormack calls the whiteness and breathiness of Tetrazzini's middle voice was what Henderson less accurately described as a childish and colourless quality in the lower register. Perhaps, Shawe-Taylor suggests, it was Tetrazzini's middle rather than her lower register (as McCormack says) that made her anxious. 'It may be that in these low keys she found that certain difficult phrases lay more easily across the break.'

Michael Aspinall on the *Bamboleggiante* School

Michael Aspinall in his notes in the booklet accompanying EMI's 1992 issue on CDs of Tetrazzini's London recordings puts forward another explanation for the 'baby talk' in her lower medium register. He writes that she was singing the way everybody expected a 'coloratura' soprano to sing in those countries to which her career had hitherto been confined. When she realised that in New York and London it was disliked, she did her best to correct her tone.

> In Italy such roles as Amina, Lucia and Rosina had increasingly become the province of teenage débutantes – light, high sopranos with a girlish timbre – and so people had come to expect and like a 'child' voice; this coloratura sopranos began to cultivate deliberately, adopting a white and open tone. Italians call this sound *bamboleggiante* – 'doll-like' – and it can be found in

recordings by Tetrazzini's contemporaries, Regina Pacini, Regina Pinkert, Isabelle Svicher, Maria Galvany, Rosina Storchio and and Josefina Huguet.

Mr Aspinall adds that from the next generation even Amelita Galli-Curci could be faulted on such grounds, and Toti Dal Monte did not please Anglo-Saxon audiences. The latter's recording of *Madama Butterfly* was an excellent example of the *bamboleggiante* school's shortcomings – 'the little girl's voice is all too obviously coming from the very fat body of a middle-aged woman.'

Of the other artists in *La Traviata* on the occasion of Tetrazzini's New York début, Reginald de Koven wrote that Bassi as Alfredo 'thrilled with his opulent outpouring of voice' whilst Richard Aldrich in the *Times* praised Ancona as Germont for singing with 'great nobility and beauty of style'.

Among other *prime donne* present on the first night was Mary Garden who split her gloves so heartily did she applaud after the final curtain. The heroine of the evening was particularly pleased to hear that William E. Vanderbilt Junior had been overheard to say as he left: 'New York heard tonight the greatest singer who ever came to these shores.'[7]

Irving Kolodin has written that the history of opera proves that there is a kind of aural appetite which nothing satisfies so keenly as the highest note and the swiftest scales. 'In Tetrazzini the New York public had its first fresh serving of the sort since Melba was new, and the response dazed even the well-versed press.' He goes on to quote Henry Krehbiel who wrote in the *New York Times*: 'It is useless to discuss the phenomenon. The whims of the populace are as unquestioning . . . as the fury of the elements.'

And so the *furore* continued, and in view of Luisa's figure some now labelled her the 'Tuscan Thrush'. On 20 January the *Telegraph* quoted her as telling their reporter that when touring in Mexico one evening at Chihuahua a purse containing a $1,000 in gold was handed to her over the footlights by an admirer exclaiming, 'Signora, a little present for you' – then at Guanajuato another purse bulging with $1,600 in gold was thrown at her. This did not lead to anyone doing the same that evening at the Manhattan when she triumphed as Lucia. Henderson in the *Sun* next day praised her *Spargi d'amaro pianto* with 'leaps, runs, staccati, double swells from piano to forte twice repeated and a finish on the high E flat'.

Pitts Sanborn in the *Globe and Commercial Advertiser*, found this Lucia's voice

> so fresh, the upper range so strong, so brilliant and so richly colored and the coloratura often delivered with such enchanting ease, that it was not in flesh and blood to listen unmoved.

It is not surprising that after this, Melba dropped the role of Lucia from her repertoire, whilst the *Musical World*'s New York correspondent reported in its issue of 17 February that inspired by the début of a rival in that city, Marcella Sembrich at the Metropolitan had been singing with such tonal beauty as to surprise even her admirers. On that same day London's *Daily Mail* was quoting Tetrazzini's views on her American critics: 'There are only two kinds, good and bad. The good praise me – the bad don't.'

Nine days later, with that baritone of grand style, Maurice Renaud as the Jester, Bassi as the Duke, and Eleanora de Cisneros as Maddalena, Tetrazzini appeared as Gilda in *Rigoletto*. Some regarded this role as not so suited to her talents as it provided few chances for her to display the ornaments of coloratura. Nevertheless, her limpid and brilliant *Caro nome* excited an explosion of applause. Commenting on her singing of this aria, the *New York Press* wrote:

> She produced a few beautiful *messa di voce* effects; she gave a scintillant chromatic scale; she seized with astonishing precision, purity and clearness of tone two or three high notes in *mezza voce*; she obtained a pretty trill on middle D sharp and E; she sang what might be called a slow trill . . . on high B and C sharp.

The following month, on 26 February, Tetrazzini appeared in Meyerbeer's *Dinorah*. Although the plot and situations bored the audience, Luisa's bravura roused enthusiasm whenever she sang, bringing beauty to and removing all triteness from the Shadow Song.

Next, on 6 March, Hammerstein revived the Ricci brothers' *Crispino e la Comare*, its first production in New York since 1885 when Patti played Annetta. Tetrazzini's talents for comedy were admirably displayed in that role. According to the *New York Evening Post*, her vivacity and humour kept the opera house in continuous laughter.

Later that month Oscar Hammerstein sent some of his company to perform at Philadelphia's Academy of Music, a charming theatre decorated in cream, red and gold, where on 19 March a capacity audience heard Tetrazzini sing Lucia. The *Press* newspaper reported next day how a 78-year old authoress, prevented by ill-health from going to the opera for over 25 years, had insisted on attending, even though the effort might endanger her life. She was seated in a proscenium box at stage level. Learning about this, when after the Mad Scene Mrs Caspar Wister struggled to her feet and joined in the applause, Tetrazzini responded by walking across and kissing her hands.

The season at the Manhattan ended on 28 March with a mixed bill of popular excerpts from five operas. The gala evening opened with Tetrazzini and Amedeo Bassi in the first act of *La Traviata*. Later came her Mad

Scene. Outside the stage door admirers awaited her departure and then pelted her with roses.

Hammerstein had gained a profit of $95,806 from the season, while the Metropolitan lost nearly $100,000. Interviewed after the last night by a crowd of reporters, he was in a confident mood. His third season would open in November at the Manhattan.

> I have already ordered 60,000 yards of canvas to be shipped from Belfast, and scenic painters will get busy early in the summer. I shall go further in the way of new and expensive productions than I have so far this year.

Next day, the *New York Times Magazine Section* passed on the news of what was in store under the heading 'NEW YORK'S $2,000,000 SEASON OF GRAND OPERA.'

Back in England, Tetrazzini's success at the Manhattan had led *Punch* to comment

> The cheapest seats are $5 each, first lap are $10, and second lap $30.... On Wall Street such is the rage for opera and the great singer that they converse and carry on their business solely in recitative.[8]

Before Tetrazzini left for America, Harry Higgins had negotiated a new contract with her for a further three seasons at the rate of £160 a performance during the first year, rising to £180 in the subsequent two years. The 1908 Grand Season, the fiftieth since the new opera house had come into use following the fire, was due to open on 30 April with her as Violetta, but quite apart from the Conried Metropolitan lawsuit she was being harassed by Isidore Lerner who, as related in Chapter 4, having entered into a contract with her in Mexico failed to meet her as arranged in Havana, forcing her to travel to New York and search for him in vain. He was now trying to throw the blame on her. On 28 March he secured an attachment on her property believing she had large sums in a New York bank. She did not keep the agreement, Lerner alleged, and therefore he now claimed $29,000 in damages.

Giorgio Bazelli, described as Tetrazzini's personal representative, told reporters that the contract was provisional and that Lerner had sent her neither railroad tickets nor money and did not arrange for her admission into the United States. Consequently she was the loser by the contract. The *San Francisco Chronicle* next day quoted Bazelli as saying: 'All sorts of schemers have been seeking to take advantage of Madame.'[9]

Fortunately for Luisa, she managed to avoid the process servers and to board the Kaiser Wilhelm II unobserved by them. After first buying more clothes in Paris and singing at a concert in the Ostend Kursaal, she visited her sister Elvira in Milan before travelling to London to take part in Covent Garden's summer season.

Prior to leaving England to make her Manhattan début, Tetrazzini had recorded during December a further six songs at their City Road studios supported by an orchestra of 25 players, conducted by Percy Pitt and supervised by Fred Gaisberg. These were issued in England during the last fortnight of January 1908 and the response from the public exceeded all expectations, for by the end of that month sales reached a total of 8,771 records. In sharp contrast, not a single one had been sold in Italy.[10]

9 Trouble in Milan – and from Melba

Although a stock of Tetrazzini's new records was despatched to the Gramophone Company's branch in Milan, none were placed on sale or listed in the local catalogue. This was revealed when the manager there, Kenneth Muir, wrote on 22 April 1908 to Theo Birnbaum in London.[1] He began that when discussing terms for a recording contract that previous November, Tetrazzini 'took occasion to complain to you of an alleged discourtesy towards her on the part of Maestro Sabajno'. This referred to the latter's visit to her in June 1906 that caused the breakdown in negotiations. Her version of events was 'absolutely different' from his, the truth of which had been corroborated by the musical critic of the *Lombardia*, Romeo Carugati, who had accompanied him, and insisted that it was Madame Tetrazzini who behaved badly. She had now given cause for a second complaint.

Some days earlier during Muir's absence from Milan, Tetrazzini telephoned his office asking for the loan of a machine so that she could listen to some of her records and requesting immediate delivery as she was soon leaving the city. They agreed to send one to her 'before nightfall'. At 6.00pm she telephoned threatening that if the machine were not delivered within a quarter of an hour she would telegraph a complaint to Birnbaum personally in London.

Muir went on:

> I wish to protest against this treatment which is disrespectful in the extreme. We had considerable shipments to customers from our stockroom on that day, and we cannot throw the organisation of our deliveries out of joint to suit the pleasure or caprice of an artiste of notoriously bad character.

As long as he was in charge, Muir ended, he declined to allow either himself or the staff under him to become the 'lackies of Madame Tetrazzini'.

On 30 April, the day that Tetrazzini was opening the Grand Season at

Covent Garden, Theo Birnbaum replied coldly that while he appreciated that Muir had thought it necessary to warn head Office in the event of their receiving 'some capricious complaint of discourtesy' from Tetrazzini, he attached very little importance to the dignity of the Milan staff in this connection. Unstinted courtesy under the most provoking conditions was exactly what the firm must ask of him, so far as the caprices of celebrities were concerned. Unreasonable behaviour was what they expected from them, and if staff got it that was no reason why managers should 'stand on their hind-legs and make a fuss'. Should a similar occasion occur again, Muir must, even at the risk of throwing his organisation out of joint, endeavour to deliver a machine to the artiste in question 'within the space of a couple of hours'.

London now enquired why no attempt was being made in Milan to market Tetrazzini's records. Kenneth Muir's response was to write to Birnbaum on 6 May:

> We beg to report that we have not yet issued these records because, just at the moment when you brought them out, we were publishing the records of the light soprano Pareto which are nearly all the same pieces as sung by Mme Tetrazzini. Besides, we consider the Tetrazzini records inferior to those of Pareto, and as these latter are cheaper we found it advisable to give up for the present the issue of the Tetrazzini records as they could not bear the competition of those by Pareto.

It will be recalled from Chapter 6 that it was Muir in January 1906 who had written to Birnbaum describing Luisa Tetrazzini as 'the most important Italian *soprano leggero* of the day' and urging the Gramophone Company to contract for her recording services. Now we have him denigrating her. This volte-face looks like having been caused by Tetrazzini's behaviour, so that Muir and Sabajno were now set on promoting the sales of Graziella Pareto's records out of pique. This attractive Spanish soprano was eighteen years younger than Tetrazzini and after making a highly successful début as Amina at Madrid's Teatro Real in January 1907 had sung Gilda there and then Ofelia, at the San Carlo in Naples.

Details of the ten 'Red Pre-Dog' and two 'Pink Pre-Dog' recordings in question are given in the Discography accompanying Dr G. Fraser's article on Pareto in *The Record Collector*, Volume XVII, No.4 for April 1967, in which he describes how she achieved international star status within a year of her début and kept her place there until she retired. He writes that, judging by her records, she had 'a beautifully focussed high soprano voice, well suited to lyric and coloratura roles, singing stylishly but without mannerism or exaggeration'. She would colour her interpretation at times 'with delicacy and pathos, the more effective because of her restraint and good taste in avoiding vocal tricks'. Her voice, though small, lacked any shrillness and 'her technical brilliance, added to the elegance of her admirable diction, placed her among the foremost coloraturas of her time'.

Kenneth Muir's letter of 6 May astonished and alarmed head office in London and Birnbaum responded sternly on 8 May, ordering Muir to make arrangements to issue the Tetrazzini records immediately.

> They are meeting with the greatest success at all our Branches, and, seeing that Mme Tetrazzini is an Italian artiste and that she has lately achieved an almost unprecedented world-wide reputation and success, it would certainly be strange if her records did not sell well in Italy.
>
> We note that you consider Tetrazzini's records artistically inferior to those of the singer – Pareto – but the question of the artistic merit of Tetrazzini's records is one which we should prefer to let the public decide. We shall be glad, therefore, if you will see that her records are no longer omitted from the Italian catalogue. Will you please confirm?

But on the same day that Birnbaum was dictating this letter, Kenneth Muir was writing an eight page long justification of his conduct to him. He began that it seemed all Birnbaum's recent letters on the subject were rather based on the misconception that if an Italian artiste made a great reputation abroad it materially enhanced that reputation in Italy. This was frequently not the case, however. Caruso might be cited as an exception but Muir could not recollect another instance of this occurring. The fact that Tetrazzini had made a great hit both in London and in New York did not really enhance her name in Italy where operatic singers were judged from a different point of view. The Anglo-Saxon public attached great importance to the beautiful natural quality of the voice rather than to the perfect school in voice production. It also attached considerable importance to good acting rather than to strong and expressive colour in singing. Muir continued:

> Melba has never succeeded in making a name in Italy in spite of her great name abroad, a name which she continued to hold a long time after her title to it had become doubtful, partly through her intelligence and ability in keeping out competition in her happy hunting ground. Consequently when by a fortuitous chain of circumstances Tetrazzini appeared before a London public in the absence of Melba, the London public found to its surprise that Melba was not at all the first soprano of the day, a circumstance which had been well-known in Latin countries for a considerable time previously.
>
> London is now of the opinion that Tetrazzini is the greatest light soprano in the world. The public there is just as ignorant of, say, Graziella Pareto as they were ignorant of the existence of Tetrazzini a year ago, but none the less Pareto has the more beautiful voice and the more perfect school of singing. This you can easily decide for yourself, by comparing her records with those of Tetrazzini – the more so as several of the subjects are the same and were made at almost an identical moment, Pareto's about ten days before Tetrazzini's. When it comes to light coloratura, Tetrazzini is far outstripped by Galvany, whose quality of voice, however, is not nearly as perfect as Tetrazzini's. What does London know of such artistes as Barrientos, Regina Pacini, Storchio and others that one could

mention? Nothing! And why? Simply because they never had a chance to sing at Covent Garden owing to the Melba monopoly.

Let us pause to consider Muir's statement that Maria Galvany 'far out-stripped' Tetrazzini. At least, he adds that her quality of voice is 'not nearly as perfect'. John Steane in *The Grand Tradition* describes her as 'a Spanish soprano who most notably on records could sound like a whistling kettle in a high E flat'.[2] Michael Scott in the first volume of *The Record of Singing* found that his main impression from the large number of records made by her was of

> a hard little voice of no particular quality, the tone fluttery, but secure, the range extending easily to the high F and with quite an extraordinary facility in staccati which she takes the opportunity to show off whenever she can, no matter how inappropriate.[3]

Muir next mentions Maria Barrientos. Richard Aldrich thought her voice 'not always of the highest finish, particularly in more difficult passages', while Michael Scott in *The Record of Singing* – I wrote of her recordings that her voice comes over 'as pure but with a somewhat thin and hard timbre, lacking character or fascination'. Also, at times, 'the intonation was not quite precise and the voice production a little light'.[4]

Muir also refers to Regina Pacini, the Portuguese prima donna, who was the same age as Tetrazzini and achieved more in so far as she married a President of Argentina. Michael Scott wrote that though she was only in her early thirties when she made her records, 'Pacini's voice already sounds worn, the tone curdled in the middle register'. He finds her 'a rather mature Gilda in *Caro nome* feeling her way cautiously and not always successfully through the staccato passages'. The top part of her voice was the best but it lacked real brilliance.[5]

Lastly, Muir names Rosina Storchio, one year younger than Tetrazzini, and admired for her accomplished technique in coloratura and her express-iveness in lyric roles. It was she who sang Cio-Cio-San in the disastrous world première at La Scala when a breeze on the stage made her kimono billow out and a voice from the audience called out in Italian 'She's pregnant! Toscanini's baby.' The final curtain fell to catcalls and whistles from the gallery, leaving Puccini dejected and Storchio in hysterics. Toscan-ini regarded her as one of the greatest of lyric sopranos and refused to engage Tetrazzini to sing at La Scala because he said she was 'too pyrotechnical'.

Muir goes on to say that he does not wish to disparage Tetrazzini but only to point out that 'her monopoly which you think is universal is really limited very definitively to countries where Italian Opera is the entertainment of a very restricted public'. This would explain one reason why her records were not instantly put on the market in Italy the moment they were sold elsewhere.

In his next paragraph Muir reveals his resentment over London head office's reaction to his letters. On 30 April Birnbaum had given him instructions as to how he and his staff in Milan should treat Italian artistes.

> With all due deference to you, the instructions given seem to me to show almost as little knowledge on this point as we here possess on the question of how to treat English artistes. If your instructions were to be carried out to the letter, we should soon produce a very different state of affairs in our recording establishment with a considerable increase in the already heavy payments made to Italian artistes. You do not appear to be in the Italian operatic theatrical atmosphere. If you were to attend rehearsals conducted by Italian Maestros in Latin countries a very great modification in your views would take place. These maestros have to exercise great firmness in handling Italian and Spanish artistes and keep before them continually the fact that they are extremely ignorant of music which is the case. If this is not done, the artistes at once take advantage of the situation and sing as they want to, which is usually an extremely bad way; unless they are continually pulled up they get into slack and slovenly habits.

All this, Muir claimed, was only too apparent in many of the records made by Italian artistes when free to sing as they pleased. Caruso was an example of this in the last record made by the Victor Company of *Vesti la giubba* which also contained a bad mistake. The Tetrazzini recordings were similarly blemished.

He would cite only

> a single instance in the record of the Mad Scene of *Lucia di Lammermoor*[6] in which there occurs a trill accompanied by a trill on the flute and therefore it is a *sine qua non* that the artiste should take this trill in one breath and as the music is written. All artistes do it, there is no difficulty about it, and yet the great Tetrazzini stops in the middle of the trill, allows the flute to go on trilling alone, comfortably takes her breath and then cuts in again quite calmly as if nothing had happened. I presume that a sample of this record was submitted to her for approval and if so, in passing the record, she a second time took advantage of the treatment of the London office and which you now propose should be also applied in Milan. I can only add that in every one of her records occur signs of the same sort of thing.

We have reached the fifth page of Muir's counter-attack. He continues that the policy in Milan was to publish records according to their commercial and artistic value. His belief was that the Tetrazzini records would meet with a disappointing sale in Italy owing to these blemishes combined with the high prices, being Rose Label records. He did not think that they would compete easily with Red Label ones by Pareto and Galvany.

The rest of this letter was devoted to a protest against the London head office's proposal that the Italian journalist Romeo Carugati should no longer be employed by the company on account of his adverse criticisms of Luisa Tetrazzini. The two most important Milanese newspapers were owned by Ricordi and Sonzogno and distinctly hostile to the Gramophone Company's interests. The third most influential journal, the *Lombardia*, had Carugati on its permanent staff, thanks to which they had been able on more than one occasion to use its columns to rebut their competitors' attacks. Muir therefore regarded it as imprudent to add the *Lombardia* to the opposition by a 'somewhat trivial economy'. Far from silencing Carugati's attacks on Tetrazzini, it would increase them.

Muir ended his letter:

> In explanation to these attacks I may say that they are not peculiar to Carugati but have been general throughout the Italian press. Madame Tetrazzini has herself to thank for them, having most injudiciously cast aspersions on Italian theatres to reporters of the foreign press, and the Italian press naturally replies.

Having put his case so strongly and at such length, Muir realized that it was useless continuing to defy London and on receipt of Birnbaum's letter of 8 May he obeyed orders and agreed 'to carry out instructions without delay' – but added sarcastically:

> We beg you to note that we are already overstocked in records and have already spent too much on supplements and have been the recipients of your complaints in these matters, but if the selections for our catalogues are to be made in London, we can hardly be held responsible.

After the Tetrazzini controversy Kenneth Muir became increasingly disgruntled and in October 1909 he resigned and joined the Gramophone Company's rivals, the Fonotipia Company. A letter in the Archives dated that month states that he was helping Ricordi, the music publishers, in a suit claiming back royalties and damages from his former employers.

Praise from Patti

Meanwhile at Covent Garden Tetrazzini had celebrated her return by appearing again on 30 April in *La Traviata* and was rapturously received. The only criticism came from *The Times* which disapproved of her costumes, claiming that they were half a century ahead of everyone else's in the opera. 'Let us hope she is still open to correction.' But she took no notice. A Czech tenor, Otakar Mařák, sang Alfredo. He had never performed in England before and was highly regarded on the Continent, but the excessive vibrato in his voice irritated the patrons of Covent Garden, and he was discreetly dropped.

In the audience was Adelina Patti who wrote next day from the Carlton Hotel:

My dear Madame Tetrazzini,

Brava! Brava! e encora Brava! I cannot tell you how much pleasure it gave me to hear you last night, and what a joy it was to me to hear your beautiful Italian phrasing and how immensely touched I was by the wonderful feeling and pathos of your voice. You made me cry in the last act. I should like also to add that in addition to the phenomenal brilliancy and purity of your high notes, your beautiful method, your phrasing, the ease and flexibility of your voice and your acting, all gave me the very greatest pleasure, and I shall take the first opportunity of going to hear you again. I heartily rejoice in your well-deserved triumph. *Brava! Brava! e encora Brava!*

Yours sincerely,

Adelina Patti-Cederström.[7]

This was a letter that Tetrazzini later said she treasured more than all the compliments received during the rest of her life. The two women became close friends and Patti visited Covent Garden during that season to hear Luisa in other roles.

On 2 May John McCormack appeared as Edgardo to Tetrazzini's Lucia, and on the 19th Melba, back from Australia, was heard again as Mimi in *La Bohème*, and then as Desdemona in *Otello*, before alternating with the Italian in *La Traviata* and *Rigoletto*. Each interpretation was judged effective in its own way, but the approach was entirely different – the Australian producing silver notes, the other golden.

The public unable to visit Covent Garden could compare the two divas by buying their records. *Punch* for May published a cartoon depicting them each behind a gramophone fighting a duel with the sound of their voices emerging from the horns. This was entitled: 'STARS IN OPPOSITION OR, THE "RECORD" OPERATIC DUET'.

That year, in celebration of the state visit to London of the French President Armand Fallières, a gala performance was held on 27 May. The entire front entrance reserved for the royal party had been adorned, according to *The Times*, with accoutrements of gold and crimson hangings, old French furniture, gilt mirrors and quantities of palms. Particularly noticeable in the auditorium were the Maharajah of Nepal, wearing a helmet composed entirely of diamonds and emeralds and a bird of paradise and an osprey; and Lady Londonderry, whose outsize tiara, necklace and stomacher 'attracted all eyes'. Supported by John McCormack as Nadir, Sammarco as Zurga and Vanni-Marcoux as Nourabad, Tetrazzini appeared as Leila in the first act of Bizet's *I Pescatori di Perle*, sung in Italian to suit her. It seems that pandering to a prima donna was worth the risk of offending a French President. This was followed by the Garden Scene from Gounod's *Faust*, with Melba as Marguerite, Giovanni Zenatello as Faust, and Vanni-Marcoux as Mephistopheles. Cleofonte Campanini conducted, and all went smoothly except that some ladies fainted, overpowered by the scent from the banks of real roses, and had to be carried out. Both divas, according to the newspaper reports next day, were at their best and rewarded by all-round applause in which no partisanship could be detected.

In late May Alessandro Bonci came to sing with Tetrazzini as the Duke in *Rigoletto* on 1, 6, and 9 June – as Edgardo to her Lucia on 5 and 11 June and 20 July; as Count Almaviva in *Il Barbiere* to her Rosina on 15 and 23 June, 4, 9, 17 and 22 July, with Mario Sammarco as Figaro; and as Nadir in Bizet's *I Pescatori di Perle* with her as Leila and Sammarco as Zurga on 19 June. All three sang superbly in this first revival for twenty years, so two extra performances were staged on 25 and 29 June.

Bonci had cause to wish Melba could be dethroned. His success when making his début as Rodolfo to her Mimi in 1900 had led to her refusing to sing again with him on the grounds that he was much too short and looked ridiculous next to her. If only some Italian prima donna of his height could replace her, what a difference it might make to his career – and now he had found her in Tetrazzini. His style was quite different to Caruso's, being more inclined to that of Fernando de Lucia. P. G. Hurst wrote in *The Golden Age Recorded* that Bonci seemed to have discovered the art of singing without needing to breathe, and so was able to execute some miraculous feats of phrasing. He always sang

> with an unforced and gracious tone in which the legato in its truest and most classical form was conspicuous, and with an exactitude of balance between notes and words which is an insoluble problem for modern singers.[8]

Tetrazzini eclipsed all her previous achievements that summer on 15 June as Rosina. The *Evening Standard* wrote:

> The perfect command with which she blended and voiced both the declamatory and the vocal passages of the florid music, the intuitiveness of her gestures, the subtlety of her inflexions, and moreover the humour and reality with which she invested some very unreal situations was little short of amazing. . . . If Mme Tetrazzini fully earned the honours heaped upon her, it was last night. She is a humorist of the front rank.

Tetrazzini was proving a much better actress than Melba, one of whose biographers Percy Colson wrote:

> She was never able to call up a look of tragedy more intense than that of the lady who has forgotten the name of the gentleman who is taking her out to supper and does not want to hurt his feelings.

Another biographer, John Hetherington, comparing the two sopranos, wrote that Covent Garden audiences now had 'a choice between the coruscating coloratura flights of Tetrazzini and the angelic purity of Melba'.

The Star was surprised to find Covent Garden crowded to its utmost, since everybody was supposed to be at Ascot, but the prospect of seeing Tetrazzini in a new role proved irresistible.

> That she triumphed in the Lesson Scene and aroused the audience to frenzy may be taken for granted. Mme Tetrazzini proved that she is not devoid of humour, and is unusually free and graceful in her movements for a *prima donna*. The too nasal quality of her voice in the recitatives was, however, not quite so pleasing.'

Verdi considered Rossini's *Il Barbiere* the finest *opera buffa*, but all Italian opera was regarded with disdain in London at this time, so we find the critic of the *Daily Mail* declaring:

> If it is true that Mme Tetrazzini has made *Lucia di Lammermoor* possible in this critical twentieth century, it is equally true that she performed the same function on behalf of Rossini's *Il Barbiere* at Covent Garden last night. Her great art, her flawless, flute-like voice, and the amazing vivacity with which the Florentine Nightingale invested the part of Rosina made Rossini's tinselled puppet live.
>
> The old *Barber* is as bold and senile as a centenarian opera can be; its characters mere mechanical dolls, and its situations operatically stagey. But last night's audience thought otherwise. Mme Tetrazzini with a wonderful 'make up' and a more wonderful art held the house enthralled. . . . Her bantering byplay with Bartolo and Figaro, her naïve little coquetries . . . never failed for an instant to find a responsive thrill in the audience and three times she was interrupted in her first important aria, *Una voce poco fa*, by uncontrollable outbursts of applause.

Referring to this revival, the *Musical Times* for July 1908 reported that Madame Patti, who was present and generous in her applause, must have felt that her successor could not give the music in the medium part of the voice the same beauty of tone as she had done, but the higher florid passages were delivered with exquisite finish and a volume of tone and great agility that frequently approached the phenomenal.[9]

On 11 July Tetrazzini was first heard at Covent Garden as Queen Margherita di Valois in *Gli Ugorotti* with Emmy Destinn as Valentina. The critics all agreed that both were superb. *The Times* found that Tetrazzini gave the famous scene *A questa voce sola* with much 'brilliancy of voice and method'. Melba, however, at a private party had amused her friends by getting down on all fours to imitate the horse that had to carry plump Tetrazzini in the opera's third act.

Tetrazzini had also sung in concerts arranged by the Grand Opera Syndicate in London on 16 June and ten days later in Paris for which she was paid £475.[10]

On 13 June the *San Francisco Chronicle* had published a report from London regarding the relations between Melba and Tetrazzini. After they had been paying one another compliments in the papers, 'the bubble of mutual admiration blown aloft by the two ladies' had burst with a suddenness that set people laughing. Melba had invited Tetrazzini 'to grace the programme' at a Covent Garden concert to celebrate her twentieth season there and had signed herself 'Your devoted admirer'. The press were told that she hoped the other would accept as she had heard a great deal about the Italian singer's 'charming manner'.

According to Tetrazzini's friends, she had practically made up her mind to grant the request, but a few days later the two met for the first time backstage at Covent Garden. Melba had said: 'Your singing delights me', but her manner was so distant and haughty that Tetrazzini was embarrassed. After a few words, Melba had swept imperiously away, leaving Tetrazzini with the feeling that she had been treated like a new scullery maid. So next morning she announced that she would not appear at Melba's concert. The same day, Caruso, who sided with his fellow countrywoman, sent Melba a note asking to be excused from participating.

Years later helping Melba in Australia with the writing of her memoirs, Beverley Nichols was to write:

> When I asked her to give me a few frank words about Tetrazzini whom she detested and despised, she waved her hands and said; 'Say she was a charming artist! A delicious artist!' I pointed out that only yesterday Melba had said she looked like a cook and faked all her top notes. To which Melba protested: 'I can't possibly say things like that. I must be generous.'[11]

It did not please Melba, who had always stayed at the Savoy Hotel, when Tetrazzini also made it her London home, occupying Suite 412 with its fine view south over the Thames and its private kitchen where she usually cooked her own breakfast, with spaghetti as the main dish. The plump *prima donna* was the hotel's best loved guest, and there was nothing the staff would not do for her. Before her arrival, the suite would be freshly painted duck-egg blue, the tint she liked best for interior decoration and an extra well-padded mattress kept specially for her put on the bed. Two grand pianos were installed, one tuned for playing in wet weather and the other in dry. Luisa would practise scales at the appropriate one for several hours every day. This would irritate Melba, who sometimes stayed in a suite within earshot. 'That woman can't sing a slow scale,' she once cried and which the other overheard. After that, Tetrazzini never spoke to her and she could not resist hitting back when the opportunity occurred. Mrs Kate Butler, the Savoy's lady superintendent, happened to be passing Melba's suite one evening with Tetrazzini when the occupant burst into full song. The Italian recoiled and then asked 'innocently': 'Have you *many* cats in your lovely hotel?'[12]

In contrast, Adelina Patti's friendship and admiration had grown stronger for Tetrazzini. On 18 July[13] she wrote from the Savoy Westend

Hotel in Carlsbad where she was taking the waters with her husband, Baron Cederström, to:

> *Ma chère et bien aimée* – Luisa!
>
> *Mille fois merci pour votre aimable petite carte avec toutes les jolies choses que vous me dîtes. Vous allez encore chanter deux fois La Traviata!* Alas! I shall not be there to appreciate it and join my enthusiasm with others. . . . May God bless you and give you every happiness is the wish of your true and dearest friend.

The question might be asked why did Patti prefer Tetrazzini to Melba? Perhaps it was because she found the Australian's voice too cold and lacking in temperament. John Pitts Sanborn the critic who heard both many times throughout their operatic careers puts it well:

> Melba sang accurately and with the dignity of good workmanship. Her singing was stereotyped without the excitement of the unexpected, the suddenly improvised, the inspiration of the heat and joy of song. Sometimes, as Tetrazzini's harshest critics insist, that soprano injures the music by the variations she introduces; oftener she lifts it above the clouds. This sort of thing was inherent in the great Italian style as in the Italian temperament. Melba's style was rather mid-century French, the style of *Faust* and *Roméo et Juliette* than that of the older Italian roles, though in many respects she sang those roles so well and so delightfully.[14]

In early August 1908 Tetrazzini went to Paris on her way to relax for the rest of the summer in Lugano. *Musical America* for the 8th of that month reported that 'just to show how absolutely American she has become' the diva on arrival at the Hotel Meurice greeted a New York correspondent with the words, 'How d'you, by Gosh?' One of her preoccupations during her stay was frequenting the Rue de la Paix buying gowns to wear off and on the stage. She would be returning to England on 28 September so as to tour, giving twelve concerts before sailing to New York on 28 October. Oscar Hammerstein had written to say that the Chamber of Commerce in Philadelphia wanted to hold a reception in her honour, when next she sang there.

According to this account, Tetrazzini claimed to have given 68 performances at Covent Garden during the season – a gross exaggeration. She had also sung at three private *musicales* in London, two given by Waldorf Astor in Carlton House Terrace, at which Caruso and Yvette Guilbert appeared, and the other in St James's Theatre under the patronage of the Princess of Wales (the future Queen Mary) when Adelina Patti, Emma Albani and Oscar Hammerstein were present.

Tetrazzini opened her autumn tour managed by Percy Harrison on Saturday afternoon, 3 October, at the Town Hall, Cheltenham, and was delighted to receive a telegram wishing her success from Patti to which she replied that evening from the Queen's Hotel. Translated from the Italian, this letter starts:

> My Queen, immortal Adelina, Thank you for the telegram you sent me. It will be a talisman for me and as such I shall take it everywhere. How I long to be with the Divine Mistress of our art and kiss her hands to thank her again for all the exquisite delicacy she has shown towards me . . .

10 Captivating the Customers

Oscar Hammerstein I had to pay Tetrazzini $1500 a performance, guaranteeing her not less than a total sum of $60,000 to attract her back for his third season at the Manhattan,[1] which opened on Monday 9 November 1908 with Maria Labia as Tosca. Then the diva, who had returned from Europe on the Kaiser Wilhelm II, appeared on Saturday the 14th as Rosina for the first time in New York, and captivated the customers, not only with her singing, now more equalized, excitingly brilliant and clear, but also with her talent for felicitously inventiveh comedy.

The Metropolitan Opera Company had for many years been performing on Tuesday evenings in Philadelphia's attractive Academy of Music. Hammerstein now decided to wage war against them there by building his own opera house on a site facing the Majestic Hotel on the corner of Broad and Poplar Streets. Ever a hustler he had this ready in only seven and a half months. On Tuesday 17 November Maria Labia excited a packed house with what was, for those days, a shamelessly sensual Carmen. The following night in New York Tetrazzini enjoyed similar success with her Lucia, then travelled to Philadelphia to sing Rosina at the Saturday matinée. Some fifty policemen struggled to control the crowds outside cheering her. Then on 26 November and 1 December respectively she delighted full houses with her Lucia and Gilda.

Back at the Manhattan on 5 December, Tetrazzini was joined by a new lyric tenor, Florencio Constantino, making his New York début as the Duke to her Gilda. He had already sung the role with her in Philadelphia four days previously. His voice, though lacking Caruso's power, was brilliant, pure and caressing. A critic wrote of him:

> From the glittering diamond upon his little finger to the great flawless stone in his stickpin, Constantino is every inch a tenor ... I like to watch his arms describe graceful circles through ambient atmosphere while his golden voice grapples with high C.[2]

His tones blended admirably with Tetrazzini's. Pitts Sanborn agreed with the other critics that her voice had gained greatly in beauty that season:

> The crudities and inequalities that marred much of her singing nearly a year ago were scarcely in evidence on Saturday. Instead, there was an attention to the finer things of voice style that one hardly dared look for then, and far from losing brilliancy in gaining refinement, her singing seemed, if possible, more brilliant than ever. *Caro Nome* she sang exceedingly well, closing it with a dazzling display of bravura. Applauded to the echo, she sang the aria a second time even better, with a more appealing delicacy, a more enchanting finesse, and she had an entire new set of vocal ornaments for the close.[3]

Up till then the conductor, Campanini, had refused to allow any repeats but he allowed four encores on this occasion.

There was more enthusiasm when Constantino sang Alfredo to Tetrazzini's Violetta on 12 December with Sammarco as Germont.

Other cities had been pleading with Hammerstein for his company to visit them and so it was arranged for Tetrazzini to cater to their aural appetite with one performance each of *Lucia di Lammermoor* and *La Traviata* at the Lyric Theatre Baltimore on 4 and 11 January. Back in New York she sang in *La Sonnambula* and *I Puritani* on 13 and 26 February 1909. According to Henderson, as Amina she 'displayed captivating lingerie and high notes and . . . walked in her sleep with admirable decorum'. After hearing her Elvira, he wrote sarcastically describing the brilliant top of her voice and what he still regarded as her undeveloped lower register:

> She is the only singer now before the public who has her chest tones at the top and her head tones at the bottom. This alone is worth going miles to study, and it is a gift which enables the soprano to produce vocal effects both novel and astonishing.[4]

Before singing Gilda in Philadelphia on 18 February the diva visited a dog show in the Horticultural Hall during the afternoon. The *North American* next morning reported that when Tetrazzini came to a chihuahua called Elsora she decided that she must have it and at once agreed to the asking price of $200. The journalist interviewing Tetrazzini did not see the animal, renamed Salome (despite its true sex), for it had been allowed to remain at the show until the close. Tetrazzini said, 'It is so small, weighing only 4 oz that I can get it in the best hotels hidden in my handkerchief if I must, and it will be so easy for my maid to take care of it'

Then on 1 March, the *Philadelphia Record* reported the sad news that in Tetrazzini's apartment at the Bellevue Stratford, Salome had died from acute indigestion. Three days later at the Opera House the dogless diva sang Amina followed by Lucia on the 6th and 11th, Elvira on the 13th and 20th, and lastly another Lucia at the matinée on 3 April.

According to the *Record* for 15 March, Tetrazzini's imperfect understanding of English caused amusement on one occasion. 'Does the Mad Scene tire you?' someone asked. 'Med'cine, med'cine,' she repeated surprised. 'No, no, I take no med'cine at all. I am quite well.'

Hammerstein's third Manhattan season ended in gala style on 27 March with Tetrazzini again as Lucia followed by the Carnival Scene from *La Princesse d'Auberge*. There was tremendous applause after the orchestra had played a waltz, *Cara Mia*, which he had written for and dedicated to her. The impressario told the audience:

> When I am in good spirits I write a waltz. When I am blue, I write a funeral march. The season closing tonight has been phenomenal. My first year's takings were $52,000. This year they rose to $400,000. Therefore I have written a waltz. My complete plans for next year are not ready for announcement, but I may safely offer you forty grand operas and twenty-two operas comiques in my repertory. So New York may tremble. I thank you.[5]

In late March Hammerstein's company held a short season lasting until 10 April at the Boston Theater where Tetrazzini appeared in her showpieces *Lucia*, *La Traviata* and *Rigoletto*. That hard-to-please critic Philip Hale reviewing *Lucia* in the *Boston Journal* declared on 30 March:

> When she rises to her greatest heights, either in sustained melodic phrases, her voice is her own, unlike other voices, and in some respects incomparable. Her tonal emission is delightfully free and spontaneous. Her phrasing is now and then chopped by a desire to take this or that long passage in one breath. Her upper notes are uncommonly brilliant, and at the same time liquid, for her brilliancy is never metallic. Her scales are unusually even, while her trill is not always of uniform excellence. She excels in the ease and abandon of her bravura, in her ability to swell and diminish a tone and then connect it with the first one of a new phrase and in many other technical matters.

The public next day besieged the box office and, reported the *Musical Courier*, when the diva appeared as Violetta on 31 March, the scene in the lobby of the theatre and outside in Harlem Place 'rivalled a Harvard-Yale football game of pushing, struggling, nerve-racking clothes-tearing stunts'.

'H.T.P', better known as 'Hell to Pay' Parker, of the *Boston Transcript* could be vitriolic as a critic, but even he was almost won over by Tetrazzini's performance. She had been 'disappointing where one might have expected much of her singing, and surprising and delightful where there was reason to anticipate least'.[6] The showpiece of the opera was Violetta's scena *Ah, fors' è lui* and its cabaletta *Sempre Libera*, on which the first act ends. 'Clearly it was one of her battle horses and through the beginning of the first act she was saving herself for the ride.' Her interchanges with the company at Flora's table in the first act were 'very pallid recitative' and only in her answer to Alfredo's first love song did her voice begin to warm.

Her singing of '*Ah, fors' è lui* was distinctly disappointing. Faultless as her ear usually was, she seemed in some parts of the house to fall occasionally below the pitch. Her ornaments of song suggested more calculation than rhapsodic spontaneity and there was a touch of glinting hardness in her usually soft and liquid tones.

Worse still . . . she phrased music and text in more arbitrary and meaningless fashion than is ever her usual custom. *Che resolvi, O turbata anima mia?* runs the text for example, and Verdi has fitted his music close to it. *Che-resolvi-O-turbata/anima-mia* was her phrasing because it suited the convenience of her breathing. Again, with all the sheer brilliance of Verdi's music in this scene, it often has distinct emotional significance. Recall Violetta's dreamy and intense representation of the *Misterioso, misterioso* of Alfredo's preceding song – a passage that Mme Melba and many other singers charged with haunting feeling. Mme Tetrazzini merely slipped over it; the emotional apart from the purely vocal character of the music escaped her.

In the second act Violetta had no set piece, being engaged wholly in melodious declamation or in short arioso with old Germont or Alfredo. The dialogue with the former in particular had passages of:

> . . . an exquisite tonal beauty in themselves and of a truly poignant emotional significance. Colorless declamation may not serve them . . . they must have the virtue of song that is exquisitely phrased and colored, that is warm and touching with expressive feeling. It was easy to be distrustful as Tetrazzini approached these passages, but the resulting surprise quickened the delight of her singing of them. Many lay in her softest and most lustrous tones, many invited the half voice that she uses with such delicate loveliness . . . But her surprising distinction in them all was the coloring so soft, so warm and so bright that she gave them; the adroit artistry with which she phrased them, and the gentle and touching intensity of feeling that she imparted to them. . . . It was lyric singing at its fullest and finest. . . .

> None the less, her unevenness persisted to the end. . . . Perhaps the truth is that Mme Tetrazzini is over preoccupied with what she has been told are her histrionic responsibilities as Violetta. . . . Out of this desire came her endeavour to make some of her ornaments of song conform to the moment in the action in which she plied them or to heighten the emotional significance of her speech. As Violetta, she picks up her train, for example, and walks eagerly to the window through which Alfredo's love-song mounts; while as Mme Tetrazzini she is doing her pet feat of *messa di voce* – the swelling and the diminishing of a single tone.

> Again in the second act, she used very felicitiously, her equally beloved morendo – the slow dying of a single lovely tone. . . . Now and then, too, she has discovered or learned a telling histrionic stroke, like the lapse into utter weariness and disillusion of body and spirit at the end of *Addio del passato*. Oftenest, however, Mme Tetrazzini is a very innocent actress who does not quite see her earnest self as others less earnest see her. . . . Her attempts at facial play are not illuminating, except when, at the end of an act she beams her delight upon the applauding audience. Her gesture is most significant when she wiggles her head and waves her chubby arm at the rejoicing house. . . . No whit the less, in the coloring of her tones, in the music of the scene with Germont (Sammarco) in the beauty and the feeling with which she clothed

them, Mme Tetrazzini was a singing actress in the very best estate of so difficult an art, because her tones were her irresistible means.

To satisfy popular demand, Tetrazzini also returned in between performances to Hammerstein's new opera house at Philadelphia to sing *Lucia* there on 3 April 1909. Here she proved once again how adept she was at endearing herself to audiences. Some divas are so greedy for floral tributes that there have been occasions when one has stealthily appropriated her rival's. Tetrazzini reversed this custom by herself sending a bouquet of sweet peas, violets, gardenias and orchids to each lady in the boxes at Philadelphia as it was the last night of the season.[7] Back at the Boston Theater she sang Gilda in *Rigoletto* on 6 April with Constantino as the Duke and Maurice Renaud in the title role. On the 8th she was heard again as Violetta, when Taccani should have sung Alfredo but owing to illness was replaced by Constantino. Lastly, on the 10th, she sang Lucia with Sammarco as Ashton.

A reporter from the *Sunday Herald* happened to be admitted backstage at the Boston Theater on the 8th, just after Taccani had been taken ill and when Constantino was protesting furiously in Spanish, French and Italian at being asked to sing Alfredo that evening. His contract, he claimed, called for a maximum of ten appearances a month with which requirement he had complied. Campanini, the conductor, and Coini, the stage manager, were insisting that he had sung only nine times. Eventually he admitted that he might be wrong. 'I am an artist not a mathematician', he declared grandly and went off smiling to his dressing-room.

Under the heading BITS OF GRAND OPERA THAT ARE NOT HEARD OR SEEN, the journalist in his paper's issue for 11 April described this incident and went on to give a frank account of what then happened. The stage had been set for the first act. The chorus began to drift on and to take their seats at the banqueting tables. The girls, tall and straight, were all Americans; the men, Germans, French, Italians, had good voices and bizarre appearances. Tetrazzini now arrived and was surrounded by the girls who put their arms round her and chatted with her as if she were their sister. 'The prima donna was bubbling over with good nature. She was as friendly and unconcerned as if she were not expecting to entrance a huge audience with golden notes within a few minutes.'

At the end of the first act Tetrazzini seemed to revel in the applause.

She laughed and capered about the stage, dragging her reluctant partners forward and backward at a run. And that it was not stage business is shown by the fact that she kept it up when off the stage. While in the wings waiting for her calls, she held court. A chorus man kissed her hand. She ordered him down on his knees. Then she placed one foot on his head and held a bouquet of flowers high in her right hand – a heroic attitude which caused every one to laugh and amused her greatly.

A second later, taking her cue, Tetrazzini staggered on to the stage in character as Violetta 'coughing pitifully, moaning in melody and behaving exactly as a prima donna dying of consumption and love should do'.

The account continues:

Golden notes are an old story to the people of an opera company after the season is well advanced, and yet the great moments of an opera seem to interest them as though they were present for the first time. When the soprano began her big aria, all was hushed. The other singers clustered in the wings and listened intently to hear how she took her high notes and how she managed the cadenza.

But the stage hands were not interested in opera particularly. 'This may go with some folks', said a six footer who was waiting for the signal to crumple up Violetta's house which looked so substantial from the front. 'This may be all right for them that like it, but give me a little ragtime.'

As the warning-bell rang for the last scene, Tetrazzini came out of her dressing-room wearing

a baby's cap with strings and a night gown which hung loosely, and with her face whitened by powder. Taking her skirts in her hands, she pranced around making fun of her role. Several of the company pretended to weep, and, folding her arms, she marched sadly to her bed where she was discovered when the curtain rose.

One of the most striking contrasts in *La Traviata* occurs when Violetta's servant has thrown open the bedroom window at her request. Into the sadness of the death scene comes the strains of a band in the street and the singing of merrymakers.

The *Sunday Herald* wrote that behind the backdrop at the Boston Theater the band was stationed with the chorus grouped around them.

All wore their street clothes as they do not appear in this act and as they wanted to rush off home at the conclusion of their number. Following the bâton of a leader, they sang the carefree chorus with abandon. Then they surged towards the exit, leaving Violetta to perish to slow music in the presence of an audience moved to tears. *Traviata* is an opera popular with the chorus. It enables them to escape early.

Tetrazzini was to have sailed from New York aboard the *Mauretania* on 14 April 1909 to open the season at Covent Garden on the 26th of that month but she had to postpone her departure through being taken ill in her suite at the Hotel Knickerbocker with acute gastritis. An investigating reporter revealed in the *Telegraph* for 15 April that this was due to her having eaten too much of Boston's baked beans, brown bread and sardines.

Signor Bazelli, Madame's manager, sent post-haste for Dr Ludwig Lang. He

1   Tetrazzini as Violetta, Royal Opera House, Covent Garden. From
The Sketch, January 1908, London

2   Tetrazzini as Rosina in *Il Barbiere di Siviglia*

Mme. TETRAZZINI

3 Tetrazzini as the Priestess in the title role of *Lakmé*

COMUNE DI FIRENZE

Ufficio dello Stato Civile

CERTIFICATO DI MATRIMONIO

Il sottoscritto Ufficiale dello Stato Civile, visti i registri degli atti di matrimonio

INDIRIZZO della SPOSA : Via dei Renai, 3

C E R T I F I C A
(nella CASA COMUNALE : PALAZZO VECCHIO)

che il *14 ottobre 1889*
(ore dieci antimeridiane e minuti quarantacinque)

in FIRENZE

fra SCALABERNI Giuseppe Santino Alberto (corrispondente teatrale)

nato in VIZZA — di anni trentacinque

e TETRAZZINI Luigia Giuseppa Assunta Maria Pierina
(FU EMILIO e di Gioiamma BIANCHI)

nata in FIRENZE — di anni diciotto
(nata il 28 aprile 1871)

Anno *889* parte *I* serie — vol. *4* atto n° *1066*

Il presente certificato viene rilasciato in carta libera, per gli usi per i quali la legge non prevede il bollo.

Firenze,

Il Compilatore

L'UFFICIALE DELLO STATO CIVILE
Vincenzo Basile

Tip.Com.Mod.12/289

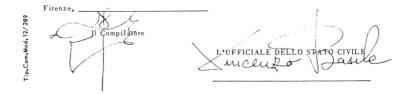

4 Copy of Tetrazzini's certificate of marriage to her first husband Alberto Scalaberni on 14 October, 1889

5   Tetrazzini being married to Pietro Vernati in Florence's Palazzo
Vecchio in 1926

A Most Triumphant Concert Tour from Coast to Coast
Now Being Concluded by

"THE QUEEN OF SONG"

Luisa Tetrazzini

A Total of 44 Engagements, Covering 30 States

Nov. 27—Pittsburgh.
Nov. 30—New York.
Dec. 7—San Francisco.
Dec. 9—Los Angeles.
Dec. 13—Los Angeles.
Dec. 16—San Francisco.
Dec. 19—Oakland.
Dec. 29—Portland.
Jan. 2—Seattle.
Jan. 5—Spokane.
Jan. 9—Salt Lake City.
Jan. 15—Denver.
Jan. 20—Dallas.
Jan. 26—Tulsa, Okla.
Jan. 29—Topeka, Kans.
Feb. 1—Kansas City.
Feb. 3—Muskogee, Okla.
Feb. 6—St. Louis, Mo.
Feb. 9—Lincoln, Neb.
Feb. 15—Chicago.
Feb. 21—Cleveland.
Feb. 26—Detroit.
Feb. 29—Erie, Pa.
Mar. 2—Buffalo.

Mar. 5—Rochester.
Mar. 8—Harrisburg.
Mar. 10—Baltimore.
Mar. 14—New York City.
Mar. 17—Washington.
Mar. 20—Philadelphia.
Mar. 22—Scranton, Pa.
Mar. 29—Richmond, Va.
Mar. 31—Norfolk, Va.
April 4—Boston, Mass.
April 7—Grand Rapids, Mich.
April 11—New York City.
April 14—Cincinnati.
April 16—Galesburg, Ill.
April 21—Springfield, Ill.
April 25—Providence, R. I.
April 30—Newark, N. J.
    (Festival).
May 2—New York City.
    (Hippodrome).
May 6—Spartanburg, S. C.
    (Festival).
May 15—Macon, Ga. (Festival).

"And then, like the great Patti, she proved her ability to charm equally with the simplest of songs."
Seattle *Post-Intelligencer*, Jan. 3, 1920.

"No other living soprano could match that magic voice possessed by Tetrazzini anywhere on earth."
Portland *Oregonian*, Dec. 30, 1919.

"She demonstrated her right to a foremost, if not the highest place in the ranks of living coloratura sopranos."
Salt Lake *Telegram*, Jan. 10, 1920.

"No such enthusiasm was ever exhibited within the historic auditorium before, unless it may have been when Patti sang there."
Salt Lake *Herald*, Jan. 10, 1920.

"There is only one Tetrazzini. Today Portland is worshipping at her shrine still under the spell of her golden voice."
Portland *Telegram*, Dec. 30, 1919.

"Tetrazzini sings better today than she did a half dozen years ago. She is the greatest coloratura now actively before the public."
Portland *Journal*, Dec. 30, 1919.

A Few Open Dates in the South Between May 6 and 15th

JULES DAIBER (EXCLUSIVE MANAGEMENT) Aeolian Hall   ·   ·   ·   ·   ·   New York City
VICTOR RECORDS   HARDMAN PIANO

6   Advertisement from the *Musical Courier*, 25 March, 1920, for one of her American concert tours

7   Tetrazzini during her 1921 concert tour of the United Kingdom

8 Tetrazzini arriving at the Gramophone Company's recording studios, Hayes, on 11 November, 1919, with Umberto Tatò on her right and the Cimaras on her left. Fred Gaisberg is on the edge, left of the Cimaras

made an examination and announced that the stomach of the diva ached. Madame must rest. Obediently Madame retired to bed and she will not rise until sailing time of the Nord Deutscher Lloyd next Tuesday. Much has been often spoken of her powers in the little matter of gastronomy. But that which has survived all European concoctions fell to Boston's famous dish.

There was no truth in the rumour that she had developed an abscess.

Tetrazzini was able to board the *Kronprinzessin Cecile* on 20 April, and reach Sheffield in time to give her first concert there and, reported *Musical America*, 'create the greatest excitement in a city "where music lovers have never shown greater interest in a singer since the days of Jenny Lind or Patti in her prime".' The Grand Opera Season had opened at Covent Garden on the 26th, and on 1 May a full house heard Tetrazzini yet again as Violetta with John McCormack as Alfredo, small dapper Mario Sammarco as Germont, and with Cleofonte Campanini conducting. Two nights later she sang Lucia with McCormack as Edgardo and Sammarco as Ashton. Then on the 14th the latter was heard in the title role of *Rigoletto* with her as Gilda and Anselmi as the Duke of Mantua.

On 29 May 1909 *La Sonnambula* was revived exactly 19 years after it had last been presented there with Etelka Gerster. There were signs of this when the water wheel did not work at all and when 'the extremely solid bridge failed to break after Amina had walked over it so that the "sensation" which thrilled our forefathers went for little'.[8] Walter Bernhard who, it will be remembered, had been the odd man out among the critics when Tetrazzini first sang at Covent Garden, and had accused his fellow critics of over praising her, now wrote:

> Really with every wish not to rhapsodise, one could hardly praise her Amina too highly. However brilliant may be many of the passages, the scope for the most refined and musical singing is equally ample, witness in particular the long solo in the Bridge Scene leading to the singularly brilliant and effective final rondo. Mr John McCormack may also be said to have come off with flying colours; yet the music assigned for Elvino is in some respects of alarming difficulty and it is permissible to doubt whether Rubini (for whom I believe it was written) really sang all the notes exactly as set down.[9]

Next on 31 May 1909 Giuseppe Anselmi, renowned for his beautiful voice and finished style, sang his first Count Almaviva to Tetrazzini's Rosina, Sammarco's Figaro, Vanni Marcoux's Don Basilio and Gilibert's Doctor Bartolo with Panizza conducting. As expected, she effectively introduced the polacca from *Mignon* and the Proch variations into the Lesson Scene. *Il Barbiere* drew the largest audience so far at Covent Garden.

Charity concert in Paris

In early June the Duchesse de Noailles wrote to Tetrazzini asking her to sing at a concert she and others prominent in French society were going to hold at the Paris Trocadero in aid of the Home for Women Consumptives at Larne. According to *Musical America* for 16 June the diva was offered 20,000 francs in gold or $4,000. She accepted; the Covent Garden Archives show her as receiving £315.[10]

Meyerbeer's *Gli Ugonotti* was revived on 21 June with Tetrazzini as the Queen, Emmy Destinn as Valentina, Marcel Journet as Saint Bris, Giovanni Zenatello as Raoul, and Antonio Scotti as Nevers. One reviewer wrote that Tetrazzini 'used to sing the music in a Donizettian manner, which did not suit it, but no one can say that of her now and her singing of *Beau pays de la Touraine* was delightful'. Another critic found that she gave the famous scena *A questa voce sola* with much brilliancy of voice and method.[11]

Emmy Destinn and Tetrazzini shared a common interest in pets. In 1928 the *Musical Times* was to quote Tetrazzini as telling a reporter on arrival at Victoria Station, 'I have plenty animal. I have fifteen dogs, five cats, and two peacocks, and I had a tiger – I called him "Poossy".' Poossy was, in fact, a young leopard which Tetrazzini acquired at the start of her career in South America. In *My Life of Song*[12] she relates how once on tour Poossy was being conveyed before her in a cart when the uneven road surface caused the cage door to burst open and away he sped and into a tailor's shop. The man's shrieks reached a policeman who was aiming his pistol at Poossy when Tetrazzini came gasping into the place and held out a tempting handful of money before the champion of law and order who relented.

Then, with commendable presence of mind, she seized a bolt of cloth and, before Poossy knew what was happening, had unwound the material and was twisting it tightly round the fugitive.

The tailor demanded compensation, for Poossy had even torn a pair of trousers apart. Tetrazzini did not quibble, but handed him at once the exorbitant sum he wanted. The man beamed, for business had been bad.

It may have been a desire to go one better than Tetrazzini that motivated Destinn into making a film called *The Power of Song* in 1913 in which she sat at a grand piano on which lay a lion – and was surrounded by two lionesses playing with their cubs. At her Château, *Stratz*, she assembled all kinds of pets and in her Aquarium Room she kept a Frog's Choir, the members of which were chosen in accordance with their vocal range. Destinn had perfect pitch and when she entertained visitors and the Frog's Choir commenced its twilight concert, she would listen intently and call out: 'That's Caruso . . . that's Melba . . . that's Tetrazzini . . . and that last one – that was me!'[13]

The Paris newspapers had reacted unfavourably to the blaze of publicity heralding Tetrazzini's French début. They pointed out that often singers lauded by the Anglo-Saxons failed to impress far more discerning audiences across the Channel. But when the gala matinée took place on 26 June in a packed Trocadero, its success surpassed all the organisers' expectations.

The critic of *La Presse* wrote that hardly had Tetrazzini ended her first number, the Mad Scene from *Lucia*, than there came cheering of an intensity that he had never heard before. From then onwards, the *Daily Mail*'s Paris correspondent wrote:

> After each piece rapturous applause mingled with shouts of 'Brava!' increased in volume until it became a mighty roar of enthusiasm. Such a demonstration is rare in Paris and it was curious to see splendidly dressed ladies and gentlemen keeping their carriages waiting in order to get a glimpse of her.

Les Nouvelles declared: 'It would be impossible for a singer how ever great her celebrity to make a more truly triumphant entrée at Paris.' And *Le Gaulois* commented on her winning ways and how, on noticing in the front row of seats the frail and elderly Comtesse de Guerne rising to applaud, the diva threw her from the stage 'a superb bloom from the bouquet which had just been handed to her, and the public noticing this applauded more furiously than ever'.

Musical America reported in its issue of 31 July that Paolo Tosti had written for Tetrazzini and dedicated to her a cadenza for his *Serenata*. This was 'decidedly difficult and runs very high but is so suited to the song itself that it seems an integral part of it, not an addition' and was one of her numbers at the Trocadero concert which had made 'a great hit'.

But one unpleasant incident had occurred which the organisers of the charity gala tried in vain to hush up, for on 2 July the Paris correspondent of *The Record* disclosed that there had been 'a brief but very pretty fight' over Mme Tetrazzini between an American, John Salter Hansen, and George Bazelli 'the prima donna's personal assistant'. This had been caused by the latter's hot temper which the previous winter had been responsible for Oscar Hammerstein's having 'many troubled moments' when angered by some fancied slight Bazelli had often threatened: 'Mme Tetrazzini shall not sing tonight.'

Hansen had come to Europe scouting for talent on behalf of American impresarios. He had known Tetrazzini a long time, having first met her in San Francisco when he had aroused Bazelli's jealousy. The latter had spotted him standing in the wings at the Trocadero talking to Hammerstein's representative and had ordered him not to speak to her.

With a smile, Hansen had replied that he had no intention of doing so unless the lady wished to see him. Just then Tetrazzini was returning to the stage for an encore and Hansen loudly praised her singing. It seemed certain that the two would meet, and this Bazelli was determined to prevent, so pointing at Hansen he ordered the stage manager to eject him. But the man, who was friendly with Hansen, took no notice, which infuriated Bazelli who shouted: 'I'll make you go!' and slapped the American's face. He responded by almost flooring his grossly overweight attacker with a right fist to the jaw. The diva witnessing this ran, screaming, to the Duc de Noailles begging him to intervene. He and others sprang between the two opponents and led them apart. Vowing vengeance, Bazelli went off with Tetrazzini. Hansen remained until the concert ended.

As her husband Alberto Scalaberni had died in June 1905 Luisa could have married Bazelli. Why she did not is probably because he was becoming too dominantly possessive for her liking, as this incident illustrates. For the sake of her public reputation, however, as they were living together, she let people assume that they were married. Her poor English enabled her to avoid giving clear answers to questions on the subject. The *Musicial Courier* for 2 September that year wrote:

> Her husband is a Roumanian by birth. They are rarely separated and he has sung with her in most of the great music centers of the world. It was in the Vienna Hof-Oper where he sang for four years that he met and married the famous prima donna. He was originally an engineer and was already following that profession in Bucharest when he decided to abandon it to go upon the operatic stage.

The couple in reality first met in Mexico City when they sang together and never married. This romance in Vienna may have been an invention of Bazelli's told to some journalist.

After singing in Paris on 26 June 1909 Tetrazzini returned to Covent Garden for further performances of *Gli Ugonotti*, *La Traviata* and *Rigoletto*. During the months from May to July she had also made a number of recordings for the Gramophone Company. These are among her best and were all made like the earlier ones with the tactful and reliable Percy Pitt at the piano. The waltz *Oh, d'amor messaggera* from Gounod's *Mireille* recorded on 5 July was chosen by Dame Joan Sutherland as one of her *Desert Island Discs* programme broadcast by the BBC half a century later. There is a superb high E at the end.

Once the season at the Garden had closed, Tetrazzini spent the rest of the summer in Lugano before returning to England in the autumn to set out on a concert tour that took her as far north as Dundee on 18 October. A week earlier she had been the main attraction in the opening Harrison concert of the season at the St Andrew's Hall, Glasgow, where she had sung for the first time the previous autumn. In the *Glasgow Herald* for Tuesday 12 October 1909 its critic wrote that Tetrazzini had come at the right time for Mr Harrison. Patti had just sung her final *Home, Sweet Home* to her faithful admirers and it seemed as if her retirement would leave a gap that could not be filled.

> Then came the hour of Tetrazzini and Mr Harrison's hour with it. Whether Tetrazzini will command the long and ardent devotion accorded to Patti is another matter. Patti belonged to a time when opera of the florid school was to some extent a living art; she was identified with the musical movement of her day. The other in order to display her peculiar gifts must go to music that has lost much of its fascination. If modern composers could use the wonderful technique of such singers, singing might take a new lease of life. Last night Madame Tetrazzini's original selection included the Mad Scene from Ambroise Thomas's 'Hamlet', *Couplets du Mysoli* from David's *La Perle du Brésil* and *Ombra leggiera* from *Dinorah*, and to these she added Mozart's *Batti, batti*, Lotti's *Pur dicesti* and *Saper vorreste* from *Un Ballo in Maschera*. All these numbers were sung with the greatest effect. Madame Tetrazzini's voice is of the inexhaustible kind that seems always to have reserves of power and range. The show pieces displayed faultless technique although sometimes one felt that a great voice might be used for better things than arpeggios, scales and trills. But the elaborate ornament of these pieces is part of the school and, as has been said, displays capabilities of the voice that are not brought out in modern music. Madame Tetrazzini is artist as well as singer and if there was nothing offered last night that called for deep feeling, each number received the interpretation just suited to it and the voice itself was a continual delight. Many people may have turned out to hear Madame Tetrazzini a year ago through curiosity but last night's extraordinary enthusiasm showed that she has gained a permanent place in the affections of the Glasgow public. The Tetrazzini concert should be one of the events of the musical season for many years to come.

McCormack's Manhattan Début

Oscar Hammerstein opened his fourth season at the Manhattan on Monday 8 November, and two evenings later Tetrazzini returned as Violetta with McCormack as Alfredo and Sammarco as Germont. She had enjoyed singing with the former at Covent Garden and it was due to her recommendation that Oscar engaged him,[14] despite some misgivings at first, saying: 'An Irish tenor in opera, I don't think so.' On arrival John told the reporters that he regarded Luisa as his 'fairy godmother'.[15] Later he would say that much of his success was due to her encouragement, and this was particularly true at his American début when he fell ill with influenza a few hours previously and staggered from his hotel bed to the opera house. Next day the *Herald's* critic in his review, headed PHYSICIAN ALWAYS NEAR, wrote that nevertheless 'this broth of a boy, twenty-seven years old, with a robust frame and a pleasant face made an excellent impression and was liked by the audience from the start'. The *Evening Post* agreed:

> That McCormack is a decided acquisition to the company is undoubted. He is a tenor with a carefully trained voice; pure, clear, even and flexible, and naturally placed. His tones are always true and sympathetic, and his mezza voce was most effective. At the outset, in addition to his apparent physical suffering, he was palpably nervous, but Mme Tetrazzini came to his rescue by crossing the stage and giving him a gentle pat of encouragement.

Tetrazzini was the most altruistic of artists, always eager to share the plaudits with the others. The *Record* for 8 December a month later, commented on 'the persistent manner in which she insists upon Mr McCormack assuming his burden of the applause' and added: 'Last night Tetrazzini literally dragged the hero forward.' This was in complete contrast to the treatment he had received from Melba. When the previous year at Covent Garden, he had started out to take a curtain call with her she waved him back, saying: 'In this house nobody takes bows with Melba.'

The general opinion of the critics was that Tetrazzini was at the peak of her powers. But the singer's taste in costumes often startled them. Even her admirer, John Pitts Sanborn, objected to what she wore in the first act of *La Traviata* – 'an instrument of percussion, a creation of many spangles'.

Tetrazzini had opened the season of Hammerstein's Philadelphia company at a matinée on 13 November by appearing as Lucia with McCormack as Edgardo. Then two days later they sang the same roles at the Manhattan – 'deepening the favourable impression he had made on his first appearance', according to the *New York Times* which disapproved of her Act I entrance 'in an extraordinary gown of blue satin, gold meshes and diamonds'. Next on the 25th he sang Tonio with her in the title role of Donizetti's *La Figlia del Reggimento*. Her plump figure hardly suited her to the part but she overcame this through her lively acting and beguiling singing. As a bonus, she added the waltz song from Gounod's *Mireille*.

John McCormack's wife, Lily, had accompanied him to New York and she was to mention in her biography of her husband, *I Hear You Calling Me*, that Tetrazzini was 'quite taken by my handsome young tenor and never tried to hide it even from me'.

On arrival from abroad the diva had announced that she had rented a house in New York for the season as her experience with hotels there the previous season had persuaded her that she must never again be dependent 'upon the uncertain cuisine of public restaurants'. Many dishes which she had been accustomed to have elsewhere she could not get in New York and much of what she did get was unsatisfactory. She described herself as a thorough student of the history and practice of cookery. As a result a reporter from the *New York World* called on her at 246 West End Avenue and in their issue of 13 November a full account of her views was published. She was so delighted to be in her own place. Even the best of hotels were 'dreadful'. There was the lobby at night she had to pass through on the way to her rooms with people staring at her and at the stage make-up still on her face. As for the dishes one is given to eat, they were never prepared the way one wanted – and one was never served by the same waiter twice. 'You lose your appetite and if you can't eat, you can't sing, and there you are.'

Tetrazzini spent a great deal of her leisure time in New York with Caruso. Although he was starring at the rival opera house, the Metropolitan, this in no way impaired the close friendship with Luisa which had begun in St Petersburg. At least twice a week he invited her to lunch in his suite at the Knickerbocker and for dinner at Del Pezzo's or at Pane's on West 47th Street, and they would feast on Neapolitan dishes. When the sun shone he took her out for country drives in his green Lancia, and they sang duets together en route to pass the time.

Luisa all her life refused to diet, with the result that her girth grew as the years passed. John McCormack used to tell a story of how one evening after a late lunch of spaghetti with Caruso, feeling the pressure from her corsets unbearable she took them off. Then when, as Violetta, she lay dying from consumption and McCormack, playing Alfredo, raised her, he felt, to quote his words, as though his arms were fondling 'a pair of Michelin tyres'. The astonishment in his face started her laughing, in which he found himself joining to the even greater astonishment of the audience.

Tetrazzini herself wrote in *My Life of Song*[16] that the secret of how she was able to look like the consumptive Violetta

> to perfection was discovered (so it professed) by the *Brooklyn Eagle*, which announced that "the diva was encased in what looked like a suit of armour over which was a gown heavily weighted down with spangles to such an extent as to make it somewhat difficult of manipulation".

She goes on to quote from various critics who acknowledged that through her acting she was able to convince audiences that she was consumptive and 'almost that she is thin though obviously to the eye she is none of these'. She insisted on coughing with the result that many in the audiences believed she was actually ill. The *Evening Mail* wrote that this degree of realism never failed to win their sympathy, but it was 'for the singer Tetrazzini, not for her tubercular Violetta'.

Vincent Sheean has described Tetrazzini as 'one of the most prodigious trencherwomen of all time'. He goes on that by chance he once watched her eat for about two hours at the restaurant called the *Castello dei Cesari* overlooking Rome and when he left she had scarcely embarked on the middle of her meal.[17]

*   *   *

When she sang at concerts, Tetrazzini would never allow the managements presenting them to tell her what she should sing. The *Chicago Sunday Tribune* for 12 December 1909 relates what happened when officials visited her at the Congress Hotel on the previous day to ask her to include the Mad Scene from *Lucia*, *Ah, fors' è lui* from *Traviata* as well as *Charmant oiseau* from David's *Perle du Brésil* all in one programme. The reporter present wrote that to demonstrate how impossible it would be to cram so much for her to sing into one concert she had stormed to the piano and accompanying herself was rushing through the Mad Scene at a ridiculous speed. He goes on that Tetrazzini behaved as if she could have 'rolled the programme maker in a piece of the carpet, chucked this under the sofa and piled the piano on top' – and when another reporter ventured into the room: 'Mr Andrea of the Manhattan Opera was bruising his fists beating the top of a chair, Max Rabinoff had backed behind a settee, Ben Attwell with dishevelled countenance was wondering whether there was more than one way out.'

The advent of a stranger brought just the tiniest lull in the storm and Attwell took advantage of it. 'But, madam you must – ' A crash stopped him. It was a tiny clenched hand coming down hard on what happened to be near. That object was the top end of the grand piano and the keys let out a shriek as Tetrazzini protested: '*Monsieur, c'est impossible ce que vous demandez. Impossible! Je ne chanterai pas tout ça! Je chanterai Lucia et la Perle. Cela suffit, n'est-ce pas?*'

The reporter wrote that the diva now 'drew the storm curtain and the sunshine of an engaging smile brought everything her way'.

Bazelli supported her, saying 'The *Traviata* aria lasts 25 minutes (sic) and the Mad Scene 30 minutes (sic) – and that is enough to tire any singer. It is terrible to ask her to do more.'

Realizing that they were defeated, the three men left.

Tetrazzini divided her time that season between singing at Hammerstein's two bases. For instance, she and McCormack appeared in *La Traviata* at the Manhattan on 10 and 19 November 1909, then in 1910, 9 and 14 February, and also at his Opera House in Philadelphia on 7 December 1909 and 5 March 1910.

Hammerstein sent detachments from his regular company also for a few days at a time to present operas from its repertoire in various cities in Canada as well as to Pittsburgh, Cincinnati and Washington during

December 1909 and January 1910. This was both to raise money to support the cost of running his seasons in New York and Philadelphia and to challenge the Metropolitan opposition in towns where they had had no competition in the past. He began this campaign in Pittsburgh on 20 December 1909 with Tetrazzini in *Lucia*, supported by McCormack as Edgardo and Polese as Ashton with Oscar Anselmi conducting. Next day *The Pittsburgh Post* described her as 'the standard bearer who expected to lead the invading forces to a glorious victory'. Unfortunately she was starting a cold and though the paper's critic, Jennie Irene Mix, praised her staccati and upper tones, she was lukewarm about some of her trills and her lower register, and thought the production second-rate. Instead of bringing his own orchestra, to save expense Hammerstein had engaged the Pittsburgh Symphony which had rehearsed only once and without the principal artists. The critic deplored the ragged singing of the scratch chorus, the tatty scenery and costumes.[18]

On 22 December, Tetrazzini sang Violetta with a sore throat that worsened, preventing her appearing again as Lucia on Christmas Eve and the performance had to be cancelled. The week spent in Pittsburgh resulted in a financial loss which increased in Cincinnati for several reasons – bad reports, employment once more of local musicians to form an orchestra who were under-rehearsed, and high prices, but the worst blow was that Tetrazzini could barely whisper. A throat specialist, unable to effect a rapid cure, warned that if she tried to sing, it might permanently damage her voice. The public stormed the box office demanding their money back. Out of three operas scheduled only *Sapho* was staged with Mary Garden who sang superbly.[19]

Hammerstein's fortunes improved dramatically in Washington. Tetrazzini had completely recovered and on 10 January 1910 she opened in *Lucia* at the Belasco Theater, when the *Washington Post's* prediction the day before was fulfilled – that this would prove 'the most brilliant first night of grand opera that the Capital of the nation ever witnessed'. The boxes and front stalls were packed with the élite of Washington society, the whole of the diplomatic corps as well as the cabinet, and leading government officials. A few minutes before the overture, President Taft and his wife arrived and were greeted with the National Anthem from the regular orchestra. Tetrazzini gave no signs of her throat trouble. Her ringing notes, portamenti, glissandi, swelling and diminishing of notes ravished her listeners. The rest of the cast, too, rose to the occasion. The President himself, visibly moved, led the applause throughout.

The following evening, Mary Garden, heard in her showpiece *Thaïs*, received an ovation. Next morning the Tafts welcomed the whole company to a White House reception and attended that night a performance of *Le Jongleur de Notre Dame* with Garden as the Jongleur, bringing once more 'tears to the eyes of those long since grown stultified to the display of emotion' as a critic had written of her rendering of the part at Pittsburgh.[20]

For the last night, on the 14th, the programme consisted of Donizetti's *La Figlia del Reggimento* with Tetrazzini in the title role, followed by *Pagliacci*. At the White House she had asked the President if he would be attending, to which he replied: 'My dear woman, a dozen Cabinet meetings would not keep me away'. Then Taft revealed that he had collected all her records and that his favourite was the one of her singing the polacca from *Mignon* to which he listened almost nightly on his gramophone. So, to please him, she added the song to the lesson scene in the Donizetti opera. He applauded so heartily that, ignoring the rule forbidding encores, she sang it again. Then, according to her, she responded to his applause by marching with arms swinging right across the stage until she could almost step into his box. Springing briskly to attention she gave him a 'cheeky' salute.

> The President shook with laughter. People in all the boxes did the same. Those in the stalls roared and rolled in their seats, while those in the upper parts of the house shouted: 'Encore! Encore!' I gave another salute. It was a full fifteen minutes before we were able to proceed.[21]

After that Taft became a close friend of Tetrazzini's.

Oscar Hammerstein had lost a great deal of money through Tetrazzini's inability to sing in Pittsburgh and Cincinnati. So to try and recoup his losses he now sent her out on a concert tour from 21 January to 8 February, 1910. When she sang in St Louis, the local *Star* for 31 January contains one of the few press reports where she herself is quoted as referring to Bazelli as her husband. This claptrap reads:

> 'Does your husband accompany you on all your concert trips?'
> A tender light shone in the eyes of the prima donna. 'Ah', she said. 'I would be lost without my husband. He is with me every minute. He is the one who discovered my voice, who brought me before the public and has managed my engagements ever since. He is truly my "alter ego" and my constant inspiration.'

Following this tour, Tetrazzini rejoined the opera company in Philadelphia where there was the largest audience of the season for *Rigoletto* on 11 February with McCormack as the Duke and Maurice Renaud in the title role. On 14 March she sang for the first time in Canada at the Théâtre Français in Montreal and received an ecstatic reception from the public and reviews comparing her with Patti. Then for the week commencing 29 March both Hammerstein's company and the rival one from the Metropolitan were entrenched in the same city. Opera-goers could choose between Caruso, Destinn, Farrar, Gadski, Homer and Scotti at the Boston Opera House – or Mary Garden, Tetrazzini, Mazarin, Renaud, McCormack and Gerville-Réache at the Boston Theatre. Olin Downes in *Musical*

America declared it to have been 'the greatest week of opera' in that city's history.[22] As John Frederick Cone points out in his history of the Manhattan Opera Company, its repertory was more interesting to those who enjoyed novelties, whereas the Metropolitan's consisted mostly of standard operas. After Tetrazzini and McCormack's performances in *Lucia* on 29 March 1910, the *Boston Post* wrote next day of the latter's singing: 'Not in years has a tenor voice been heard in the city so pleasing and acceptable.' Cone comments that these words could have been disconcerting to Caruso who was sensitive to criticism and who had sung there just two nights before.[23]

The policy of presenting star singers in short seasons of opera and concerts at theatres outside New York meant that both at the Manhattan and the Metropolitan casts lacked big names to attract the public and box office receipts fell as a result, stretching the finances of both rivals to breaking point.[24]

11 Tetrazzini Breaks with Hammerstein

As Montrose J. Moses has written in his life of Heinrich Conried, Hammerstein's opponent in charge of the Metropolitan, few men have the constitution to survive the wear and tear of Grand Opera management. In those days it was supported by affluent members of society and to please such a clientèle the impresario had to gather, in the opera house for which he was responsible, as much of the best of musical talent in the world as he could. Under Conried and his predecessor Maurice Grau, the Metropolitan became an exhibition of stars, all of whom were paid huge fees. Conried had to be ready at a moment's notice to readjust all his plans because of the whims of some singer – to listen to reports from the enormous artistic staff that looked to him for instructions or corrections – to know what the business manager and his assistant were doing – to cope with the complaints of the chief electrician and the stage manager – as well as the varied complications arising from exacting musical conductors.

As if that were not enough, he had to attend long and tedious rehearsals, often lasting from eleven in the morning until seven at night. Scarcely had the season closed than he was travelling abroad searching for 'talent' having signed contracts with members of his old company.[1]

Herman Klein, the English critic, in his *Unmusical New York* wrote that Conried was not a polite man and knew no more about opera 'than an ordinary chauffeur knows about aeroplanes'. Trying to cope with his ever increasing burden of troubles culminated in an attack of paralysis. Among these were the financial losses caused through the destruction of scenery and properties in the San Francisco earthquake and the refusal of the New York police authorities to allow Salome to be repeated after the first performance. In the spring of 1909 Conried died.

Oscar Hammerstein was the first American impresario to upset tradition by presenting operas of a more unusual character which the conservative

125

Metropolitan could never have contemplated offering to its customers. He had the gift of finding more new singers – not always of the first rank – than the rival establishment. It was he who broke up the opera monopoly making it possible for cities like Boston, Philadelphia and Chicago to have their own opera seasons without being dependent upon the Metropolitan's generosity.

For over three years battle raged between the Manhattan Opera House and the Metropolitan. At the end of the first year the latter had lost $84,039, and for the season that followed this grew to $95,806, whilst for 1908–9 they were in the red for the alarming amount of $205,201. Otto H. Kahn, the banker and the Met's chief stockholder, spent nearly $2,000,000 of his own fortune to keep the older opera house alive.[2]

As the 1909–10 season progressed, the position deteriorated still further and the directors of the Metropolitan in desperation opened secret negotiations with Oscar. He was willing to come to terms and to agree, in return for $1,250,000 not to present opera in New York or Philadelphia for a period of ten years. In addition he transferred, among other rights, the contracts with his company of artists, including Tetrazzini, to the Metropolitan, which then announced that it would employ them in a new Philadelphia-Chicago Opera Company presenting seasons in those two cities and occasionally elsewhere.[3]

Tetrazzini Outwits Lerner

On receiving a letter from Hammerstein to this effect, Luisa wrote back indignantly protesting at such treatment without prior consultation. Since he now had no intention of honouring the agreement signed with her, she regarded it as no longer valid and would conclude new contracts with those most fit for her purposes.[4]

Tetrazzini still had two disputes over contracts on her hands. Owing to the death of Heinrich Conried of the Metropolitan on 27 April 1909, the one with him was in abeyance but that with the wily Isidore Lerner was still being fought. It will be recalled how in late March of the previous year she had managed to avoid his process servers and leave for Europe. Now he was harassing her again. Due to sail aboard the *Mauretania* on 13 April 1910 to sing at Covent Garden, she was kept practically a prisoner inside her rented house at 246 West End Avenue, New York, on account of Lerner's efforts to serve an attachment on the trunks containing her gowns and jewels. However, on the evening of the 12th, disguised in her maid's clothes, she left the house in an ordinary hackney cab and went up the steerage gangway unobserved. A small army of private detectives guarded her stateroom and the approaches to it under the direction of her counsel.[5]

All through the night, process servers exhausted every resource to serve on her attachments that would hold her in New York. Next morning she told a reporter from the *Philadelphia Inquirer* that when she fainted on the stage in *Lucia di Lammermoor* that season it was not because of her exhaustion but because one of Lerner's detectives, after hounding her in her West End Avenue home, had thrust papers in her hand as she entered the opera house. It had been agreed that the hearing of the case should be postponed until November but Lerner apparently thought that if allowed to leave the country she would not return and was determined therefore to attach all her trunks. She had laughed when she then revealed: 'I have all my trunks – all my jewels – I have everything. But I shall not tell you how I have them. But believe me that Lerner man shall not lay his hands on one thing or on me.' She added that on her return she would then be perfectly willing to dispose of 'the ridiculous suits of the Lerner person'.

The *New York Morning Telegraph* for 14 April told its readers rumour had it that Luisa's baggage went on board disguised as freight which it was hard to attach. Then when the liner was out on the ocean, a wireless message was received that she and Signor Bazelli had appeared on deck and had sung the duet *Addio, Addio* from *Rigoletto*.

A week later, under the heading of TETRAZZINI'S FRIEND DIES ON THE OCEAN, the *San Francisco Chronicle* published the following:

> The death of J. G. Bazelli on the Cunarder *Mauretania* was announced today on arrival of that steamship at Liverpool. Bazelli accompanied Luisa Tetrazzini, the famous soprano, on the voyage. The cause of death is not stated in the despatch. Bazelli had been Madame Tetrazzini's constant companion since her first appearance in San Francisco years ago, when he sang with her as a tenor. In Europe and New York he defined his relation to the diva as being that of her secretary and agent. When she left New York last year and again when she returned to the operatic stage, she was named on the steamship passenger list as Mme Tetrazzini-Bazelli. They never admitted that they were married, however.

On the same day the *New York Telegraph* published a similar report which contained additional information:

> Bazelli was an unobtrusive man, keeping much to himself and on the exterior only interested in the affairs of the artist he represented. At the same time when drawn out he showed a lively interest in matters which the usual singer chooses to neglect. He was the only foreign singer, it is related, who ever asked why Philadelphia was called the Quaker City. He would spend his days over here in long rambles round the public buildings and interesting sites of the city.
> It was the same in London. His peculiar reserve as also his single-hearted devotion to the advancement of the career of Mme Tetrazzini stood in the way

of his making many friends. By birth he was a Roumanian and had the cast of feature and the general demeanour of that half Latin people. He was also a tenor though he was never engaged either at the Metropolitan or Manhattan Opera House. Always, he cherished the hope that he would be. Indeed, one season he brought over his costumes in the hope that finally he might be called upon. His hope never matured. His enforced idleness seemed slightly to gall him, but he said little about the subject to others.

In many senses he seemed a lonely figure, demanding little of anyone for himself and chary of inflicting his claims upon either acquaintance or friends. He was a type not unknown in the operatic world, almost but not quite contented to be the slave of the lamp; happy and yet not quite happy to bask in another's glory; helpful, retiring, harmless and pathetic, a Major Dobbin of the most heartless, glittering and fickle society in the world, the society of operatic artists. Mme Tetrazzini's friendship for him was sincere and of many years' standing.

The next day these reports were corrected. Bazelli had not died. He was in good health and staying at the Savoy Hotel with Tetrazzini. The man who died was a Mr Brazell.[6]

The summer season of grand opera at Covent Garden was to have opened on the night of 23 April 1910 with Tetrazzini in *La Traviata* but the manager, Neil Forsyth, came before the curtain at eight o'clock to announce that she was suffering from bronchitis and that Mme Donalda would take her place.[7]

Tetrazzini recovered sufficiently to appear four evenings later as Gilda in *Rigoletto* with Ettore Panizza conducting, and according to the *Musical Times*, 'soon showed that her E flat in alt was unaffected by her indisposition'.[8]

King Edward VII, who had reached London only late that afternoon from Biarritz, went specially to Covent Garden to hear Tetrazzini. This proved to be the last time that he attended one of her performances for on 6 May 1910 he died. This caused audiences to fall at Covent Garden, largely because the subscribers were among those closely affected by the event. Nevertheless, the management made no changes in their prospectus.

Due to its popular success when revived the previous year, Bellini's *La Sonnambula* was presented on 26 May with Tetrazzini once more pleasing a capacity audience, supported by John McCormack as Elvino and with her brother-in-law, Cleofonte Campanini, conducting.

Fashions change in music as in everything else. The London critics were united in their disapproval of the opera itself. *The Times* believed that rarely could an opera 'so supremely ridiculous as *La Sonnambula* have been put on the stage', while the *Daily News*'s musical critic complained: 'It is so dull and there is really nothing for the soprano to sing until the last Act.'

'The faded old work was trotted out again yesterday for the benefit of Madame Tetrazzini and her admirers, and seemed, if possible, more faded and tawdry than ever,' sneered the *Westminster Gazette*. Bellini's work dealt with the problem of a sleepwalker, but a still more pressing one for most was the task of keeping awake while the work was being performed.

On Saturday 18 June 1910 *Lakmé* was revived at Covent Garden. The critic of *The World* wrote that judging from the audience's response it should have a certain vogue at any rate as long as Tetrazzini was there to sing the title part.

> The Bell Song aroused frantic enthusiasm, and deservedly for it was perfect of its kind; really the purity and finish of her cantabile were most remarkable, especially if one recollects that in some other roles she has played outside her regular range, she has failed – or come as near to failure as such an artist can – in this respect. Still it is not hypersensitive to suggest that a little more variety would not be amiss and that her performance can hardly be taken seriously as an attempt to depict an Indian priestess. But it may be said with some justice that the music is not very Indian either.

Since first singing in concert at the Teatro Apollo in Lugano in 1901, Tetrazzini had spent much free time between engagements resting there. When the season at Covent Garden ended on 30 July, 1910 she went to Lugano and in August it was announced that she had bought the Villa Barioni near the little church of Geretta. She was to take a deep interest in the management of the house and the estate which she renamed *Il Paradiso*, making it a haven for some fourteen dogs brought from all parts of the world and, fascinated by the new medium for mass entertainment, she had a fully equipped film theatre installed. Here she entertained lavishly and gave generously to local charities.[9]

In September Tetrazzini went to sing at the Teatro Regio, Parma, where Cleofonte Campanini was conducting for the season before travelling to America to become principal conductor of the newly formed Chicago Opera Company. On arrival, she learnt that the star of the Regio orchestra was Rosalinda Sacconi the harpist, whose lengthy solo introduction to the park scene in Act One of *Lucia di Lammermoor* was so exquisitely played it always gained such applause that it had to be repeated many times. Meanwhile with the curtain up, the soprano in the title role stood on the stage waiting to start singing *Regnava nel silenzio*.

This Tetrazzini had no intention of allowing. What was she supposed to do in the meantime, she asked Cleofonte. Sweep the stage? She had no intention of forming part of a backcloth for a harpist to show off her skill. Happily, Rosalinda had not a combative character and immediately stepped down, allowing another instrumentalist of lesser talent to take her place.[10]

And so on 8 September Luisa sang her favourite role and received an ovation. Next on the 13th she played Rosina with similar success, and on the 17th for her benefit Maria in *La Figlia del Reggimento*, with John

McCormack as Tonio followed by Ofelia in the fourth act of Thomas's *Hamlet*. Then she returned to London, staying with Bazelli at the Hyde Park Hotel before going on a concert tour.

On 24 September 1910 Tetrazzini gave a concert at the Crystal Palace with Henry Wood as conductor.[11] A few days earlier she went to his house in Elsworthy Road, Hampstead, for a piano rehearsal. In his autobiography he wrote that she never tried to avoid such rehearsals like some younger and less celebrated singers then did. He described her as 'a plump, cheery little woman always ready to chat about singers past and present in the most animated fashion'.

After Tetrazzini had sung *Caro nome* and the *Carnevale di Venezia*, Wood asked her to sing the *polacca* from *Mignon*, but she replied firmly: 'No, I am not singing that this season.' When he asked why, she explained: 'I never try to keep up more than three coloratura airs at once. I just practise those three.'

This response impressed Wood and he comments that in his experience really great artists decide upon their season's repertoire and devote their entire attention to perfecting every detail. 'How different from the procedure of artists of lesser degree who accept engagements to sing *anything* – no matter whether they have ever seen it or not!' He observed that both Tetrazzini and Melba had voices that lasted 'fresh and bright long after the age when so many voices became hard and chill.'[12]

The *Musical Times* reviewing this Crystal Palace recital reported that Tetrazzini had lived up to her reputation, receiving a great reception from a packed audience, the majority of whom had no doubt never listened to bel canto before.[13]

Autumn 1910 Concert Tour

Tetrazzini had been engaged by the concert director Percy Harrison of Birmingham, to take part in his first provincial tour, opening at Cardiff's Park Hall on 27 September and then going to Bristol's Colston Hall on the 29th. Dates in October were: Town Hall Cheltenham (1st); Town Hall Birmingham (3rd); Free Trade Hall Manchester (5th); Philharmonic Liverpool (7th); Tower Pavilion Blackpool (9th); St Andrew's Hall Glasgow (12th) McEwan Hall Edinburgh (15th); Victoria Hall Sunderland (17th); Town Hall Newcastle (19th); Victoria Hall Sheffield (21st).

On Tuesday afternoon, 25 October, 1910 Tetrazzini sang for the first time in Dublin. Her programme at the Gaiety Theatre included *Caro nome*, the *Carnevale di Venezia* variations and Eckert's *L'eco*. Next day 'H. R. W.' wrote in the *Evening Mail* that in modern times one was apt 'to sneer at the coloratura school'. It required no less than a Tetrazzini to revive interest in that form of entertainment. The review went on:

> I do not think that the oldest opera-goer present – those who had recollections of Albani, Tietjens, Patti and the rest – could suggest that any of these could possibly equal the perfect vocalism of this wonderful singer in her special sphere. Gifted with a voice of extraordinary range and power, of flexibility and resource, Madame Tetrazzini has conquered every difficulty in vocal technique.... There is a certain joyousness in her voice, a brightness and animation which is optimistic, but the tragic or sensuous vein appears to be absent. If she sang the Mad Scene from *Lucia* it would seem to me that insanity was a thing to be envied rather than pitied. In *Caro Nome* she gave a most delightful example of perfect vocalism, and in the *Carnival de Venice* rose to heights of vocal technique which have probably never been surpassed.... Her pianissimo notes in the extreme upper part of her compass are like the harmonics of a violin, and her trills like those of Fransella on the flute.

From Dublin Tetrazzini travelled north to sing with the Belfast Philharmonic Society at the Ulster Hall on 27 October, with a concert on Saturday evening, 29 October. This time she sang *Io son Titania*, *Bel raggio* and the Bell Song from *Lakmé*.

On learning of her dispute with Hammerstein, 'Doc' Leahy had followed Tetrazzini to London to offer her such terms to sing at concerts for six months that, defiant of Oscar's threats, on 1 August 1910 she had signed the contract Leahy drew up.[14] The proceeds of the tour he estimated would amount to nearly $300,000, two-thirds of which would go to her. In the autumn, Hammerstein commenced legal proceedings to prevent Tetrazzini from singing for Leahy alleging that for her to do so would be a violation of a contract between them. These were held before Judge Hough of the United States Circuit Court in New York shortly before her arrival on the Mauretania, which was due to dock on Thanksgiving Day. A preliminary injunction was secured by Hammerstein's counsel, Robert C. Beatty, but the judge ordered him to file a bond for $5,000 to cover any possible damage that might be sustained by Tetrazzini were the ban to continue after her tour.

When the Mauretania reached New York on 24 November, Tetrazzini remained aboard in her stateroom all night after abortive attempts to avoid service of papers enforcing the injunction. Neither her name nor that of Bazelli were on the passenger list. She would not admit that they had arranged for such omissions but that was suspected by Hammerstein's lawyer, Louis J. Vorhaus, who had boarded the liner with Deputy Marshal William Crawford to serve the papers. Earlier on, Benjamin F. Spellman, her personal counsel, accompanied by 'Doc' Leahy, had gone down the bay in a revenue cutter and, boarding the ship at quarantine, had locked themselves in Tetrazzini's stateroom. Leahy told her that he had been to Washington to get a special permit to take her off the ship on a tug to avoid service of the injunction, but that the government officials had refused his request.

When Vorhaus arrived and hammered on the stateroom door, Spellman opened it angrily. Vorhaus quickly explained his business and there was a heated verbal duel. He retreated out of the room and the Deputy Marshal then entered and served papers on Tetrazzini.

The two opposing camps later held press conferences.[15] 'We'll make 'em eat that injunction, seals and all', threatened Spellman. 'Madame Tetrazzini was never notified that her contract would be renewed for the season of 1910–11, and it's plain as daylight that she is therefore released.' He distributed letters for inspection that Hammerstein had written to his 'favourite songbird' in which he indicated that he was willing to release her. Spellman said that the impresario had often acknowledged his gratitude to her for the way in which she had adhered scrupulously to the terms of her contract, and that he had openly declared that of all his artists she was the one who gave him no trouble.

Spellman quoted from a letter in German which Hammerstein had written that May from Paris saying:

> If all my singers had been so compatible as Madame Tetrazzini I should not have been obliged to retire from grand opera. Such creatures as Garden, etc., were not worth getting grey-haired about. It was not the money I lost, but the ingratitude of those artists which compelled me to retire.[16]

Spellman contended that Hammerstein had practically given up the option on her services by saying in substance that he would not require these.

Tetrazzini herself told the journalists that it was her intention to go immediately with her manager, Giorgio Bazelli, and 'Doc' Leahy to San Francisco and open there on 12 December. She threatened that if forced to do so she would sing in its streets.[17]

At the opposition's press conference, when asked by a reporter if he had heard from Tetrazzini, Oscar Hammerstein replied: 'No. She has not even taken the trouble to send her "best friend", as she used to call me, a card announcing her arrival.'

'Will you go to call on her?' interjected a journalist.

'No. I shall not call on her. Her little dog might bite me,' Hammerstein returned.

'Is it true that you have booked a concert tour for her?' was the next question.

'Yes, I have – and I think she will sing for me and not for Mr Leahy,' came the confident reply.

The Circuit Court proceedings were resumed on 1 December 1910, and eventually on the 6th Judge Laccombe allowed Tetrazzini to leave New York, remove her personal belongings and sing for Leahy, but for every performance she had to deposit $1,250 in the bank pending final settlement of the case.

Both sides regarded this verdict as favourable. 'I aim to get $1,250 every time Madame Tetrazzini sings and not have any trouble about managing her,' commented Oscar. 'I consider it a remarkable decision.'

Benjamin F. Spellman, the prima donna's attorney, was equally pleased. 'The decision is a victory. It means that Luisa Tetrazzini is not forced to sing under Oscar Hammerstein's management. We will gladly comply with Judge Laccombe's suggestion.'[18]

'Doc' Leahy generously deposited not only the required sums on Tetrazzini's behalf but also paid her $500 a concert. Her comment was that the controversy had gained her a $100,000 worth of publicity.

Benoist's Touring Experiences

André Benoist, the pianist, wrote entertainingly in his autobiography of his experiences on tour with Luisa.[19] Leahy sent him a telegram offering generous payment to accompany her which terms he accepted and went along to meet the lady in a luxurious suite at the old Manhattan Hotel. 'Doc' was there to introduce him. His good looks clearly appealed to her. She did not speak – she twittered, exclaiming, '*Ma, è carino il piccino!* ('My, the boy is very cute!') As, after a while, she had not mentioned the subject of music, he asked if she would like him to accompany her at the piano, but she refused at first. Later, after some prompting, she agreed to sing a few bars of *Una voce poco fà*, but at the fifth or sixth, broke off exclaiming in Italian, 'That's enough!' – as a short fat man with the blackest, shiniest hair and the pastiest complexion Benoist claimed to have ever seen came in. This was Giorgio Bazelli to whom Luisa now 'twittered in voluble Italian'.

Once André had left with Leahy he enquired what was the fellow's official position in the diva's ménage and was told:

> I don't exactly know but it seems he is a former Italian or Roumanian tenor who had fallen on evil days when Madame picked him up somewhere, and he is constantly complaining of being tired though he eats like a horse. There doesn't seem to be any sentimental attachment between the two, for, as you will learn in time, Madame has no use for the male of the species, except at rare times when something in her nature appears to reverse itself and there's the devil to pay. But wait, and you'll find out.'

Benoist discovered that Luisa had three pastimes on tour. The main one was consuming huge amounts of spaghetti, next was going to the movies and last but not least, playing dominoes. There was something else that played an important role in maintaining the quality of her singing. The first time this was brought to his attention was when 'Doc' Leahy rang up, beside himself with worry. 'She says "Ah no singa tonight" and when I asked her why, she said, "Ah wanta a man!" Now, Ben, what shall I do?'

How to cater for this diva's amorous appetite was not easy. One look at her tubby figure put many off. 'Sometimes by adding a bit of pecuniary reward to diplomatic persuasion the matter was concluded to everyone's satisfaction. The result was high good humor and a superb performance.'

André Benoist found that playing the same accompaniments to the same arias, performance after performance, during the tour became tedious for him so he started elaborating slightly on some of the piano parts. He thought that Tetrazzini would approve of his enrichment of her musical background, so he was taken aback one morning to be summoned to her suite where she, Bazelli and Leahy glared at him and 'Doc' shouted: 'Luisa claims that you are a spy sent out by Hammerstein to spoil her effects on the stage!' Benoist's first reaction was that this was a practical joke, but their grim faces then made him realise that they were serious. Doing his uttermost to look as innocent as possible, he asked what could have given her such a false impression. A torrent of excited Italian gushed from Luisa's lips, which Leahy translated: 'Madame says you are continually changing her accompaniments, and that you have been paid by the Hammerstein clique to do this so as to upset her and thus ruin her singing.'

Benoist could not understand how anyone could be so naive as to suspect him of involvement in such a scheme. Nevertheless he claims, 'it took me hours to convince all concerned that what I had done was only with the intention of adding beauty to the performance.' Then Luisa burst into tears, kissed him on both cheeks – but asked him in future to keep, all the same, to the score.

Nocturnal Disappointments

André Benoist wrote that one of his most diverting experiences touring took place in St Louis where they rested a few days between engagements. One evening they went to a variety show starring Marie Dressler whose performance appealed so much to Tetrazzini that she went round backstage to congratulate her. This resulted in Marie being invited to dinner at the Hotel Jefferson next night. Benoist sat between the two ladies to act as interpreter as the one spoke no Italian and the other hardly any English. Bazelli was installed on Luisa's left so that in her words 'I keep an eye on him' – otherwise he might drink too much. It was already evident from his behaviour that he had been imbibing a number of 'comforting cocktails'.

Marie Dressler brought with her 'a stalwart red-headed Irishman' whom she introduced as her husband. He also seemed to be somewhat intoxicated and almost fell over as she made him sit on her right. She asked André to explain to Luisa that it was for the same caring purpose as hers concerning Bazelli's welfare. Up to then, both ladies had behaved with the utmost decorum, but by the time the third course was reached they had drunk so much champagne that with tears in their eyes they revealed all the trouble experienced in struggling to make the two men satisfy them in bed. Benoist says that he found it exhausting translating every descriptive detail to each lady in turn. The last he recalled of the occasion was of their drooping over him in each other's arms blubbering over their nocturnal disappointments.

On 9 December 1910 the Florentine Nightingale and her entourage reached San Francisco.

SONGBIRD TRILLS IN PULLMAN CAR AND BUBBLES WITH GLADNESS WHEN TRAIN NEARS HER FIRST LOVE – 'MY SAN FRANCISCO'

Thus ran the headlines to journalist Ralph Renaud's article in the *Chronicle* next day. He began:

> Our own Luisa Tetrazzini has come home again to the American city that she loves most.... She came singing to herself her favourite bits of Italian opera and our less musical but more meaningful *Home Sweet Home*. It was my privilege to meet Mme Tetrazzini at Sacramento and return to San Francisco with her, the Southern Pacific agents courteously making an exception to the rule which prohibits local travel on the Overland Express Limited.

He sat in her private Pullman drawing-room listening to her impromptu song recital and to the imitations she gave of the behaviour of Oscar Hammerstein and of 'the language of the farm animals' that they viewed from the train. They discussed

> the victorious fight with Hammerstein, a fight that so much occupied Doc Leahy's time and energy that only twelve hours of sleep could be obtained between three days and nights.... He said he would bring Tetrazzini to San Francisco in spite of the most stubborn fight that could be offered by the foremost impresario of New York. He has kept his word. He was happy yesterday as he travelled through the Sacramento Valley and on to San Francisco but he was not so happy as Tetrazzini.

Later that afternoon Tetrazzini arrived. Cheering crowds lined Market Street all the way from the Ferry Building to the Palace Hotel where Colonel Kirkpatrick, its owner – who had once presented her with a black pearl – had the Presidential Suite ready for her. According to Renaud her professional appearances in the city were to be attended by more 'plain, ordinary people than ever attended those of any other artist'. Accompanying her were Giorgio Bazelli, two maids, 'a particular pet, a mascot dog

of Mexican hairless breed', André Benoist, and the American baritone
Frederick Hastings.

Under the headline DIVINE TETRAZZINI BRAVOED BY 5,000,
Thomas Nunan wrote in the *San Francisco Examiner* on 13 December
about the concert Tetrazzini gave the previous evening in the Dreamland
Pavilion. 'San Francisco had seen nothing of this kind on any other night
since the conflagration of 1906,' he claimed. 'Almost half that number
were turned away, unable to obtain even standing room.' To appease those
thus disappointed, 'Doc' Leahy had arranged for two more concerts to be
held.

On Sunday the 18th, the *Chronicle* published a long account of Ralph
E. Renaud's interview with the diva in the sitting-room of her suite. On
arrival he waited there for a hairdresser to finish work on Tetrazzini's
tresses in her boudoir. With Renaud sat Leahy, Del Mué (the artist whose
life-size sketch of the singer's face was reproduced in the middle of
Renaud's article) and Bazelli, whose relationship with the diva, Renaud
wrote, was 'half professional and half, well, anyway, she signs herself
'Mme Tetrazzini-Bazelli.'

Renaud says that they discussed every angle of the row with
Hammerstein:

> ... and there were more than fifty-seven varieties. My mind was a jumble of
> contracts, renewals, depositions and injunctions, but from what they told me I
> imagine the Eastern managers, scenting profits from afar, framed up a stand-
> and-deliver game, which, happily, for San Francisco, failed miserably. Whether
> or not Tetrazzini was in the right – and the Court unquestionably thought she
> was – I suspect it would be a rather difficult matter to prevent her from doing
> what she wanted. In comparison, Joshua must have had an easy job of it when
> he held up the astonished sun.

While they were chatting, a tiny chihuahua flipped into the room and
begun tugging at Del Mué's shoelaces with her teeth. Ralph Renaud wrote
that the dog did not long precede the diva herself who wore an elegant
light blue gown covered with lace and whose auburn locks flowed away
from her forehead 'in an amazing mass of little ripples'. He found her
tending towards 'a tight sort of stoutness' but she was still very pretty
and 'decidedly what the French mean when they say "*charmante*"'. Since
her previous visit she had added 'the accomplishment of English to the
Russian, Spanish, German and Italian languages, which she already
knows'. She could not speak a great deal – 'still she manages to make
herself understood, and understands everything you say if you take pains
to speak slowly'. Mrs Leahy was going to travel with her during the rest
of the tour, and by its end Tetrazzini expected to talk as good American
as anyone – 'probably better, for when she utters a word now it is followed

by three or four shrugs, captivating smiles, and all the engaging artifices which give spoken language its color'.

Renaud told Tetrazzini 'What a wonderful night last night!' Describing her voice as surprisingly light and baby-like, he quotes her as replying: 'Oh, sure yes! But I am so scare. I tremble so and so.'

'For a while there the emotion was so strong she couldn't get her breath,' said Leahy. 'But she's glad to get back to San Francisco.'

'San Francisco is my countree,' Tetrazzini told Renaud. 'Here is where I have the grrrrrest love. They interest in me like some relative! Eet is the – what you call eet – the magnetism. Yes, yes, I feel eet. Eet is different here. All over the world when I sing there come to me flowers and kind words from persons of San Francisco in the audience.' Suddenly she exploded into happy laughter, and then explained that she had just recalled how once at the Manhattan there were two men in the gallery, one a New Yorker and the other from San Francisco. The former, pointing at her on the stage, had shouted insults about her dress, so the latter knocked him out. Again she laughed merrily at the recollection.

Renaud then asked if Tetrazzini had been invited to sing before King George V, but the effort of explaining proved too much for her English vocabulary and she turned to Bazelli with a voluble stream of Italian.

> 'She says to tell you,' he explained, 'that the court is in mourning now, but when the Coronation occurs next June she must appear and sing for His Majesty. Mme Tetrazzini sang at a gala night that was given to President Fallières of France. The opera was *Les Pêcheurs de Perles* by Bizet, one of her favourites. You know, no one is allowed to applaud or clap but when she reached her first big number, they forgot, the President forgot, everybody forgot, and the whole house was yelling and standing on its feet.'

After hearing this, Renaud turned to Tetrazzini and queried: 'Then you like applause?'

'Oh yes, sure!' she replied. '*C'est la chose principale, n'est pas?* That is half of the life.'

Before leaving, the journalist remarked how everybody had admired the peacock gown Tetrazzini wore at her opening concert.

'Yes? You like eet? All right. Sure! I show you more!' With this the diva retired a moment to tell the maid to bring out her other dresses, and returned skipping and singing 'Yeep I-addy, I-ay, I-ay. I don't care what becomes of me!', with a good round 'Whoop!' at the end. Renaud wrote:

> This was undoubtedly to prove to me her complete mastery of the vernacular. The three gowns displayed for my inspection were really marvellous. Besides the peacock dress there was one she called her 'aquarion' gown, a strange conception of the depths of the sea, with weird fishes swimming through shimmering water, lobsters crawling over the sands, crabs clasping the bodice, nets for sleeves and bits of real coral set in effectively.

.

'Dis feesh I like,' she described pointing to one of the figures. 'And see! My arms in the net! I cannot get out. Very funny! See! The lobster is not cook. I do not like that kind of one. I t'ink up these dress myself and they make them in Milano.'

Then Tetrazzini showed Renaud still another gown, this time a dazzling white thing of net on silk with innumerable rhinestones set into the fabric. She made him lift it to see how heavy it was.

'Oh, I got plenty dress,' she said. 'But zis one eet is almost impossible to wear. Eet is so 'eavy. Maybe they t'ink I am seek because I walk slow, but eet is these dress!'

And so she rattled on, entertaining as a quaint and artless child. Renaud continues:

> I don't remember just when I got out, but I do know that my interview with the queen of singers was the sunniest and most cheerful I ever had.
>
> One could see from her photographs that she was good-natured, but that did not show the brightness, the animation, the fresh gaiety of spirit which constantly radiated from her presence. For a moment, at first, she would try to be dignified, sitting with folded hands, but the task was evidently too much of a tax on her temperament, and in another moment she was off chattering to everybody, fluttering her hands with gesticular flashes, much more rapid and eloquent than words or bursting into uncontrolled gales of tinkling laughter. She gave one the impression that while she continues to live she must be happy and she moves continually in an atmosphere of pleasurable excitement.

Three days after this interview was published, a message from Tetrazzini appeared in all the papers:

> I will sing for the poor people of San Francisco and for all the people who cannot afford to buy tickets for my concerts. I am going to sing at Lotta's fountain, as in New York I said I was going to do when I heard that I might be prevented from giving concerts here under Mr Leahy's management. The injunction didn't stand but I have decided to sing. This will be my Christmas offering to the people of my dear San Francisco.

12 Singing in the Streets of San Francisco

December 1910 was an eventful month in San Francisco. Abe Ruff, political boss of the city, had been sentenced to prison for 14 years, and Battling Nelson was preparing to defend his lightweight boxing crown. But it was unquestionably the concert Luisa Tetrazzini gave on Saturday, Christmas Eve, that became one of the best remembered events in San Francisco's musical history. She was to sing in the open air in the days before microphones and to be clearly heard far out on the fringes of an audience expected to number 100,000, but which in reality turned out to be a quarter of a million.

The temperature in the evening was a pleasant 60°F and the air was quiet and still as people swarmed towards the spot where Geary, Kearny and Market Streets met, and from where Tetrazzini was due to sing from a large platform erected outside the *San Francisco Chronicle* building. At 8.25 pm green-coloured fires, lit on its roof and those of the highest buildings in the city, signalled Tetrazzini's arrival. An elevator specially installed for the occasion took her up to the editorial offices. She was in a merry mood and to pass the time sang snatches of popular nonsensical ditties of the day – 'Yip I Addy I Aye I Aye' and 'There was an Old Soldier who had a Wooden Leg.'[1]

Male reporters wrote next day that she wore 'glittering jewels' and 'a gown which was a vision of white and things', while women scribes were more precise – such as 'over her long white trailing gown stiff with hundreds of flashing brilliants and iridescent passementerie, that showed the rounded lines of her form, she wore a cloak of old rose'. Also – 'Her broad-brimmed white hat was ornamented with sparklers and willow plumes, and a white ostrich feather boa graced her neck.'

The streetcars had been re-routed and 150 policemen assigned to handle the crowd. San Francisco was not alone in wanting to listen to Tetrazzini. Throughout the afternoon, trains and ferry boats had brought large groups from San José, Santa Rosa and the Sacramento and San Joaquin Valleys to swell the gathering.

'It was a crowd where the best is like the worst,' wrote another journalist, 'bootblacks rubbed elbows with bankers, and painted creatures with the fat and wholesome mothers of families.' One man whose fat and wholesome wife could not make a way from their home through the impenetrable crush, phoned her husband at his office near the focal point for help. Being a resourceful businessman, he dangled the transmitter out of the window so that she could listen.

Tetrazzini's concerts in San Francisco had also been patronized by a greater proportion of ordinary folk than had ever attended the performances of other artists in the city. People came from the Mission, the Potrero, the Barbary Coast, Pacific Heights, Nob Hill, North Beach and the East communities. This explains why she attracted so large an audience (apart from the fact that there was not a dime to pay).

Now and then Tetrazzini went to the window, waved and blew kisses to the delighted gathering below, and her own enthusiasm grew in proportion with theirs.

The concert began at 7.50 pm when Paul Steindorff, the popular conductor, and his symphony orchestra settled themselves on the platform and played the 'Light Cavalry' overture before some fifty choirboys in white surplices singing carols joined them. Then as nine o'clock struck, Tetrazzini, waiting expectantly at a window, saw more green flames shoot up from the top of the Monadnock building across the street and from buildings in all other directions to herald her appearance. Ralph E. Renaud, the journalist who had interviewed her at the Palace Hotel, was standing nearby and he wrote next day:

> As she turned round there was an expression on her face I had never seen there before. She was quite serious. No smile. There was a film over her eyes. Was Tetrazzini frightened? Ah, no! Clasping her hands upon her breast, she cried 'Look! Look! My grrreat familee! See! Everybody my brudder! Everybody my sister!'
>
> And spreading her arms and stretching her gloved fingers she spoke once more with almost a sob in her tones: 'My 'eart eet is so beeg lak dees—way out to 'ere an' 'ere! Oh, I am so 'appy!' In a moment she was smiling again with the familiar, dimpled roguish smile.

Tetrazzini's old rose cloak was placed about her shoulders and, clinging to Mayor Patrick H. McCarthy's arm, she descended to the street level, swept through a doorway out into the big sound shell at the back of the platform and mounted the steps to the raised dais. A spotlight picked out her figure. She held her white-gloved hands aloft in greeting to the crowd and a reporter rhapsodized next day that the roar in response 'could be heard in the Sierra'. After the Mayor had introduced her there was a fanfare of trumpets, the signal for all men to take off their hats.

Clasping a fine specimen, Tetrazzini began by singing *The Last Rose of Summer* as all traffic ceased throughout the city. There was a complete silence except for her voice, and then at the end came a storm of applause. As she followed this with *Je veux vivre dans ce rêve*, the waltz song from Gounod's *Roméo et Juliette*, the silhouetted figure of one of the orchestra was seen rubbing his bald head with one hand and wiping his eyes with the other. After each number the applause intensified, and the concert then closed with the orchestra playing and all singing *Auld Lang Syne*. As the last notes died away and cheer after cheer echoed across the square, Tetrazzini bowed and smiled and waved her handkerchief. Then she turned away and shook hands with Steindorff, and someone presented her with a basket of scarlet poinsettias.

Next day in the *Examiner*, Harvey Wickham reported that listeners as far away as Second Street told him that Tetrazzini's voice had carried even to them, although the music of the orchestra was inaudible at that distance. He had literally listened to her on his knees, assuming such a position so as not to obscure the view of those 'who had not the good fortune to be stationed in her immediate vicinity'. In the Bohemian Club then existent in Los Angeles her voice was also heard – but in this case carried the 500 miles over a telephone line.

TETRAZZINI UNITES SAN FRANCISCO ran one headline next day and newspapermen competed with one another in hyperbole as they acclaimed the diva's performance. But one caused some amusement by inadvertently calling her 'the original nightingale although she looked more like a pigeon'.

Tetrazzini had begun something new in popular entertainment that was to lead to the mass open air 'rock' concerts of our era – and she triumphed without any form of sound amplification, such was her personal magnetism and rapport with her audience.

'Doc' Leahy had feared that after so many people had listened to Tetrazzini for nothing in the open air on Christmas Eve there would only be a small audience when she gave a Concert at the Dreamland Skating Rink on Monday afternoon, 26 December 1910, but on the contrary, every seat was sold.

A Profusion of Tributes

On 28 December Mayor McCarthy called on Tetrazzini repeating orally the thanks of the city conveyed by letter the day before. The Parks Commissioner had ordered that, as a tribute from the people of the city, flowers and evergreens should be gathered from the Golden Gate and other parks to decorate her car as it made its way escorted by hundreds of admirers to the Oakland mole (also similarly adorned) and the ferry boat which took her across the bay. Many travelled on it so as to get a closer look at the singer. Awaiting her on the Oakland side were hundreds more who had come from outlying parts. She then boarded the *Shasta Limited* for Portland where her next concert was to be given.

The Mayor had already sent the Board of Supervisors a letter:

Gentlemen,

Through the immeasurable generosity of a distinguished woman, today the most famous and accomplished vocalist in the world, the city of San Francisco has been privileged to become the recipient of an honor without parallel. . . . I refer in this instance to the public song recital of Mme Luisa Tetrazzini, the greatest singer alive, who on Christmas Eve last appeared in the center of our city in the midst of an unprecedented crowd and there gave to the masses of our people the inestimable advantage and benefit of hearing her peerless voice. This remarkable event has been heralded throughout the world and placed the name of San Francisco upon the lips of every community at home and abroad, as the place selected by the greatest diva of the times for a magnificent bestowal upon a music-loving public.[2]

On receipt of this encomium the four Supervisors, Kelly, McLaughlin, Hayden and Murdoch, met the Mayor in emergency session at the City Hall to see about a fitting testimonial for the diva. They settled upon a gold plate and Messrs Shrieve and Co. were commissioned to prepare a design for approval. It was hoped that it would be ready in time for presentation to her on 11 January 1911 when she returned en route for a concert tour of the southern states.

The Chamber of Commerce were delighted. A spokesman declared that Tetrazzini had

told the world, as it could not have been told in a better way, of the wonderful climate on the Pacific Coast, where the people could stand bareheaded in the street and listen to a great singer when snow and ice held the rest of the country in its grip.[3]

In Portland on 30 December 1910, as Tetrazzini was leaving her hotel for the Heilig Theater, a newspaper photographer stationed outside let off his flashlight apparatus. An unfriendly gust of wind at the moment the powder ignited carried the flames so near the diva that it seemed she would be burned by them. She started back but was caught by the attendants just as she nearly fainted. Her gown was scorched but she was not injured. 'Dirty, dirty, dirty,' was all she was reported as repeating as Bazelli helped her into the taxi.[4]

Every one of the 2,200 seats in the Heilig Theater was filled. When the box office opened, the line extended three blocks and no more seats were available before half its length had reached the window. Those in the parquet, priced at $4 each, were readily resold for $10. Throughout the concert, a crowd of several hundred stood outside in the pelting rain straining their ears to catch the sound of Tetrazzini's singing within.

From Portland, Tetrazzini set off next day to continue her concert tour in Seattle and British Columbia before going back to California. Then on 12 January 1911 the *Chronicle* carried an account of Tetrazzini's return. 'Ah! It is good to be home!' she had exclaimed as she stood on the upper deck of the ferry boat crossing the bay the previous night and looked at the lights of San Francisco. She had spoken of the snows in the north with a shiver. 'In Vancouver there was a blizzard' she said, 'but the people came and the house was full. It was beautiful – but this is home.'⁵

At the Palace Hotel where Tetrazzini was going to stay again, its resourceful manager, Colonel John C. Kirkpatrick, greeted her with the news that their renowned chef, Ernest Arbogast, had created a new dish in her honour, 'Chicken Tetrazzini', which would be served for the first time that evening.

Then at 2 pm on the 19th the diva was driven to the Dreamland Skating Rink for a special event, the presentation to her of the commemorative plate fashioned from Californian gold. In the centre of this was inscribed:

Presented to
MADAME LUISA TETRAZZINI
by the
People of San Francisco, California
As an Expression of Love and Appreciation
Christmas, 1910.⁶

On the platform in ascending rows stood some five hundred school children with a head teacher, Estelle Carpenter, in charge. In front of them sat the orchestra, conductor Alfred Roncovieri, and at the grand piano accompanist André Benoist. With the musicians playing *The Star Spangled Banner* and the children throwing cascades of flowers towards her, Tetrazzini, on arrival, walked to the front of the platform beaming at everybody, then, after eulogizing speeches – 'The rewards of music are greater than the rewards of oratory', declared Daniel A. Ryan – interspersed with cheering and the singing by the children of *Santa Lucia, Colombia, the Gem of the Ocean*, and *Funiculi funiculà*, by the end of which Tetrazzini was weeping with joy on Estelle Carpenter's shoulder, Acting Mayor Kelly made the presentation.

Tetrazzini pressed the gold plate to her heart and as Benoist began to play the first notes of *The Last Rose of Summer*, she dried her eyes, shook her head, then nodded as if to say to the gathering: 'I cannot sing now – but, no, I must, for you.'

The reporter from the *San Francisco Chronicle* wrote next day: 'And even finer than the singing it was to watch the expressions on the faces of the school children as they listened to her.'

Two evenings later, on 21 January 1911, Tetrazzini returned to the Dreamland Skating Rink for her promised concert. The *San Francisco Chronicle* that morning stated that she would include two songs in her programme not given by her before at any event in that city. These would be the Adagio and Rondo from *La Sonnambula* and Proch's variations. Her third song, in compliance with innumerable requests for it, would be the polacca from *Mignon*.

This concert nearly had to be cancelled. In the middle of the afternoon on 21 January, Leahy phoned Benoist in a state of near-panic.[7] Tetrazzini was suffering from a severe attack of cramp and could hardly move, and every one of the 6,500 seats in the Dreamland Skating Rink had been sold at $5 a seat – then the average weekly wage. Luisa had said she would sing but he did not see how she could.

At the time arranged, the anxious pianist went to Tetrazzini's dressing-room and found her hunched up on a chair, head on knees, while her feet were pressed against the edge of the seat. Perspiration beaded her face and even the make-up failed to mask how ill she was. Forcing his voice to sound optimistic, he asked how she felt. In broken English she replied: 'Ah no fella good but Ah singa. Ah allaways singa!' Then Leahy came in and quavered: 'Luisa, it is time.' With a tremendous effort, the soprano managed to stand and, forcing a smile, made her way slowly to the stage. At the sight of her, the audience went wild with enthusiasm and she responded valiantly with a low curtsy. Benoist approached ready to catch her if she collapsed, but she managed to straighten herself without his help, though he detected beneath the assumed smile the pain she was suffering.

Tetrazzini began with *Caro nome* and Benoist writes that never had he witnessed such an astounding display of beauty of tone, admirable technique and true heroism.

> Her roulades and trills came forth perfectly, and she ended with the high E which she attacked pianissimo, started for the exit door and, as she approached it, swelled the E until it sounded like a clarion. She held it as she bowed low and disappeared.

Tetrazzini had triumphed once again, and the audience saluted her with applause that it seemed would never end. Back in the dressing-room, she sat up on the chair as before and told Benoist: 'Ah no fella good, but Ah singa. Ah allaways singa!'

Fortunately Luisa had no recurrence of the attack of cramps, so accompanied by 'Doc' Leahy and his wife, she continued on her tour.

There was a record audience on 24 January in the Los Angeles Auditorium and so as to accommodate more people a false floor, enabling a further 100 to sit there, had been built over the orchestra pit while 300 more were seated upon the stage. The *Musical Courier* for 29 January reported that three concerts instead of two as previously announced were being held.

Supreme Court's Lerner Case Judgment

When Tetrazzini reached Chicago to sing at its Orchestra Hall, good news came to her from New York where on 22 February 1911 Supreme Court Justice Gerard gave judgment for her in the protracted suit brought against her by Isidore Lerner, the theatrical manager. Her counsel had asked for his contract with her to be declared void on the grounds of want of mutuality, and the court ruled that it had been 'cleverly devised for the benefit of the plaintiff alone'.[8]

Asked for her comments on the case by the *San Francisco Chronicle*, Tetrazzini said of Lerner: 'He was just a miserable fruit dealer – never knew anything about music or opera.'[9]

'Mme Tetrazzini has returned to New York after a long tour in the West, whose momentous episodes have been duly chronicled and last evening she appeared for the first time this season,' wrote Richard Aldrich in the *New York Times* for 7 March. The venue was the Carnegie Hall and her recital was given 'with the assistance of a "concert company" of the kind that used to be accepted in New York: Mr Frederick Hastings, baritone; Mr Walter Oesterreicher, flautist, and Mr André Benoist, pianist'. As usual the programme was 'rich with opportunities for her to display her operatic style – the Mad Scene from Thomas's *Hamlet*, *Bel raggio* from Rossini's *Semiramide*, *Voi che sapete* from Mozart's *Le Nozze di Figaro*, and the air from David's *La Perle du Brésil*'. She had sung 'with much bravura but was not so finished and accurate in her florid passages as she had sometimes been'.

The *New York Times* for 6 March had contained a long account of an interview with the diva on the previous day in her suite at the Hotel Manhattan where she had been receiving the press. The reporter wrote that Tetrazzini revealed she had one weakness which amounted to a passion. Whenever she had any spare time, she went to the movies. During the tour when in Spokane, the manager of a picture house invited her to see some special new films that he was exhibiting one afternoon. Of course she went. To her astonishment on arrival she saw in flaming red letters painted on a white strip of bunting that extended right across the front of the building the words: 'TETRAZZINI WILL BE HERE TODAY

BETWEEN 3 AND 4'. There was a huge crowd outside clamouring for admittance and paying 5 cents each. She and Bazelli laughed and went in. Then the manager came up and asked if she would sing. That request she was obliged to refuse.

On Sunday 12 March Tetrazzini supported by several soloists was the main attraction with Nathan Franko and his orchestra at a concert held at the Hippodrome. She then resumed her tour singing first at the Academy of Music in Philadelphia, then on the 21st in Washington (when, reported the *Musical Courier*, 'she advocated the production of a vocal aristocracy by the intermarriage of the world's greatest singers'). Next she roused the French Canadians to wild enthusiasm with her showmanship at Montreal's Arena on the 24th before travelling south by private car to fulfil yet another engagement in Rochester's Convention Hall.

The *Musical Courier* for 25 March had turned its attention on 'Bazelli, the famous husband'. He liked to dwell on the drawbacks of fame and 'tells you of the strenuous life he suffers – all of which is in strange contrast with his rather round and happy face, the merry twinkle in his eye and his ever-growing embonpoint'.

Process Servers Outwitted

Back in New York Tetrazzini gave her third concert there within a month when on 2 April she sang at the Hippodrome before nearly 6000 people. It was announced beforehand that she would be sailing on the *Lusitania* for England on the 5th so as to open the summer season at Covent Garden on the 23rd. However, Oscar Hammerstein was determined not to let her leave the country until his law suit had been finally settled, so his lawyers arranged for process servers to bar her access aboard. The squad found 'Doc' Leahy at the dockside. He looked calm. They asked him whether she would be sailing on the liner.

'Why, that would hardly be possible in view of the fact that she sailed from Halifax, Nova Scotia, for London this morning,' answered Leahy without the ghost of a smile. It was later revealed that Tetrazzini had gone straight from the Hippodrome to Montreal and then on to Halifax where a stateroom had been reserved on a steamer.[10]

Oscar Hammerstein had another reason for stopping Tetrazzini from singing at Covent Garden. The enormous opera house that he had built and opened in Kingsway as its rival was proving a white elephant. In fact, he was to lose £40,000 during the coming season while Covent Garden lost £15,000, proving that at that time London could not support two grand opera companies.

Hammerstein had to wait until 26 July that year until his case against

Tetrazzini was settled and he was awarded $19,250 in final settlement of his claims. She had actually deposited $52,500 in accordance with Judge Laccombe's ruling of 6 December 1910, while the impresario alleged his damages for the past season due amounted to $75,000.[11] So he was the loser and Tetrazzini the gainer in the affair.

13 Discord Over Royalties

Most divas have justifiably tried to make as much money as possible during their careers. Patti put the position aptly when the directors of the Norwich Musical Festival, troubled by her terms, wrote: 'Why so much at a Musical Festival?' Adelina wired back: 'I am a Musical Festival.' This was certainly true in the case of Tetrazzini, whom she named as her successor.

In an earlier chapter, the negotiations between the Gramophone Company in partnership with the Victor Talking Machine Company and Tetrazzini to market her recordings were described.[1] By the autumn of 1908, Alfred Clark and Sydney W. Dixon had become joint managing directors of the first-named firm. In November that year Clark wrote to Calvin G. Child, chief recorder and artists' manager of the Victor Talking Machine Company, regarding the contract with Tetrazzini which would expire on 31 December 1909. They had seen her a few days before she sailed for New York, 'when she expressed herself as very sorry not to be able to make more records for us but her voice had absolutely gone; in fact at the interview she was quite hoarse'. She had, however, recorded six songs for them about three months previously regarding which there had been some discussion as to whether they should be sold to the public. Finally, it was agreed with her and Bazelli (described as 'her manager') that three of them were of sufficient quality, so these would be released once Melba's concert tour of Britain was over as Clark wanted to concentrate entirely on promoting the sales of that artist's records until then.

Regarding Tetrazzini, Clark thought that she would prefer to remain contracted to the Gramophone Company after December 1909, rather than change to another company. 'She told us of several offers that Pathé's had made her and mentioned Fonotipia also.' Correspondence continued between the two companies and in March 1909 the Gramophone Company made it clear in a letter to Victor that 'any new contract which they might make with Tetrazzini should provide that her exclusive services were given to both companies jointly'.

In May 1909 Tetrazzini made more records in London, using the new 'gutta percha' pressings which Fred Gaisberg considered to be of superior quality to the American material used previously. A letter dated 8 June claimed that they were 'far above anything she had made and rank with the very best records which we have put out'.

Tetrazzini was pleased with these and agreed to renew her contract through the Gramophone Company on condition that her royalty per record be raised from 50 to 60 cents as from 1 January 1910. All negotiations had to be conducted through Bazelli who refused to give way. Sydney Dixon was certain that the extra 10 cents were for Bazelli's personal use. The Gramophone Company and Victor were each to pay Tetrazzini £500 ($2,500) in advance of royalties, and the number of titles she was to record were to be split equally between the two companies, one half to be made in London and the other half at Victor's Camden recording laboratory, New Jersey.

Meanwhile, in America, the Victor Talking Machine Company were extremely unhappy about the Tetrazzini metals sent from London. There were many defects in size and quality, according to Calvin G. Child, who complained that they were 'shells that would have been a disgrace to the original matrix plant of the Berliner Gramophone Company in its earliest infancy'. So a second set of shells were demanded. Victor were also unhappy about the holding back of the Tetrazzini records until too late in the season. Moreover, they were in the high price class and customers expected them to be perfect both in appearance and sound, not 'rough and unsightly as the pressings from the shells which you sent'. So a third set, produced at the Gramophone Company's new factory at Hayes under changed and improved conditions, were shipped over in November 1909, the man who had made the others having been replaced by some of the best experts from the Gramophone Company's Hanover factory. Fortunately this put things right and Child wrote that these shells were 'as perfect as possible'.

Another matter was causing Victor concern – the increased royalty of 60 cents per record to Tetrazzini. On 17 November 1909 Eldridge R. Johnson, the company's President, wrote to Alfred Clark in London expressing their fear that 'it will be impossible to retain the enthusiastic support of Caruso and Melba after they learnt Tetrazzini was being paid a larger royalty than they received'. Victor would rather pay more money in advance than pay such a royalty which they felt certain would eventually cost them 'eight or ten times' any possible advance payment that they might be called upon to make. Johnson ended: 'If you value your "Red Seal" business get into line with us and correct this mistake. We would be willing to share any reasonable sum necessary as advance royalty to rearrange contract on a 50 cents basis.'

But Bazelli would not agree to such a proposal, so when he was in New York in March 1910, Calvin G. Child made him an offer. If Tetrazzini would remake all her present records with Victor at Camden and reduce her royalty to 50 cents, they would pay her an advance of $30,000 (£6,000) and a further advance of $1,000 on any additional new numbers. The proposal was rejected by Bazelli, who told him that 'Madame knows too well the selling value of her records to reduce the royalty for a little ready cash'.

On 25 May that year, Child wrote to Sydney Dixon in London stating that Eldridge R. Johnson still strongly objected to the increased royalty, and repeating the offer made to Bazelli. Child went on that he had been informed Tetrazzini would no longer be employing Bazelli as her manager after the end of the year.

> A New York photographer by the name of Foley is to take care of her business matters – and McCormack's interest in the 'lady' is quite strong at present. In case an opportunity should arise for you to see her personally, we would be only too glad to have your kind offices in getting such an arrangement as this through, but it is useless to attempt to do anything through Barzelli [sic].
>
> We are taking the stand that we cannot, as we explained to her representative when I was in Europe, handle her records at the 60 cents basis and if she is not willing to accept a 50 cents royalty, we must discontinue putting any more of her records in the catalogue and will simply keep the present ones there to fill such orders as may come in.
>
> McCormack feels very sure if the proposition is put to her and explained in this way that she will consent to the reduction.

That autumn Victor arranged with the Gramophone Company for the subject to be raised again with the couple while they were in England for a concert tour. Sydney Dixon wrote to his fellow managing director, Alfred Clark, on 7 October that he had met them both that Monday afternoon in their Birmingham hotel, afterwards attending Tetrazzini's concert which was 'a tremendous success'. At an interview with Bazelli next morning he had gone thoroughly into the matter of a royalty reduction. 'You can imagine that with a man like Bazelli it was an almost impossible conversation to carry on.' Eventually Dixon succeeded in getting them to consider the reduction, and intended to go up to Sheffield on 20 October for more talks.

Dixon added that he had stressed to both Bazelli and Tetrazzini once again that the Victor Talking Machine Company were not prepared to go on advertising Tetrazzini's records and pay her a 60 cents royalty because it would cause trouble with Caruso and Melba. Bazelli had made all sorts of threats as to breaking the contract for recording in America if the Victor organization did not spend more money on advertising Tetrazzini. 'Eventually he cooled down and the discussion continued in a quieter manner.'

Dixon assured Clark that he now felt reasonably optimistic that the couple would accept the reduction in the royalty rate provided the advance suited them. They had parted on the most friendly terms, agreeing to talk further in Sheffield when the programme of songs which Tetrazzini was to record at the Hayes studio on 1 November was to be fixed.

At last, when Tetrazzini and Bazelli reached New York in early December, the dispute ended. On the afternoon of Sunday the 4th Calvin G. Child called on them at the Manhattan Hotel where they were staying. In a letter dated the 6th of that month from the Victor Talking Machine Company's recording laboratory at Camden, he sent the Gramophone Company's managing director, Alfred Clark, a full account of the 'very satisfactory interview' at which final agreement had been reached. Tetrazzini would make not less than fifteen records at Camden for an advance payment of royalties amounting to $30,000 in return for which the royalty on all of her records after 1 April 1911 would be 50 cents instead of the present 60 cents. She had left for a concert tour in California on the previous afternoon and would return in the spring. She intended to make these records at times during her concerts in the East when she had an opportunity and after her concert tour was over. For the future, half her records were to be made in London and half at Camden.

Bazelli had requested that the Gramophone Company should give Tetrazzini written consent to this understanding and permission for her to sing in the Victor studios for the purpose of making records. Their experience in the legal action taken against her by Oscar Hammerstein made them cautious and that was why they had asked for such a written statement. Child went on that Bazelli was

> quite willing to listen to my explanations of the trade situation here and the difficulties arising because of our large discount to the trade and he quickly saw the disadvantage to Madame Tetrazzini of having her records sold to the dealers at a discount of 40% where the records of her confrères were sold at discount of 55%.

The full terms of this agreement were given in a letter of the same date sent to Bazelli care of W. H. Leahy in San Francisco. The $30,000 would be paid when Tetrazzini had completed twelve master records of selections to be mutually chosen from her repertoire by Bazelli and an authorized representative from Victor. The royalty on each record sold in the United States would be 50 cents, and in the Gramophone Company's territory 2s. 0d instead of the 2.50 francs provided for in that company's current contract. She further agreed to make master records of three more selections to be mutually chosen from her repertoire before sailing for Europe in the spring of 1911, but if impossible she would make them as soon as could be arranged after her return to the United States in the fall of that year.

Bazelli acknowledged this letter on 14 December, stating that he had booked passages for 'Mrs L. Tetrazzini' and himself on the *Lusitania* sailing from New York on 5 April 1911, so that she could stay four or five days in Philadelphia to record for Victor at Camden. Tetrazzini's success in San Francisco had been enormous.

> In Oakland the concert was *sold out* in 2h. 30, and I believe this also is a record. I did send you the dates of the concerts until February. Now you will see Mrs Tetrazzini must sing two concerts also in Canada and British Columbia (Vancouver, Victoria). I stay here until the last of December.

There was a change of plans over Tetrazzini's return, for *The Times* of 13 April 1911 reported that she had arrived at Bristol the previous day on the Canadian Northern R.M.S. *Royal George* from Halifax, Nova Scotia, and had travelled to London.

14 Coronation Gala

The Grand Opera Syndicate running Covent Garden were determined to attract the many visitors expected to crowd London for the Coronation of King George V and also to prevent any of its clientèle deserting to frequent Hammerstein's new opera house close at hand, so £70,000 was spent on improvements.[1] In readiness for the first season to be held by Diaghilev's Imperial Ballet a new stage made of oak had been laid which, unlike that in most London theatres, was perfectly flat. It had three bridges to raise or lower portions of the space for the setting up of spectacular scenes. There were ten traps for bringing up or sending down through the stage characters taking part in operas, and every trap was fitted with what is known as a 'steam curtain' used for vapour or smoke effects.

There was also a 'steam curtain' 40 foot long stretching across the front near the proscenium opening, which could be used if necessary to exclude view of what was happening behind it. New footlights with 250 lamps in white, amber, red and blue had been installed, and behind the proscenium 4,000 lamps were now to be employed in the lighting of the stage. Red carpet covered the floor in the stalls and was considered a great improvement on the old dingy green, and the same change of colour had been made in the paper on the walls of the private boxes. Also, facing the audience was a new and sumptuous red curtain emblazoned for the first time with the royal monogram 'G.R.' and raised hydraulically.

The management had also tried their best to make the programme appeal to the cosmopolitan audience. French and Italian operas were to be the fare for the Grand Opera Season in the summer; Wagner and possibly Strauss being reserved for the autumn – and in order to give greater variety they were to have all the delights of the ballet from St Petersburg. Two works new to Covent Garden were to be staged – Massenet's *Thaïs* and Puccini's *La Fanciulla del West* (making five of that composer's operas in the repertoire). 'How possibly can that upstart Hammerstein compete with all that?' declared general manager Harry Higgins proudly.

The season opened on Saturday 22 April 1911 with Delibes's *Lakmé*. Since this was unusually early in the year there had been fears that the audience (as far as the boxes and stalls were concerned) might have been sparse through subscribers not having returned to Town after the Easter vacation. But the fact that Tetrazzini was to appear in the title role attracted a full house.

The *Daily Telegraph* critic[2] admitted that the scenery was 'gorgeous', the singing 'remarkable' and the dancing 'excellent' but regretted that all this had been lavishly expended upon 'Delibes's flimsy and trifling opera'. But it was not the 'absurd' story that mattered – only the singing of Mme Tetrazzini 'doubtless the whole raison d'être of the performance'. She was therefore wise not to attempt 'to give verisimilitude to the tragic self-sacrificing priestess, but to be simply her most amiable and good-natured self – hardly, if at all, embarrassed by the singularity of her costume which consisted of a species of cuirass, much jewelled, and a very short skirt'. She was to retain the cuirass and to give it to her pupil, Mme Franchesi Runge, the American soprano, who in turn gave it to the San Francisco Opera, years later. When during the 1908 season Luisa had worn an outlandish confection on her head in the party scenes in *La Traviata*, some Melba supporters had tried to cause trouble claiming that it made her look ridiculous. They complained to Harry Higgins who retorted: 'She can wear a top hat if she likes so long as she sings.' In *Lakmé* she wore what resembled an ornate English policeman's helmet, but nobody minded.

Singing with characteristic brilliance Tetrazzini ended the Bell Song with a high F natural, which was the signal for an ovation. John McCormack as Gerald, Lakmé's military lover, did all, wrote the same critic, that was 'humanly possible to represent convincingly an Englishman singing love songs in Italian to a Hindu priestess in décor suggesting the winter garden of a Riviera hotel'. Edmund Burke as Lakmé's father, presented 'a startling contrast to his daughter by appearing as an immensely tall, gaunt, and sinister species of fakir' who at the end 'impressively declaimed over Lakmé's corpse'.

The *Advertiser* considered that *Lakmé* was one of the 'silliest and emptiest of *opéras comiques*, only saved by its disarming naïveté – and by dear, good-natured Mme Tetrazzini'. There were two further performances during the season.

Three evenings later a packed house acclaimed Luisa as Gilda in *Rigoletto* with Sammarco in the title role and McCormack as the Duke. Next on 5 May she sang Violetta and wrote *The Times* next day 'enraptured the audience throughout'. Sammarco played Germont and McCormack Alfredo. The latter was to appear as Rodolfo to Melba's Mimi in *La Bohème* five nights later.

On 31 May Tetrazzini's 'short-skirted and very arch Rosina' in *Il Barbi-*

ere di Siviglia was rated 'her most incontestable triumph' this season by the *Daily Mail* next day. Then on 3 June *Rigoletto* had its 200th performance at Covent Garden when *The Times*'s reviewer wrote:

> Of course Madame Tetrazzini had to repeat *Caro nome* though she preferred to sustain the high E rather than to trill upon it and its immediate neighbour.... As for Mr McCormack's Duke, the singer is unquestionably developing his voice, but it is impossible to say the same of his deportment, and really he need not be so afraid of his lady-love as he would appear to be in the scene with her in the second act.

On 16 June Tetrazzini sang Amina in *La Sonnambula* with Burke as Rodolfo and McCormack as Elvino. The *Daily Telegraph* found that while in appearance she was not 'an ideal representative of the anaemic and neurotic Amina, the music suits her voice so well that the part is among her most admired impersonations'. It was true that her celebrated E flat in the ensemble had to be attacked with care but the note was there and the intonation was as true as ever.

Tetrazzini was immensely proud of the fact that she had sung first at the start of her career before the King and Queen of Italy, then, in turn, before every President in South America, the Czar and Czarina of Russia, the Kaiser, the Presidents of France and the United States, Kind Edward VII and Queen Alexandra. Now she was to sing at the Coronation Gala to be held at Covent Garden on Monday 26 June 1911 in honour of their successors, King George V and Queen Mary. It was to prove the most spectacular evening on both sides of the footlights in Covent Garden's long history.

The colossal task of embellishing the auditorium with 100,000 roses proceeded up to shortly before the public were admitted.[3] Mauve, heliotrope, citron, cream and white orchids and crimson hangings adorned the huge royal box which took up all the space normally occupied by the eleven middle boxes. Suspended over this was a floral replica of the Imperial Crown, whilst its interior was decorated with pink carnations, Queen Mary's favourite flowers. George Calderon in *The Times* reported next day that the splendour of the roses was outshone by the splendour of the audience. At a quarter to eight, Yeomen of the Guard entered the stalls to mark off the rows reserved for the guests of the King and the Government. Calderon's account continues:

> The stalls were now fast growing into a scintillating mass of wonderful dresses and more wonderful uniforms. Some were strangely exotic. In voluminous white drapery, a Moorish gentleman passed into a box. A Teutonic officer's vividly green plumed helmet was a new note in the blazing crescendo of colour. There were Japanese and Indian, Chinese and Malay personages, clad in varying degrees of strange gorgeousness.

The decorations stopped short below the great amphitheatre, though it, too, was crowded with distinguished people. High above in the dark gallery there were more sparkling uniforms and toilettes to the very last of the six-inch planks which serve as seats in that lofty region. The 'gallery slips', the high passages which run at right angles to the stage, were much sought after, for though the stage can hardly be seen thence, they commanded an admirable view of the incomparably glittering audience.

A third of the seats had been reserved for royal guests and the rest had rapidly been sold to the public with the result that on the black market £1,000 was offered for a box and a £100 for a single seat. By a quarter-past eight the royal box was nearly full. Because of the pale yellow wall and yellow lights, it was not the most glowing part of the house, but most of the occupants of the stalls stood with backs to the stage looking upwards through opera glasses at the growing assembly. An anarchist present with a bomb could have eliminated at least 90 per cent of the world's most blueblooded families – crown princes, archdukes and their consorts by the dozen, princes and princesses by the score. Diaghilev commented that there were almost as many maharajahs as there were roses.

Punctually at half-past eight, the monarch and his consort arrived. There was an elaborate fanfare from the orchestra and the audience rose for the National Anthem.

The most splendid of *Aida*'s scenes – the return of the victorious Egyptian warrior Radamès to Thebes and his welcome from the Pharaoh and people – opened the performance. Glaring white masonry and a dark azure sky gave a glowing impression of oriental splendour under the blaze of a torrid sun. Louise Kirkby Lunn was impressive as Amneris, and Emmy Destinn superb as Aida with her voice soaring above the great mass of the ensemble.

The tranquil balcony scene from Gounod's *Roméo et Juliette* came as a contrast, after a short entr'acte. Juliette was Melba's favourite part and she sang it ravishingly with the cool clear tones for which she was celebrated.

A longer entr'acte followed. Then came the humorous singing lesson scene from Rossini's *Barber of Seville. The Times* wrote:

> Applause was very restrained during the whole evening and in any case begloved hands cannot be very sonorous. But the roulades of Mme Tetrazzini in *Je suis Titania* of Thomas aroused the chief enthusiasm of the evening and the stern and imperturbable Japanese and Hindus relaxed their faces into a smile as the irresistible Mario Sammarco as Figaro roughly shaved the reverend Bartolo (Pompilio Malatesta), while his daughter Rosina (Mme Tetrazzini) flirted with Almaviva (John McCormack) at the spinet. Her voice and execution were more wonderful than ever. Both the King and Queen laughed at her merry business and joined in the applause at the fall of the curtain.

After a further interval, the evening ended with the scene of the 'Animation of the Tapestry' from Tcherepnin's *Le Pavillon d'Armide* danced by the

Imperial Russian Ballet. From Covent Garden, King George and Queen Mary went through the streets lined with sightseers – despite the lateness of the hour – to a ball given by the Duke and Duchess of Westminster at Grosvenor House.

Quite a different scene was enacted in Tetrazzini's flower-filled dressing-room. She had a male friend named Mose Tapiero, a talented ocarina soloist, who was known to eat three whole chickens and piles of pasta at one sitting, and he had spent the long evening on one of these gorging sessions with the result that he was writhing about suffering from agonizing indigestion, and had come to beg her to give him the only treatment that eased the pain. This was to make him lie down and then to massage his stomach with a warm iron borrowed from her dresser![4]

Three days later, on 29 June 1911, Meyerbeer's *Gli Ugonotti* was revived for the fourth season in succession. The critics considered that, though the opera was pretentious and meretricious, it did provide opportunities for many star singers to appear in it and was one of those works which people patronized only for the singing. Destinn was Valentina; robust François Darmel – Raoul; Sammarco – Nevers and the six foot six Russian bass Sibiriakoff – Marcello. Tetrazzini sang the florid arias of the Queen with 'delightful ease and beauty of tone' according to the *Daily Telegraph*.

July 1911 Records 'Finest Ever'

On 11 and 14 July Tetrazzini made more records at Hayes – some new, some repeats of earlier titles. The reaction to these was excellent. Will Gaisberg wrote to his brother Fred in Berlin on 21 August:

> We want to tell you, and also our Managing Directors express the same opinion, that the last Tetrazzini records which you have just made are the finest that we have ever turned out, and far away ahead of the last work done by the Victor Company.[5]

On 20 July Tetrazzini had visited the enlarged factory at Hayes which she toured, and then sang to the 500 work girls, pressing afterwards a record of her own voice, which was handed to her on departure. She returned on 22 November to give another concert with Percy Pitt at the piano.

The Director of the Deutsche-Grammophon-Aktiengesellschaft of Berlin wrote to Will Gaisberg of the Gramophone Company on 19 September, offering Tetrazzini £300 per engagement for two concerts to take place, the one in Budapest and the other in Vienna between 5 and 17 October. However, Tetrazzini demanded £400 and the Berlin director wrote back that such a sum was simply out of proportion. No agent would risk such an amount without knowing if the public would like her or not. In fact he would candidly advise her against singing in Vienna as he did not think she would be successful there:

> The Viennese people are the hardest to please and satisfy and are so crazy with Selma Kurz that they would not admit any coloratura singer being superior than her. I will perhaps be able to manage an opera performance for Tetrazzini in Berlin as soon as the new Opera House has opened.[6]

Actually it would have been difficult for Tetrazzini to fulfil such engagements for she was already committed to a provincial tour opening in Birmingham on 9 October. This over, she sailed on the *Amerika* to New York where she arrived on 12 November and then went to sing at the opera house in Philadelphia (renamed the Metropolitan) on the 15th in *Lucia* with Amedeo Bassi as Edgardo and Mario Sammarco as Ashton.

The *Musical Courier* for 22 November wrote:

> Confident of her popularity Mme Tetrazzini did not hesitate to share in an original and not commendable innovation in the opening act. For the moonlight scene near the ruined tower of Wolf's Crag, as the libretto has it, the sunny setting of the first scene was employed, and the orchestral introduction to this second scene was played to an empty stage à la Cavalleria intermezzo. These liberties enabled the florid soprano to effect her appearance in less obscurity and shadow than the correct scenario of the opera demands.
>
> *Lucia*, however, is not taken very seriously these days and few in the vast audience seemed to resent these peculiar changes. Mme Tetrazzini took her prima donna's bow with her customary mid-Victorian graces and coquetry, and then proceeded to exhibit the resources of her art as brilliantly as of yore.

In Chicago's New Auditorium

After singing Violetta with Bassi as Alfredo and Sammarco as Germont in Philadelphia on 18 November Tetrazzini travelled to Cleveland with Bassi where she sang Lucia and he Edgardo on the 21st. Then they both went to Chicago where she undertook five roles in a fortnight with its new Grand Opera Company at the Auditorium. The Auditorium, which seated 4,000 people, was said to have the best acoustics in the world. A *Chicago Daily News* reporter called on her arrival at the hotel where she was staying and in its issue for 22 November he wrote that with Bazelli and 'Doc' Leahy acting as her interpreters she said that she would like a sane interviewer. 'One newspaper lady met me at the station and first she asked me was I married!' smiled Tetrazzini. She continued:

> Let us not talk of such things. There are many, many things more important than being married. I am – oh, so anxious to know whether Chicago will like me in grand opera. They are so warm, these Chicago people. In my concerts they have been so good to me. I love them!

Regarding Bazelli's relations with Tetrazzini, among her press cuttings preserved in the *San Francisco Examiner*'s archives is one unfortunately undated from the *New York American* but probably of about this time. It quotes a report from London to the effect that the diva on occasion was hypnotized to give her confidence before singing. Her comment was that 'the only hypnotic influence under which she sings is that of her audience' and that although the report was mistaken there were times when her voice was 'subservient to the influence of her manager and friend, George Bazelli'.

Tetrazzini opened in Chicago on Friday 24 November, with her brother-in-law Cleofonte Campanini conducting. Next day Glenn Dillard Gunn wrote in the *Daily Tribune* that the reserve which marked the public's attitude to the first two performances of the season was changed into

> the most enthusiastic demonstrativeness last night by Mme Luisa Tetrazzini, who set the audience to shouting and applauding with her interpretation of the Mad Scene and kept them at it for five minutes.

Not since Caruso was first heard in Chicago had there been anything like it. 'Nor did his achievements, even in the days of his prime, match the display of vocal technic which so excited Mme Tetrazzini's listeners.' They possessed in common 'the power to move an audience as can no other operatic stars of the present generation'.

Tetrazzini next appeared on the following Tuesday the 28th as Violetta in *La Traviata*, again with Bassi as Alfredo and Sammarco as Germont, and to the largest audience so far of the season bringing into the box office $10,000. Glenn Dillard Gunn's review in the *Tribune* began by saying that the opera's 'faded beauties were endowed with the brilliant qualities of Mme Tetrazzini's voice' and the public applauded 'a repetition of those remarkable vocal stunts' that had so astonished those hearing her Lucia. Chicago had also been treated to a display of her breath control similar to that employed by her in the same opera when making her Manhattan début in 1908.

> If holding a high E flat for more than a minute and at the same time stooping over and picking up sundry yards of green silk train – which one would judge would be tiring exercise to a person of Mme Tetrazzini's matronly figure – is not an astonishing feat, then an opera audience never yet responded to the peculiar physiological and psychological thrill of a high tone. Such thrills were dispensed in abundance as is always the case when Mme Tetrazzini sings, and they constitute the essential grandeur of grand opera to many people.

On 30 November *Rigoletto* was presented with Tetrazzini as Gilda, Bassi as the Duke, and Sammarco in the title role. Gunn in the *Tribune* wrote that every member of the cast was in fine voice and that the performance moved from one number to another with never flagging interest. 'The tender duet between Rigoletto and Gilda added to the rich sonority of Sammarco's voice, Mme Tetrazzini's warm, pure and perfect tones.' Elsewhere she indulged in 'some sensational bits of technical display'.

Nixon began his notice in the *Daily News* by saying that the 'peppery progressionists' determined to eliminate Verdi's works as 'meretricious melody' suffered disheartening experiences in relegating old fashioned opera to 'the dusty shelf of oblivion'. This was because 'the mere people seem to love it, cherish it and acclaim it'. *Rigoletto's* revival the previous evening was as notable in artistic performance as it was successful in inspiring enthusiasm in the largest audience of the season.

Tetrazzini's next new role in Chicago was that of Rosina. Gunn wrote in the *Tribune* for Tuesday 5 December that the majority of the audience attracted to the Auditorium the previous evening by the announcement that *Il Barbiere di Siviglia* would be sung arrived 'with memory echoes of the Rosina of Sembrich tinkling in their ears'. They left, however, 'with the wonderful notes of Tetrazzini dimming the luster of the other star'. Gunn goes on:

> Mme Tetrazzini is quoted as having said recently that 'the public now likes me to do stunts'. If by doing 'stunts' the madame refers to her ability to shower upon her audience tones from the realms usually occupied by the birds and the mountain peaks – staccato notes which stand out with the clearness of star points – then the public loves Mme Tetrazzini's 'stunts'. . . .
> The role of Rosina gave Mme Tetrazzini not only many opportunities to please this stunt loving following of hers, but it allowed her an opportunity to prove her abilities as a dainty comedienne. She acted.

Regarding the other artists, Gunn wrote that the Chicago public loved Mario Sammarco almost as much as it did Tetrazzini but to them he had been seen previously as 'a gray wigged count or a sorrow laden father'. His Figaro, therefore, 'full of light and life and color' was a great surprise that they thoroughly enjoyed. Nixon in the *Daily News* also praised his characterization as 'not only finely sung, but was acted with such ease, point and finish that it compared favorably with a long line of eminent predecessors in the famous part'.

As for Tetrazzini, Nixon wrote that she was equal to 'all the emergencies put upon her in the tricky and blithesome score'. Her legato had velvety quality when it came to a test like *Una voce poco fa*.

> Her trill defies tremolando while the effectiveness and certainty of the voice appear to make it higher than it really is – the tone swells like a translucent bubble but it never flattens or bursts. She was rather matronly for the role of the sprightly, Spanish Rosina, but she has far from forgotten the archness and coquetries of the sex and her Rosina carried the gaiety from time to time with surprising lightness, and, strangely enough be it confessed, her voice at times took a tone of whiteness when she attempted to put the unction of humor into music.

On 6 December Tetrazzini sang the title role in *Lakmé* with Bassi as Gerald. Gunn in the *Tribune* began his review:

> Phenomenal is the word that most accurately describes the performance.... The size of the audience earlier in the season would have been considered phenomenal, but sold out houses are so fast becoming the rule for grand opera performances that they have ceased to occasion comment save in the ever cheerful haunts of the management. However the art of the great coloratura soprano is none the less phenomenal because we are fast becoming accustomed to its many astonishing aspects and it was possibly with a desire to emphasize its unusual qualities, that the stage management saw fit to surround it, as it were, with the equally astonishing collection of vegetable phenomena represented in the setting of the first act. With Mme Tetrazzini prepared to prove at any moment that the age of miracles is not past, vocally at least, the credulity of the spectator was not subjected to the strain which the sight of lusty palm trees growing like orchids in mid air would occasion ordinarily.

For the Saturday matinée on 9 December, Tetrazzini sang for the second time as Lucia. It was her last performance that season in Chicago. Box takings amounted to $12,000 and over 1,500 people were turned away. When the opera ended, in response to the tremendous acclamation awarded her, Tetrazzini sang *The Last Rose of Summer*.

Before leaving the Chicago Grand Opera Company, Luisa went with them to sing Lucia on 11 December at Cincinatti. Next day its *Times* stated: 'The greatest ovation which was ever accorded to any singer in the old Music Hall was hers. She is magnificent, peerless and unapproachable.'

15 Début at the 'Met'

In the summer of 1911 Giulio Gatti-Casazza, Conried's successor at the Metropolitan, had invited Tetrazzini to give six gala performances there and enquired what her fee would be for each one. According to what she wrote later in *My Life of Song*[1] she demanded $3,000 and he protested that they were paying Caruso less – it was $2,500 – and that if the tenor discovered she was receiving more, he would want more, too. But she claimed she held out and that Gatti-Casazza agreed on condition that she kept the amount of her fee a close secret.

Prior to making her début at the Metropolitan, Tetrazzini returned to Boston on 20 December 1911 to sing Lucia at its Opera House, where Henry Russell, the English impresario and singing teacher, brother of Landon Ronald, was general manager. The largest audience of that season were told that she was still suffering from the effects of an attack of influenza and consequently would have to refrain from attempting the highest notes. Florencio Constantino sang Edgardo and Roberto Moranzoni conducted. The general opinion was that never had she shown more intelligence and warmth. Admired were her finely sustained legato, the way she launched and ended a phrase, her extraordinary breath control and her lavish bravura.

Not since Melba's heyday had a soprano aroused such admiration – and there was an exceptionally high proportion of men in the audience, many of whom had rarely been to the opera before. The only fault-finding came from a captious critic who took exception to her first act costume with its bizarre medley of tartan bands which he thought would have caused a riot in the Scottish Highlands. Incidentally, she always refused to wear her sporran in the traditional position because she said it looked 'rude'. It was all right behind because the audience could imagine it was her cushion.

Russell himself had an aversion to, as he put it, prima donnas with 'ripe Italian figures', adding that he had engaged Tetrazzini only due to popular demand. 'I hired her,' he told friends, 'but I don't have to listen to her.'

Quaintance Eaton wrote[2] that to one spectator Tetrazzini and the supporting flautist in the *Lucia* soliloquy scene gave the impression of 'two goldfish disporting themselves in a globe of clear water'. The general opinion of Boston critics was that her voice had lost its first upper softness but had acquired in its place a diamond brilliance.

For the matinée on 23 December Russell revived, much to the older generation's delight, Ambroise Thomas's *Mignon*, with Fely Dereyne in the title role and Tetrazzini singing Philine for the first time in the United States. Her acting was praised by the critics as refreshingly lively. Jeska Swartz, a pocket-sized brunette, was cast in the mezzo part of Frédéric, which caused Tetrazzini to be overheard tittering, backstage, 'This leetle boy – ees supposing to be in love with me? Like a peanut to a mountain!'

In an interview published in the *Boston Traveller*, Tetrazzini revealed some of her opinions. For example:

> The American woman is superb. But she should not be so bold in her make-up. She should never let a man see her make-up. A woman should always deceive a man. A man will love you more if you keep him guessing.

Immediately after Christmas, Tetrazzini left Boston for New York. Gatti-Casazza had suggested that she should make her Metropolitan début in *La Traviata* with Toscanini on the podium, but she had declined saying that she was too pyrotechnical – a sarcastic reference to the reason given by him for not engaging her to sing at La Scala. 'Give me conductor No. 2' she requested. So instead, on 27 December 1911, she appeared as Lucia under Giuseppe Sturani's baton with Florencio Constantino as Edgardo and Pasquale Amato as Ashton before a near-capacity audience that was one of the largest of the season. She must have experienced a feeling of complete achievement as she walked onto the spacious stage of the last great opera house in America where she had not sung and surveyed the faded gilt and red plush, the monumental chandeliers and the famed Diamond Horseshoe of boxes with their small three-leafed clovers of lights dimming arrogantly after the house lights were put out.

And in one of those boxes sat Toscanini. To his credit he joined in the applause and went round to Tetrazzini's dressing-room afterwards to congratulate her. 'What a shame it is that I did not have the honour of conducting this remarkable performance on this night of nights', he said.

In his review next day in the *New York Times*, Richard Aldrich wrote that there was only one acceptable excuse for reviving such an opera as *Lucia di Lammermoor* and that was a management's ability to engage a prima donna sufficiently accomplished to sing the heroine's role. Originally, it had been essential to find the right tenor as Edgardo, but now this was regarded as of secondary importance. Sopranos with the vocal skill needed to sing Lucia were becoming more and more scarce.

Tetrazzini's performance had been received with exceptional enthusiasm. Aldrich considered that her voice had gained in fullness and even in power. Its lower ranges had improved in quality. They had lost 'the infantile character that used to be so striking a defect in her singing, and some of the constriction that used to make her lower tones sound pinched she has apparently overcome'.

To this extent Tetrazzini's voice had gained 'in the uniformity and evenness that it formerly lacked'. On the other hand, the tremolo that had begun to be noticeable when she commenced singing at the Manhattan remained and 'the suspicions of it in her upper tones were now, unfortunately, more than suspicions'. But she still 'rejoiced in brilliant passage work' and in runs, scales, and arpeggios which were 'often beautifully limpid, clear and delicate' though her scales were 'sometimes blurred'. She had dealt out a good many high notes the previous evening, but in some instances not without a certain amount of caution – 'thus at the close of *Spargi d'amaro*, after the Mad Scene, which she sang brilliantly, she speedily dropped her high E flat and took the octave lower'.

One of Tetrazzini's favourite vocal ornaments was

the swelling and diminishing of tone on one note, which she does beautifully and uses frequently – sometimes at inopportune occasions – as in the sextet in the second act where she seizes a moment to display her *messa di voce* that interferes with both the musical development of the piece and even with its dramatic significance – for it has one.

All the same in 'the more serious regions to her art', she deserved praise for her command of legato and for her phrasings which often showed 'beauty of no mean order'.

All that Constantino did and the manner in which he achieved it was in keeping with 'the grand old traditions of which so few traces are now left on the operatic stage'. A better Edgardo than he could not have been found, and he fully deserved the audience's rapturous applause and the compliment paid him by the management of including the fourth act, often omitted when the opera was regarded as having no further interest 'after the prima donna had gone mad to the accompaniment of the flute'.

Henry Krehbiel of the *Tribune* remained aloof, however. (It was he who had condemned Puccini's *La Bohème* as 'foul in subject, and fulminant but futile in music'.) He wrote:

Mme Tetrazzini was received with much cordiality on her entrance, but after she had begun to sing she was, we fear, made to realize there are different standards of judgment touching the art of song among the patrons of New York. It was not until after the sextet (which had to be repeated) that the audience was aroused to a demonstration of enthusiasm, and though she sang her part very admirably indeed, it is probable that some of the credit for its success was due to the music, and the other singers, for even Mme Tetrazzini, despite the variety of registers in her voice (unhappily in evidence in her entrance air), cannot sing a sextet with chorus alone. As for the rest, there is not much to be said of Mme Tetrazzini's singing that has not been said over and over again in these columns – said in praise and said in mournful depreciation, in praise of her command of artistic device, and in dispraise of the inequalities of her voice, in praise of the fine texture of her upper tones, in regret because of the infantile character of her lower, in laudation of skill artistically used and in denunciation of the same skill abused.

Krehbiel's judgment was a minority's one. The *Musical Courier* for 3 January 1912 thoroughly approved of the diva's performance:

Mme Tetrazzini comes back to us in the full height of her powers, and while her marvellous facility in runs, passages, trills and all the other dazzling requisites of coloratura singing are undiminished in the slightest degree. Lovers of pure bel canto were delighted to find that she had added to her equipment a smoother joining of registers and a more liquid flow of tone production in sustained cantilena than she exhibited at the time she was one of the stars of the Manhattan Opera House. The audience listened in sheer amazement to the Mad Scene and the other scintillating episodes where her astonishing ease and accuracy of vocal pyrotechnics were in place.

However there were also a deeper note of pathos evident in the Tetrazzini voice, and if . . . the story of *Lucia* as put into libretto form were not so stupid and unconvincing she would have established herself as a dramatic soprano of no mean ability.

Tetrazzini reappeared in *Lucia* on 1 January 1912, with the same artists except that Campanari replaced Amato. On the 6th, Sturani again conducted when she sang Violetta in *La Traviata* with Dmitri Smirnoff as Alfredo and Giovanni Polese as Germont – repeated on the 18th with Amato as Germont. On the 11th she was heard as Gilda with Smirnoff as the Duke and Dinh Gilly as Rigoletto – repeated on the 27th with the latter role taken by Maurice Renaud, of whom Krehbiel wrote: 'Where Renaud sits, there is the head of the table.'

In between these performances, Tetrazzini had travelled to Boston to sing another Lucia at the Opera House on the 12th, to Providence to give her first concert on Rhode Island on the 16th in its Infantry Hall with Charles Strony accompanist, Ramon Blanchart baritone, and José Mardones bass – and then back to Boston to sing in *La Traviata* on the 20th. The younger members of the audience were not put out by the fact that she hardly resembled a consumptive. All that they wanted were those skyscraping notes. One bit of realistic business outraged some dowagers who were sticklers for good manners and restraint even when one is dying. This was when, after giving a racking cough, the diva inspected the make-believe phlegm in her handkerchief at length and with growing horror. But she did not completely lose herself in the part. During the most poignant moments of her deathbed scene, those in the front stalls caught her giving an unmistakable wink at someone in the wings. This Violetta received admirable vocal support from Giovanni Zenatello appearing for the first time as Alfredo in Boston, but, as his father Germont, Polese overacted.

On 29 January when *Il Barbiere di Siviglia* was staged, Vanni Marcoux's antics as Basilio, enormously tall and all rolling whites of eyes, succeeded in making the reserved, staid Bostonians rock with laughter and inspired Tetrazzini to even livelier acting than usual as Rosina.

Back at the Metropolitan, Tetrazzini sang Lucia again on 2 February 1912 with Constantino, and on the 6th, now aged forty-one, she chose to sing Gilda for her last night there. Caruso was the Duke and Renaud the Jester. Outside, mounted police were hastily summoned to try and disperse over 2,000 frenzied fans who, ignoring the 'House Full' notices, were battling to break a passage into the auditorium. There were casualties through the police being forced to use clubs.

A few days later, Tetrazzini made a record with Caruso of the Quartet from *Rigoletto* and the Sextet from *Lucia* for the Victor Talking Machine Company. She was earning over $60,000 annually in royalties from the latter in the United States alone. Paying a tribute to her in the *New York World-Telegram* for 4 May 1940, Pitts Sanborn wrote that

> people who hear only a microscopic voice in the roles of Lucia and Gilda can have no just idea of how the *Lucia* and *Rigoletto* quartet ought to sound. Tetrazzini's soprano dominated those numbers with a grand line as of Greek sculpture.

These ensemble records demonstrate this. After singing at the Hippodrome with the Franko Orchestra on 18 February, Tetrazzini set out from Central Station on a concert tour organised by 'Doc' Leahy. A reporter wrote that she looked

> like an ermine-trimmed pigeon pecking the cheeks of admirers and tearfully hugged Caruso who told her solicitously to behave and not to give away her money so freely to all and sundry.

She was to claim that he had proposed marriage to her in 1911.

16 'San Francisco, My Heart Is with You'

Before leaving New York, Tetrazzini had asked the correspondent of the *San Francisco Chronicle* to see that a message to its people was published prominently in his paper: 'You were the first in America to appreciate my art and there is no place where I would rather sing than San Francisco.'[1] On 6 March she arrived in that city aboard the 'Lark' of the South Pacific Company. Standing on the platform of the private Pullman car used for her travelling she smiled down through the rain at the press photographers and at Mayor Rolph who held up towards her a great cluster of Killarney roses. Thanking him, she sang for his benefit a few bars from *San Francisco, my heart is with you*.[2] Next to her, applauding, stood Bazelli and also 'Doc' and Mrs Leahy who had accompanied her on the tour.

As they left the train, Tetrazzini insisted on taking charge of a black leather bag which she handled with care. A reporter asked if it contained her jewels. 'No, it is not that', she replied. 'I carry in this my chilli sauce, my Worcestershire sauce, my paprika and everything that is good for the voice.' Questioned as to whether she preferred as engagements operas or concerts, she revealed: 'Operas – but I sing the old operas. These new operas, they are not written for the singer – they are written for the orchestra. No, no, no, I do not like them.'[3]

Tetrazzini was then driven to the Fairmont Hotel where a reporter from the *Chronicle* found her exploring the depths of a huge trunk. She pulled out an enormous roll of paper containing the names of 1,500 school-children in Monterey County begging her to visit them and sing. Asked if she would, she replied that it would depend on whether there was time for her to do so.

Next to interview the diva was a journalist from the *Examiner. Il Paradiso* was the name she had given her villa in Lugano. Mentioning this, he said that he had been told it was large. Did she intend to have children? 'I could not have them and sing', she explained. 'Art cannot serve two masters. I sing! It is very tragic to have no children. It makes me unhappy.'[4]

On 12 March, Harvey Wickham reviewed in the *San Francisco Chronicle* the concert Tetrazzini had given the previous night at the Dreamland Pavilion.

> One would not have thought yet another grace could be added to her art, yet the very first selection which she gave to the vast audience showed that something had been added to the list of her accomplishments. When she was here last year, it seemed as if she was the one perfect singer beyond the reach of improvement. And so far as the 'florid art' that was probably true.

The *Ritorna vincitor* from *Aida* in which the soprano sings of her conflicting emotions revealed that Tetrazzini was a dramatic artist as well:

> When those wonderful mezza tones began to pour forth in the recitative preceding the aria it was plain that here was one of the few who are never satisfied with what they have done in the past but must always be accomplishing something new. The audience had come to hear tones of a pearly sweetness and trills and runs and high notes and the spell of the more solemn and heroic *Ritorna vincitor* came as a complete surprise after the waltz song by Luigi Venzano which she gave as her first encore, the runs and the trills were all there as of old, but the marvel of *Ritorna vincitor* was still ringing in my ears.

Next Tetrazzini sang Cowen's *Swallows*. Then came *The Last Rose of Summer* and 'it was as if Patti had come back in the first flush of her youth'.

Tetrazzini's singing of the Bach-Gounod *Ave Maria* had to be rendered twice – 'thanks perhaps to the marvellously "white" coloring of the final note'.

The programme ended with the *Mad Scene* from *Lucia*. 'So much has been written about this that the best thing to do is to say that she sang it in her very best style in spite of the rain which beat upon the roof.'

On 17 March, St Patrick's Day, Tetrazzini sang again at Dreamland wearing a white afternoon dress and a long lace coat trimmed with green – and a brooch of shamrocks wrought in jewels and enamel work. She sang 'Killarney' as a second encore. The *San Francisco Call*'s critic wrote next day that never had he heard 'Killarney' interpreted so well without a brogue. 'It was as Irish as the green which nearly girdles Italy.'

Lotta Crabtree Consents

Although Tetrazzini had been presented with that gold plate in commemoration of her 1910 Christmas Eve concert, many felt that there ought to be some permanent record of the event in the city itself. The committee formed to further this proposal reached the conclusion that the best place for a memorial plaque would be on the fountain standing on the island where Market, Geary and Kearny Streets converged. This spouted drinking-water (dubbed 'Market Street Champagne') from four carved lions' heads. The busy downtown intersection was known as Newspaper Square from the large number of newsboys who congregated there. The fountain had been donated to the city in 1875 by Lotta Crabtree, the singer, and thanks to its strong cast-iron shaft, had remained standing proudly among the ruins after the 1906 earthquake. The Mayor, however, doubted the propriety of adding any inscription to it without her consent, so he wrote and requested this. Lotta immediately replied by telegram: 'I will be honored to have Mme Tetrazzini's name to be associated with me.'[5]

Despite such approval, there were misgivings. Supervisor Murdoch declared that the correct position for a tablet was on the wall of the *San Francisco Chronicle* building, whilst Supervisor Vogelsang said that despite the consent of the donor he did not think it was proper to superimpose the name of one artist on the memorial of another. Supervisor Giannini thought the plate should be mounted on the wall of the safety station and when it was objected that there were no lamps there he replied: 'Doc Leahy will undoubtedly buy some.'[6]

It was finally decided to give Supervisor Hayden power to go ahead with the plan after the Park Commission gave their approval. This saved the Mayor considerable embarrassment for he had already arranged with Tetrazzini for the unveiling to be held at Lotta's Fountain on Sunday 24 March.

For the ceremony, a stand was erected outside the *Chronicle* building, and by the time Tetrazzini, escorted by the Mayor, arrived wearing a black jet trimmed gown with a large black hat similarly decorated, some 40,000 people had gathered around it and in the nearby streets, while others watched from every floor of the buildings opposite. Her appearance was the signal for frantic applause and the waving of hats and handkerchiefs.

Meanwhile 250 Italian children from Garfield School at the top of Telegraph Hill, led by their music teacher Estelle Carpenter, marched down, singing as they did a welcome to the diva from the land of their parents. They positioned themselves in the lower part of the stand. Directly in front sat Paul Steindorff and his orchestra with Tetrazzini, Bazelli, the Mayor, city officials and friends in the upper rows.

After the overture the children sang an air from *Cavalleria Rusticana*, the *Star and Stripes* and *San Francisco, San Francisco, my heart is with you*. It had been announced that Tetrazzini would not sing as her throat was troubling her and the wind too keen for her to risk damaging her voice, but she hummed with the children a few bars of '*San Francisco*'.

There followed speeches and the unveiling of the bronze tablet on which was engraved: 'To remember Christmas Eve 1910, when Luisa Tetrazzini sang to the People of San Francisco on this spot'. The last three words were inaccurate, of course, and should have read more accurately 'nearby'. This aroused some good-natured criticism from those who had been present.[7] Before leaving, Tetrazzini pulled apart her bouquet of Californian poppies and threw them to the crowd accompanied by her customary blowing of kisses.

Next morning, the *Chronicle* devoted its front page to reporting the event and included a large photograph of Tetrazzini smiling approvingly at the tablet with George Bazelli on her right and 'Doc' Leahy on her left. Beneath this was reproduced a message from her:

> On the eve of my departure from dear old San Francisco I desire to express my thanks for this gift to me. This tablet, I hope, will always remind you of the affection which Tetrazzini holds for you and always will hold for you. After listening to the remarks of your splendid Mayor about the need of an Auditorium and the people's center, I want to add my plea to his and ask you to vote so that you may get that great Auditorium, which is offered you merely for the ground. When I come back here I want to sing in it. I will be proud to sing there for you.

There was a pressing need for a large and well appointed concert hall to be built. Hence the reference in Tetrazzini's letter urging the people of San Francisco to vote in favour of the proposal that public land should be provided as the site on which a Civic Auditorium might be built.

Later, in further remembrance of the Christmas Eve concert a bas-relief portrait of Tetrazzini by Haig Patigian was added to Lotta's Fountain.[8]

On 30 March Luisa sang at Portland's Heilig Theatre with 275 people on the stage behind her; on 1 April to nearly 7,000 in Houston's Auditorium; then on the 6th she travelled to Los Angeles for a Good Friday concert.[9]

The Greek Theatre in Berkeley has been described in Guide Books as 'one of the most remarkable structures of its kind in the world'. It is built in the shape of an amphitheatre against the side of a hill and its crest is fringed by sombre eucalyptus trees. Here, next day, some 10,000 people gathered for this event. There was a full orchestra conducted by Paul Steindorf with 300 singers drawn from the San Francisco Choral Society, the San Francisco Clef Club, the Oaklands Wednesday Morning Club and the Berkeley Oratorio Society.

The sopranos and contraltos were all in white. 'Tetrazzini alone wore the black dress suggested by the church calendar,' wrote Harvey Wickham in the *San Francisco Chronicle*.[10] He continued:

> Professor William D. Armes prefaced the programme by announcing that no encores would be given no matter how much the great audience applauded,

and he suggested rather emphatically that it would be much better if they did not applaud at all. The response, of course, was a hearty round of applause.

Audiences were notoriously contrary, especially those which had paid 'good money for their right to be present'.

This 'perversity' developed into a 'positive unpleasantness' after the 'Good Friday Spell' from *Parsifal* with which the orchestra began. Those who clapped were 'soundly hissed' by those who wanted to preserve a church-like solemnity about the occasion. Wickham thought it would have been wiser to say nothing about applause for every time the enthusiasm of the clappers broke bounds they aroused 'the criticism of the party of silence' and this split in the audience slightly marred an otherwise perfect afternoon.

Next came Rossini's *Stabat Mater* and Wickham considered Tetrazzini's *Inflammatus* deserved the tremendous applause it received in spite of Professor Armes's admonitions. 'But the solo suits her less than some others that might be named and she made no effort to soar above the chorus except in one or two beautiful high Es.'

On 10 April Tetrazzini sang in Denver's Auditorium; on the afternoon of Sunday the 14th in Chicago's Auditorium; then the tour ended on the 21st at the Hippodrome, New York. Two days later just before leaving on the *Mauretania*, she gave 'a kinematic exhibition all her own at the Garden Theater' reported the *Morning Telegraph*. She was accompanied by

> a score of intimate friends and operatic associates whom she had invited to witness with her for the first time, a series of motion pictures in which she played the star part in two notable Pacific coast events. One was the unveiling of the Tetrazzini tablet and the other on Good Friday last when thousands gathered to hear her sing in the open air amphitheater at the University of California.[11]

The Grand Opera Season opened at Covent Garden on 20 April 1912 and Tetrazzini was heard as Gilda on 27 May in *Rigoletto* with McCormack as the Duke and Dinh Gilly in the title role. On 1 June she appeared as Rosina with McCormack as Almaviva and Sammarco as Figaro. Panizza conducted both operas while Campanini did so when she sang Margherita di Valois with Destinn as Valentina and Sammarco as Nevers in *Gli Ugonotti* on 11 June. Two days later she sang Violetta in *La Traviata* with McCormack as Alfredo, Gilly as Germont, and Panizza on the podium.

Aldous Huxley's Encomium

It was probably this summer that Osbert and Sacheverell Sitwell together with their sister Edith and other admirers of Tetrazzini's singing obtained permission to call on her at the Savoy and present a wreath of bay and myrtle to her as a tribute from the young writers of England. The seven or eight persons who formed the deputation included Aldous Huxley who wrote the speech that Sacheverell was to deliver. Osbert in the fourth volume of his autobiography describes what happened when they entered the diva's suite, the sitting-room of which had been converted for the occasion into a bower of white lilac. Journalists and cameramen were present. The bedroom door was flung open and Luisa entered wearing an over-elaborate brown crêpe dress lavishly adorned with lace. She radiated good nature as she approached slowly, 'making a conventional theatrical gesture of greeting and pleasure, with her right hand to the poets drawn up in line, and with her left hand to the cameraman up his ladder ready to pull the trigger'. Then came anticlimax as she caught her foot in a rug and fell flat onto the floor.

Happily Tetrazzini had not injured herself and was completely unruffled by the accident. Sacheverell was about to read their tribute when curiosity made her seize the paper, but he, determined to go through with his task, snatched it back saying '*Prego, Divinissima*' and began to read. The camera clicked – and so, wrote Sir Osbert in his account, 'There a delightful occasion remains, enshrined in the dusty office files of newspapers.'[12]

On Sunday afternoon, 16 June 1912 the Covent Garden board of directors presented Tetrazzini in concert at the Royal Albert Hall, supported by Jane Bourgeois, Giuseppe Cellini and James H. Goddard. Luisa's programme consisted of the Mad Scene from Ambroise Thomas's *Hamlet*, Mozart's *Voi che sapete* and Venzano's *Valse di Luigi*. The recital ended with all four singing the Quartet from *Rigoletto*. Marcel Charlier was at the piano.

Sydney Dixon of the Gramophone Company attended this Tetrazzini concert, her first to be presented at the Royal Albert Hall. All seats had been sold a week beforehand. Nevertheless, he wrote in *The Voice*,[13] some 4,000 seatless people had sought unsuccessfully to struggle through the turnstiles impeding the entry of the 13,000 who had bought tickets. It reminded him of a Rugby football match in which he had once played, for never had he seen 'such a crushing and a pushing' at a concert.

> Came the great little lady and in an unmistakable pantomime took the huge audience to her heart. She bowed and smiled and then followed a unique execution of roulades and florid vocal gymnastics. What a shouting and a cheering! Were those gesticulating women really the same people who had been staring at each other's frocks through lorgnettes by the Achilles Statue on that same Sunday morning? Were those cheering stockbrokers and bank officials the same men who travel daily from Surbiton to Waterloo and never speak to each other, year in, year out? It takes a Relief of Mafeking, an Armistice, or a Luisa Tetrazzini to break down English reserve....
> To arrive at the very pinnacle of fame in England is to become universally

known by a Christian name or by initials. At the Albert Hall there came shouts from a dozen parts of the house of 'Bravo Luisa!'

Robert Hichens the novelist tells in his memoirs how he was seated in the front row at this concert and how next to him was an elderly lady who evidently had a cold. When Tetrazzini came on to sing her first aria and having been affectionately applauded was about to begin, suddenly there erupted from this lady a terrific sneeze. Quite unperturbed, the diva bowed to her and said in English: 'Bless you, my dear!' – and then calmly launched into song.

On Sunday afternoon a fortnight later Tetrazzini sang for the second time at a Royal Albert Hall concert. The *Morning Post* next day reported that her interpretation of Grieg's *Solveig's Song* was 'very individual'. It was followed by the Waltz Song from Gounod's *Roméo et Juliette* 'brilliantly sung', Tosti's *Serenata* 'with sundry ornamental additions that must be taken as further expressions of individuality'. Then came David's *Couplets du Mysoli* from *La Perle du Brésil* – 'which proved an excellent means for the display of her voice, whose flexibility she illustrated by a shake on the C in alt followed by a cadenza introducing an E in alt'. As an encore she sang *Home, Sweet Home*, and at the end was heard as Marguerite to McCormack's Faust and Dinh Gilly's Mephistopheles in the trio from Act V of Gounod's opera.

Melba had not sung at Covent Garden that season, spending it instead in Australia. Her English admirers were disappointed and it was rumoured that she had done so deliberately to indicate to Harry Higgins and the Grand Opera Syndicate that she was tired of having to share the limelight with that 'dwarf' as she called Tetrazzini. In fact, they had been debating whether the latter's sixth successive season ought not to be her last, for though her popularity was undiminished, her repetition every year of the same coloratura roles lent ammunition of those who accused them of lack of enterprise and to becoming stale and unimaginative, so it was decided not to invite her back for the 1913 season.

January 1913: Return to Chicago

In late November and early December 1911 Tetrazzini's triumphs singing five of her major roles with the Chicago Grand Opera Company led to her being invited to sing again in its fine Auditorium, to be followed afterwards by a long Pacific Coast tour, the climax of which would be a short season in San Francisco where she would open the new Tivoli by singing Gilda, the role in which she had first soared to fame in the old theatre.[14]

Sailing from England to New York aboard the *Mauretania* on 6

December 1912, Tetrazzini went to Boston Opera House to sing Lucia and Violetta before going to Chicago to perform these roles as well as those of Gilda and Philine at the Auditorium in the last two weeks of January 1913.

In 1930, Edward C. Moore wrote in his *Forty Years of Opera in Chicago* of Tetrazzini:

> She came and laid everyone low. With the most disdainful ease she made the art of coloratura to glow as it has never glowed since. Physical illusion was not in her line at all; she was the size of three or four Maggie Teytes. But what a voice! Even after all these years one can recall the warm reediness of its qualities, the joyous certainty with which it swooped into all the cascades and fireworks of coloratura display, the piercing intensity which somehow or other never became shrill.

Tetrazzini was paid $2,000 a performance by the Chicago Grand Opera Company and for the whole time she sang with them she received $72,000 in all.[15]

Tetrazzini then set out on a long tour with the Chicago Grand Opera Company that took her to the Alhambra Theatre in Milwaukee, the Metropolitan Opera House of Philadelphia, Baltimore, and Washington. When they reached Dallas, where she had never sung before, her Lucia created such a sensation in the Fair Park Coliseum that the 4,500 strong audience rewarded her with the Texan salute – by rising and waving with wild enthusiasm handkerchiefs held high in the air.[16]

17 Clashes with Campanini

After singing in *Rigoletto* and *Lucia di Lammermoor* on 5 and 8 March 1913 respectively in Los Angeles, Tetrazzini and Bazelli travelled with the other members of the Chicago Grand Opera Company to San Francisco two days later aboard the 'Sunset Limited' to celebrate the opening of 'Doc' Leahy's new Tivoli Opera House on the evening of the 12th by again appearing as Gilda. She had with them a maid, a valet for Giorgio, a collection of Chinese dolls, jewels worth £250,000 and, as a reporter phrased it, 'a large cargo of enthusiasm'.[1]

Parading her Jewellery

No sooner was the diva installed in her suite at the Fairmont Hotel than a reporter from the *Chronicle* called to interview her. Bazelli as usual acted as interpreter, and announced that for the first time Tetrazzini would wear all her jewellery on the stage. Not as Gilda, that would look wrong, but in *Traviata* the following Saturday. 'Every big gem I have!' she cried. 'Wait a minute and I show you!' Clapping hands and speaking rapidly to her maid who was doing the unpacking, she went with her into the bedroom, and presently emerged holding two white plush pillows on which her jewellery was set out.

'Look!' Tetrazzini pointed at a pearl as large as an elk's tooth.

'That was given me by Colonel Fitzpatrick for singing to him in the old Palace Hotel the year before the fire – it is one of the most prized jewels in my collection. And I shall wear this diamond tiara and this diamond bandeau. Imagine how they will look under the lights on the stage! I shall also wear my diamond and sapphire necklace – and this pair of solitaire diamond earrings of 82 carats each and worth $60,000. And this was made for me by the Emperor of Germany's private jeweller'.

She held up a ring with a single emerald 'as big as a hickory nut' according to the reporter and next a pendant with three huge pearls, white, black and pink. There were more necklaces, 'dog collars,' and other personal bric-à-brac beyond count.

Brandishing a parasol with a diamond-tipped handle, Tetrazzini declared: 'No one can complain that I will be stingy with my jewels. They will be on me for everyone to see, and I intend to blaze like an electric sign!' Speaking of jewels, Tetrazzini revealed that a trunkful of imitation ones was on its way to her from London. They had once belonged to the great prima donna Maria Malibran, who had worn them in her roles.

Regarding Tetrazzini's parading of her jewellery, she was following the example of Adelina Patti when she sang at Covent Garden in 1895 after an absence of ten years, during which time, thanks to her tours of North and South America, she had amassed a fortune. Appearing as Violetta in *La Traviata* on 11 June before a packed house including the Prince and Princess of Wales, Patti wore in the Ball Scene a white dress upon the corsage of which blazed massed diamonds extending round her back. She had decided to display in this way all the stones acquired during her career. Nearly 4,000 had been temporarily removed from their settings and mounted upon a sort of cuirass. With these she wore ropes of pearls, a tiara and diamond bracelets.

Tetrazzini pointed out to those who called on her that she had lost weight which she attributed to having been taught how to dance the 'Texas Tommy' foxtrot by George Barnett, commandant of the Navy Yard at Philadelphia, during a reception aboard the battleship *Kansas*. 'The floor was cleared and we were gazed at by a thousand eyes as we went through the delicious dance', the *San Francisco Examiner*'s representative reported her as telling him.[2] 'It was exciting – I may not have danced with grace but – well, I can only repeat that it was exciting, very exciting.'

When in Peking about the time of the Boxer troubles, Mrs Barnett had received several hundreds of dolls as a present from the Dowager Empress and she had given two of them as a present to Tetrazzini, who also collected these. At her home in Lugano she kept over a hundred – 'dolls that winked, dolls that talked, and last but not least, a doll known as the little Tetrazzini which had a phonographic record hidden in her chest. When one pressed a button one heard a recording of Tetrazzini herself singing *Caro nome*.' 'She sings better than myself' Tetrazzini had laughed.

Unable to overcome her impatience, Tetrazzini hurried to the new Tivoli Opera House at nine that evening together with Bazelli, 'Doc' Leahy and his wife, and a few friends. Carpenters and decorators were busily at work putting the finishing touches to the auditorium. Leahy showed her around the stage and the other parts of the house. She studied the mural decorations, tried the seats for comfort, and asked questions about the stage lighting, before trying out the acoustics with *Home, Sweet Home, The Last Rose of Summer* and part of the Mad Scene from *Lucia*, and expressed herself satisfied. She then returned to the Fairmont 'to find her apartment littered with flowers sent by her admirers'.

On 11 March the *Chronicle* reported good news for the diva from New York:

The long-standing case of the Conried Metropolitan Opera Company against Luisa Tetrazzini which was started in the United States Circuit Court in that city in September 1908, was dismissed yesterday by United States District Judge Van Fleet under the new rule calling for the dismissal of all equity cases that have not been brought to trial within a year after filing.

As was expected, Tetrazzini triumphed next evening at the New Tivoli as Gilda, the same role in which she had made her début in the old theatre. The following night Mary Garden also enjoyed success in the title role of *Thaïs*. Then on the afternoon of Saturday the 15th, Luisa dazzled a full house both with her singing and her jewellery as Violetta. Next she sang Lucia and also Annetta in *Crispino e la Comare* on the 20th. On 29 March 1913 many American newspapers carried a report inspired by Bazelli that Tetrazzini would continue to appear with the Chicago Grand Opera Company after the present tour ended. She had received 'the most alluring offers', but finally decided to accept the one of Andreas Dippel, its general manager. The salary she was to receive 'for singing half-a-dozen of her roles with this company is matched only by that paid Caruso in New York'.[3] But Tetrazzini did not continue singing with them on account of growing differences between her and Cleofonte Campanini. He was now manager as well as principal conductor and could be very touchy. Tetrazzini thought that he was giving himself airs. He had started dyeing his hair and moustache, and the colouring would dribble down the sides of his mouth and drip onto his white dress shirt when he perspired from exertion on the podium. This made Luisa burst out laughing which irritated him. While she could learn a new role remarkably rapidly, he would take several months to master a score. This she often mentioned in their frequent arguments.

Campanini did have one thing in common with his sister-in-law – he was extremely superstitious. Convinced that old nails were the most potent bringers of good fortune he kept an alert eye on the ground wherever he went, ready to pounce on any he spotted. As a result his coat pockets bulged with what he had collected. Once a practical joker dropped old nails all the way along the underground passage that went from the Congress Hotel in Chicago where Campanini lived to the Auditorium Building and along the hall that led to the opera company's offices. The conductor found the sight of them an irresistible attraction and despite the fact that he was suffering from severe lumbago, bent down and spent nearly an hour picking them all up.[4]

After San Francisco, the Chicago Grand Opera Company performed in ten cities. The tour ended at the Metropolitan in New York where on 3 May Tetrazzini sang Lucia. In Minneapolis one night Tetrazzini and her brother-in-law had quarrelled during the interval over some points of a performance and it ended with her telling him, in the whole company's hearing, that she was the star and the draw at the box office and that he was only the conductor. There had been in fact for some time more and more clashes of temperament between them. Campanini was infuriated and decided that when the opportunity arose he would get even with Luisa. This occurred when she was singing Gilda and had soared into the cadenza with which she ended *Caro nome*. Then something distracted her attention and, losing her place and pitch, she finished on a high enough note but some degrees short of the correct one.

Campanini's expert ear had detected the lapse. Most conductors would have let Tetrazzini's note fade away then, cloaked by the applause, have led the orchestra in considerately and quietly, and it was likely that nobody among the audience would have noticed her mistake. It was too good an opportunity, however, for Campanini to miss. Grasping his baton resolutely, he nodded to the orchestra and from them crashed a chord that shook the roof.

After this, any close association between the two became impossible and on 5 September 1913 the first reference to the rift appeared in the *Toledo Blade*:

> Not Tetrazzini but Melba will be the coloratura star of the Chicago Grand Opera Company next season. This surprising information has just been made known by a member of the opera directorate upon receipt of information from Cleofonte Campanini, the new director of the opera forces at the Auditorium. This tends to confirm the rumours current here last season that Campanini has had serious and probably irremediable falling out with the great cantatrice ... Tetrazzini's whims and temper are matters of general knowledge in the operatic world and for years Campanini, possibly on account of his relationship, was the only person who could influence her. It was only through Campanini that Hammerstein was able to secure her for the Manhattan, and but for him she would not have remained there. Therefore there is more than ordinary interest in the fact that they have had differences so great that Campanini has engaged her greatest rival in Tetrazzini's place.

But the reference to Melba was premature. She had not agreed to join the Chicago Grand Opera Company for the next season. Instead, in October that year she began a long concert tour of the United States with Jan Kubelik, the famous violinist, which included Chicago, where the critic of *Musical America*[5] wrote: 'Her voice still combines the rich quality that puts her foremost among the prima donnas, nor has she lost any of the flexibility that enables her to do such beautiful coloratura work.' Nevertheless, he also found faults. 'In her opening number, the Mad Scene from *Lucia*, she seemed to lose some of the depth and sweet quality of her voice and at times sang off-key.'

About the same time, Tetrazzini was touring in Britain. Arriving at the Savoy Hotel on 17 September, she gave a recital at the Albert Hall next day, followed by 14 provincial concerts of which those at Plymouth, Portsmouth, Middlesborough and Leicester were for the first time. In Scotland she paid return visits to Edinburgh, Glasgow and Dundee.[6] At the end of October she left for Budapest where on 4 November she sang Violetta as guest artist in a new production of *La Traviata* that had opened at the Royal Opera House on 11 October with period costumes designed by Jeno Kemendy. Unfortunately she proved too fat to wear those made for the Hungarian soprano playing the role in all other performances so Tetrazzini and the rest of the cast wore evening dress. The critics were scathing about this. While agreeing that her technique was perfect, they thought she looked too old for the role compared with their local heroine the slender Erzsi Sàndor, and that her voice sounded tired. She had come ten years too late to Budapest and had proved as much of a fiasco as Caruso had when he sang there. Before leaving the city she gave a concert on the 8th. Unfortunately no reviews of this have survived in the archives.

On 19 November Tetrazzini made her first appearance in Vienna in the Konzerthaus. Here she had better luck. It will be remembered that on 21 September 1911 the Director of the *Deutsche Grammophon Aktiengesellschaft* had written to the Gramophone Company in London: 'I certainly would not advise Tetrazzini to sing in Vienna, as she will have no success there. The Vienna people are the hardest to please and satisfy.'[7] Instead, the *Musical Courier*'s Austrian correspondent wrote:

'She scored her usual triumph with *Ah, fors' è lui*, the polonaise from *Mignon*, and *Caro nome*. Her voice is certainly phenomenal; Vienna has never heard a singer more at ease in the third octave. She had to concede many encores before the audience would leave the great hall.'[8]

Back in England to honour the Philharmonic Society's centenary in 1913, it received the title of 'Royal' and on 5 December at a party in celebration at Pagani's, Tetrazzini was presented with the Society's gold medal by Sir Hubert Parry – following her first appearance at the Queen's Hall when he conducted his New Symphony and Percy Pitt accompanied her rendering of the song he had written for her, *Sérénade du Passant*.

On 12 December 1913 Tetrazzini and Bazelli arrived in New York on the *Mauretania*, and on the 19th she opened a short season at the Boston Opera House. Next day the *Daily Advertiser* wrote of her Violetta:

Her voice retains its peculiar bird-like quality and pleases by the wealth of vocal splendor and elasticity of expression. It shows some slight changes from the voice of a year and more ago. Her lower tones, once childish and distressingly thin, she has developed to a considerable degree. Last night they were full, vibrant and of definite quality. This gain has been made at some sacrifice of the pure coloratura quality of the upper register but the net gain in her singing is indisputable.

Olin Downes in the *Boston Globe* found that Tetrazzini had increased her powers of vocal dramatization:

There have been occasions when she treated Verdi's music according to her convenience. Last night she made the soliloquy of the first act something more than two awaited airs for the display of a prima donna's agility. There was appropriate distinction between the moods of fleeting pensiveness and restored abandon. In the scene with Germont the elder, Madame Tetrazzini managed without suspicion of forcing her voice to give true dramatic significance to the sustained and intensive passages in which Verdi demanded more breadth of tone than that usually found in the coloratura voice . . .

This critic ended:

There was a regard for the rhythmic values and the continuity and proportion of the songful passages that the celebrated soprano has not always shown; there was the same fluency in scale passages and vocal embroidery that has marked Tetrazzini at her best; there was an increasing body in the lowest tones which was used with a sense of colour, and there was still the impressive brilliance of the high voice.

On Christmas Eve the *San Francisco Chronicle* published the annual telegram that Tetrazzini sent them in memory of her celebrated concert with 'best wishes to your ever beautiful San Francisco', to which Mayor James Rolph had responded reciprocating her 'Yuletide greetings'. That evening she was heard once more as Lucia in Boston.

On 29 December Tetrazzini sang Gilda in *Rigoletto* and critic 'Hell to Pay' Parker wrote next day in the *Boston Evening Transcript*:

It is customary to say nowadays that Tetrazzini's voice is not what it used to be. Such a remark is likely to be made on every occasion, whether at the time it happens to be true or not. Last night it was certain that Gilda did not take her high E in the *Caro nome*. It also seemed that she was not always on the pitch; some said that she was sharp and others that she was flat; perhaps both were right, certainly both were uncomfortable. But be it said for Tetrazzini that she strikes her tones so clearly that the least deviation is noticeable to the practised ear, whereas many another singer habitually warbles about her note so that no one can say which part of her warbling is intended to be the note in question. And more than a few times last night Tetrazzini's tones seemed a bit pinched, sung as the layman puts it – back in the throat. One does not expect of her voice a real sweetness, but at their best her tones are so pure and efficient that they give a pleasure hardly second to those of anyone now singing on the operatic stage.

Still Tetrazzini's old virtues were there and were justly admired by a large audience that had come to get its money's worth. The magnificent firmness, the steel-like brilliance of her tones were evident in all her singing . . . It was worth a long journey last night only to hear the C flat which the singer struck in the

Quartet. Here, and in the whole final section of the piece, her voice had something of an epic quality.

It is of particular interest to note the reference to her not taking her high E in the *Caro nome* and not being always on the pitch because it was this that gave Campanini the chance to humiliate her.

Tetrazzini ended her season in Boston with a Lucia on 10 January 1914, probably the last time she sang in an opera, although some allege that she appeared for the first time as Amelia with Maggie Teyte as Oscar in a single performance of *Un Ballo in Maschera* somewhere in Italy that year. So far, however, it has proved impossible to find evidence of this. From now on she was to concentrate on concerts where much more money was to be made. For example, between 5 October 1912 and the end of August 1913 Melba gave 51 concerts in Great Britain, and from 29 September that year to 5 March 1914 she sang in a further 58, according to Thérèse Radic in her biography of the diva.

Musical America for 24 January 1914 gave a glowing report of Tetrazzini's concert the previous Sunday at the Hippodrome in New York, but Emilie Frances Bauer wrote more cynically in the New York *Evening Mail* that a concert by Tetrazzini always had been and always would be the same. She was certainly full of vivacity. Her faults were typical of coloratura sopranos of the old school, as were her finer qualities. She was indifferent to everything but flexibility of tone, floating high tones and fanciful effects which accentuated in one way or another her astonishing ease. What he sang made very little difference, nor did it seem to be a matter of concern that the harp gave her an accompaniment in the Bach-Gounod *Ave Maria* that 'was in the jerky rhythm of ragtime, rather than a smooth legato line such as Bach wrote it'. But it all went to make a Tetrazzini concert 'with encores, applause, and flowers galore'.

Touring with Titta Ruffo

Tetrazzini then left New York on a concert tour managed by 'Doc' Leahy and with Titta Ruffo (often called the 'Caruso of the baritones') who was six years younger than her. He had a powerful voice and during the First World War that was to break out later that year he served throughout in the Italian Army. When peace came he would often declare that he had been made a sergeant because his voice could be heard the whole length of a parade ground by three battalions.

The tour opened on 21 January 1914 at the Music Hall, Cincinnati with Yves Nat as the pianist and the couple were rapturously received by a full house. Then two days later 'Tet' and 'Tit', as they had been dubbed by the press, sang at the Armory in Minneapolis, where Melba and Kubelik had just given a concert. According to the *Minneapolis Journal*,[9] the audience heard this time 'two typical Italian artists who threw themselves with enthusiasm into their task of producing sweet song – a startling contrast to the blasé perfection of the preceding couple'.

Tetrazzini opened with *Caro nome*. 'Her attack, her staccati, her messa di voce were as incomparable as ever, while her runs in rising chromatics seemed an improvement upon those of her earlier appearances'. There followed Francesco Veracini's *La Pastorella*, the Venzano waltz – 'sung at breakneck speed with occasional slowing down only in time-honored places and ending in a triumphant E in altissimo'. Here she had to give two extras, Cowen's *The Swallows* and *Home, Sweet Home*, the latter being put over 'with fewer frills by far than Patti used to apply'. Her last solo was the *Charmant oiseau* aria from David's *La Perle du Brésil* with flute obligato sung with 'great brilliancy and many amusing details'.

The other local paper, the *Minneapolis News* was less enthusiastic. 'The Melba-Kubelik entertainment of last week was repeated in the same Armory with a change of cast.' It was 'a retrogression to the frontier days of a generation ago when the vocal exhibitions of a Patti used to fill the big roller skating rinks with a motley throng of the curious'.

On 28 January 1914 'Tet' and 'Tit' were singing in Toronto, and on the 30th in Buffalo.

On 8 February, the *San Francisco Examiner* published a report from Philadelphia headed TETRAZZINI HAS SONG OF WOE, CAMPANINI IS HER NEMESIS. A furious 'Doc' Leahy had the previous day accused Cleofonte Campanini of having conspired to present *Tosca* in the Opera House at Philadelphia with Caruso and Geraldine Farrar heading an all-star cast on the same night that Tetrazzini was singing at the Academy of Music, in order to diminish her audience.

Leahy told the press:

> Last fall he begged me to influence her to join the Chicago Opera Company. I cabled to Tetrazzini who was in London. She refused. She has no desire to come again under his management. He made life disagreeable for her before. He never allowed her any dress rehearsals and once he left out the latter half of the opera *Crispino* to annoy her. He has also meddled in her private affairs and made himself obnoxious. The people of Chicago and San Francisco are clamoring to hear Tetrazzini, and Campanini is in an awkward position because he cannot get her. He must blame himself for he was always picking on her and making her do things against her contract.

Leahy also suspected Campanini of inspiring the *Toledo Blade* newspaper article attributing to Tetrazzini many 'whims and caprices'. The San Francisco impresario had complained indignantly: 'Think of that! Why Tetrazzini has sung when she has had toothache, ulcerated jaws and other ailments and she has never whimpered even when she should have been in bed.'

The presence of such formidable opposition, however, had no effect on Tetrazzini's concert two days later. In fact there was such a demand for tickets that an extra three rows of seats were installed on the platform usually occupied by the orchestra. *Musical America* wrote that Tetrazzini was 'in superb voice' and added: 'Ever since her first appearance in Philadelphia when she sang in opera during the Hammerstein season, she has been an immense favorite in the Quaker City.'

On 13 February 1914 'Tet' and 'Tit' sang to a capacity audience of 2,700 in Milwaukee's Auditorium. Then on the 15th of that month they packed the Auditorium in Chicago, and George Bazelli pointed out at a dinner party afterwards that the audience was the biggest it had ever held, overflowing onto the stage where some 500 were seated and into the orchestra pit.

After this engagement Titta Ruffo left for Philadelphia to sing with Melba in *Rigoletto* on 18 February, followed by *Don Giovanni* on the 21st and *Hamlet* on the 28th; then he toured with the Chicago Opera Company. Raffaelo Diaz now sang with Tetrazzini on her tour.

Delighted with the enormous success of the concert in Campanini's stronghold, 'Doc' Leahy next day left Chicago with Tetrazzini who, as an expression of disapproval of any place connected with her brother-in-law, cancelled the booking for her to sing at the Orchestra Hall there on 26 August. Before departure, Leahy accused him as general manager of the Chicago Opera Company of planning in revenge to send an opera troupe, reduced in numbers, of third-rate singers to Californian theatres. Leahy vigorously objected to having San Francisco lowered operatically to the level of a 'tank town'.

Bernard Ulrich on behalf of the Chicago Grand Opera Company immediately refuted this. 'Denials of any intentions of diminishing the artistic standards of the Chicago company were instant, voluminous and credible, but the incident did not lower the temperamental temperature of Leahy', stated the *San Francisco Chronicle*.

Tetrazzini sang next in Des Moines, Dallas, and then for L. E. Behymer in the Auditorium, Los Angeles. On 2 March *Musical America* contained a report from its correspondent there that she had been asked to comment on Cleofonte Campanini's alleged statements that he had not engaged her to sing with the Chicago Opera Company because her voice was breaking, that she was losing her power over the public, and that in any case Melba was the world's greatest coloratura soprano.

Tetrazzini had flown into a temper, exclaiming: 'For many months I have borne this persecution. I have stood it rather than break with my sister, his wife.' She showed the journalist a telegram from Campanini sent to her in Lugano urging her to accept an engagement for 25 performances. She had not replied and he had then made the statements mentioned. 'When we arrive in San Francisco', she went on, 'I will collect all my evidence which will include the offers of the Chicago Opera Company to me and the derogatory things said about me. I may bring suits in every city where these things have been said and the public will soon learn the truth of the matter.' She would sue for $150,000 in damages.

On the way from Los Angeles to San Francisco, Tetrazzini narrowly escaped injury or even death, when the front part of the train was derailed. She told the reporters:[10]

> I am a fatalist, but I listen to what you call premonitions. The morning of the wreck I had an opportunity to ride in the first section of the train but something told me not to do it – and I refused at the last moment and stayed in the second section. I felt something might happen.

She thought the amulet an Indian Chief had given her when she visited the Grand Canyon might have protected her.

'The gracious embonpoint that we knew of old has given place to an equally gracious but divinely sylph-vision', enthused one reporter. It had been achieved by the Chief teaching her a 'Hopi Indian' war dance which she performed regularly not forgetting the war whoop 'and the effect had been magical'.[11]

On Thursday evening 5 March, Tetrazzini gave a concert at the Tivoli in San Francisco despite a severe cold that had suddenly developed. Next day Anne Cora Winchell wrote in the *Chronicle* that nevertheless in her final number, the *Mignon* polacca, she had gathered all her forces with such determination that 'much of the delivery was little more than clouded while her trills were absolutely flexible and perfectly pitched'.

The day before singing in Canton, Ohio, on 13 April, Tetrazzini went with Bazelli to a little movie theatre which was crowded. 'Suddenly an incandescent bulb on the wall exploded', went the account in the *Cleveland Leader*,

> and the hot wire fired the thin drapery curtains. As the flames shot towards the ceiling a panic started. Women and children rushed towards the exits. Tetrazzini stood up and urged the people to remain quiet. No one paid any attention so, going down the center aisle towards the orchestra pit, she began one of her concert selections.
>
> It had an immediate effect. The frightened people stopped their mad rush and turned to listen. Ushers quickly extinguished the flames and she returned to her seat and saw the rest of the show without anyone in the house having recognised her. 'It was nothing', she said when interviewed after the show. 'I was as much frightened as any of them.'

The tour ended on 8 May at the National in Washington – and soon after, having thus travelled over some 30,000 miles, Tetrazzini sailed for Europe with Bazelli. Nothing had come of her threats of legal action against Cleofonte Campanini. He had maintained a discreet silence.

When on 4 June Tetrazzini sang at the Royal Albert Hall, the *Musical Times*[12] reported that she appeared as the 'most distinguished of a "star" company' and by opening with Verdi's *Ah, fors' è lui* she gave an instant reminder of her first triumphs in England and showed that her technique was 'as facile and marvellous as ever'. Then on the 23rd of the month she sang there again with the London Symphony Orchestra with Arthur Nikisch conducting. Unlike the first occasion which was packed, this was poorly attended. According to *Musical America*, she seemed 'not one whit cast down by the size of the audience'. She indulged in her usual pranks and varied them 'by mounting to the conductor's desk as a more conspicuous and commanding position from which to respond to the plaudits of her admirers'.

This journal was to attack Melba in its issue of 29 October for the hackneyed contents of her programme and now, four months earlier on 26 June, it castigates Tetrazzini in similar terms:

> But even for Londoners such extravagances will not always serve as a sauce with which to dish up tasteless and insipid coloratura fare that merely tickles the artistic palate and leaves the mind craving for more solid and satisfying sustenance. Dazzling vocal technique is not likely to make a lasting impression upon audiences that have become accustomed to the soul inspiring methods of a Gerhardt and a Culp, for whom the art of singing means something more than a mere vehicle for the exploitation of dazzling head-tones and phenomenal breathing achievements.

John Pitts Sanborn's Appraisement

The Great War of 1914–18 ended Luisa Tetrazzini's career on the stages of the world's opera houses. Henry C. Lahee in his *Grand Opera Singers of Today* published late in 1912 included some admirable assessments of her talents that John Pitts Sanborn had contributed during the previous nine months to the *Globe*.

> The true history of a diva, could it ever be written, would make curious and engrossing reading... We doubt whether any of the glorious line is more mysterious than Mme Tetrazzini. An oyster she is and will probably remain so. Whether she is just an imbecile singing by the grace of God alone or what she is, those that write most about her are not in a position to know positively for she is an Italian and operatic Italians, with rare exceptions, are about as available for purposes of psychological observation as a skylark singing in high heaven. It has been necessary to study her art across the footlights.
> Luisa Tetrazzini has been quoted as saying that she taught herself to sing. Her voice and her trill she had from God as she listened to her oldest sister, Eva. A few months of repertory completed her preliminary studies. Such training

is a contrast to the seven laborious years of the great tradition, and might account for the crudities in her singing, most evident the first night she sang here, and which have been harped on ever since, but does it account for her perfect attack, her wonderful control of breath, her clean execution of ornaments, her exquisite portamento, her proficiencies in sustained singing, especially her ability to phrase with the roundness and incomparable grace of the pure old Italian style? Who shall ever know this?

But certain it is when she first sang at the Manhattan she was chiefly remarkable for her extraordinary upper octave. In it the tones were perfectly produced, strong, pure, dazzling in their flame-like play of color. When she sang a thing like the Carnival of Venice variations, her staccati, her chromatic runs, her echo effects, her swelling and diminishing of a tone, the ravishing curve of her portamento showed a vocal virtuoso in that exalted region without a peer. The feats of Sembrich and Melba paled in comparison. But those inexplicable crudities and inequalities! A woman who in *La Traviata* had just sung *Ah! fors' è lui* surpassingly well could declaim *Dite alla giovine* in a choked, metallic parlando that would not be tolerated in any respectable vocal studio. Some of the sounds she emitted in the lower portion of her voice were like nothing but the clicks of an old fashioned talking machine before those devices had been perfected. However, Tetrazzini never sang here so badly as that first night. When she returned the next season, the crudities had largely disappeared, and her medium register, previously deficient, she had recovered or developed.

Sanborn goes on to say that her 'return to vocal civilization' was thanks to singing in London and New York under the guidance of Cleofonte Campanini and in competition with such singers as Melba and Sembrich. But her 'apotheosis' had come in the spring of 1912 when, after a year's absence, she had returned to the United States to tour in concert:

Then the voice was almost perfectly equalized, a glorious organ from top to bottom. Even in the lower register, she was ready with a firm, rich tone as in *Voi che sapete*. She not only sang great florid arias with perfect command of voice, technique and style; she sang Aida's *Ritorna vincitor* as scarcely a dramatic soprano has sung it here; she sang Solveig's song from *Peer Gynt* like a true Lieder singer and the page's song from *Figaro* she sang with an adorable and enchanting display of great soprano singing in every style, and the most wonderful display of sheer vocal virtuosity New York can have heard since the prime of Adelina Patti.

However, Sanborn was forced to conclude from some things that Tetrazzini had done during her engagement at the Metropolitan at the end of December 1911 and the start of January 1912 that there were still times when, affected by nervousness or indisposition, Tetrazzini had allowed some of the old crudities to 'crop out' in her singing. By seizing on such moments and ruthlessly applying the microscope one could concoct 'a veritable Jeremiad about her'. Yet nine times out of ten, her singing was 'not only flawless but so transporting in its warmth and beauty that you forgot the art of it in sheer delight'. Her *Voi che sapete* was the finest piece of Mozart singing he had ever heard, and he had heard both Melba and Sembrich sing the same piece. Victor Maurel had once remarked to him that Tetrazzini in *Crispino e la Comare* had impressed him even more in some of the andantes than in her great coloratura flights.

Tetrazzini was, in Sanborn's opinion, one of the last possessors of a perfect trill – 'two golden hammers beating a faultless interval'. Only Sembrich and Melba, in his day, had been worthy to be compared with her as sopranos and in some respects she was a greater singer than Sembrich, and in all, save sheer voice, a greater one than Melba.

18 Exit Bazelli – Enter Tatò

From the outbreak of hostilities in 1914 until the Armistice Tetrazzini lived in Italy. When Rumania declared war against Germany and Austria on 27 August 1916, Bazelli left her and went back to his homeland. They were never to meet again for in 1920 he settled in Craiova, the town of his birth where with his sister Eugenia Bazelli, a pianist and singing teacher, he presided over a literary salon and died there in 1953.[1]

The Gramophone Company's musical director, Fred Gaisberg, had become the diva's close friend. Short, with an expressive face, whimsical and very entertaining, he had eyes that radiated kindliness from behind his spectacles. During the war he worked in Italy supervising the construction of a pressing and matrix-making plant for his employers, and Luisa, always hospitable, entertained him regularly in her various homes. She lived in the grand manner in her villa on the Via Gaeta in Rome. It had furniture inlaid with jade and mother-of-pearl, bright silk hangings on the walls, whilst in the bathroom the Spanish shawls she had worn as Rosina were discreetly draped over the lavatory pan. Her guests at dinner ate off solid gold and drank out of the most expensive crystal, and the lace curtain covering the rear window of her limousine had woven into it at intervals a design representing her features.

Wartime Activities

When, with the object of promoting Anglo-Franco-Italian amity, the bands of the Coldstream Guards and the Garde Républicaine, under the command of Major Mackenzie Rogan, visited Rome and Milan, Tetrazzini, with Gaisberg's assistance, held lavish receptions at her own expense for the two hundred and more instrumentalists.[2]

After Trieste was taken by Italian troops late in October 1918, Tetrazzini arranged a charity concert on a grand scale and sang supported by Titta Ruffo and with Mancinelli conducting.[3] Then during the Peace Conference in Paris she took part in another concert to which she invited President Wilson though he had offended her by saying that he preferred the Chinese to the Italians. Mrs Wilson came instead.[4]

In July 1919 Luisa was awarded a gold medal with a Diploma of Honour of the Italian Red Cross in recognition of her participation in numerous charity concerts for the benefit of disabled and wounded soldiers. Later the American Red Cross also gave her a medal for her services to the wounded soldiers of the Walter Reed Hospital.

The summer of 1919 was spent by Tetrazzini at her villa Il Paradiso in Lugano preparing to tour the United States giving concerts. When the *Colonia Svizzera* of San Francisco published a report that she had lost her voice and could never sing in public again, she was furious and accused those promoting her rivals of plotting against her. Then, to prove how baseless these rumours were, she sang at a concert held in the Teatro Apollo at the beginning of July in aid of the Ospedale Italiano, when she proved beyond doubt that she was still a great coloratura. The critic Béha wrote in the *Corriere della Sera* that he was at a loss for words to describe adequately the magnificence of her acrobatic voice, able to manage limitless runs, trills and turns.[5]

For the coming tour, Tetrazzini engaged as her accompanist Pietro Cimara, an excellent pianist who had played for the now Dowager Queen Margherita several times, and he and his wife stayed at Il Paradiso while the programmes were chosen and rehearsed.[6] Before leaving, Tetrazzini held a soirée on 13 September in the garden of her villa when among those invited and who sang were the local Concordia choir.[7]

Tatò Passes the Test

With Bazelli gone, Tetrazzini needed a capable manager she could trust. She found him in an unconventional manner. One day in Rome, she noticed that a film she had long wanted to see was being shown in a small movie house. As it was the last night of its run she ordered a taxi and, still adorned with the masses of jewellery she had worn at a reception earlier that day, off she went. When she arrived at her destination, the burly driver was horrified that she intended to enter a cinema in a locality notorious for crime and expressed his concern. She was touched by this and felt by the look of him that he was honest, so acting on a sudden impulse she started taking off her jewellery and handing it to him. He was to take care of it and to collect her when the film had finished. He did so, and satisfied that he could be trusted, she engaged the 29 year old Roman Umberto Tatò as her chauffeur and bought him an Isotta car.

Soon he became her highly paid manager as well and travelled everywhere with her.

Before embarking on her first post-war tours, Tetrazzini went to Paris where she gave a concert in aid of the Red Cross which raised £17,600 – in those days a huge sum. The *Excelsior* wrote:

> The Opera is full; all Paris is there. Here in the box of the Queen of Rumania are Marshal Foch and Admiral Fournier, and in adjacent boxes may be seen Madame Raymond Poincaré and Mrs Wilson. Tetrazzini is accustomed to sing before Queens. If ever one possessed the gift of 'bel canto' it is surely she. It is indeed a human voice that trills as no nightingale ever could.

In London, Tetrazzini, Tatò and the others in her entourage stayed at the Savoy. Britain's leading impresario Lionel Powell, doubting her box appeal after five years of war, had refused to pay her the £400 a concert she demanded through her then agent, Felix Corbett. However, Thomas Quinlan was more adventurous and engaged her on those terms for some of his Subscription Concerts. These opened with a concert on Saturday afternoon, 20 September at the Royal Albert Hall and was supported by the French violinist Madame Renée Chemet and Frank Mullings, the popular tenor, when it was announced that she would be singing *Ah, fors' è lui* and the Mad Scene from Ambroise Thomas's *Amleto*.

The extensive prior publicity was masterminded by Fred Gaisberg. Invitations to join those welcoming her on arrival at Victoria Station were sent to all the music critics, enclosing a special pass for admission to the platform.

> Many notabilities, English and Italian, will be there', ran the covering letter, 'also Major Mackenzie Rogan with the band of the Coldstream Guards.... The band will play at the Savoy Hotel, and if you are able to be present at the Savoy also, an informal reception will be held there at which we shall be very pleased to see you.[9]

In an entertaining article in the *Evening Standard* of 18 September 1919, Ernest Newman, least susceptible of critics to the *prima donna* fetish, told how he had been invited and had decided not to attend.

Actually, this Press reception and others were popular with journalists thanks to Luisa's personal charm. At her request Fred Gaisberg always acted as interpreter, but this was only so that Luisa could lapse into Italian and pretend not to understand when questions were asked about her private life, which he would then skilfully avoid answering. No interview ended without her having made at least one observation that would make the front pages of newspapers, such as, 'I would not diet. If I diet, my face sag.' And on another occasion: 'I am proud that I am wealthy. If you see me wearing jewels, no matter how many, you can know that they are

real. I have never worn artificial jewellery.' This was exactly the same way
such interviews had been conducted when Bazelli was with her.

The stock question from reporters was 'What do you think of London?'
Gaisberg wrote in his reminiscences:

> They could have answered it better themselves since the diva lived hermetically
> sealed for the duration of each visit in her private suite at the Savoy. Her only
> outdoor experience was to and from the Albert Hall in a closed conveyance.[10]

This is not entirely correct as he did take her on a visit to his company's
factory at Hayes.

The women reporters would ask Luisa's views on English cooking.
Gaisberg thought they were wasting their time as she remained faithful to
her Italian dishes. He stressed that she enjoyed lending herself to occasions
of a kind that had publicity value and that her temperament was just the
right one to ensure success. The *Musical Times*[11] was to make a similar
comment: 'No public performer makes more astute use of the daily press
than Madame, by means of interviews and photographs.'

The Albert Hall concert proved enormously successful with over 10,000
people in attendance. It was widely reported in America. The London
correspondent of the *Christian Science Monitor* wrote that Tetrazzini had
proved her voice retained 'its old beauty, agility and liquidity'.[12]

Death of Patti

Six days later on 27 September, Tetrazzini was in Leeds to give a recital
in its Town Hall. When the concert was over a young journalist burst into
her dressing-room and gave her the news that Adelina Patti had died at
Craig-y-Nos in South Wales. According to her account in *My Life of Song*,
Luisa had felt uneasy all day with a strong foreboding of an impending
loss and after hearing of the death 'wept for three days'.

Tetrazzini's recording contract was jointly with the Gramophone Company in England and the Victor Talking Company in the United States
and had just expired, so the opportunity was taken while she was in
London for a new one to be prepared and signed for another three years
and on the same terms as previously.[13] This, as we shall learn shortly, was
to become the subject of a dispute as a result of Umberto Tatò's taking
an increasingly active role in the conduct of her business affairs.

Upset to find so many English friends had died during the war, Luisa,
on All Souls Day, November 2 and soon after, visited their graves in and
out of London, laying white chrysanthemums on them. Deeply religious,
she arranged for a Mass for the souls of all her deceased friends to be
said at Lugano on that day, when it was also her custom to pray for them

in the nearest Catholic church wherever she might be staying. Then in the afternoon the sentimental soprano would seek out the local cemetery, no matter of what denomination and place on neglected graves some of the flowers brought with her, and do as much tidying up and cleaning of headstones as possible until dusk. She was to write in *My Life of Song*: 'Perhaps one day one of my friends will show kindly attention to the burial place of Tetrazzini.'[14]

On 11 November, Fred Gaisberg took Luisa by car through streets hung with banners and streamers to the Gramophone Company's studios and works at Hayes in Middlesex. Here she sang to the factory girls in the canteen, *Somewhere a Voice Is Calling*, in English with Pietro Cimara at the piano, followed by his own *Canto di Primavera*. She was then taken to the recording room where she found George Formby Senior, the Lancashire comedian, making what proved to be his last recording, and was photographed with him. Then she lunched with the management and was presented with a special shell-case which the company had manufactured for the Italian War Office.[15]

Tetrazzini had arrived in London to find it in the throes of an industrial strike. The trains were at a standstill so the fourteen trunks brought with her had to be loaded onto a motor lorry and taken to Liverpool where they were transferred to the *Mauretania*. Umberto Tatò chartered the Handley Page airship piloted by Lieutenant Hobbs of the Royal Flying Corps which conveyed her, dog Joy, and entourage to that city where she gave a concert to a capacity audience. Next morning she rushed to the docks only to find that the liner's departure would be delayed for a week owing to scarcity of coal. All passengers were compelled to remain on board as the actual date and time of departure was uncertain.

Arriving later than expected in New York on 25 November, without repairing to her hotel, Tetrazzini hurried to Boston with her accompanist, Pietro Cimara, and tour manager, Jules A. Daiber, to give her opening concert with two young American artists, lyric tenor Warren Proctor and violinist Mayo Wadler on the 27th. Immediately following this, she returned to New York where three afternoons later she performed at the Hippodrome, a vast barn-like structure at 43rd Street and 6th Avenue, known as the 'Pachyderm of the Amusement World'. There was an audience of over 4,000 and though a considerable number of her listeners were stowed upon the stage, they did not wholly fill the rest of the house.

Richard Aldrich in his review next day in the *New York Times* wrote that all those present were

> primed for enthusiasm and let it loose on all occasions, principally, as was natural, after Tetrazzini's singing of the Mad Scene from *Hamlet* and Benedict's variations on the *Carnival of Venice*, the two florid numbers of her programme.

Caruso led the clapping from a box after the variations and threw a bunch of roses at her which she caught and clasped. Then she beckoned the king of tenors to come down and share the applause with her. They stood on the stage embracing each other, and it was some time before the concert could continue.[16]

This was the kind of music in which Tetrazzini was most at home. Aldrich found her distinctly not at home in an Italian version of Solveig's song by Grieg and only less so in two Italian songs by Mazzini and Cimara. Nevertheless, he considered that she had returned with her voice 'not only not impaired but even in some respects improved during her absence.' It seemed more powerful, though the power had been gained to a certain extent at the expense of its quality. It sounded somewhat harder in its brilliancy.

'The inferior quality of her lower tones, which, on her first appearance here, had a singular infantile quality, that many will remember, she had already succeeded in bettering before her departure.' In fact, this fault had now almost disappeared, and the whole range of her voice was more nearly equalized. That she was still not in perfect control of her vocal resonances was shown occasionally by loss of quality, 'a pinching effect' heard in certain tones and especially upon certain vowels. Upper tones were at their best 'clear and vibrant' and she retained 'that exceptional control of the *messa di voce*, the swelling and diminishing of a note long held that was remembered as one of her most admired effects.'

Tetrazzini's delivery of florid passages Aldrich regarded as not wholly flawless, but it had 'the brilliancy, celerity, the appearance of ease and spontaneity' that were enough to make a great effect in times when such things were scarce. She was able to impart to such music 'the entrain and sweep that are its only reasons for being'. Her supremacy in it could hardly be questioned.

What concerned Tetrazzini most was what critics wrote when comparing her with the new operatic sensation Galli-Curci. The majority thought her the greater artist. But Pierre V. R. Key in the *Cleveland News Leader* had certain reservations:

> The Tetrazzini voice has more intensity than the Galli-Curci (which makes it sound bigger) and it is a more brilliant instrument. Mme Galli-Curci could never give such a brilliant sweep of tone to parts of the Hamlet aria which Mme Tetrazzini gave the afternoon of her re-entry into our midst. . . . On the other hand, though her high tones are better than her younger rival's, Mme Tetrazzini no longer caresses the ear with them as she once did. The bloom of those altitudinous notes has faded. Into their place a hardness has crept, a hardness that at times is a trifle wiry.
>
> Mme Galli-Curci's tones are like velvet. . . . And just now I seem to catch a more liquid-like flowing of voice in the Galli-Curci scales and other florid executions than in Mme Tetrazzini's coloratura work. Most of my critic col-

leagues disagree with me on this point. They seemed in their reviews to prefer the elder singer's roulades and vocal flourishes. . . . I'll concede that they are right in recognising an improvement in the singer's lower tones.

Cleofonte Campanini

Just as Tetrazzini was about to leave New York to begin her Pacific Coast concert tour, the news came that Cleofonte Campanini was critically ill with pneumonia. On reaching Chicago on 1 December, Luisa left the train and, rushing to the hospital, was reconciled with her dying brother-in-law from whom in 1913 she had become estranged. Then she travelled on to San Francisco, which she reached on the 5th and went to stay at the Fairmont Hotel where she had an emotional reunion with 'Doc' Leahy. *The Spectator*[17] commenting on their long friendship, wrote: 'It is claimed by her intimates that there is no being whom Luisa Tetrazzini is more fond of, upon whose sagacity she relies more on than William H. Leahy. She calls him "Daddy".'

On Sunday afternoon 7 December 1919 Luisa sang in the huge Exposition Auditorium in the Civic Center, a cold austere place with poor acoustics which the superb carrying power of her voice easily overcame.[18] Immediately the date for her concert had been announced queues had formed at the box office and all seats were swiftly sold. She made an impressive entrance from the top of winding stairs backstage and paused before descending as the audience gave her a standing ovation. Those who had not seen her since the last visit would have been startled by the weight put on in the intervening years. She wore her much talked about gown patterned with the image of a peacock, the head of which was on her shoulder, the neck and body across her broad bosom, while the exquisitely coloured tail stretched across her solid stern.

Obviously moved by the reception, Luisa made her way hesitantly to stage level, dabbing her eyes, then with arms outstretched she moved towards the footlights. Her knees seemed to give way and she subsided onto the stage with the peacock's tail beneath her. Her head drooped and she sobbed. Now women in the audience began to weep too. After a while Luisa arose with difficulty, waited for calm to return in the auditorium, then signalled for the accompaniment to begin. But she was still in a highly excitable state and had sung scarcely more than a few notes when she again broke down. At this there was general pandemonium, then when the audience had settled down and she had recovered Cimara started playing once more and Luisa embarked on her first aria, *Caro nome*. Ever since her début at the Tivoli in *Rigoletto*, she had always opened her concerts in San Francisco with this.

At the end Leahy's manager, Frank W. Healy, announced that as so many had been unable to get seats, Tetrazzini would give a second concert on the evening of Tuesday 16 December. This was advertised as an 'At Home' recital, and Ray C. B. Brown wrote in the *Chronicle* next day that no other phrase so aptly described the atmosphere of genial welcome that permeated the auditorium, expressed itself in repeated applause and culminated in a wave of enthusiasm that swept hundreds forward to the platform to hear more intimately her final encore, *Home, Sweet Home.*

In an interview with Tetrazzini, Brown asked what was the greatest moment in her life to which she gave the expected reply: 'When I sang in the streets of San Francisco.' He returned: 'There must have been other moments' – and she responded diplomatically that it was when General Pershing held in her honour a military review in an aviation field, when some 30,000 people were estimated to have been present. The American flag passed before her in review. She saluted it.

> On this occasion I did not sing but for the first time in my life I flew through the air. General Pershing said to me: 'I do not speak Italian. I speak a language all the world understands. This is my language.' – and he kissed my hand.

Tetrazzini also told Brown that she would in future sing only in concert as opera was too much of a strain.

Aerial Publicity

On 9 and 13 December Tetrazzini gave two concerts in Los Angeles. Then she had an adventure. On the 16th at Tanforan Race Track there took place an exhibition of acrobatic feats by the young aviator Ormer Locklear, who had gained fame through being the first to change planes in the air and to walk out on the wings of his machine in flight. The *San Francisco Examiner* were the sponsors, and they offered a free trip in Locklear's plane to everyone who gave $10 to their Christmas charity fund.

On the day the grandstand was packed with paying spectators whilst others watched for free from the nearby slopes.

Dressed as Father Christmas, Locklear danced along the wings and performed breathtaking stunts. Tetrazzini, who was willing to take on most things that would keep her in the public eye, volunteered to go aloft. 'I have gone as high with my voice as I can hope to go, so now I want to go higher', she quipped and, wrapped up in a voluminous overcoat, climbed with Ormer's assistance into the cockpit at the rear of his two-winged Curtiss Jenny.

Always at pains to keep the ever-hungry Press well fed with titbits about herself, Tetrazzini provided them with a lively description of her flying adventure at a conference given later at the Fairmont Hotel. 'When first we mounted into the air, my heart missed a beat', the *Examiner* reported her as saying 'Oh, it was alarming when the propeller blew wind in my face. For *prima donnas* I can think of nothing more helpful in reaching high C than a trip in the sky!' But despite such expressions of enthusiasm, she herself never flew again.

On 19 December Cleofonte Campanini died and the news reached Tetrazzini when she was giving a concert at Oakland. She immediately hurried to Chicago to console her widowed sister Eva before resuming her tour at Portland on the 29th when some 4,000 people were packed into the auditorium overflowing onto the stage and with rows of extra chairs in the passageways. Then in January 1920 the tireless diva sang in seven cities; in February, eight; in March, ten.

Everywhere Tetrazzini continued to show herself adept at handling audiences. For example, following her concert to some 5,000 strong at the Coliseum in St Louis on 6 February, the *Globe Democrat* reported next day that a storm of applause rewarded her first offering, the Mad Scene from Thomas's *Amleto* and that after several recalls she came down from the stage and walked up the centre aisle blowing kisses from her gloved hands 'impartially to parquet, balcony and gallery'. The audience responded by 'standing on their seats, clapping and shouting "Bravo!".' Then, retracing her steps, she imprinted resounding smacks on several women.' The encore, *Somewhere a Voice Is Calling*, sent 'the cognoscenti into frenzied delight' when for its last note 'without any effort whatsoever she reached, intoned and held for twelve beats an opulent unforgettable E flat'.

In Buffalo, the owner of the hotel where the diva was staying was so eager to please her that when she commented on the smallness of her private sitting-room he immediately brought in carpenters and masons and, taking down partitions, made several moderate-sized rooms into one the size of a ballroom.[19]

During the tour Tetrazzini had written to Caruso and he replied on 5 February from the Hotel Knickerbocker in New York. It was a letter that she treasured and kept for the rest of her life. After her death Pietro Vernati, her second husband, took possession of the few things she had left, and later he sent a photocopy to EMI suggesting that the contents might be used for publicity purposes to stimulate sales of her records and increase the royalties he was receiving. Replying in Italian, Caruso wrote that he felt he must thank her at once for her letter dated the 2nd of that month. He thought of her as a kind of benevolent goddess and he hoped that her visit to America would be a long one

because we Italians need to show these people the difference between truly brilliant performances and humdrum ones. My wife has a special regard for you and took to you from the moment you appeared on the stage when you sang at the Hippodrome. She is constantly saying 'Tetrazzini is a really great artist and sings like a small bird that is making love'. My family has fallen captive under your spell, so do not forget to let me know when you reach New York so that we can spend an evening together.

They were able to do that the following month.

On Sunday 14 March Tetrazzini returned to the Hippodrome to give an afternoon concert. Next day's *New York Times* wrote that she was 'in fine spirits and voice as she gave us airs from *Semiramide* and *Mignon* and among her encores sang *Just as the Shadows Fall*'. In the evening she returned to hear her old friend Titta Ruffo, now demobilized from the Italian Army, give a recital.

Hollywood

The English journal *Musical Mirror* for 23 March 1920 bore a cartoon on its cover captioned THE GIRL OF THE GOLDEN WEST, and depicting Tetrazzini dressed as a cow-girl riding a bucking bronco and firing a pistol. This was a reference to a press report from America that she told an interviewer her great ambition was to be a film actress. She was 'just mad on Wm. S. Hart and his cowboy stunts'.

Tetrazzini's desire to start a second career in Hollywood persisted. More than two years later, the *Los Angeles Times* for 18 December 1922 published a report from London that she was studying 'the technique of Bill Hart and the knockabout comedians'. Music critics at Cardiff, Wales, searching for her after a concert found the diva in a motion-picture house. 'Wherever I go', she told them, 'I find time to see the pictures because I hope to go on the screen before I retire.'

On 28 March 1920 Luisa Tetrazzini sang with Caruso for the last time when they appeared with the baritone Riccardo Stracciari at an Italian Loan Rally at the Lexington Opera House, New York. On awakening in the morning, she found herself suffering from a cold which so affected her voice that by an hour before the concert she could barely whisper. Remembering that Enrico kept himself well stocked with remedies for disorders of the vocal chords she tore in a taxi to his suite at the Knicker-bocker Hotel. Falling into his arms, she indicated in dumb show what was wrong with her. He told her not to worry as he had a sovereign remedy that would restore her voice. It was a mixture of ether and iodoform, he explained, leading her into the bathroom.

Dorothy Caruso, the tenor's wife, was to write later:

I can still see Tetrazzini balancing on the rim of the tub in full evening dress, while Enrico, wearing his gold-rimmed spectacles, hung over her like an anxious owl. As he sprayed, she had to pant quickly and not stop for a moment or the ether would have gone down into her lungs and anaesthetised her.[20]

Fortunately nothing went wrong, and such was Luisa's confidence in Enrico that she burst into full song at the first attempt – and went on to sell Italian Government bonds for a huge sum at the Rally, thanks to her singing and his.

On the first Sunday afternoon in April, Tetrazzini sang to a large audience at a concert in Boston Opera House assisted by James Goddard, bass, and Count Cimara at the piano. The *Musical America*'s critic reported in its issue of the 9th:

> Not only were her hearers most enthusiastic in their applause, but they apparently enjoyed hugely the silly actions of the diva, actions which at times threatened to turn the concert into a vaudeville performance. Of her singing let it be said that her middle and lower registers are the same as of yore, with also the same whiteness of tone. But the altitudinous heights are not now reached without effort, and even after they are attained the tone is of very uncertain flow.

The trouble was that Tetrazzini, now nearly 49, was overworking as though she were half that age, and within a few days the consequences were to involve her in an unfortunate dispute.

19 Conflict over Contracts

Opera stars have often refused to attend rehearsals. Adelina Patti insisted on a clause being inserted in her contract giving her the right not to attend any, and she would send her personal maid to stand in for her instead. As a result she often did not meet the other singers performing in the same opera till the first night.

Tetrazzini had a similar aversion to rehearsals and refused to attend any held on the day of a performance. She had been engaged to sing in Rossini's *Stabat Mater* on the afternoon of 11 April 1920 at the closing concert of the Oratorio Society's Music Festival in the 71st Regiment Armory in New York. It was not stipulated in the contract that she must attend the rehearsals, but it was customary that if requests were made for attendance they should be met. On the other hand it was regarded as admissible for an artist of renown to send to the conductor music with tempi marked in lieu of a rehearsal. Tetrazzini's concert manager, Jules Daiber, wrote to her while she was on tour asking her to be at rehearsals with Walter Damrosch and the Symphony Orchestra of New York at 10 am on the Saturday before the performance. According to Luisa, she arrived at the Hotel Knickerbocker in New York at midnight on the Friday after a long and fatiguing journey from Grand Rapids, Michigan. She was insufficiently rested to attend rehearsals next morning so she sent along her accompanist, Pietro Cimara, instead.

Walter Damrosch's version of what happened as reported in the press[1] was:

> Madame Tetrazzini showed herself quite indifferent to the dignity of the Oratorio Society's Music Festival. It may be all right when one is barnstorming to shun rehearsals. But the best music is a series of fine adjustments of voices and instruments and conditions. I have not heard Madame Tetrazzini sing for 15 years – that was when she was with Oscar Hammerstein at the Manhattan Opera House. It was necessary that she and the orchestra became acquainted. I wished only twenty minutes from her – a matching of the voice with some of the instruments, a running of a few cadenzas with the oboe accompaniment – what every prima donna does.

I had called a rehearsal of Madame Tetrazzini for Wednesday. She let me know that she would not attend because she had a concert engagement. This was all right. Although I had two concerts that day I changed the call to Saturday morning. I had every right to expect her to be at the Armory. I know that her manager had notified her to be there at ten. But as she was not we proceeded with the dress rehearsals of other artists. The others finished but there was no sight or sound of her. Had she sent a telegram or a note or telephoned giving a reason for absence I would have given the message due consideration. But she did nothing of the kind. When she had kept us waiting three-quarters of an hour, a little frightened man with thick gray hair carrying several sheets of music beneath his right arm, hurried down the aisle.

The new arrival was Cimara who bowed to the towering conductor and quavered: 'Madame Tetrazzini cannot come to the rehearsal.'

'Is she ill?' Damrosch demanded.

'No, Signor. She is quite well. But she cannot come to the rehearsal.'

'But we must rehearse', Damrosch insisted.

'She cannot come. She is not dressed.'

'Tell her to put on a wrapper and fur coat, and come to the rehearsal.'

'She asked me to show you her music with the tempi marked.' Cimara held out the sheets of music. 'This is the way Madame sings these selections.'

Damrosch stared down at him, then he looked at his watch. 'Tell Madame Tetrazzini that I will give her until twelve o'clock to come to this rehearsal.'

Cimara bowed and hurried away.

Walter Damrosch told the press that there was no further word from Tetrazzini by twelve o'clock, so they contacted Ernestine Schumann Heink through her manager and she obligingly consented to take the other's place.

'Did Madame Schumann Heink rehearse?' enquired a reporter.

'Assuredly she did. No excuses. No airs. Some of my artists have had not one but three rehearsals for a concert. They have been more than willing. They have been anxious to rehearse. Prima donnas' whims are a thing of the past.'

Schumann Heink's programme consisted of an air from Mozart's *Titus* and a group of songs while the chorus repeated Rachmaninoff's *Laud ye the Name of the Lord* instead of the announced selection from Rossini's *Stabat Mater*.

A reporter quoted 'a little awed rotund man' connected with the management of the New York Symphony Society as saying in a hushed tone, 'Nobody has done this to Mr Damrosch before and no one will again.'

According to Tetrazzini, it was six minutes to twelve when Cimara reappeared at the Hotel Knickerbocker with Damrosch's ultimatum. She dressed immediately, but by the time she reached the rehearsal Schumann Heink had been engaged in her place. Furious at being so treated, Tetrazzini returned to her suite where reporters soon flocked to ask what she now intended to do.

'I love my public', she declared.

> My dear public. I would never disappoint. So what I do when the management of the Oratorio Society telephone to me and say your engagement is cancelled? I stay still in this hotel – or do I take the train to dear Cincinnati where I am to sing on Wednesday and where I am to be entertained the day before? No! I say I will stay and go to the concert. If Mr Damrosch gets his whim I will rise in a box and sing without rehearsal. I go. I send someone to buy the tickets.

Tetrazzini told the press that she took with her to the concert her lawyer Mr Spellman and his wife as well as the Cimaras.

> I met in the lobby many persons I know. I shook hands with them. I am happy. I enjoy the concert. It is very good. I take my friends to dinner here. I have a pleasant afternoon. And I sue the Oratorio Society for $4,000 because I have not been allowed to sing at the concert.

Benjamin Franklin Spellman explained that his client's fee just for *appearing* at a concert was $4,000. This she had done. Had she actually given the concert she would have received a guaranteed $8,000.

> This is a fight for principles. I take the cases of music artists against managers because I am for the freedom of the artist. I am opposed to the Czar-like domination of the director who roars 'Come here' or 'Go there' at his will. Tetrazzini's contract did not require her to attend a rehearsal. She would gladly have done so were it not for the fact that she had just returned to New York after a 24 hours long railroad journey. She had a right to believe that the orchestra was capable of merely accompanying her in her roles without a previous rehearsal, and the position of the Oratorio Society became inexcusable after she sent her accompanist who is a fully fledged conductor to point out to the conductor of the orchestra the various phases of the accompaniment.

The day before the concert, Luisa's widowed sister Eva had arrived bringing with her the body of her husband which she was taking to Parma, his former home, for burial.[2]. She also stayed at the Knickerbocker before sailing on 13 April. Nine days earlier, Spellman filed a suit against the Oratorio Society. The matter was settled out of court in her favour.

Continuing on her tour, Tetrazzini sang at Cincinnati, Galesburg, Springfield, Providence, Rhode Island, and in a Festival at Newark, New Jersey. In May, New York heard her again at the Hippodrome before she achieved a grand total of 45 concerts, with engagements at the Festivals in Spartanburg, South Carolina, and Macon, Georgia. She then sailed from New York on the *Presidente Wilson* after paying her income tax and posing with Collector Edwards before a battery of cameramen and telling him: 'I'm sorry my income tax isn't more because I love America.'[3]

That June when in Rome, Tetrazzini was invited to a private audience with the Queen of Italy who had helped her at the start of her career and who was now the Queen Mother Margherita.[4] She asked her visitor to sing again in Italian the Liebestod from *Tristan und Isolde* which Tetrazzini claimed to have sung to her in 1891. Afterwards the diva says she mentioned that she was planning to embark on her 'farewell' concert tour that autumn through the United States and the Queen wished her every success, but added that she must not think of finishing her career for many years, saying: 'I shall not allow you to do that yet. You must come and sing to me again.' Within three months, however, an event occurred making such an invitation unlikely: Tatò's wife sued him and Tetrazzini in the urban magistrate's court of Milan.

Tatò's Wife Sues

An account of the case and its outcome appeared in the *Corriere della Sera* for 23 September, 1920. It would have been interesting to read a transcript in full of the proceedings but it proved impossible to discover in Milan whether even one still existed. The reporter wrote:

> The exuberance of Signora Tetrazzini's temperament was such that her relationship with her man of trust gave rise to comments which eventually reached Tatò's wife Cornelia. Being young and attractive and having also a little boy, she did not wish to find herself abandoned after one year of marriage and following vain attempts to bring her husband back to her she decided to ask for a legal separation whilst intending it to become a civil action for adultery. Luisa Tetrazzini, being indisposed, did not appear at the hearing which was crowded with people from the singing world curious to learn details of her amorous adventures. . . . The defendant Tatò's denial that he had never had anything but a correctly professional relationship with Tetrazzini was disputed by the prosecuting counsel who produced evidence of suggestive behaviour in the hotel rooms of half Europe and in the secluded villas of Rome. A whole bizarre world flashed past in the depositions of secretaries, porters, gardeners and cooks . . . a way of life, real and imagined, so full of gossip and extravagance that a witness might define it as a branch of a madhouse.
>
> A note of high drama was not lacking . . . Tatò's wife with angry and tearful outbursts moved the public with her protests as a wife and mother. The lawyers representing her, Trespioli and Serembi, asked for the conviction of the accused, proposing 3 months imprisonment for Tetrazzini and 6 months for Umberto Tatò. Gallina for the defence had argued from the start that the case for the prosecution relied entirely on statements made in the past beyond the time limits required by the law, and therefore could not be accepted as evidence. Magistrate De Mita agreed and acquitted the defendants.

On her lawyers' advice Signora Tatò reluctantly did not appeal against this ruling and her husband went on acting as business manager to Tetrazzini.

Tetrazzini must have been greatly relieved at the outcome for she was due in London to sing at the Royal Albert Hall on 9 October before sailing for New York to start a concert tour there in early December. The pair arrived at the Savoy on 2 October and soon after Fred Gaisberg visited her to try and settle a dispute over her recording contract.[5] This had been from the start a joint one with the Gramophone Company and the Victor Talking Machine Company. As a result of the success of the last American tour, Tatò in January that year had approached Victor at Camden, New Jersey, with a view to Tetrazzini's making recordings with them there. He then learnt that this could be done only with the concurrence of the Gramophone Company.

As a result, in February 1920, Tetrazzini had written a long and angry letter to 'Dear Friend Gaisberg' in London. He must be aware of her esteem for the Gramophone Company and 'with what enthusiasm I go to visit them, and with what pleasure I renew my contract'. But they had deceived her. Profiting by the fact that she did not know English well, they had made her sign a contract 'against all laws'. This allegation of Tetrazzini's is unconvincing. Earlier on, before the war, she had also disputed the contract with Conried of the Metropolitan on the grounds that it was written in French which she had then alleged she could not understand. Always determined to have her own way, she would resort to such subterfuges to achieve it.

Tetrazzini claimed that she had been told verbally by the Gramophone Company: 'We will leave you with full liberty to sign or not to sign with the Victor Company.' Now the latter had informed her that she could not make a separate agreement with them. She had consulted 'two great American lawyers' who had advised her that the Gramophone Company's contract was a trick, as it was all for them and nothing for the artist.

> I cannot write in a letter, but I will explain verbally my indignation. I believe you are a friend and can give me honest advice. Signor Umberto Tatò, who does not know a word of English, directs my affairs and laments that people whom he thought infallible must so deceive an Artist who has never done them any harm.

On 10 February Fred Gaisberg had passed on the contents of this letter to Sydney Dixon, the Gramophone Company's joint managing director, and he was given the task of placating the disputatious diva. It seems that her hope had been that the success of her concert tour in the States would lead to Victor offering her a higher royalty for sales there than she was receiving in England from the Gramophone Company. But they had misgivings as to how long her renewed popularity would last and were relieved that the joint contract provided an excuse for not going into the matter with her and Tatò. Fred wrote back to Tetrazzini promising to do all he could to help and that a new agreement could be negotiated on her return to England in the autumn.

This was the position when, after Tetrazzini's arrival at the Savoy on 2 October 1920, Fred called on her to discuss the subject and reach agreement. Three days later he reported in a letter to Sydney Dixon that she had told him her coming tour of America, then being advertised as her 'farewell' to that country, would definitely be that. (There were in fact to be more 'farewells'.)

She intended nevertheless to do 'a lot of singing in England' as it was easy travelling and she was fond of the country. They could expect that she would 'bombard' this market for the next five years as she was healthy and her voice would hold out until old age.

Asked what he thought of Tetrazzini's endurance, Harry Higgins of Covent Garden had assured Fred Gaisberg that she would sing as long as that because she used her voice properly. Fred was to write in his *Music on Record*:[6] 'To his dying day, Higgins considered her the greatest prima donna of her time. He said nothing ever excelled the brilliance of her attack and the abandon of her cadenzas. Of this her gramophone records alone are proof enough.' This judgment Higgins must have taken care not to reveal to Melba!

A New Recording Contract

In his report to managing director Sydney Dixon, Fred went on to propose that Tetrazzini's joint contract should be replaced by a five year one with the Gramophone Company alone, guaranteeing her £500 per annum and expiring on 30 April 1926. Her sales so far for 1920 showed that she had earned about £700 in royalties, so they were well protected with a £500 minimum guarantee.

> Perhaps you will let me know what you think of this? Tetrazzini sends her love. . . . Since her stay here the newspapers have inundated her apartments with reporters and photographers. I have never seen such spontaneous publicity and it is my impression that her greatest genius is her publicity adaptability, and for this alone, we should try to extend the length of our contract with her.

Gaisberg ends his report to Dixon by saying that the Counting House had just sent him Melba's record sales for that year. They totalled £1,246, so her guarantee was more than covered. Her cheque for that half year would amount to £746.

A new contract was drawn up for Tetrazzini on the lines indicated and much to her satisfaction. However, having acquired the right to deal separately with the Victor Talking Company, she was to find, much to her annoyance, that they did not want her to make any new records with them after all.

A large contingent from the Gramophone Company attended Tetrazzini's one and only concert in England that year held at the Royal Albert Hall on the afternoon of Sunday 9 October. She was accompanied by Percy Kahn and assisted by violinist John Dunn and by Adela Verne who gave pianoforte solos.

Sydney Dixon in *The Voice* for November wrote that ten thousand people had crowded into the Royal Albert Hall to hear again 'their old favourite, while thousands were unable to gain admission'. Huge bouquets were showered on her and encore after encore demanded. Though she had given ten, even then the audience clamoured for more.

> Then those in the orchestra stalls broke through the barriers, swarmed down to the platform, and demanded autographs as well. Taking her final bow, she said: 'If you want me back, I will come again' and the audience roared 'Yes'.

In her dressing-room, Tetrazzini found Fred Gaisberg and his family together with Sydney Dixon and others waiting to congratulate her and she insisted on taking them all back to dine with her and Umberto Tatò in her suite at the Savoy. Dixon called her 'a delightful hostess' who was 'as full of fun and frolic as if she were still a schoolgirl'. She danced, sang *Swanee*, little lullabies, English comic songs, and related entertaining reminiscences of her experiences until far into the evening. She told them as they left: 'If you are happy, then I am happy too. We are all happy together. You love me, I love you.'

During this visit publishers offered to commission the writing of Tetrazzini's memoirs. Her English was extremely elementary and she had kept no diaries so she asked Fred Gaisberg if he would help her in return for part of the royalties. He agreed – and soon discovered that she was willing to show only the façade of her crowded life to the gaze of the world. He commented: 'As with most Latins, it was of vital importance for her to preserve face.'

20 The First 'Farewell' Concert Tour

Tetrazzini reached New York in early December 1920 and gave the opening concert of her 'farewell' tour on the 5th at the Hippodrome to an audience of over 7,000 which, according to John Pitts Sanborn in the *Globe and Commercial Advertiser*,[1] was 'rich in celebrities', with musical comedy star Lillian Russell leading the applause. Tetrazzini had as her assisting artists Francesco Longi, pianist, Max Gegna, cellist and J. Henri Bove, flautist. Sanborn wrote in his review that her first number was the polacca from *Mignon* sung in 'truly dazzling fashion', especially the chain of trills at the close – 'but there were still better things to follow'. Her second encore, *Voi che sapete* from *Le Nozze di Figaro*, she sang 'with consummate vocal control, and with an exquisite and adorable simplicity of style'. It was one of the finest pieces of Mozart singing Sanborn felt he had ever heard.

From *La Sonnambula* Tetrazzini sang not only the rondo, *Ah non giunge*, but the recitative and the *Ah, non credea* which precedes it. 'One wonders if Jenny Lind herself, over whose *Ah, non credea* the contemporary scribes waxed lyrical, could have sung that more ravishingly', Sanborn commented.

As another encore Tetrazzini sang Santuzza's *Voi lo sapete* from *Cavalleria Rusticana*. This was 'an object lesson as to what may be accomplished in dramatic effect through just musical phrasing, a sure sense of design, and the kind of emotional expression that hits the nail on the head every time'. And 'let no one imagine that Tetrazzini now lacks the lower range for this "dramatic" music. Her voice responded richly and warmly throughout its extended scale.'

Tetrazzini's last number was the *Shadow Song* from *Dinorah* and there were other encores. At one point in the concert a bouquet of roses was handed over the footlights to her. She read the attached card and then announced to the audience, 'From my dear friend, Caruso!'

213

In mid-December, Tetrazzini attended a reception in her honour aboard Woodrow Wilson's yacht, *The Mayflower*. It was the first time any singer had received such a mark of presidential esteem. Then in the New Year she resumed her 'farewell' tour, starting at the Coliseum, Toledo, on 13 January 1921 to a full house. She sang *Caro nome*, the *Couplet du Mysoli* from David's *Perle du Brésil* with flute obligato from Henri Bove, the Mad Scene from *Lucia* with flute. The final encore, a distinct achievement, sung with cello and flute, was Drigo's *Serenade*.

For this tour 'Doc' Leahy had provided Tetrazzini with 'a hotel on wheels' as the *San Francisco Examiner*[2] described it. This was a private rail car with bedrooms, drawing and dining rooms, a kitchen run by a chef selected because of his knowledge of the dishes that appealed to her, and three servants. There was a music room with a miniature piano, and a library of scores.

Reporters queued everywhere to interview the ever-cooperative Luisa. The headlines went:

'WORLD GOING CRAZY, SAYS DIVA'
'DECLARES THE NEW GOWNS HERE HORRID'
'DISAPPROVES, TOO, OF SUFFRAGETTES'
'MME TETRAZZINI LOVES PIGEONS'
'TETRAZZINI ABHORS THE TANGO'.

However, by the time she reached California she realized that the public must not be made to regard her as too old fashioned, and on 15 March 1921, beneath the caption 'JAZZ APPROVED BY TETRAZZINI' one read in the *San Francisco Examiner*: ' "More power to members of the Ragtime Royalty and the shimmy shaking clan", declared the diva. "Why do the so-called highbrows condemn these things that are so great a part of American life?" '

When on 6 March, Tetrazzini had passed through Los Angeles en route to San Diego for a concert, a reporter from the *Los Angeles Times* visited her private railcar where were displayed her decorations and medals received for taking part in festivals and singing in aid of charities, as well as over fifty dolls, including one four feet high dressed in the height of fashion and standing next to a trunk full of its other costumes, all replicas of those worn by Tetrazzini in her various roles. It stood upon an ornate gramophone used to play matching records of her singing.[3]

Having sung in San Diego, Tetrazzini returned to Los Angeles where L. E. Behymer presented her for one recital at the Philharmonic Auditorium on the evening of 18 March. Then three days later on arrival in San Francisco she was presented with a bouquet by 6 year old soprano Lillian Ruggero, the local prodigy dubbed by admirers 'La Piccola' Tetrazzini and who now became the diva's protégée and later famous under the name of Lina Pagliughi.[4]

The 'farewell' concert took place on Sunday afternoon 27 March with 6,500 people crowding the Exposition auditorium. Next day Tetrazzini travelled to California's capital, Sacramento, for a civic reception on 2 April in the Capitol building. The Governor William D. Stephens led her to a chair. 'Now you have replaced me as Governor!' he smiled as she sat down. When he brought her into the Assembly, Joe Pedrotti who represented Los Angeles, begged 'Give us a song.' But she protested that there was no orchestra, and suggested that they might instead attend the concert she would be giving at Oakland on 4 April before leaving the Golden State.[5]

Back in England *The Voice* for May 1921 showed a photograph of the diva standing in a Los Angeles alligator farm, smiling down at a group of young ones frolicking at her feet. The accompanying text reported that she would be ending her American tour that month and sailing for London. In a 1993 catalogue of a New Jersey firm specializing in operatic memorabilia there were offered for sale two photographs – the one signed by her 'Luisa Tetrazzini, *coccodrillo di 17–5 anni vivo*' and the other is captioned 'Luisa sitting on Big Bill'. Both show her perched astride the creature. This led to a story circulating that she had bought a baby crocodile which she had smuggled into her Savoy Hotel suite and kept in a bath. All this was excellent publicity for the concert she gave at the Albert Hall on 14 July with the London Symphony Orchestra under conductor Arthur Nikisch.

Mourning Caruso

Tetrazzini then travelled to Lugano to relax in her villa. There she received the bad news that Caruso had been taken ill with peritonitis. A postcard reached her from him in Naples that read: 'I am waiting for you with open arms, waiting every moment to salute you with a golden note.' She immediately hurried south only to reach his bedside after he had died. During the funeral on 4 August she was in great distress. Caruso's son, also named Enrico, has revealed that Tetrazzini wanted to sing at her close friend's funeral but the Pope would not allow a woman to sing in the cathedral; instead, Fernando de Lucia came out of retirement and sang '*Pietà, Signore*' at the service.[6]

Lionel Powell was the leading English concert promoter of those days. Originally a violinist, he later turned his attention to the more lucrative business of bringing over to the United Kingdom celebrated international artists and orchestras. When Tetrazzini had returned to London in 1919

Powell had rejected the proposal that he should send her out on a concert tour, but Fred Gaisberg's judgment was respected by him. He had accepted his advice with considerable success before the war when he had toured the Russian soprano Michailova. Now Gaisberg was urging him to take on Tetrazzini, and the astonishing success of her Albert Hall concerts led him to change his mind. As a result, on 15 September 1921 Tetrazzini and Tatò arrived at the Savoy to prepare for a long concert tour under Powell's management.

Concurrent with the diva's coming was the well promoted publication of her book, *My Life of Song*. Stocks at bookshops were soon sold out but the critics were less enthusiastic. *The Times Literary Supplement* for 21 September found that the language in which it was written had 'a quaint interest of its own and one wonders who supplied it'. Financial success was a commonplace in such accounts and one was hardly impressed at learning that the wonderful voice had earned its owner over a million pounds but it was 'truly pleasing' to be told that though the soprano owned a palace and a mansion and when travelling stayed in the most luxurious hotels, she often helped the servants to scrub the floors.

The *Musical Times* criticized the book for devoting only a few lines occasionally to music and containing far too many trivial incidents. It thought that the day of operatic stars was drawing to a close. 'Tetrazzini may very likely be the last of the female line.'

On Fred Gaisberg's recommendation, too, Lionel Powell had engaged a brilliant young pianist to accompany Tetrazzini on her concert tour in Britain. This he was to continue doing until she finally retired. Ivor Newton, in his reminiscences *At the Piano*[7] has described how Fred Gaisberg took him to the Savoy Hotel's royal suite which the diva occupied. Overlooking the Thames, it had one of the finest views in London and was crowded with enormous baskets of flowers. They were received by Umberto Tatò, whom Newton describes as 'a huge unfriendly Italian who eyed me as though I were a horse on which he was disinclined to risk even a small bet'. Then Tetrazzini herself came in and greeted Fred with genuine affection but studied Newton with a certain hauteur. Tatò now carried in her music which was in albums bound in pale blue silk and the rehearsal passed smoothly. When Newton complained to Fred Gaisberg as they left the hotel that the diva might have tried to make him feel at ease, he was told that it was because she was wondering whether her public would approve of her having so young an accompanist. But such standoffishness was a mere mask of the moment and she soon revealed to Ivor the uninhibited geniality that was the keynote of her lively nature.

On 25 September 1921 Tetrazzini opened her tour with a Sunday afternoon concert at a packed Royal Albert Hall, with Ivor Newton as her accompanist and supported by singers Leila Megane and Stefan Bielina and pianist Pouishnoff. She sang arias from *Lucia di Lammermoor*, *La Sonnambula*, and *La Perle du Brésil* with obbligatos by the flautist John Amadio and cellist Lauri Kennedy. Her encores were Gounod's *Chantez, chantez, ma belle*, Gaetano Braga's *La Serenata*, and Godard's *Berceuse*.

Tetrazzini then opened an extensive provincial concert tour in Birmingham on 28 September 1921. When she sang in Cardiff's impressive Empire Theatre on the afternoon of Saturday 29 October, 'Orpheus' in the Monday's *Western Mail* wrote that every seat was filled by music lovers from all over South Wales. Not content with such intricate passages as were to be encountered in the final variation of a piece, she sometimes added to 'her own intensely difficult fioriture the phrases scored, say, for the flute'. She had begun with the aria *Ah, non credea* from *La Sonnambula* with encores of Enrico Toselli's *Serenade* and Francesco Quaranta's *Si Fossi*. Further opportunities for her 'amazing vocalism' came with the Mario Costa songs *Sei morta ne la vita mia* and *Serenata Medioevale*, followed by the sprightly *Carceleras* from the Zarzuela in R. Chapi's *Las Hijas del Zebedeo*, and then, as more encores, Braga's *La Serenata* 'charmingly sung with violin obbligato by M. Bratza' and Drigo's *I Milioni d'Arlecchino*. 'Orpheus' found that there was 'something of the Patti touch in her final song – a quality that is always more or less noticeable in Tetrazzini's singing – the simple strains of *The Last Rose of Summer*'.

Tetrazzini now returned to the Savoy for a week's rest before giving another Sunday afternoon concert at the Royal Albert Hall on 6 November. The review in *The Times* began:

> The most vivid description will tell nothing of the secret by which she holds her audience captive. After the wild scenes of enthusiasm that her signing aroused who could say that English audiences were not emotionally susceptible.[8]

Three days later she was performing once more in the provinces before filling the Albert Hall again on Sunday 4 December with Pablo Casals the cellist as guest artist. Then she ended this long tour with two out-of-town concerts.

The diva remained in London for the end-of-year festivities. An advertisement in the *Evening Standard* for 20 December announced a 'Tetrazzini Gala Night' on Christmas Eve at the Savoy. A *table d'hôte* dinner costing £1.10s, exclusive of wine and cigars would be served in the restaurant. 'Mme Tetrazzini will be pleased to see every guest.' This she did and at midnight climbed onto a chair and sang *Home, Sweet Home*. When the customers left, she gave an impromptu concert for the waiters, singing all their requests.

Entertaining the tax inspector

Ever since her arrival in England that autumn Tetrazzini had been pursued by the income tax authorities, and on receiving a Final Demand notice for £1,500 she had invited the local Inspector of Taxes to call earlier that Christmas Eve at suite 412 in the Savoy. On a table stood bundles of £1 notes neatly tied with red ribbon which she helped him to pack into his briefcase. Then, according to the *Musical Mirror*: 'She capped it all by presenting the man with a slice of Christmas Pudding made by herself. Was this by way of friendliness, or did she want to kill him? We wonder.'[9] Aware of the publicity value Fred Gaisberg had arranged for the Press to photograph the event.

21 'How to Sing'

There can be no doubt that Tetrazzini had been very fond of Caruso and that his death upset her. She spent most of the summer of 1922 in Naples paying almost daily visits to his grave and on 2 August, papal permission having this time been given, she sang at a Requiem Mass held on the first anniversary of his demise in the Church of San Francisco di Paola there.[1] Enrico Caruso junior writes in his book how afterwards: 'Mme Tetrazzini and I wept together'.[2] She often said that the great tenor had asked her more than once to marry him and that she had refused. She inherited his watch, scarf pin and cufflinks and often wore them during the rest of her life.

Ten years later, on 9 December 1932, Tetrazzini was filmed briefly in the HMV shop in London's Oxford Street listening to the re-issue of the 1917 record of Caruso's singing *M'appari* with dubbed-in symphony orchestra. Tears come into her eyes and her many-chinned jaw begins bobbing up and down as she joins him in the last high phrases. 'Thank you very much,' she is heard saying and then rings out a wonderfully infectious laugh.[3]

On 8 September 1922 Tetrazzini, together with Tatò, arrived at the Savoy and next day she gave a press reception, masterminded by Fred Gaisberg as usual. 'Figaro' in his monthly feature *The Operatic World* in *Musical Opinion* for October wrote:

> She can always be trusted to come back to England with any amount of éclat borne triumphantly on the wings of her press agents' vivid imagination. The true herald of the Tetrazzini top notes is the bright red and juicy paragraphs about her attempts to reduce her weight, her cooking and her dusting and above all her amazing geniality of spirit. The downright bravura of her publicity agents' methods have long made us sit up and take notice. The great singer is boosted like a circus; the thing is that it succeeds.

With Tetrazzini was Attilio Baggiore, a handsome Italian tenor in his early twenties who was clearly her lover of the moment. She told reporters she was certain that he had a great future. According to a report from London of 2 October to the *Musical Courier* he had been singing in Naples when she heard him first. 'As Sig. Baggiore himself says, he has been "a lucky boy ever since". He is now under contract with Madame and will sing with her throughout.'[4] A photograph of the signing ceremony was issued to the press and appeared in some newspapers. It was arranged that the couple should make two records together for Victor of Camden, New Jersey, at the Gramophone Company's Hayes studios. Tetrazzini had, the previous year when in the States, recorded *Gl'angui d'inferno*, the Queen of Night's aria from Mozart's *Il Flauto Magico*, together with Tate's *Somewhere a Voice Is Calling*, and Gaetano Lama's waltz song *Come le rose* but Victor had not so far published them.

The recordings at Hayes took place on 11, 13, 15 and 22 September – those on the first two dates being for the Gramophone Company. Full details from the sheets in the EMI Archives are given in the Discography. Nine were musically trifles but charming love ditties, two sung in French and the others in Italian with guitar accompaniment by the accomplished Toto Amici, one of these being a duet, Lama's *Piccolo Amore*, with Baggiore. The rest, with orchestra conducted by Percy Pitt, included the duet, *E il sol dell'anima* from *Rigoletto*, with Baggiore. Victor, however, it seems did not consider two recordings she very much liked – Lama's *Come le rose* and Drigo's *Serenata* – marketable, neither did they care for her protégé Baggiore's efforts so after protracted and embittered negotiations none were published and the 'metals' destroyed. Tetrazzini, fortunately, retained the 'white label' samples and, as related in the Discography, all except the *Rigoletto* were transferred in brilliant fashion by Keith Hardwick onto compact disc in 1992. Why they were spurned at the time is hard to understand for they are among the most enchanting of her records. Michael Aspinall comments: 'the tone is solid, the legato masterly – and does she know how to sing a tune!'

On Sunday afternoon, 1 October, Tetrazzini gave her first International Celebrity Concert at the Royal Albert Hall for impresario Lionel Powell before touring for him. Accompanied by Ivor Newton, after a violin solo from Bratza, she sang *Ah, fors' è lui*, later Eckert's *L'eco*, ending with *Ah, non credea*.

Desmond MacCarthy in his book *Portraits* recalled that he had read Tetrazzini's *My Life of Song* just before London welcomed her back at this concert which he attended. After it was over her car could not move through the press of people until she began to throw her 'pledges of affection' – her bouquets – to them.

> Such receptions only fall to those who are themselves reflections of emotion, flashing it back in looks, and in keeping with such a role she waved and blew kisses, showing in every gesture her surprise and pleasure at the warmth of the greetings.[5]

After this concert, Tetrazzini set out on a long provincial tour with Attilio Baggiore billed as 'The Celebrated Italian Tenor'. Opening in Reading on 4 October, they sang next in Edinburgh, Dundee, Glasgow, Belfast, Dublin and Liverpool before returning to the Albert Hall for a concert on the 29th. Then on 1 November in Preston hundreds of devotees failed, as elsewhere, to gain admission. Three days later in Manchester, a reporter calling in the morning at the Midland Hotel found her still in the bath. Telling him to remain on the other side of the door she sang a Neapolitan waltz song to entertain him as she dressed. It was one she had recorded at Hayes on 13 September – Lama's *Cara piccina* which translated starts: 'I have loved you for a month and have not been able to sleep.' On she went for concerts in five more cities before returning to the Albert Hall on 26 November. Three evenings later she was performing in Nottingham. On 2 December she sang yet again in Manchester. The tour ended in Cardiff on the 16th.

The concert tour over, Attilio Baggiore went back to Italy where he became a comprimario with the Rome Opera, but despite Tetrazzini's patronage he never again recorded.

Ivor Newton's experiences

Ivor Newton who accompanied Tetrazzini at the piano on this tour wrote in his memoirs[6] that as fast as money was earned by her she spent or gave it away, ingenuously believing in the integrity of anybody to whom she took a fancy. Umberto Tatò whom he describes as 'her burly secretary, who was never seen to write a letter or pick up a telephone' had no doubt been given by her his platinum watch and chain inlaid with pearls. Newton thought he ought to have been called her 'treasurer' for his breast pocket was stuffed with five-pound notes that had to be paid over to him before his employer commenced to sing.

Describing his early days as her accompanist, Newton says that, on arrival in the artistes' room, the first thing Tetrazzini did was to try out her high D flat. If this were managed with immediate ease, she would smile and declare: 'It's there – all is well.' When the time came to begin her programme, Luisa would make the sign of the cross and hurry along the corridor onto the platform, where those unable to find room elsewhere often placed themselves. As they pressed back against the walls to let her pass, everyone in turn would be greeted like an old friend, and children hugged as though her own.

Such warmth of feeling for her public, Newton assures us, was completely sincere and it rendered audiences favourably disposed towards her before even one note was sung. Having made the platform squatters feel thoroughly at home, Luisa would signal to Ivor to begin playing by tossing the end of her long rope of pearls over her shoulder.

Newton comments that Tetrazzini's behaviour before singing did not appeal to everyone. On one concert tour the Algerian baritone Dinh Gilly, who had sung with her in opera, was now acting as an assisting artist. He stood beside Ivor in the wings watching 'her startling flirtation' with the audience and launched into a bitter attack on prima donnas. 'They should be burnt at the stake!' he exclaimed. 'I detest them all. I lived with one for five years.' (This was Emmy Destinn.) He expatiated on the subject as he and Newton ate supper together afterwards. There was nothing about the breed that did not outrage and disgust him. 'In the old days', he claimed, 'if they hadn't lovers around them, they used to drag the scene shifters into their dressing rooms before their "Mad Scenes".'

The grande toilette Tetrazzini wore for recitals was in sharp contrast to the extreme *déshabillé*, as Newton puts it, in which she attended morning rehearsals, dishevelled and singing the 'Mirror' aria from Massenet's *Thaïs, 'Dis-moi que je suis belle*, to announce her arrival in the building.

Possibly Luisa's most exotic gown was the peacock creation. It was her favourite, and Newton was always scared of treading on the splendid train. 'Did you ever see a train like that?' he once asked a concert hall fireman. 'It's not the train I'm looking at', the man replied, 'it's the engine what's pulling it!'

Aware that people made fun of her stoutness, Tetrazzini could joke about it herself. When Newton asked why she no longer appeared in opera, she replied that it was because no stage carpenter was capable of building a bridge which would not collapse under her weight.

Newton found that when on tour Caruso's records and her own were the only ones Luisa would play on the machines that the Gramophone Company's local representatives placed in hotel suites for her use. 'In an age of great singers', wrote Newton, 'Tetrazzini had an unrivalled place in the hearts of the British public.' He found her technique faultless. She would sing ornate *Carnival of Venice* variations which made Lucia's Mad Scene 'sound as simple as a folk-song' – and she sang them with intelligence. 'It is not a question of vocal agility', she told him, 'but the power to express emotion while producing a beautiful tone in coloratura.'

Newton says that Tetrazzini's showy temperament combined with the glow of her personality added life to her concerts. When he accompanied her, there was invariably instantaneous applause in appreciation of the stirring rhythm and fiery precision which, for example, was given by her to the polonaise from *Mignon, Io son Titania*. He says that Luisa enjoyed singing with obbligatos, mentioning how she sang with a 'cello *Batti, batti* from *Don Giovanni*, and Catherine's aria, *La, la, la*, from Meyerbeer's *L'étoile du nord* with a flautist on each side of her, which was very popular.

Sometimes when an audience went on demanding encores, the diva would reveal another surprising side of her genius with a forcefully delivered dramatic aria such as Aida's *Ritorna Vincitor*. This, Newton believed, was evidence of her being as capable of greatness in dramatic roles as in the coloratura ones in which she had achieved fame. Percy Pitt, the musical director at Covent Garden, used to say so, too, according to J. B. Steane in *The Grand Tradition*. John Pitts Sanborn wrote that she sang this aria 'as scarcely a dramatic soprano' had sung it in America. Steane observes that her records show something of a dramatic soprano's fullness in her voice from about the upper F to B flat.

At the end of her concert tours in the British Isles with Ivor Newton, Tetrazzini would invite herself to tea with him in his London home. The problem was how to spend the time and he decided that a good way of doing this would be by inviting young and promising artists to be present and to sing to her. She gave each one her full attention and generally pertinent advice afterwards. On one occasion, Elena Danieli went up to her, made a deep curtsey and asked, 'Madame, can I sing *Ah, fors' è lui?*'

'Why ask me?' Tetrazzini replied. 'You should ask Verdi.'

Always at the end of these parties, Newton enquired if Tetrazzini would sing to them and she would agree with alacrity.

Marguerite D'Alvarez in her memoirs *Forsaken Altars* tells how, before making her own New York début, Tetrazzini came into her dressing-room at the Manhattan opera house.

> I was trying to paint some wrinkles on my unlined face. She laughed whole-heartedly, but said a little wistfully: 'How wonderful is youth.' She gave me a little bottle of water in which she had put spoonfuls of sugar and told me to take sips between the acts and have an enormous meal afterwards, as she did. I loved her and have many memories of her kindness. . . . Once I helped her to dress, and suddenly a dismayed expression crossed her smiling face. She had lost her earrings, Canary diamonds, the size of small saucers. 'Margherita', she begged, opening the top of her bodice, 'look for them here.' When I finally found them, hidden under one of her very opulent breasts, she said thankfully: 'Remember, that is the only safe place for your jewellery in a foreign country.'

When the Artistes' Committee of the Gramophone Company met on 15 December 1922, the Chairman, Mr Beck reported[7] that he and Fred Gaisberg had visited Tetrazzini in her suite at the Savoy, the Sunday before she left for Italy. She had greeted them both 'most courteously' inviting them to dinner, given them photographs of herself with friendly inscriptions on them, and the whole evening was spent in 'an atmosphere of cordiality and friendliness'.

Beck went on that he had asked what more Tetrazzini desired to remove any sense of grievance she might retain against their company. She said that she would be satisfied if they replaced those ten records in the HMV catalogue which had been removed owing to their surfaces not being up to the catalogue standard. He assured her that this would be done. She then asked that the Victor Talking Machine Company matrices be used in those cases where the Victor recording was better than those of the Gramophone Company. Beck told her that this had already been done.

Dispute with Victor

Tetrazzini then said that Tatò would be going to America in January 1923 for the express purpose of making trouble for Victor if they did not accede to their demands. 'He and Madame Tetrazzini both have a personal grievance against Mr Child who, they complain, practically ignored them when they were in the States.' She had mentioned several instances that irritated her – for example, Victor had deducted from her record royalties 8 per cent in respect of American income tax without notifying her. As a result, being unaware of this she paid the sum in question all over again when remitting tax on her total income to the United States Revenue Officers who later took no notice of her application for a refund.

Beck went on that in his opinion Tatò should not be considered simply an ex-chauffeur. 'He impressed me with the fact that he had very carefully studied the business relations of Tetrazzini with the Victor and Gramophone Companies as far back as 1907, and had the facts at the tip of his fingers.' Tatò was far from being unintelligent and on arrival in the States, he planned to have criticisms made by eminent musicians and critics on those records rejected by the Victor Company of Tetrazzini's last recordings in England. Beck told his committee that he had already written to Victor's Calvin Child a personal letter as to how matters stood and was writing a further report of his last interview with her, warning them of what Tatò intended doing in America. 'I can conclude by saying that, as far as our Company is concerned, Madame Tetrazzini left London quite happy and satisfied.'

Touring for Sol Hurok

In his reminiscences published in 1947, the New York impresario Sol Hurok claimed that Tetrazzini and Titta Ruffo toured in concert for him between 1922 and 1923, but this is incorrect. She did not do so in either of these years. Hurok says that he found her a charming little woman with a weakness for romantic attachments with men much younger than herself on whom she squandered her money. He could scarcely keep up with her rapid changes of heart.

A frantic call from Detroit or some other city would warn me that there was going to be serious trouble over the pianist unless I came at once. By the time I arrived, the trouble was no longer the pianist but the cellist.[8]

Hurok is possibly referring to her 1920 tour when she sang in Detroit on 26 February. In 1923 Ruffo toured with Yvonne D'Arle. The only other time he did so with Tetrazzini was in 1914 as described in Chapter 17. He also gave a recital with her on 23 April 1921, in the Hippodrome, New York, when the *Musical Courier*'s critic wrote four days later in his review: 'There never has been quite such a multitude as applauded and cheered the two famous artists.'

Views on singing

The success of Tetrazzini's *My Life of Song* with her admirers led to the publication in the late summer of 1924 of her *How to Sing*. As a young soprano she would study with famous Italian maestri she met during her travels and would write down in cadenza books – little booklets of manuscript paper – the cadenzas they taught her. She had learnt a great deal from singing with Mattia Battistini and her phrasing is reminiscent of his in its Italian sweep and eloquence and the frequent addition of little mordents, as Michael Aspinall has pointed out.[9] She had also worked incessantly on her scales whilst in her teens, thanks to which she owed her accuracy and brilliance in large-scale florid singing.

In articles first published in 1909 she had claimed to have developed her own breathing capacity, saying that the breath must be sent out in a steady, even flow. She had learnt to control this flow of air so that no muscular action of the throat could cut it off.

> The physical sensation should be first an effort on the part of the diaphragm to press the air up against the chest box, then the sensation of a perfectly open throat, and, lastly, the sensation that the air is passing freely into the cavities of the head. . . . This feeling of singing against the chest with the weight of air pressing up against it is known as 'breath support', and in Italian we have an even better word – 'appoggio' which is 'breath prop'. The attack of the sound must come from the appoggio.[10]

Aspinall comments that singers reading this would understand at once what she meant and be able to hear in her records that she is putting it into practice. He adds:

> The long line of her perfectly steady singing, the *disinvoltura* with which she passes through wide intervals with absolute security, and her flawless attack – delicate or walloping – are all made possible by her breathing and *appoggio*.

How to Sing was published in London by C. Arthur Pearson, a firm no longer in existence, and it was never disclosed how the actual writing took place. It was probably based on notes in Italian supplied by Tetrazzini and from conversations with her in the same language which after translation into English was expertly edited. As to be expected, she vigorously defends coloratura singing. It was nonsense to say that such music was false and dramatically unreal.

> What is the difference in principle, I would ask, between the fioriture passages of the vocalist and those introduced as a matter of course in the most serious instrumental music? Why should a cadenza for the voice be reckoned less worthy than a similar passage for the violin or the 'cello? All the greatest masters have introduced florid passages in plenty in the noblest instrumental music. Yet the view is very generally adopted that these are inadmissible, or belong to an inferior phase of the art when the instrument employed happens to be the voice.[11]

Vocal fioriture was by no means confined to the music of composers like Donizetti and Bellini. Bach used it often even in his most solemn work, while Handel revelled in coloratura.

> That Mozart can be reckoned in the same category it is hardly necessary to recall, while even Beethoven did not disdain to utilise the art of vocal decoration in many of the numbers of *Fidelio*. In the modern Russian School we have Rimsky-Korsakov's 'Hymn to the Sun' from *Coq d'Or*. And have we not also such an eminently serious master as Richard Strauss challenging comparison in our own times with the most extravagant productions of the past in this particular genre in the music of Zerbinetta in his *Ariadne*?

As to the charge that coloratura in dramatic music was unnatural, those who argued thus overlooked the fact that such an objection could be levied against everything in opera. No one sings all the time in real life any more than they speak in blank verse as they are made to do in Shakespearian drama.

Referring to her Covent Garden début in *La Traviata*, Tetrazzini added:

> All critics said they were especially struck by the manner in which I managed, while singing Verdi's florid music brilliantly and effectively in the purely vocal sense, at the same time to make it expressive – and this I took as the greatest possible compliment which could be bestowed on me. For that I think is what coloratura properly sung should be.

Tetrazzini revealed that she had found invaluable Lilli Lehmann's 'Great Scale' remedy for all manners of vocal ills which meant singing 'long slow scales of sustained notes steadily repeated'.[12] Some years previously Lilli found herself quite hoarse on rising in the morning of the day when she was due to sing Norma that evening in Vienna. She was unable to rise above A flat, although at the performance she would have to reach high D flat and E flat. Nevertheless, she persevered with the 'Great Scale' remedy at half-hourly intervals until 11 am and noticed that she was gradually improving. By the evening she had her D and E flats at her command so that people said they had seldom heard her sing so well.

Tetrazzini warned those training to become professional singers to beware of bad maestri.[13] In New York, for instance, there was said to be a professor of this type who sold to his pupils, in order to give timbre to their voices, bottles of water from Italy at $2 each. Even in her own native land the same sort of thing occurred. She had heard of one in Milan whose practice it was to make his pupils tie pieces of elastic to the legs of the piano. They were then instructed to pull out and let go again in order to feel the gradations of *crescendo* and *diminuendo*. But even he had been surpassed in invention by another 'professor' whose custom it was to illustrate the art of *mezza voce* by means of an umbrella which he opened and closed 'as his happy pupils, standing before him, swelled and diminished on the chosen note'.

The *Musical Times*[14] was not impressed with *How to Sing*. Tetrazzini dealt 'almost entirely in generalities, expressed without distinction of any kind'. She did put up 'a goodish case for coloratura singing, but apparently fails to see that there is a difference in values between the twiddles of Donizetti and the *melismata* of Bach'. The critic was pleased to find her describing the *tremolo* as a crime.

Regarding the case for coloratura, the distinguished American critic W. J. Henderson, who reviewed extensively Tetrazzini's performances at the Manhattan, wrote in his book, *The Art of Singing*:

> The vocal music of today is not embroidered with runs, trills, groups and ornaments, as the operas of the late 17th century were, but does contain thousands of progressions which can be executed with perfect smoothness and fluency by the agile voice, but by the singer untrained in coloratura only awkwardly and uncertainly.[15]

Herbert Caesari was to write in 1958:

> It is interesting to relate that as a test Tetrazzini once sang one hundred high Cs in succession, and each time the graphically recorded waveforms proved to be identical, the pattern of the curves being absolutely unvaried. Like the great singer she was, Tetrazzini had long cultivated tactile and visual memory of all her tonal sensations, and was thus able to reproduce at will exactly the same tonal quality when and where needed. Is it any wonder that her voice was unimpaired after fifty years of singing?.[16]

Soon after the publication of *How to Sing* Tetrazzini learnt that some nuns from Sweden were busily searching for a suitable property to turn into a convent in Lugano. She acted on a sudden impulse and sold *Il Paradiso* to then at a giveaway price, so it was said. Since then, the *Casa Santa Birgitta* has been enlarged and visitors to the resort can now stay there as paying guests.

22 Tetrazzini Makes Broadcasting History

On Tuesday 10 March 1925 the London *Evening Standard* organized the first all-star concert to be broadcast from the BBC's 2LO studio on Savoy Hill. Apart from Tetrazzini and Ivor Newton her accompanist, the other artists were the Scottish pianist Lamond, cellist W. H. Squire, violinist Isolde Menges, contralto Phyllis Lett, baritone Dinh Gilly, singer of sea shanties John Goss, and the Kedroff Quartette. The *Standard* devoted its front page to the event under banner headlines with a photograph of Signor Tatò, Tetrazzini's manager, and Ivor Newton on either side of her arriving at 2LO. 'This is the proudest moment of my life for I have come to sing to ten million English people,' she was reported as telling the paper's representative who interviewed her in her suite at the Savoy. She claimed to have been one of the first to have 'a listening-in set' in Rome. People used to come to her house to hear concerts transmitted from Paris, London and Berlin. The transmission from 2LO was the clearest in Europe and London concerts the best. Her previous experience of broadcasting had been confined to taking part in wireless experiments in America five years earlier when she was thanked publicly afterwards by Joseph Daniels, Secretary of the Navy.

> I was singing in a studio in New York, and my voice was relayed to a training ship in the Hudson River, which in turn transmitted the sounds out to sea. Imagine my astonishment when, half an hour later, I received a message from the captain of a Cunard liner, 800 miles away, thanking me for my concert. This was, I believe, the first time that a ship ever listened in to a land concert, and I have the Marconigram to this day.

The previous Christmas Tetrazzini had broadcast a greeting to the Italian people from the radio station in Rome. Appropriately correcting her broken English, the journalist went on to quote her as saying:

> But I would rather sing to a thousand audiences than one microphone. An

audience has being and sense and feeling, but a microphone is a dead thing without a soul. When you stand on a platform to sing, you know whether the audience is with you or against you, but the microphone just remains the microphone expressing neither dissent or assent. I tell you I am terrified at the prospect. But all will be well, I know, and I hope the public will be as pleased with my singing as I am to be among them once more.

Much to her regret, she was growing old, and the days of her grand opera parts were past. 'Now I shall sing some light songs of sentiment. This I have on my side – that the English are probably the most sentimental people in the world.' She would like to sing something from Ambroise Thomas's *Amleto* – a great favourite of hers – or from Meyerbeer's *Dinorah*. 'These two operas are those I sing during the day for practice when I am dusting the ornaments in my drawing room.' Actually she was to sing from neither.

Fred Gaisberg later revealed that for taking part in this historic broadcast Tetrazzini was paid by the BBC a fee far in excess of that received by other artists up till then; he also claimed the credit for setting up the event.[1]

The concert commenced at 7.30 pm, lasted three hours with an interval between 9.30 and 10 o'clock, and was broadcast from all the BBC's 21 stations including the Chelmsford high-power 5XX. Radiofonica Italiana, as well as two stations in America, KDKA of Pittsburg and WEAF of New York, had made special arrangements to pick up and relay the concert, which was also heard in liners at sea.[2]

'Tetrazzini parties were the fashion in London,' the *Daily Express* informed its readers next day. 'Many theatres played to depleted audiences, and owners of wireless sets found themselves in unprecedented popularity.' At Selfridge's, fifteen hundred people listened to the concert in the luncheon hall. A crystal set with a two valve amplifier connected to four loudspeakers 'secured almost flawless reception'. The headlines to the papers covering the occasion ran:

10,000,000 PEOPLE HEAR TETRAZZINI – NATION ENTRANCED BY A VOICE – WIRELESS TRIUMPH OF THE GREAT DIVA.

Listeners heard first violin soli from Isolde Menges, three songs from Phyllis Lett and Lamond playing a Beethoven sonata. Then just after ten past eight Tetrazzini was escorted to the studio hung with grey curtains and softly carpeted in blue. Dinh Gilly, standing by, cried after her, wishing her good luck: '*In bocca di lupo!*' She stood, somewhat nervously at first, while the announcer spoke, and at the mention of her name smiled broadly at the unseen audience, pressed both hands to her heart and blew them her customary kisses. Then she sang *O luce di quest' anima* from Donizetti's *Linda di Chamounix*.

The *Daily Express* Music Critic, 'F.T.' wrote:

There may perhaps be a slight diminution of resonance in the lower middle part of the voice, but the florid passages and the compass of the end of the aria sufficed to set at rest any doubt regarding the continued flexibility of the voice and the sweet tone of the famous high notes. These were heard on a crystal set with all the beauty we associate with the name of Tetrazzini.[3]

In the second part of the programme Tetrazzini opened with the song she had chosen as her test piece when seeking admission as a girl to the Conservatoire in Florence, Margherita's prison cell aria, *L'altra notte in fondo al mare*, from Arrigo Boito's *Mefistofele*. She followed this with Tosti's *L'ultima canzone*, *Un bel di vedremo* from *Madama Butterfly* – the first time it seems that she sang this in concert – Rachmaninoff's *Primavera* and lastly Cowen's *Swallows*, Landon Ronald's *Life* and Moore's *Last Rose of Summer*.

For the first time ever a singer's voice was recorded by wireless. The account in the *Evening Standard* went: 'The actual air waves of Mme Tetrazzini's voice were photographed last night on a long strip of film, as received on a sound recorder when the prima donna's voice was being reproduced on a loudspeaker.'[4]

The experiment was carried out in the Chiswick home of Professor A. M. Low who was reported as saying:

These waves are a permanent record of this remarkable event. They could be actually reproduced into sound, and are quite as accurate as a gramophone record. By means of this device voices heard on the wireless from a great distance (which no gramophone recorder could record, owing to faintness and buzz) can be registered on the film. So great is the delicacy of the wave that the recording diaphragm is made more thin than the skin of a soap bubble – tens of thousandths of an inch – and a spot of light is reflected from a tiny mirror attached to it.

The rest of the national press were generous in their praise of the *Evening Standard*'s innovative concert. The *Daily Telegraph* wrote:

The all-star programme broadcast last night from 2LO thanks to the enterprise of our contemporary, the *Evening Standard*, showed the full possibilities of this wonderful discovery of modern science. The special attraction was Mme Tetrazzini. But quite apart from this, it may well be taken for a model of what such a concert should be. . . . The quality was excellent throughout.

The *Morning Post* declared: 'Mme Tetrazzini can do anything with her voice except sing out of tune'.

The *Manchester Guardian* critic agreed: 'All in all the transmission of the great singer was so good that everybody who listened in last night may proudly boast today that they have heard Tetrazzini. It now remains for them to see her – which is well worthwhile'.

Tetrazzini was deluged with telegrams and bouquets of flowers which poured into her Savoy suite. However, though press and public regarded the 2LO experiment as an epoch-making success, it had a disastrous effect on the diva's next concert held at the Royal Albert Hall at 8.15 pm on Wednesday 25 March, even though this was advertised as her 'POSITIVELY ONLY APPEARANCE IN LONDON THIS SEASON'. Prices ranged from 12s down to 2s 4d.

Two days later the *Daily Mail* asked

> Did the broadcasting by Mme Tetrazzini on March 10 militate against the attendance at her concert? Messrs Lionel Powell and Holt, the concert agents, state that on her last visit two years ago Mme Tetrazzini filled the Albert Hall to capacity three times within a few weeks.

According to the agents, the audience in the Albert Hall on the 25th represented only one-third of the smallest of Tetrazzini's London audiences since 1909. The result had been a heavy financial loss to themselves. She had broadcast against their express wishes and in the face of their advice that it would have an adverse effect on her drawing power at the box office.

> Whether last night's extraordinary lack of support for one of the world's most famous singers was due to faulty broadcast transmission, bad reception on poor instruments, or to any other causes, the fact remains that the broadcasting of Mme Tetrazzini's voice was a disaster.

But the diva herself told a *Daily Mail* reporter that she attributed the empty seats at the Albert Hall to the fact that she was singing on a week night and not as formerly on a Sunday afternoon. That was the most convenient time for people to go to concerts. She certainly had shown no signs of being disappointed at so small an audience.[5]

Peter Page wrote in the same paper: 'Wearing a blue velvet cloak and in an exuberant mood, she blew kisses to her public and fastened and unfastened bangles and bracelets in a manner that put her on good terms with everybody at once. As a coloratura singer, she is amazing and came through the difficulties of Donizetti's *O luce di quest' anima* with attractive nonchalance and followed it up with a sentimental English ballad. Gounod's *Serenade*, Rachmaninoff's *Printemps* and the Mad Scene from *Hamlet* were other items in a programme which, though singularly devoid of musical interest, was a good vehicle for displaying the full possibilities of this exceptional voice.[6]

'Mr Gossip' in the *Daily Sketch* found that Tetrazzini's audience made up in cordiality what it lacked in numbers. 'On one side of the organ, however, was packed a solid mass of enthusiastic supporters, who waved handkerchiefs and clapped until the good-natured diva, who is far from being sylph-like, became very much out of breath through rushing violently up an inclined plane so many times'.[7]

The *Evening Standard* published a spirited reply from Tetrazzini to her agents when a reporter called at the Savoy Hotel and showed her their letter. She claimed that the Albert Hall concert had been arranged at short notice in response to public requests that she should hold one while in England, and as a result there had been less than a week in which to advertise the concert. 'I do not regret one little scrap that I broadcast, and this attack would never deter me if the question of broadcasting were to arise in the future. Nothing shall shake my faith in broadcasting. We artists must not be niggardly about a great public benefit, whether it affects our interest or not.' She had written to her agents regretting their action in making such a statement. 'If they think broadcasting has spoilt my chances, why then have they just engaged me for a tour of the Kingdom next November? They appear to have faith in me in spite of this eloquent denunciation of wireless.'[8]

The *Musical Times* for May carried a brief review of Tetrazzini's Albert Hall concert. This read:

> The audience was only moderately large and musically it must be confessed the attractions were singularly scanty. But though Madame Tetrazzini's voice is far from what it was in her prime, she possesses a technical competence which commands respect. Her easy production and elegant phrasing might be a lesson to many singers who could justifiably ridicule her musical outlook.
>
> If Madame Tetrazzini were now to limit her feats to those of the normal lyric soprano she could still, and for long, hold a considerable place. But she has partly lost her coloratura agility, and in florid music the highest notes were hard and inclined to false intonation. Her legato is still admirable. Tetrazzini at her best could have made some of the newer adulated singers of 1925 seem clumsy. She must have worked hard in her youth.[9]

Two evenings after this concert, Tetrazzini sang at a musical party given at the Italian Embassy in Grosvenor Square for the Crown Prince of Italy (later King Umberto II for one month only in 1946). Ivor Newton who accompanied her at the piano wrote that she was extremely concerned about her programme, being eager to please the Ambassador's wife, the Marchesa della Torretta, who herself had been a famous singer. The guests included members of the Diplomatic Corps and of the British Cabinet as well as Guglielmo Marconi who, when later a wireless set was brought into the drawing-room, 'tuned it in himself'.[10]

That autumn Tetrazzini set out on a long concert tour of the British Isles. Queen Alexandra had occasionally visited Covent Garden to hear Tetrazzini sing. On 20 November the Queen died at Sandringham and the diva who was in Perth for a concert on the 28th in its City Hall took part earlier that day in a memorial service held in St John's Parish Church there. *The Times* reported next day that 'a beautiful rendering of Gounod's

Ave Maria was given by Mme Tetrazzini who sang behind a screen in the chapel'.[11]

23 A Second Marriage Fails

Both Tetrazzini's contracts with the Gramophone Company and with the Victor Talking Machine Company expired on 30 April 1926.[1] Fred Gaisberg, on behalf of the first named, wrote to the latter on 4 February that during the past 3½ years they had sold approximately 36,305 records and that the advance of about £333 each year had been covered. They did not see any indication of a falling off of her sales due to the introduction of electrical recording, or for any other reason, but as they had been employing this new form of recording for only about five months it was probably too soon to say whether this factor would have any effect.

It was quite certain that Mme Tetrazzini would never be able to record for any other company, and she had not expressed any desire, either directly or indirectly, for a further agreement. What conversation they had had with her indicated that she was willing to allow the contract to lapse and to receive royalties as they accrued from year to year.

Clifford Cairns, Manager of Victor's Artists and Repertoire Department, replied on the 19th of the same month that they, too, would allow Tetrazzini's contract to lapse with no further plans for recording and no further guaranteed yearly payment.

It was that summer when Nellie Melba made her final farewell tour of the British Isles ending with a concert at Aberdeen. Gerald Moore in his reminiscences *Furthermore*,[2] relates how at the hotel afterwards there was a supper party. Harold Craxton, her pianist, after inspecting the menu, hurried over to the maître d'hôtel and told him: 'On no account is Dame Nellie to see this. If she does, she will tear you to pieces!' The offending items read: 'Pêche Melba – 3s. 0d. Poire Tetrazzini – 4s. 0d.'

Incidentally, when Fred Gaisberg first persuaded Melba to record for the Gramophone Company in 1904, knowing that Caruso's discs were each priced £1, she insisted that none of hers should be sold for less than a guinea.

Marries Vernati

In October Tetrazzini announced that she had become engaged to Pietro Vernati and that the romance had begun through his falling in love with her voice after hearing her practising in her home on the elegant Via Gaeta in Rome. He was only 32 and 23 years younger than her. Some papers described him as a haberdasher's son and others 'as a member of a family which controls a large chain of stores in Italy'. The civil wedding ceremony took place on 23 October before Alderman Sebregdoni in Florence's Palazzo Vecchio. Some ten thousand people thronged the square outside and while attempting to enter the building from her motor car, the bride was caught in the crush and almost fainted. Supported on the arm of her sister Elvira, she eventually made her way inside where the groom, representatives from the Italian Royal Family, the Government, civic dignitaries and innumerable friends awaited her. According to a special cable to the *San Francisco Chronicle*,[3] 'so great was the noise coming from the cheering crowds that it was difficult to follow the proceedings'. Amadeo Bassi, the tenor who had so often sung with her in opera was her witness, while Vernati's was a Colonel Bombassei Frascani.

The reception afterwards was held at the Hotel Savoy when the new Signora Vernati sang *Caro nome*, Tosti's *Romance*, and together with Bassi the love duet from *La Bohème, O soave fanciulla*. Among the wedding presents were some from the 'sovereigns of Italy, Belgium and Spain' (*Musical America*, 13 November) and a signed, framed photograph from Benito Mussolini on which he had written in Italian: 'To Luisa Tetrazzini – To the voice that makes me believe in Paradise'.

The religious rites were celebrated before Cardinal Mastrangelo and Bishop Fossati of Fiesole in the Church of Santa Maria del Flore next day. Luisa wore a silver wedding dress plus a train with ermine tails, and a diamond tiara. A grand-nephew of hers and a nephew of Vernati's acted as train bearers. A photograph of the couple, front view, with her looking at least twice as broad as her 'toy boy' bridegroom appeared in the *Daily Mail* and so amused comedian George Robey in London that he cut it out and stuck it on the mirror in his dressing-room. Ivor Newton thought that Pietro Vernati seemed 'pathetically juvenile'. A short bit of film of the event was shown by Martinelli at the National Film Theatre in 1967. The bride told reporters: 'Now my real lyrical life begins. Hereafter I shall have something to trill about.' She would continue to sing in concerts and hoped to begin an American tour after their honeymoon in Perugia and two months in her villa in Rome. The tour, however, did not take place but she did give a concert two years later at the Royal Albert Hall on 21 October and told the press that she had brought her husband to spend the end of a prolonged honeymoon in the city where she gained international fame.[4]

But the 'prolonged honeymoon' was in fact a last attempt to save a marriage that had failed and the *Musical Mirror* for July 1929 reported that the diva brought an action for a separation from her husband on the grounds of incompatibility and this had been granted by the Court at Rome. Luisa complained that their three years together had been 'anything but pleasant'.

From conversations the present author has had with Mary Casalini Costa and others who knew the couple well, the trouble was largely caused through Vernati being a prudish young man who could not cope with his wife's strong sex drive. He wanted her to dress more conservatively and tried to stop her from frequenting bars and picking up men. She had also become interested in Spiritualism which was to lead to her being duped by some unsavoury characters. Umberto Tatò had left her employment when she had married Vernati. As a result she now lacked a reliable adviser and manager.

Now separated from her husband, Tetrazzini once more used Fred Gaisberg's good offices to present her in another 'farewell' concert. *The Times* on 21 October that year (1929) reported that she had made her reappearance at the Albert Hall the previous night.

> She sang Micaela's aria from *Carmen, Voi che sapete* and a group of ballads in Italian and Spanish. Although her singing is no longer as brilliant as it used to be and she cannot take a long phrase or a high note with the old ease, her voice has lost little of its quality nor, it must be added, of its hardness. And there is still the same sense of style which can make a song like Tosti's *L'Ultima Canzone* enjoyable. Mr Ivor Newton played the accompaniments and Mr Cherkasaky added some fluent performances of Chopin and Liszt to a somewhat meagre programme.

On 20 January 1931 Tetrazzini went to sing at a charity concert at the Teatro Pagliano, now renamed the Verdi in Florence where she had made her brilliant début as Inez in *L'Africana* in 1890. Next day the *San Francisco Examiner* quoted the Associated Press as reporting from there: 'Tonight every song of the former diva was cheered to the echo. In the audience were many who had heard her at the height of her career'. Vittorio Martucci, sister Elvira's husband was at the piano.

The failure of her marriage led to Luisa's attempting to make another American 'farewell' concert tour as well. She arrived in New York on Christmas Day 1931 aboard the *Leviathan*, and the *New York Times* described her as dressed in the same black caracul coat with the white fur collar in which she had been clad on her last visit to the States some years previously. She wore a double row of pearls and the emerald set in a platinum ring the Kaiser had given her in 1902. The reporter quoted her as saying: 'I spend my time between Milan and Rome and have palaces in both cities. The one in Milan is on the outskirts of the city and a good way from *La Scala*. I have had all I want of grand opera.' Then, still adept in the art of making herself popular, she went on: 'I have one grand passion left and that is for your country.' And pulling a small 'Stars and Stripes' flag out of her handbag she waved it, shouting 'Viva America!' as she rushed into the arms of old friends who had come to the dockside to meet her. She told them that through sea-sickness she had spent the entire voyage in her cabin, although the crossing had been a smooth one.

Tetrazzini was then driven off to stay at the Hotel Ritz-Towers where the *World Telegram* reporter who interviewed her three days later wrote that 'her ponderous frame' was draped in 'a jade chiffon dressing gown dripping with ostrich feathers'. When the *San Francisco Chronicle*'s New York correspondent called and asked for her views on modern society, she expressed disapproval of 'the way so many women are now behaving like men'. As a result they were losing their past privileges. 'Mme Tetrazzini touched lightly on her last venture into matrimony saying that she was now rather cynical and disillusioned about love'.[5]

Singing in variety

Questioned about her concert tour, Tetrazzini confined herself to replying 'with a chuckle' that three managers were fighting over her. The truth was that she had failed to interest any concert promoters. All were suffering from the effects of the depression caused by the Wall Street financial crash and they also wondered whether the new generation would take to her. She announced that the purpose of her visit was a charitable one. Every cent she earned would go to funds for the relief of the jobless.

In the New Year Tetrazzini's financial position had so deteriorated that she was forced to accept an offer to sing in a large Boston cinema where she was one of a number of variety turns including acrobats.[6] She opened on 16 January when reviews all agreed that age had been kind to her voice which still retained the 'rich colorful resonance it had in the past'.[7]

André Benoist, who had accompanied Tetrazzini at the piano during her 1910/11 American tour, wrote in his memoirs that the last time he saw her was in this Boston variety show.

> She had become so stout that, being unable to walk on the stage gracefully, she had been placed on a small platform around which her long skirts had been draped and upon this scene the curtains parted. It was rather a pitiful sight. . . . Once more the depressing thought came to me: Why, oh why do artists not know when to end their careers in time?[8]

Back in New York Tetrazzini persevered in her efforts to organize a tour for herself, and eventually in desperation she accepted an engagement to appear four times daily in vaudeville at the Paramount Theatre, commencing on 13 March 1932. Looking massive in white robes festooned with ostrich feathers and wielding an enormous fan, she sang two arias, *Caro nome* and *Addio del passato*, closing in English with *The Last Rose of Summer*. Her companion Lina Primo told a friend: 'Sometimes the legs give way, the voice never.'

An account of an interview with Tetrazzini in her dressing-room at the *Paramount* appeared in *The Theatre* for April that year. The journalist reported her as saying that she was doing 'a tremendous lot of reading'. Ten hours in one dressing-room was a long time and she did not know whether she would be able to endure three months of it. Was it true that she trembled with nervousness? Of course, it was, and she had been trembling for the same reason all her life. She had never gone on to a stage to perform without trembling, and she did not think she was showing it more than she used to in the old days in England.

Speaking of her visits to London, she would like the interviewer to mention how very sorry she had been to hear of the death of Lionel Powell, the impresario, who had arranged so many of her concert tours. 'I thought he was one of the most charming men I ever met.'[9]

Did she know how the story had started that she was appearing in vaudeville because she was penniless?

> Goodness knows! They will say anything in the papers here to make a sensation. No, I am not doing anything to stop the story getting about. It amuses me too much. I should be terribly upset if I really were poor. I am only unhappy when I think of all the poor people who are suffering so much distress through unemployment in America. The distress is too awful for words, but when I think of all the hungry people I can help by singing in a cinema I become happy again. I shall try hard to endure ten hours on duty as long as I can for their sakes.

The money paid her she was donating to a fund for the relief of those out of work in New York.

Unfortunately for her, Tetrazzini found singing in vaudeville four times a day too much of a strain, contracted a cold and had to give up the engagement.

24 Frieda Hempel's Appreciation

Prima donna Frieda Hempel had become a friend of Luisa's in 1922 when they had attended each other's recitals in the Royal Albert Hall and Frieda now invited the other to stay in her New York apartment while she recuperated. In an appreciation published in *The American Music Lover* (Vol. 6, June 1940) Frieda wrote how Luisa's happy, almost childlike nature completely charmed her. The voice was 'as good as ever' only the breath control was not what it had been.

> Nevertheless, she could take a splendid high C and soften it in a beautiful dimuendo – something many young sopranos cannot do. She sang all the time even in the elevator, for there was nothing self conscious about Tetrazzini.

Sometimes the two women would stay up almost all night singing together or playing records. One night Frieda remembered especially. They had put on Luisa's recording of *Ah, non credea mirarti* from *La Sonnambula* (Victor 88305) and she sat there 'in her old bath robe, singing with it, with a beauty of tone and expression that made me choke with emotion'.

Frieda Hempel goes on to give details of the six records she chose for a half-hour radio programme as the best to exhibit Tetrazzini's voice and art. She began with the taunting song of the page Oscar, *Saper vorreste* from *Un Ballo in Maschera* which she regarded as typical of Tetrazzini's brilliance and abandon. Because of its 'stronger, more forward recording', the 1907 Gramophone Company's version (issued in New York as Victor 92068) was played in preference to the later American recording (88304 or 6341) which is an even more florid performance.

Frieda Hempel's second and third selections were again Gramophone Company recordings of *Ah, fors' è lui* (the only one in which the *Ah, fors' è lui* is preceded by the recitative *E strano*) and *Sempre libera*, which were released by Victor on records 92060 and 92021. The first Hempel regarded as 'one of the finest examples of legato singing ever recorded by Tetrazzini.[1]

Hempel played next the striking *Carceleras* from Chapi's *Las Hijas del Zebedeo* (Victor 88294; HRS 1015) which shows Tetrazzini's remarkably low register. She had once told Hempel that her voice when young had originally been a contralto's, which in view of her high range the other had found hard to believe though she knew Luisa had sung in concert arias from heavy dramatic roles like *Aida*. Noticing Frieda's sceptical expression, Luisa sang some deep contralto tones which were judged 'wonderful in quality and volume'. Hempel's account continues: ' "Oh, Luisa", I said, "what a voice! Is there anything you cannot do?" She laughed and, looking down at herself, answered, "Well, Friedalina, some singers hava da figure, but I gotta da voice." '

Frieda Hempel writes that the last two records she played over the radio were *Ah, non credea mirarti* and the notoriously difficult *Ah, non giunge*, both from *La Sonnambula* (Victor 88313 or 6345). 'Tetrazzini makes it sound like child's play and in my opinion her dazzling performance has never since been equalled.'

Other outstanding recorded examples of Tetrazzini's vocal art that appealed to Frieda Hempel were: First, the lovely Pastorale from Veracini's *Rosalinda* available in the HMV Historical Catalogue coupled with *Una voce poco fa* from Rossini's *Barbiere di Siviglia* (No. DB 690); the latter also issued by Victor on 88301 and 6337, and also in a re-recorded electrical version with new accompaniment – disc 7883. Next there is a surprisingly effective rendering of the dramatic soprano aria *Pace, pace mio Dio* from Verdi's *La Forza del Destino* (Victor 88502 or 6397); her famous polonaise from Thomas's *Mignon* (V. 88296 or 6342), the Bell Song from Delibes's *Lakmé* (V. 88297 or 6340), Proch's Air and Variations (V88297 or 6340), and her superb *Carnevale di Venezia* (V. 6339).

For those who did not like the old recordings because of their poor accompaniments, Hempel suggested that they listened to the re-recorded disc (Victor 7883) that includes besides Tetrazzini's *Una voce poco fa*, her singing of *Caro nome*. 'In the latter disc some of the true fullness of the singer's voice is better conveyed than in the original acoustic records of these same arias. Tetrazzini is said to have approved of this re-recording.'

Frieda Hempel went on to point out that Tetrazzini's first recordings with Victor are marred by their frequent failure to convey the true roundness of her tones. In their eagerness to avoid blasting, the producers may have positioned her too far away from the horn resulting in a thin, distant tone.

Having, thanks to Frieda Hempel's kindness, recovered her health after performing four times daily in vaudeville, Tetrazzini tried once more to obtain concert engagements but without success, so in late May she left for Europe aboard the *Berengaria*.

25 The Last 'Farewell' Appearances

On Wednesday 7 December 1932 *The Times* reported that Tetrazzini had arrived at the Savoy Hotel from Italy and two days later, reviewing the charity concert at the Albert Hall in aid of the Safer Motherhood Appeal, it commented that 'musically speaking the thing of most substantial interest was the repetition under Sir Thomas Beecham of Smetana's unfamiliar tone poem *Bohemia's Woods and Fields*.' The audience's enthusiasm, however, reached its peak at the end when Tetrazzini appeared. Her voice, the critic wrote, had 'kept its clarity and her high notes their purity'.

'H. S. G' stressed in the *News Chronicle* that all the artists taking part in the event 'freely admitted that it was Tetrazzini's show'. Her contributions had been Micaela's song from the third act of *Carmen* and *Ah, non credea* from *La Sonnambula*. The applause and the cries of 'Encore!' which rewarded her must have seemed 'like an echo of that historic night 25 years ago when she began her brilliant reign at Covent Garden'.

The *Morning Post* agreed that the reappearance of Madame Tetrazzini in London after so many years was the event of the evening.

> When she trotted on to the stage clearly much moved, throwing her hands in the air, blowing a kiss or two, in obvious trouble with her voluminous draperies, the audience gave her a rousing welcome. And the brave old lady deserved it.

The writer wondered how many contemporary singers at her age would be able to sing Bellini's very exacting *Ah, non credea*, or even Micaela's song as she did.

> It would be affectation to pretend that the voice is anything like what it was, but there are some beautiful notes still, curiously high rather than low, and the phrasing, and above all, the style remained impeccable.

Following the success of the Caruso re-recordings, the Gramophone Company wrote to Victor in December 1932 asking them to consider re-recording two titles of Tetrazzini's from the following list: (i) *Il Barbiere di Siviglia: Una voce poco fa.* Matrix C10071; (ii) *Rigoletto: Caro nome.* Matrix C10074, DB536; (iii) *La Sonnambula: Ah non giunge.* Matrix C10076, (iv) *La Sonnambula: Ah, non credea mirarti.* Matrix C10064.

They pointed out that she had recently appeared at the Albert Hall, which had been a very successful concert and was to undertake 'a large farewell tour of the world'. For such a tour a few re-created records would be useful. The reply from the Victor Company was, however, not 'enthusiastic'. Nevertheless eventually (i) and (ii) were re-recorded electrically with added orchestra and numbered DB1979, V7883.

It seems now that Lionel Powell was dead, Tetrazzini had not limited her negotiations for the booking of a concert tour to his successor, Harold Holt, but had also dealt with another impresario, Thomas Arthur Russell, which led to his taking a legal action against Tetrazzini and Holt in the King's Division of the High Court of Justice in the summer of 1933.[1]

Estranged Husband Sues

Meanwhile, Tetrazzini's marital troubles had come to a head when on 26 June Pietro Vernati filed a suit in Rome to prevent her from dissipating what remained of her fortune on the grounds that she was 'mentally unsound'.[2]

Fortunately for Tetrazzini, the High Court case in London was resolved amicably. The settlement was as follows.[3] She agreed during the autumn season of 1933 to sing in concerts in England to be advertised as 'a farewell appearance', and that the plaintiff Thomas Arthur Russell would have the first refusal of her services for the Albert Hall or elsewhere in London at a definite guarantee of £300 as a fee. Harold Holt was given the option of cooperating with Russell in co-presenting her should he so desire and on a basis to be mutually agreed.

Harold Holt received the right to engage Tetrazzini for a maximum number of 12 concerts in his International Celebrity Subscription Series throughout the provinces commencing in October 1933 provided that all printed matter, newspaper advertisements and other announcements bore immediately under her name the words, 'By arrangement with T. Arthur Russell'. For each such concert she would receive 50 per cent of the proceeds from the sale of tickets with a guaranteed minimum of £100, whilst Holt would pay Russell ten per cent of the takings.

Tetrazzini also committed herself to giving eight further concerts under Russell's management for which she was to be paid a similar 50 per cent with a £50 minimum.

The next clause went:

The Plaintiff agrees not to use any of the "International" towns controlled by Mr Holt in which to present Madame except with Mr Holt's permission, but he may at his discretion arrange for Madame to appear at towns which could be fitted in conveniently with these International dates so long as Madame's wishes are respected that she has two clear days' rest between each concert.

Taking advantage of this last clause, Russell submitted to Fred Gaisberg who was acting for Tetrazzini a list of 12 provincial 'dates' which he forwarded to her at the Villa Rondo, Via Cesare, Babtisti 98, Monza, north of Milan, which had once belonged to Italian Royalty and which she had purchased. She wrote back from there on 3 July, thanking him for all that he had done but expressing surprise that the tour would consist of 24 concerts instead of the 20 she had expected. She had also expected at least two clear days' rest between concerts. There were too many appearances in too short a time. She hoped her strength would hold out. Fred replied immediately on the 7th of that month:

Dear Friend,

You are quite right that the dates of the tournée are not very favourable, but you must endeavour to economise your vitality and voice, and give, for these very small towns just so much. You must conserve your energy. To allow two days between each concert would indeed be too extravagant and would take up too much of your time and the time of the impresarii. In other words it is not economical or commercial.

On this tour, which must be in the nature of a farewell tour, you must give the maximum of your strength. I have told Harold Holt that he must not let you be disturbed by journalists and everything must be done to make travelling easy.

Meanwhile the engineers of the Gramophone Company had been busy on the re-recordings mentioned earlier. On 18 August 1933 two matrices were sent to Victor at Camden: 2B 5032–1 *Il Barbiere di Siviglia – Una voce poco fa*: and 2B 5033–1 *Rigoletto – Caro nome*. This became DB 1979 and was sent to Milan for Tetrazzini's approval. Happily, she thought the result 'very favourable'. The Italian branch of the company issued the record in their December supplement. The re-recording was reviewed in the October issue of *The Gramophone*, which praised these 'fine examples of her voice and skill at their best'.

Record Royalties 1928–36

It might be of interest at this stage to give details of some of the half-yearly payments of record royalties received by Tetrazzini in her declining years from the Gramophone Company.

To:	£.	s.	d.
31 December 1928	46	4	9

31 December 1929	8	8	5
30 June 1930	22.	7	1
30 June 1932	None		
31 December 1932	5	15	1
30 June 1933	3	18	4

Now for the six months ending 31 December 1933 they were to rise to £151. 3. 8d as a result of her long 'farewell' tour of the British Isles. Then to fall back to:

	£.	s.	d.
30 June 1934	14	8	10
30 June 1935	12	16	3
31 December 1936	14	6	1

On 20 August 1933 Pietro Vernati failed in the first round of his law suit to get the civil court in Rome to declare Luisa incapable of managing her own affairs on the grounds that she was the victim of hallucinations and that under their influence she was foolishly squandering her fortune, once valued at five million dollars.[4] According to Vernati's lawyer her luxurious villa in the most prestigious part of Rome had become a meeting place for spiritualists and 'mysterious rites held there inevitably wound up in the clinking of champagne cups'. He had learnt she was now trying to sell the property and he wanted to prevent this.

'I won't keep my house just to please him,' Tetrazzini was quoted as saying. 'He knows I am 62 years old and he thinks that if I sell it I shall spend the money on my friends and so there will be less for him.' She protested against her husband's statement to the press that she had come down to singing in a Boston movie house as 'the last stage of a glorious career'. She accused him of misrepresenting her charitable acts. Every cent thus raised had been used to support the jobless in Boston and New York.

Vernati would not accept defeat and appealed to a higher court. After reading in the press of the litigation in Rome with Pietro Vernati, Fred Gaisberg wrote on 21 August:

Dear Luisa,
    Do not let the trouble with your Marito disturb your tranquility and peace of mind. You must make every effort to live quietly, so as to prepare yourself for the very big English concert tour. You must be in the best of health when you start this tour.[5]

Tetrazzini hoped that her husband would have second thoughts and withdraw his appeal. But, as he did not and as it was to come before the Public Minister on 11 October, she filed a counter charge three days earlier claiming that the purpose of his litigation was to extort money from her.[6]

Thanks to Fred's negotiating skill, Arthur Russell agreed to reduce the number of provincial concerts under his management and on 30 August

Fred wrote to Luisa at the Villa Rondo in Monza giving the final rearrangements as follows:

Wednesday afternoon	18 October	Reading
Sunday afternoon	22 October	Bournemouth
Wednesday evening	25 October	Doncaster
Saturday evening	28 October	Eastbourne
Thursday afternoon	2 November	Taunton
Saturday afternoon	4 November	Torquay
Monday evening	6 November	Plymouth
Thursday evening	9 November	Folkestone

Gaisberg added that there was no need for Luisa to arrive in London before 14 October. 'Please take my advice and bring with you a useful maid, who can act both as your maid and secretary. An intelligent girl is what is needed.'[7] She took his advice and brought with her a Clary Schlatti – and no man friend, which would have been unwise in view of her marital rift.

As mentioned in Chapter 4 André Benoist accompanied Tetrazzini at the piano on an American tour. In his memoirs he wrote that when they parted she gave him a 'princely present' – a gold Jurgenson repeater watch which he treasured. 'But only as a museum piece, for I soon noticed that when wearing it, its weight made me limp on one side.' Years later after her decease and without referring to her by name, Harold Holt was to relate at a large banquet in Fred Gaisberg's honour how a famous diva when on tour used to take with her for companionship some young Adonis whom she fussed over and spoilt and gave, when they parted, an expensive watch. On one occasion her cicisbeo pretended to be ill and refused to leave the Savoy.

The lady was so upset that she wanted to cancel the tour so as to remain with him. Someone suggested that elderly Fred Gaisberg should travel with her instead. He was not too pleased at the prospect of a long tour in winter visiting some dismal towns. However for the sake of good relations he agreed and when they returned to London the grateful diva presented him with a grandfather clock.[8]

On 4 September 1933 Fred informed Luisa that he had arranged for her to hold a press reception on 17 October. Then on the 12th he wrote that 'Ivor Newton will be *l'accompagnatore* which will make you very happy because he is *molto simpatico*.'[9]

On that same day Tetrazzini was sending Fred details of what she intended as her programme at each concert. She would be singing four songs as follows:

Part I	Ofelia's aria from the Mad Scene in Thomas's *Amleto*
Part II	Leoncavallo Mélodie – *Qu'à jamais le soleil se voile*
	Tchaikovsky Mélodie – *Toujours à toi*
	R. Chapi – *Las Hijas del Zebedeo: Carceleras*

On 14 October 1933 Tetrazzini arrived in London and went to stay at the Savoy. But there was no royal suite this time. All she could afford was a small room without a view. That legal battle with her second husband was the chief topic reporters were eager to discuss. Fred Gaisberg who directed the Press conference at the hotel needed all his skill to deflect awkward questions. At her request he went with her and Ivor Newton to Reading for the opening concert on Wednesday 18 October under Arthur Russell's management.

Fred wrote in his diary:

> It was an afternoon affair. The theatre was drab and depressing. We sought the dressing-room assigned to her. It was also drab and without a proper convenience. Things seemed suspiciously quiet and I peeped out into the house. It was only half filled. Tetrazzini was not feeling too well, and to cap the situation only narrow ladder-like stairs led to the stage, up which we all had to climb and to assist the somewhat portly singer up and down. In the past on these occasions there had always been Umberto Tatò or Bazelli to kiss her behind each ear before she faced her audience and to give her confidence.

Now she relied on her rosary to achieve this and as she kissed it, Fred could see a tear trickling down her cheek. Concerning her singing, he wrote that her voice was no longer equal in purity and timbre to what it had been pre-war, but she had the *pratique* of long experience on the concert platform that enabled her to give entire satisfaction to her public.[10]

After singing in the other seven towns as arranged – and in addition for Harold Holt at Leeds Town Hall, Tetrazzini returned to London on 10 November. Two days later, Fred Gaisberg and his sister Carrie accompanied her to the Albert Hall for her Sunday afternoon farewell concert. He wrote in his diary: 'I was in the Artists' room with Tetrazzini. She was in a terrible state, and although she pulled through the concert it was pathetic. She attempted to play her old role of Prima Donna but the going was heavy.' She managed nevertheless to retain her sense of humour. As she came onto the platform she brushed against one of the orchestra and apologized, saying: 'I would have gone sideways – but I have no sideways!' The programme also included violin solos by Lisa

Minghetti, piano solos by Niedzielski and songs from Joseph Hislop, the Scottish tenor.

F. G. Prince-White wrote in the *Daily Mail* that the many thousands of people in the audience showed Tetrazzini very clearly that they hoped it would not be the last time they heard her.

> Grey-haired men and women shut their eyes and were carried back on memory's wings to magical nights at Covent Garden Opera House nearly thirty years ago. Young men and girls who had never heard her before were struck with amazement; they could not think of her as a veteran. . . . She came, half running, onto the platform in a flutter of black lace, waving her heavily jewelled hands, laughing and crying at the same time and throwing kisses to right and left. There was a roar of welcome, which swayed her like a strong wind. Then silence, as she drew herself up and nodded to her accompanist to begin.

'From time to time she glanced at a large emerald on her right hand,' the *Morning Post*'s 'S. G.' observed.

> It was her mascot. She never sang in public without it and she was reassuring herself that the stone was still there. She sang the Mad Scene from *Hamlet*, the Jewel Song from *Faust*, and some smaller pieces. Last of all she sang *Ah, fors' è lui* from *Traviata*, the opera in which also in early November, 26 years previously, she had made her triumphant début at Covent Garden. Enthusiasm had by now reached a climax. The audience invaded the platform and her last encore was sung from among a compact maze of admirers.

Prince-White in the *Daily Mail* says that Tetrazzini was almost covered with roses by hundreds of her admirers. 'They snatched at her hand to kiss it – they pressed on her with gifts. And all the while they were shouting "Bravo"!'

She was utterly exhausted when she sank into her chair in the Artists' Room, and could scarcely hold the glass of water for which she had asked. When she had recovered a little, Prince-White enquired whether she would ever sing in London again. ' "Ah, no, my friend", she exclaimed sadly, "this is indeed my last appearance in London. Or shall we say" – and her laugh came back – "shall we say the last official appearance? Perhaps if my dear English public ask me sometime to come – well I will!" ' The *Musical Times* for December commented sourly: 'The dear English public may be depended upon to continue to do its duty where a prima donna is concerned as consistently as it neglects its duty to musical events of real importance.'

A large cheering crowd awaited Tetrazzini outside, and police had to make a way for her car, which was filled with the flowers that had been showered on her. She told the chauffeur to drive her to Westminster Cathedral and escorted by Fred Gaisberg, went in and, lighting candles, prayed for Caruso and Patti.

Richard Capell next day in the *Daily Telegraph* described the concert as one of those which, common in the old days, had become ever rarer, so much so that those of the younger generation who had missed it might perhaps never have another chance.

> It was a miscellaneous concert; it threatened to be interminable. Singers sang pieces that had been written for the opera house, pianists played pieces that had been composed for the orchestra.
>
> One section of the audience insisted upon encore after encore from the tenor of the afternoon, while those who had come intending to witness a great star's disappearance below the horizon began to look at their watches and wonder: 'What about tea?'
>
> On the face of it, then, not the most poetic of farewells. But it was better thus. It was better that the diva should bid good-bye in the manner of her era, in the manner of Patti, of Melba. This jovial old lady, with her still undefeated vocal technique, must be almost the last of the divas.
>
> Time was when this voice was a complete carillon of faultless ringing tones. It was remarkable yesterday how many of the little bells were still intact and musical. Some of the metal has worn dangerously thin; it would be affectation to deny that the hour for good-bye has struck but hardly once was a flaw betrayed in the delicate old instrument. Thus do good material and good workmanship stay the course.

Ernest Newman wrote in a similar vein. 'Every living singer should have been present to hear her for there was so much that she could teach them, singing not only with intelligence but also with perfect technique.'

The Times found that Tetrazzini remained a great singer with the brilliance of her technique undimmed:

> One doubts, indeed, whether, apart from the quality of tone here and there, she sang *Ah, fors' è lui* any better at her first appearance at Covent Garden than she did yesterday afternoon.... She did not essay the second part of the air, but she had already shown in the 'Mad Scene' that she has not lost her command of the spectacular side of her art. She even managed to infuse a remarkable amount of dramatic expression into that almost forgotten *cheval de bataille*. Even better was her singing of the *Jewel Song* from *Faust*, which was truthful in dramatic expression and perfectly vocalized.
>
> Of her other contributions to the programme, Chapi's *Carceleras*, which one had heard her sing long ago, was as brilliant as ever in its sly imitation of Spanish intonation. If the patter was a little less brisk, the sense of fun was undiminished.

On the very day that Tetrazzini was reading these favourable reviews in the English papers her husband's appeal against the dismissal of his suit by the civil court came up before the Tribunal of Rome. His lawyers alleged that since the couple had been legally separated Tetrazzini had pawned jewels worth 1,500,000 lire for a mere 100,000 lire in a reckless manner, and she had now sold their home in Rome worth 2,000,000 for a quarter of its true value. 'The poor exalted woman believed in spirits which she evoked with melodramatic gestures, falling in tremendous contortions on soft carpets' was how the Rome correspondent of the *San Francisco Chronicle* translated the advocate's words. Tetrazzini admitted that she was interested in spiritualism but scoffed at her husband's charges. Her generosity was prompted by artistic temperament. Vernati had exaggerated the extent of her fortune. Perhaps when they married he had believed that she was richer than she really was. She still had to rely partly on her work for a living. Vernati was trying through this case to extort money from her.

The Italian Public Minister recommended that Vernati's appeal should be rejected and a decision was deferred for the Tribunal to give full consideration to the matter. In such cases, however, they usually agreed with the Public Minister.

Following her Albert Hall concert Tetrazzini resumed her 'farewell' tour now solely under Harold Holt to give International Celebrity Subscription Concerts with Ivor Newton as her accompanist, and with assisting artists the Edinburgh-born tenor Joseph Hislop and the Russian violoncello soloist Piatigorsky.[11]

The posters and newspaper advertisements bore the message:

FAREWELL OF

TETRAZZINI
    TETRAZZINI
LAST IN THE ROYAL LINE OF PRIMA DONNAS
    TETRAZZINI
       TETRAZZINI

No matter how unwell she might have been during her long career, the 'Florentine Nightingale' had rarely withdrawn from an engagement and on this last tour there were several occasions when it was touch and go as to whether willpower alone could surmount the increasing physical handicaps of age and the treacherous British climate in winter. Stories were to circulate that she had failed to perform more than once, involving Harold Holt in serious financial loss, but these had no basis in fact.

On the evening of 14 November Tetrazzini gave the first International Celebrity Concert of her 'farewell' provincial tour run by Harold Holt. This was at the Town Hall, Middlesborough.

On the 16th she sang at the De Montford Hall, Leicester; on the 20th at St Andrew's Hall in Glasgow; on the 23rd at the Caird, Dundee. Next she went to Manchester where two evenings later she was due to sing in the Free Trade Hall. Brand Lane who ran the International Celebrity concerts informed her that the orchestra rehearsal would be held on the morning of the 25th. That, she told him, was out of the question because she never left her hotel on the day of the concert until just before the advertised time.

When Brand Lane handed her a copy of the programme there was more trouble, for it incorrectly stated that she would be singing the Mad Scene from *Lucia di Lammermoor* instead of the one from Thomas's *Amleto* which she had chosen on fixing her programme with Fred Gaisberg for the whole tour.[12]

Brand Lane apologized, but pointed out that the orchestral parts for *Lucia* were the only ones available in Manchester. Tetrazzini, however, was obdurate. 'I shall sing Ofelia from *Amleto* or I shall not sing at all,' she insisted, storming into her bedroom and locking the door. As Sir Henry Wood was to conduct the orchestra, further discussion was postponed until his arrival late that evening from London. He immediately telephoned his secretary there and arranged for the *Amleto* orchestral parts to be left with the guard of a night train from Euston. Then, since Tetrazzini had refused to rehearse with the orchestra, Sir Henry got Ivor Newton to do so alone with him so that he could mark on his score the phrasings used by her and the pauses where she took breath for which he must allow during her singing.

Diva and conductor did not meet until the opening of the concert when Sir Henry escorted her onto the platform. Ofelia's Mad Scene proved an enormous success, and the evening ended with Luisa kissing him and everyone in the orchestra – and even Brand Lane.

Tetrazzini was heard next on 27 November at the Colston Hall, Bristol. According to Newton, she sang for an encore *Caro nome* as in her prime. 'Madam, that was wonderful,' he complimented her. 'It was not wonderful,' she returned, seeming extremely surprised, and crossing herself. 'It was a miracle.'[13]

Three days later, Tetrazzini appeared at Liverpool's Central Hall. *Musical Opinion* reported that audiences supporting concerts that winter had been sparse and even she had not been able to attract a full house.[14]

In contrast a very large audience assembled to bid farewell to the diva in Edinburgh's Usher Hall on Saturday afternoon, 2 December.[15] Those who saw her looking limp and weary in the dressing-room could hardly believe their eyes when she appeared before the public. Then on the 5th she sang in Birmingham before travelling to Dublin. The Irish Sea was rough and, never a good sailor, she was extremely sick but despite this fulfilled her engagement on Saturday afternoon, 9 December, in the enormous old Theatre Royal. The *Irish Times* reported next day that she had brought with her 'much of the old vivacity and sparkle and just wanted to share her high spirits with the audience'. The *Evening Mail* thought it fitting that she should be making this farewell in a theatre that had seen 'some of her finest triumphs during the last twenty-five years'. She still had that youthful outlook that had always been her chief characteristic and was more than 'perhaps the greatest coloratura singer the world has ever known, being a great personality, a gracious lady and a simple, lovable soul'.

On the Sunday Tetrazzini went north to Belfast where she was billed to sing on the Monday evening at the Ulster Hall.[16] Now she was suffering from a bad cold and impresario Harold Holt was doubtful if she were fit enough to perform but she insisted on doing so. Her cold had worsened by the time she had crossed the Irish Sea once more to reach Newcastle-upon-Tyne where she sang in its City Hall on 14 December. The *Newcastle Daily Journal* found that she had made a brave show with the resources 'which the inexorable march of time has left her'.[17]

This final 'farewell' tour was due to end in Sheffield's City Hall on Monday, 18 December. The photograph on the front page of that morning's *Sheffield Daily Telegraph* show the diva arriving the previous day at the station looking old and tired. Interviewed later at the *Royal Victoria Hotel* by a reporter she was asked if anything had gone wrong so far during her travels. 'Tell him about that hat,' suggested Clary Schlatti, her companion and secretary. Tetrazzini then revealed that she had brought twenty of the most fashionable hats with her from Milan for wearing during the tour, but had left them all at the Savoy Hotel except the one she travelled in. The difficulty always was to try and make it look different when the Press wanted to photograph her. 'I pull it a little more round on my head each time to make it seem the very latest fashion!'[18]

Critic 'A.M.C.' wrote in the Tuesday edition of the *Yorkshire Telegraph and Star*[19]:

Tetrazzini's voice is a Box of Tricks. It is 63 years of age, but she conjures with it as though it was half that number.

This is what happened when she bade adieu to Sheffield at the City Hall last night. She came slowly, painfully slowly, to the platform. Sympathy was aroused. But as if to dispel that sympathy Tetrazzini flung out her arms to the audience. She waved her hands gaily; she blew kisses. Tetrazzini appeared a brave little woman as she walked slowly to the arm of the grand pianoforte. She was about to sing the Mad Scene . . . and she clutched a black scarf tightly round her neck as if to prepare herself for this excruciating aria.

A cheerful nod to her accompanist and Tetrazzini's first notes were heard. Amazing notes – especially in the vibrant middle register; amazing cadenzas, beautifully curved; breathing completely under control.

Tetrazzini is old but she has the will of youth. Never does she become pathetic. You forget Tetrazzini, the old lady of song, when you hear these notes. What beauty they still retain – and sometimes an exquisite brilliance. True her top notes have faded, true her middle register has lost some of its quality, but Tetrazzini's technique is such that defects are readily hidden . . .

Legal conflicts

The New Year began badly for Tetrazzini. The Tribunal had not yet ruled regarding her husband's appeal, and now he had discovered that she had been tricked into buying part of a mountain in the belief that precious metals would be found there, so on 2 January he renewed his application for a guardian to take charge of her finances. She was given until the 29th of that month to testify in Rome.

Fred Gaisberg did his best to comfort his old friend by entertaining her in London before she returned to the worries of legal conflict in Italy. He had the happy inspiration of taking her to the London Coliseum which had a curtain attractively adorned with the faces of the famous in the world of entertainment, and among these was Tetrazzini's own which pleased her immensely.

The show was a revue starring Gracie Fields, who appeared in one sketch as an opera-house cleaner scrubbing its stage. She confides to the audience her longing to be a *prima donna* with a voice like Tetrazzini's and clowns her way through arias in a mixture of Lancashire, Italian and French, getting all the top notes. This so amused Luisa that her cascades of laughter echoed round the theatre, drawing the attention of the audience to her presence and they gave her a warm-hearted reception.

The delighted diva had a note sent round asking Gracie if she would sing *Ah, fors' è lui* for her. 'There was only one thing to do, go on stage and guy the aria she had requested, as I usually did,' the great variety artiste wrote in *Sing As We Go*. 'I went, but I was quaking.' After the performance had ended, on returning to her dressing-room, she found Tetrazzini already waiting. The little woman stood on tiptoe, her dark eyes filled with tears, and put up both arms to embrace the other. 'My darling', she said, 'you *must* sing in real opera and leave all this.'[20]

Back in Monza, Tetrazzini refused to reconcile herself to the fact that she was now past going on concert tours and she wrote to Fred Gaisberg asking him to do all he could to get Harold Holt to book her a spring tour. Meanwhile her legal battle with her husband dragged on and on.

On 13 January 1934 Fred wrote to 'Dear Cara Luisa' that he had just had an interview with Harold Holt who told him he was experiencing great difficulty in arranging concerts for such a tour.

> It seems that a lot of the concert agents are reporting that their recent efforts in the concert world have been without success and they strongly advise the abandoning of concerts in their towns until better times.
>
> Mr Holt says that he can fix up 10 concerts only. Under the circumstances, I think you had better make up your mind to come over just to do 10 concerts and postpone the rest until the summer when Harold Holt thinks conditions will be more favourable around some of the resorts.[21]

However, Tetrazzini did not give the proposed ten concerts. As Harold Holt's business correspondence and records are no longer in existence the exact reason for this cannot be ascertained. But she did come over in March for a single concert. The *Sunday Times* for 11 March 1934 commented on Tetrazzini's recital the previous Sunday afternoon at the London Palladium.

> This artist's formal farewell was duly recorded some time ago. On this occasion she availed herself – and the public – of the privilege of writing a postscript. Its characters were formed with inimitable individuality. Miss Lisa Minghetti contributed violin solos with brilliance and distinction, and Ivor Newton accompanied.

Tetrazzini sang the Mad Scene, Leoncavallo's *Qu'à jamais le soleil se voile*, Tchaikovsky's *Toujours à toi*, and the *Carceleras*. Her encores were *Ah, fors' è lui* and *Chantez, chantez, ma belle*.

Three days later Tetrazzini left London for Paris.

On 4 November 1934 the United Press reported from Rome that Mme Tetrazzini had just made it known that she was demanding

> criminal punishment of her young husband who for many months has been trying to place her financial affairs in the hands of a trustee. She had instructed her counsel to proceed in penal court tomorrow with charges of attempted extortion against him. Attorneys for the diva claimed to have evidence that Vernati offered to withdraw his action for appointment of a trustee if the singer would pay him $8700.'[22]

On the 2nd of the following month, a civil court in Rome ruled that Tetrazzini was 'well behaved mentally and had not squandered her estate as charged'. This was actually a formal closing of the case because a short while previous to this Vernati had been advised by his lawyers that he had not the slightest chance of success and had withdrawn his petition to prevent his wife from administering her estate on the grounds that she was mentally deranged. Although legal differences were now settled, the couple continued to live apart.[23]

The only persons to gain from the conflict were the lawyers and in order to pay them, Tetrazzini had to sell the Villa Rondo in Monza. She then discovered too late that Pietro Vernati's distrust of the type of people with whom she was mixing was well founded, and that her spiritualist friends had been in collusion with the previous owner and had tricked her into buying the Villa Rondo at a vastly inflated price. Alfredo Forletto, a medium, Giovanni Rognoni and Marcello Dazza were those involved and she sued them on charges that they had conspired to defraud her through messages received during seances she had attended. She contended that she had given Rognoni power of attorney to buy the villa and that he had sold the furniture it contained to Dazza while she was absent in the States.

The case dragged on for years and then on 15 April 1940, when Tetrazzini was dying and unable to attend the proceedings, a Roman court acquitted the three men of the charge that they had embezzled money from her.[24]

Operatic school in Milan

Having sold the Villa Rondo for far less than what it had cost her, Tetrazzini was left in such financial straits that she rented a large house in Milan. Here one half was used by Ettore Verna as a school providing private instruction for all branches of the operatic theatre while the rest was occupied by her and where she lodged the students. Some of these she coached. Verna employed as repertory maestri Antonio Narducci, conductor of the San Carlo in Naples, and Giovanni Fratini; for languages and diction Professor Maria Borchetta and Dr Max Cushing; for acting, costuming and make up, Albertina Baldi.

When Verna was interviewed at the Villa Tetrazzini in 1938 by the Editor of the *Giornale Degli Artisti e Degli Spettacoli*, he spoke about some of the students he and she had launched – the Oklahoma Chickasaw Indian Princess Mobley Lushanya who, after a brilliant début as Aida in Trieste sang Cio-Cio-San there as well as in Turin and Florence, then in 1944 sang Tosca to acclaim in Mexico City opposite Ramón Vinay whom she married; Luisa Bickford of Maine, known professionally as Luisa Franchesi, who had already appeared in opera in New York, Boston, Philadelphia and Chicago as well as at Ferrara, Trieste and Genoa; Anne McMullan, a lyric coloratura soprano who had made her début as Gilda at the Teatro Alfieri in Turin; Thomas McGrath, an American tenor discovered by Lily Pons; and a thirteen year old coloratura, a protegée of Tetrazzini herself, Edvina Marino.

Nikitina, born in Russia, star of Diaghilev's Monte Carlo Ballet Company and later an equally famous singer at La Scala, tells in her memoirs[25] how, when aged six, she heard for the first time on a gramophone record Luisa's voice which captivated her more and more as she listened to it,

> especially by its coloratura, with trills where two notes were clearly heard at the same time, her rapid staccatos, her sharp notes, but particularly by the easy, silvery sound, equally harmonious and strong on the high and low notes.

Then years later in 1936 on the advice of concert manager, Harold Holt, Nikitina went from London to Milan to seek advice from Tetrazzini on the choice of a professor to prepare her to sing in opera.

Nikitina relates how she had just arrived and had not yet unpacked or searched for Tetrazzini's address, when she herself appeared in the hotel.

> I will never forget my emotion at seeing this woman who had ever since my

childhood been a legend to me.... She was very fat, breathless, small, with bulging black eyes. She spoke very fast, with the soft, sing-song Tuscan accent, interwoven with American words which she used to make herself better understood. She took me under her wing at once and wanted me to find a cheaper room for which I was grateful, but what I wanted was that she should hear me as soon as possible.

Next day Nikitina went to Tetrazzini's villa.

When I arrived she came down from the second floor, singing away – and rolling pizzicatos that reached the E sharp, with a wonderful timbre. Her voice was still very young. The lesson began. She made me try out the whole of *Rigoletto*, directing it as we went on: she sang the part of Caruso; I sang her own part, Gilda. She ended by promising me a great career as an opera singer and undertook to give me daily lessons. She refused to accept any money from me.

On 29 May that same year the *San Francisco Examiner* had reported the sad news for Luisa of the death at the age of 73 of the impresario 'Doc' Leahy who had done so much to further her operatic career. Then in 1938 her sister, Eva Campanini, died at Salsomaggiore. But despite such blows, her talent survived. When friends called who had not seen her for a long time, she would tell them: '*Sono vecchia, sono grassa, ma sono sempre la Tetrazzini!*' She was old and fat but still Tetrazzini. And to prove it, she would strike a chord on the piano and sing an ascending arpeggio to a perfect high C. This was what she did on one of the three occasions in September 1937 when Max de Schauensee visited her in Milan. It was hot and when he arrived she was sitting in her garden in a rather tacky pink dressing-gown, a fan in her hand, holding court with some pupils and friends.

Writing in a leaflet accompanying Rococo of Toronto's issue of Tetrazzini's unpublished 1922 recordings, de Schauensee remembers that she laughed a great deal, revealing several missing teeth.

It was all rather idiotic – zany, if you will – but every now and then there were flashes of shrewd appraisal and observation.... She hated Melba and gave us an imitation of Melba's rather straight tone ('like a horn', she said). I asked her whether she had ever heard Patti and she said, 'Only once – a concert in 1908. It was dreadful, for it was at the very end but she sang a long trill and made a gradual decrescendo on it. This was enough for me to understand why she was Patti and what a singer she must have been.' She rated Lina Pagliughi (her pupil) as the greatest coloratura of the day. And Lily Pons? ... 'Piccola, piccola voce,' and again she burst out laughing.... In Tetrazzini's upstairs bedroom, I was shown the fearfully ornate furniture which had belonged to Queen Margherita at Monza.

Max de Schauensee ends that Tetrazzini was a perfect sample of the overwhelming virtues that can stem from what are now considered the defects of an era.

Today, she would be rather lost in the over-produced, quasi symphonic conception of operatic presentation ever moving towards 'total theater'. And yet – could anyone blamelessly cut the wings and cage such a veritable human nightingale?

De Schauensee also writes that Tetrazzini, when all is said and done, emerges as a vocal and technical genius. 'When Emilio de Gogorza took the great Pol Plançon to hear her in *Lucia* the famous basso, who had heard everybody from Patti down, turned to his friend, and exclaimed, '*Mais c'est un génie!*'

26 The Most Enduring of Memorials

The Galleria in Milan is a wide, glass-covered arcade on either side of which are to be found a miscellany of offices and shops. Regarded when originally erected as an architectural wonder, it is always busy with people passing between the square before La Scala and the one adorned by the city's impressive cathedral. A witty writer, Eugenio Gara, has written that whether it was built 'on a spot which was already the marketplace of operatic folk, so that they might have a roof over them, or whether it was built first and the opera fraternity flocked to it, as soon as it was finished, as an ideal place for gossiping and bargaining' is uncertain. It was here that Tetrazzini would often sit outside Savini's Café and Restaurant Bar and as passers-by waved to her, she would remark proudly to her companion: 'You see how many people know me!'

Occasional events occurred to brighten Tetrazzini's old age, such as when she was elected President of the Italian Academy of Bel Canto, and when on 10 January 1938 she sang on the radio in Milan and a recording of this was relayed to the United States. As a result a correspondent of the Associated Press visited her and she told him how she had forgiven Toscanini for preventing her from singing at La Scala on the grounds that she was 'too pyrotechnic'. One day recently he had been resting in the Galleria when, catching sight of her, he rose, approached, kissed her hand, then asked if she would sit with him. 'I think it is time you sang for me,' he suggested. 'No, I sing nothing but pyrotechnics!' she had replied, then added, 'But perhaps we will find something to do together'.[1]

Later, Luisa became friendly with Toscanini's former mistress Rosina Storchio, who had sung Cio-Cio-San at the disastrous *La Scala* première of *Madama Butterfly* in February 1904, conducted by Cleofonte Campanini. The two elderly sopranos would occasionally meet at a café. One day Rosina looked worried. 'The roof of my mausoleum in the Cimitero

Monumentale is leaking,' she complained. 'And so is mine', Luisa revealed.[2]

Sol Hurok, the impresario who had presented Tetrazzini in concerts in the United States, wrote in his reminiscences how he visited her during her retirement and how she herself cooked spaghetti for their dinner. Afterwards she insisted, with a purposefulness he did not understand, that they went out driving in her Packard 'almost the last memento remaining to her of the great years'. They reached one of the most beautiful cemeteries he had ever seen and she led him into a finely proportioned mausoleum. There inside, confronting him from all the walls were photographs of the diva in every one of her great operatic roles. 'See, my darling Hurok,' he quotes her as saying with a serene satisfaction shining in her face, 'this is my future home. I wanted you to see it.'[3]

Adelina Patti named Tetrazzini as her successor after listening to her Violetta at Covent Garden in 1908. Tetrazzini did the same for Lina Pagliughi after hearing her sing in California when only seven years old. The childless diva wanted to adopt the prodigy but the girl's mother would not hear of it. Nevertheless Tetrazzini did all she could to further Lina's career and when brought to Milan by her father to perfect her musical training with Maestro Manlio Bavagnoli they became very close. Their friendship lasted until the diva's death.

Pagliughi told Lanfranco Rasponi that even when in her late sixties Tetrazzini could tackle Es and E flats with a serenity and a roundness that left her gasping.

> There was nothing she could not do with that instrument of hers. She kept insisting that I learn to use my chest tones the way she did. But I was always pulling out excuses for I was well aware that while she could use them fearlessly, I never would be able to do the same and that I risked injuring my vocal chords. She was the most marvellously kind and humane person, and everyone who knew her could not help but love her. In fact, her home was always full of young people asking for advice, but also enjoying the pleasure of her company. Tetrazzini took her retirement with philosophy and wisdom and never stopped helping people of all stations. I learned a great lesson from her.[4]

The end nears

On 15 February 1940 Luisa fell ill with cerebral haemorrhage and was taken to the private clinic of Dr Vittorio Mattei in Milan's Via Carpi. It looked as though she might make a slow recovery. Then on 23 April the press reported that she was lying seriously ill with pneumonia.

Lina Pagliughi was singing the Queen of the Night in *The Magic Flute* at the Maggio Musicale Fiorentino when she learnt that Luisa was in a critical condition, so she rushed to Milan between performances to be with her best friend, who embraced her trying in vain to speak. 'She never stopped weeping,' Lina recalled to Lanfranco Rasponi. 'What a tragic ending for someone who had one of the most beautiful voices in the world.'

Only a nurse was at Luisa's bedside when she died at 8.35 am on 28 April – three months before her 69th birthday. For some days she had been unable to take nourishment other than occasional sips of champagne. Incorrect reports that she died a pauper and had to be buried at public expense have been repeated as fact in books of reference since then, but this is not true. After a Requiem Mass at the church in the Via Casoretti, attended by her widowed sister Elvira Martucci, niece Elsa, the Minister of Popular Culture, actor Rodolfo Chiantoni and a few others, her body, clad in a brocade and silver gown was placed in the mausoleum of which she was so proud and above which perched the graceful figure in bronze of a woman with arms outstretched pointing up into the sky – and inscribed with words from *Lucia di Lammermoor: Alfin son tua* – 'At last I am thine.' This she had commissioned from a sculptor Toscanini had recommended.

The day after the diva's death was announced, a black wreath tied with white ribbon bearing these words on an unsigned card: 'In memory of San Francisco's own Luisa Tetrazzini' was placed by Lotta's Fountain by an old lady who then hurried away. Next, a bunch of pink roses with a card inscribed 'In grateful remembrance' was laid above the wreath.

Luisa had been cared for during the last year or two of her life by a friend, the old soprano Giulia Scaramelli, the wife of the baritone Taventi. Scaramelli told John Gualiani that Tetrazzini still had when she died a long pearl necklace worth then a million lire, but that someone had stolen it whilst she was in the clinic. This necklace was the one the end of which she would pick up and toss over her shoulder as a signal at concerts that she was ready to begin.

Apart from the necklace she left very little. Once Umberto Tatò had dared to chide her over her lavish gifts of money to all with a hard-luck story, however threadbare, but she merely smiled, patted his cheek and replied in Italian: 'Poor Tatò, but don't you see it makes me happy? Tatò would not like me to lose any happiness, would Tatò?'

And he, knowing from long experience that it was useless arguing with her, shrugged and kissed her hand. To his intimates he confided his fear that Luisa would die in penury, a fate that might have been spared her had she not possessed, as Peter Dawson wrote, a heart as big as her voice.[5]

The *Musical Times* obituary notice[6] sets out admirably Luisa Tetrazzini's talents:

Even in 1933 when the colour of her voice had faded she retained that superlative technique in which she surpassed all rivals. Tetrazzini's coloratura singing was the most brilliant that our times have known. It had that ease and naturalness that should be, but seldom is, a first condition of that type of vocal art, and which removed all sense that a clever feat was being performed in defiance of nature. Her voice had colour at command and she could use it sensitively for dramatic effect; moreover, she had humour and the gifts of an actress.

Luisa left no will, so her husband took possession of the few things she still owned. After the Second World War, the EMI Music Archives show the Gramophone Company as remitting to him £310.8s.2d for royalties on Tetrazzini's record sales for the period July 1939 to 31 December 1946. As time passed, the payments diminished as might be expected. For example, for the half year ended 12 December 1956 they were only £6.9s.7d. For the next six months they rose to £43.4s.7d, falling to £9.3s.2d for the rest of that year and to £3.7s.2d from then to 31 March 1958.

During the years that followed, Pietro Vernati was continually urging EMI to bring out new editions of his wife's records. The last communication in their files came from him at his home Via Acton 46, Lido di Ostia-Roma. Dated 7 October 1968, it acknowledged receipt of £30.1s.7d on account of royalties and enclosed photocopies of letters from Enrico Caruso and Adelina Patti to his wife as well as one of a letter in which the Lord Mayor of Rome announced the naming of a street in that city after Luisa Tetrazzini. Vernati suggested that these might be used for promotion purposes, and also that attention be drawn to the fact that 'the younger generation of opera singers, such as Maria Callas, used the records of the voice of my wife for their study'.[1]

Mausoleum destroyed

In May 1990 I went to Milan's *Cimitero Monumentale* to visit what Luisa Tetrazzini had described to Sol Hurok as her future home. The man in the *Ispettorato* shook his head and said that no one of that name was interred there. I persisted, so he pored over a book of entries, then filled out a ticket and handed it to me. I read 'CELLA 9, SPACIO 83, RIPARTO 5' and off I went.

The cemetery still is, as Hurok found it, extremely beautiful, well spaced out and tended. Section 5 was easy to find but where the Tetrazzini mausoleum should have been was a communal one which, from the list of contents outside, was where distinguished citizens of Milan were laid to rest within. But Tetrazzini's name was not included.

Had I been given the wrong particulars? I searched in vain round all the mausoleums in that section. I returned to the Ispettorato and found it closed. I walked round the entire cemetery looking for a mausoleum with a bronze figure on top – but all in vain.

That afternoon I visited the Museo Livia Simoni next to La Scala and there I was told that as Tetrazzini's mausoleum had fallen into need of repair and as there was no one willing to pay for its restoration, her body had been removed and the mausoleum demolished and the present one erected. The bronze angel had 'disappeared'.

John Gualiani has lived most of his life in Milan and has an unrivalled knowledge of opera. He was able to give me further facts as to what had happened to Tetrazzini's tomb. One day in 1981, a visitor from San Francisco was taken by him to see it and finding the structure in an extremely dilapidated state the American, on returning home, had written to the City Hall offering to have it restored at his own expense, but he never received a reply. The mausoleum had been razed in the interim and the diva's remains reinterred elsewhere. Mr Gualiani gave me a photocopy of a photograph of himself standing before the building and taken by this visitor. Above the entrance in huge capitals is her name – TETRAZZINI – and half hidden by overhanging branches the bronze figure can be glimpsed.

John Gualiani also explained to me that the procedure at the Cimetero Monumentale is first for the plot of ground to be bought and the mausoleum erected and then every time a member of the family dies 'a large sum of money' must be paid for the right to interment within it. In Tetrazzini's case, he says, the City of Milan authorities at that time forwent this extra charge in view of her fame. The first and only other member of the family to be interred there was her brother Rodolfo, who died on 28 July 1917. In February 1992 I heard from Dr Giorgio Cavallari of Milan that the bodies had been moved to plots 558 and 559 in section N. 30 of the cemetery for the poor, the Cimitero Maggiore. He sent me two photographs of the graves showing just bare earth and no monuments of any kind. Rosina Storchio's mausoleum has also been demolished and her remains interred here. Also in another plot lie those of Elvira de Hidalgo, Callas's singing teacher.

It is sad that Tetrazzini's remains should have been treated in this way – and especially when one remembers that in Argentina she once sang to raise money to protect a cemetery from desecration, and then, later, made it her practice on All Souls Day to tend neglected graves should, when dead, have been treated in this way. Fortunately there is a far more lasting memorial to her in the recordings of her voice – a voice not to be mistaken for any other, that sang straight from the heart to the hearts of her listeners.

Notes

Chapter 1 – The 'Florentine Nightingale' Flies Off

1. Information received in letters from and phone conversations with Aristo Biancoli's granddaughters, Mrs Pauline Forster and Mrs Gloria Parkes.
2. Tetrazzini, Luisa (1921) *My Life of Song*, London: Cassell, pp. 7–11.
3. Ibid., pp. 23–4.
4. Ibid., pp. 28–30.
5. Shaw, Bernard (1931), *Music in London*, 1890–94, London: Constable, vol. 1, pp. 6, 8–9.
6. Tetrazzini Luisa, (1921), *My Life of Song*, London: Cassell, pp. 41–52.
7. Information from John Gray and Alessandro Scalaberni, Luisa's great nephew by marriage, in Florence. Also information from John Rosselli: references to Alberto and his father Luigi in Frank Walker's *The Man Verdi* (1962) and in *Messa per Rossini* (*Quaderni dell'Istituto di Studi Verdiana*, Parma, 1988). Luigi was a busy impresario, active in a number of north and central Italian towns between 1858 and 1877. He is best remembered for having refused the (gratuitous) use of the Teatro Communale, Bologna for the proposed Requiem Mass for Rossini which Verdi and 12 other Italian composers put together. Also Ugo Morini, *La Accadema Degli Immobili Ed Il Suo Teatro 'La Pergola'* 1649–1925, Pisa, Tipografia Ferdinado Simoncini, p. 249.
8. Interviews with Millie Robbins, *San Francisco Chronicle*, 1 and 7 November, 1968 – also with Arthur Bloomfield, *San Francisco Examiner*, 1 November, 1968.
9. *La Riforma*, 30 December, 1890.
10. *My Life of Song*, pp. 59–62.
11. Rinaldi, Mario *Due Secoli Di Musica Al Teatro Argentina*, Vol. II, Firenze, Leo S. Olschki Editore, MCMLXXVIII, p. 1194.
12. *My Life of Song*, p. 65.
13. Details from Dr Carlo Marinelli's archives.
14. Mario Rinaldi, p. 1195.
15. *Dizionario La Musica*, Unione Tipografico Editrice Torinese, 1968, p. 382.
16. *My Life of Song*, p. 71–3.
17. Information from Mary Jane Phillips Matz, author of biography of Verdi.
18. Gaisberg, Fred W. (1964), *Music on Record*, London: Robert Hale, pp. 106–11.

Chapter 2 – In South America

1. Bosch, Mariano G. (1910) *Historia del Teatro en Buenos Aires*, Establecimiento Tipografico El Commercil, Buenos Aires, Capitulo xxxvi, pp. 416–20, 436–7.
2. *Standard*, 24 September, 1892.
3. Letter, 5 December, 1989. Also 10 January, 1990.
4. *My Life of Song*, pp. 106–11.
5. Letter, 5 December, 1989, also 24 February, 1990.
6. *Standard*, 16 January, 1894 *La Prensa*, 16 January 1894 – *La Nación*, p. 5, c. 2, January 1894.
7. *Standard*, 27 January, 1894, and *La Nación*, 25 January, p. 5, c. 3.
8. *Standard*, 20 February, 1894.
9. *La Nación*, 20 February, 1894.
10. *My Life of Song*, p. 75.
11. *Standard*, 7 March, 1894.
12. *My Life of Song*, pp. 102–3.
13. *Standard*, 17 March, 1894 – *La Nación*, 17 March, p. 5, c. 4.
14. *Standard*, 5 April 1894.
15. *My Life of Song*, p. 92.
16. *Standard*, 28 August, 1894.
17. *Standard*, 4 September, 1894.
18. *Standard*, 10 October, 1894.
19. *Standard*, 21 October, 1894.
20. *Standard*, 20 November, 1894.
21. *Standard*, 5 December, 1894.
22. *My Life of Song*, p. 75.
23. ibid., pp. 79–82.
24. ibid., pp. 87–8.
25. Henstock, Michael (1990) *Fernando de Lucia*, London: Duckworth, p. 218.

Chapter 3 – Singing With Caruso

1. *My Life of Song*, p. 125–31.
2. *My Life of Song*, pp. 91–2.
3. *Standard*, 8 June, 1898.
4. ibid., 21 June, 1898.
5. Caruso, Enrico Jr. and Farkas, Andrew (1990), *Enrico Caruso: My Father and My Family*, Portland, Ore.: Amadeus Press, p. 388.
6. *Kurjer Warszawski*, Nr 125 p. 4 – Nr 127 p. 3 – Nr 130 p. 5 – Nr 131 p. 4 – Nr 133 p. 5 – Nr 134 p. 4 – Nr 135 p. 3 – Nr 280 p. 3 – Nr 282 p. 3.
7. Agliati, Mario (1967), *Il Teatro Apollo di Lugano*, Instituto Editoriale Ticinese, pp. 222–3.
8. *Kurjer Warszawski*, Nr 280 p. 3 – Nr 282 p. 3.
9. Forster, E. M. (1924), *Where Angels Fear to Tread*, London: Edward Arnold, pp. 167–71.

Chapter 4 – At The Teatro Arbeu

Abbreviations

EOF   Enrique de Olavarria y Ferrari (1961), *Reseña Historica del Teatro en Mexico* (1538–1911), Mexico, Editorial Porrua, 5 volumes.

LRM = Luis Reyes de la Maza, *El Teatro en Mexico durante el Porfiriato*, tomo III, Mexico, Universidad Nacional Autonoma de Mexico, 1968.

1. Carlo Gatti (1964), *Il Teatro alla Scala*, Milan: Ricordi, pp. 63–4. Annuario Lirica Italiana, Milan, 1896–7.
2. EOF, pp. 2484–6.
3. EOF, p. 2486.
4. EOF, p. 2488.
5. EOF, p. 2491.
6. EOF, p. 2493.
7. EOF, p. 2495.
8. EOF, pp. 2496–7.
9. EOF, pp. 2498–9.
10. EOF, pp. 2500.
11. EOF, pp. 2501–2.
12. EOF, p. 2499.
13. LRM, p. 221–2.
14. EOF, p. 2508.
15. EOF, p. 2509.
16. EOF, p. 2510.
17. *My Life of Song*, pp. 140–1.
18. EOF, p. 2510.
19. EOF, p. 2511.
20. To find out these facts about Bazelli's career involved long research through newspapers and journals including the *Mondo Artistico, Gazzetta dei Teatri, Gazzetta Musicale di Milano* and the *Corriere della Sera*.
21. EOF, pp. 2635–40.
22. EOF, pp. 2641–2.
23. *San Francisco*, Hastings House, p.143 – Galgey, Edmond (1950), *The San Francisco Story*, N.Y.: Columbia University Press, p. 178.
24. Article by Freddie Francesco, *San Francisco Chronicle* Library, December 1946.
25. EOF, p. 2642.
26. Benoist, André (1938), *The Accompanist*, N.J.: Paganini Publications, p. 143.

Chapter 5 – The Tivoli – and Lawsuits

1. Dickson, Samuel (1955), *The Streets of San Francisco*, Stanford: Stanford University Press, pp. 8–13.
2. *San Francisco Examiner*, 12 January, 1905.
3. *Argonaut*, 30 January, 1905, p. 72.
4. ibid., 20 February, 1905.
5. *My Life of Song*, pp. 143–6.

6. *San Francisco Call*, 20 April, 1905, p. 1, c. 3–6.
7. *San Francisco Chronicle*, 28 April, 1905.
8. ibid., 29 April, 1905.
9. *Evening Post*, 15 September, 1905.
10. *San Francisco Call*, 20 September, 1905.
11. *San Francisco Call*, 22 September, 1905, p. 16, c. 2.
12. *San Francisco Call*, 27 September, 1905, p. 9, c. 2.
13. *San Francisco Call*, 2 November, 1905, p. 4, c. 1.
14. Maxwell, Elsa (1954), *I Married the World*, London: Wm. Heinemann, pp. 35–6.
15. EOF, p. 2767.
16. EOF, p. 2768.
17. EOF, p. 2770.
18. EOF, p. 2778–9.
19. *My Life of Song*, p. 153–4.
20. Caesari, Edgar Herbert (1965), *The Alchemy of Voice*, London: Robert Hale, p. 83.

Chapter 6 – In A Despotic Diva's Absence

1. Gaisberg, Fred W. (1946), *Music on Record*, London: Robert Hale, pp. 66–8.
2. All correspondence between Muir and the Gramophone Company in London is preserved in the EMI Archives at Hayes and is unpublished.
3. Moore, Jerrold Northrop (1976), *A Voice in Time*, London: Hamish Hamilton, p. 95.
4. ibid., p. 113.
5. Covent Garden Archives.
6. Unfortunately for posterity Eva made no records for by the time this might have been possible her voice had deteriorated.
7. Covent Garden Archives.
8. *My Life of Song*, pp. 173–4.
9. Covent Garden Archives.
10. *My Life of Song*, pp. 177–9.
11. ibid., pp. 190–4.

Chapter 7 – Covent Garden's 'Voice of the Century'

1. *My Life of Song*, p. 194.
2. ibid., pp. 184–5.
3. Covent Garden Archives.
4. *My Life of Song*, p. 94.
5. Moore, Jerrold Northrop *A Voice in Time*, p. 113.
6. *My Life of Song*, pp. 204–11.
7. *Musical Standard*, December 1907, p. 363.
8. EMI Archives, Hayes.
9. ibid.
10. Melba, Nellie (1925), *Melodies and Memories*, London: Thornton Butter-

worth, pp. 236–9. Also 'Hammerstein Tells How He Engaged Songbird Melba' in the *World*, Theatre Section, 6 May, 1906, p. 2.

11. Cone, John Frederick (1964), *The Manhattan Opera Company*, University of Oklahoma, p. 144.
12. Sheean, Vincent (1956), *The Amazing Oscar Hammerstein*, London: Weidenfeld & Nicolson, p. 126.
13. *My Life of Song*, pp. 240–1.
14. EMI Archives.
15. 'How Great Artists Make Their Records', *The Voice*, 12/13, 12/21.
16. EMI Archives.

Chapter 8 – Oscar Hammerstein's 'Star of Stars'

1. Cone, John Frederick (1964), *The Manhattan Opera Company*, Oklahoma: University of Oklahoma, p. 140.
2. *The World*, 19 January, 1908.
3. Kolodin, Irving (1953), *The Metropolitan Opera, 1883–1950*, New York: Knopf, p. 230.
4. *The World*, 16 January, 1908.
5. *New York Press*, 16 January, 1908.
6. 'A Gallery of Great Singers: 13', *Opera*, September 1963, pp. 596–8.
7. *New York Times*, 16 January 1908.
8. *Punch*, 22 January, 1908.
9. *San Francisco Chronicle*, 29 March, 1908.
10. EMI Archives.

Chapter 9 – Trouble in Milan – and from Melba

1. All the correspondence between Kilmuir in Milan and the Gramophone is to be found in the Tetrazzini files, EMI Archives, Hayes.
2. Steane, John (1974), *The Grand Tradition*, London: Duckworth, p. 42.
3. Scott, Michael, (1986), *The Record of Singing*, London: Duckworth, Vol. 1, p. 91.
4. ibid., p. 90.
5. ibid., p. 162.
6. The Gramophone Company recording to which Muir refers is that of 'Splendon le sacre faci' = Matrix no. 2176f HMV 053144 Victor 92018. Now on CHS 7 63802 EMI CLASSICS CD 1, Item 5.
7. This letter passed into the possession of Tetrazzini's second husband Pietro Vernati who sent a photocopy to the EMI Archives. It was also reproduced as an illustration to Giovanni Artieri's article, *Lettere a una cantante* in *Libro dei Giorni Italiani, Anno XII, 'Il Teatro Lirico'*. ENIT edition, Rome, 1960.
8. Hurst, P. G. (1963), *The Golden Age Recorded*, Lingfield: Oakwood Press, p. 95.
9. *Musical Times*, 1 July, 1908, p. 456.
10. Covent Garden Archives.
11. Nichols, Beverley (1949), *All I Could Never Be*, London: Jonathan Cape, pp. 67–8.

12. Shenker, Israel (1988), *The Savoy of London*, Chesler Publications, p. 10.
13. Reproduced as illustration to *Lettere a una cantante*, by permission of Pietro Vernati.
14. Quoted by Lahee, H. C. (1912), *The Great Opera Singers of To-day*, Boston: Page & Co., pp. 128–49, from Sanborn's essay in the *Globe*.

Chapter 10 – Captivating the Customers

1. Rawlings, Syllester, 'What These Singers Are Paid Today Told by Arthur Hammerstein', *New York Evening World*, 7 May, 1910.
2. Tuggle, Robert (1987), *The Golden Age of Opera*, N.Y: Holt, p. 54.
3. *Globe*, 6 December, 1908.
4. *The New York Sun*, 14 and 29 February, 1909.
5. News item in the *New York Evening World*, 29 March, 1909.
6. *Boston Transcript*, 1 April, 1909.
7. Cone, J. F., *Oscar Hammerstein's Manhattan Opera Company*, p. 224.
8. *Musical Times*, 1 July 1909, p. 466.
9. *Musical Opinion, Out and About*, July 1909, p. 705.
10. Covent Garden Archives.
11. ibid.
12. *My Life of Song*, pp. 306–7.
13. Holzknecht, Vaclav (1981), *Emma Destinnova*, Praha: Panton, p. 174.
14. *My Life of Song*, p. 242.
15. *New York Herald*, Theatre Section, 9 January, 1910, p. 11.
16. *My Life of Song*, p. 262.
17. Sheean, Vincent, *The Amazing Oscar Hammerstein*, p. 271.
18. Cone, John Frederick, *The Manhattan Opera Company*, p. 252.
19. ibid., pp. 253–4.
20. ibid., p. 255.
21. *My Life of Song*, p. 271.
22. 'Concert Tour for Tetrazzini', *The New York Clipper*, Vol. LVII, 15 January, 1910, p. 1.
23. Downes, Olin (1910), 'Boston's Judgment', *Musical America*, Vol. XI, April 9, p. 6.
24. Cone, John Frederick, *The Manhattan Opera Company*, p. 256.

Chapter 11 – Tetrazzini Breaks with Hammerstein

1. Moses, Montrose J. (1916), *The Life of Heinrich Conried*, N.Y.: Thos. J. Crowell, p. 186.
2. Sheean Vincent, *The Amazing Oscar Hammerstein*, p. 243; Cone, J. F., *The Manhattan Opera Company*, p. 226.
3. Sheean, Vincent, *The Amazing Oscar Hammerstein*, p. 302.
4. *My Life of Song*, p. 243.
5. *San Francisco Chronicle*, 13 April, 1910; *My Life of Song*, p. 294.
6. Cutting, name of newspaper not shown, preserved in *San Francisco Chronicle* library archives, headed 'Report of Death of Tetrazzini's Husband False, London, April 20, 1910'.

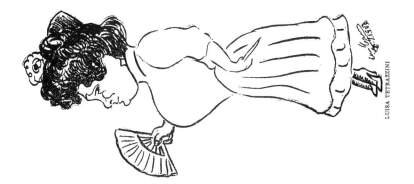

CARICATURE OF CARUSO IN OPERA, DRAWN BY HIMSELF.

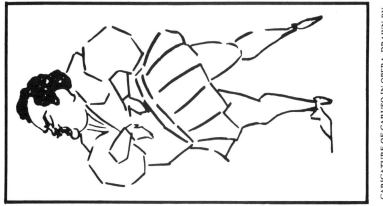

LUISA TETRAZZINI

9   Caricatures by Caruso of himself and Tetrazzini

10   Studio photograph of Tetrazzini by W. & D. Downey, London, soon
after her 1907 Covent Garden début

11 Tetrazzini in her dressing-room with brother-in-law, conductor
    Cleofonte Campanini

12   top: Mayor P. H. McCarthy introducing Tetrazzini before her famous open-air concert in San Francisco on Christmas Eve, 1910.

bottom: part of the huge crowd assembled. Her tiny figure in white is visible

13   Oscar Hammerstein I

14 top: A *Punch* cartoon satirizing the rivalry between the two divas

bottom: Tetrazzini visiting an alligator farm in Los Angeles, 1921. She was also photographed sitting on one named 'Big Bill', aged 17½ years

15   John McCormack

16   top: Tetrazzini's mausoleum in Milan's Cimitero Monumentale before demolition

bottom: photograph (taken in 1993) of the plot in the Cimitero Maggiore where her remains were transferred

7. *The Times*, 24 April, 1910.
8. *Musical Times*, 1 June, 1910, p. 377.
9. Agliati, Mario, *Il Teatro Apollo di Lugano*, Istituto Editoriale Ticinee, p. 300.
10. Hughes, Spike (1956), *Great Opera Houses*, London: Weidenfeld & Nicholson, p. 133.
11. *The Times*, 26 September, 1910, p. 8.
12. Wood, Sir Henry J. (1938), *My Life and Music*, London: Gollancz, p. 318.
13. *Musical Times*, 1 November, 1910.
14. *San Francisco Call*, 5 August, 1910, p. 1.
15. *San Francisco Examiner*, 25 November, 1910; *San Francisco Call*, 26 November, 1910, p. 2.
16. *San Francisco Chronicle*, 26 November 1910.
17. ibid., 2 December 1910.
18. ibid., 7 December 1910.
19. Benoist, André (1938), *The Accompanist*, N.J.: Paganini Publications, Chapter X.

Chapter 12 – Singing in the Streets of San Francisco

1. A very full account of the event appeared in 'Millie's Column' of the *San Francisco Chronicle* for 22 December, 1960.
2. *San Francisco Chronicle*, 28 December, 1910.
3. ibid., 29 December, 1910; *San Francisco Call*, same date.
4. ibid., 31 December, 1910, both papers.
5. ibid., 19 January, 1911.
6. A large photograph of this appeared in the *San Francisco Chronicle*, 20 January, 1911.
7. Benoist, André, *The Accompanist*, Chapter X.
8. *San Francisco Chronicle*, 24 February, 1911.
9. ibid., 9 March, 1911.
10. *San Francisco Chronicle*, 6 April, 1911.
11. *San Francisco Call*, 27 July, 1911, p. 1.

Chapter 13 – Discord over Royalties

1. The whole of this chapter is based on the correspondence in the Tetrazzini files in the EMI Archives, Hayes, England.

Chapter 14 – Coronation Gala

1. Covent Garden Archives.
2. *Daily Telegraph*, 24 April, 1911.
3. Covent Garden Archives.
4. Information from Tetrazzini's great niece, Mrs Pauline Forster.
5. EMI Archives, Hayes.
6. ibid.

Chapter 15 – Début at the Met

1. *My Life of Song*, p. 240.
2. Eaton, Quaintance (1965), *The Boston Opera Company*, N.Y.: Appleton-Century, pp. 167–8.

Chapter 16 – 'San Francisco, My Heart Is with You'

1. *San Francisco Chronicle*, 15 February, 1912.
2. *San Francisco Call*, 7 March, 1912.
3. *San Francisco Chronicle*, 7 March 1912.
4. *San Francisco Examiner*, 7 March, 1912.
5. *San Francisco Examiner*, 17 March, 1912.
6. *San Francisco Chronicle*, 19 March, 1912.
7. *San Francisco Call*, 25 March, 1912.
8. *San Francisco: The Bay and Its Cities* (1940), Hastings House Publishers, p. 191.
9. *San Francisco Call*, 5 April, 1912.
10. *San Francisco Chronicle*, 6 April, 1912.
11. ibid., 24 April, 1912.
12. Sitwell, Osbert (1949), *Laughter in the Next Room*, London: Macmillan.
13. *The Voice*, February 1920, pp. 12–13.
14. Davis, Ronald L. (1921), *Opera in Chicago*, N.Y.: Appleton-Century, p. 280.
15. Moore, Edward C. (1930), *Forty Years of Opera in Chicago*, N.Y.: Horace Liverright, pp. 90–1.
16. Davis, Ronald L. (1965), *A History of Opera in the American West*, Prentice-Hall, p. 47.

Chapter 17 – Clashes with Campanini

1. *San Francisco Chronicle*, 11 March, 1913.
2. *San Francisco Examiner*, 11 March, 1913.
3. *San Francisco Chronicle*, 29 March, 1913.
4. Davis, Ronald L. (1921), *Opera in Chicago*, NY: Appleton-Century, p. 81.
5. *Musical America*, 29 October, 1913.
6. *Musical Times*, 1 November, 1913, p. 723.
7. See Chapter 14.
8. *Musical Courier*, 22 November, 1913.
9. *Minneapolis Journal*, 24 January, 1914.
10. *San Francisco Chronicle*, 4 March, 1914.
11. *San Francisco Examiner*, 4 March, 1914.
12. *Musical Times*, 1 July, 1914.

Chapter 18 – Exit Bazelli – Enter Tatò

1. It has been assumed in the past that Tetrazzini was married to Giorgio Bazelli and that he must have died before 1926 enabling her to marry Pietro Vernati. It needed considerable research for me to learn eventually from Professor

Nicolae Baloiu of the *Academia de Musica Bucuresti* the facts but incorrect in one respect. He wrote to me that Eugenia Bazelli was his wife. Further research in Craiova itself proved that she was his sister. For discovering this my thanks are due to Daniela Constantin of Craoiva. She was unable to find his grave anywhere and was told by an old lady who had known him that she believed he spent his last years in Nice and may have had two children there. It has proved impossible to obtain any evidence to support this story.

2. Gaisberg, Fred W. (1946), *Music on Record*, London: Robert Hale, p. 148.
3. *My Life of Song*, p. 292.
4. ibid., pp. 275 and 288.
5. Agliati, Mario (1967), *Il Teatro Apollo di Lugano*, Istituto Editoriale Ticinese, p. 378.
6. ibid., p. 379, footnote.
7. ibid., p. 332.
8. Information received from a friend of Tetrazzini's, Mary Casalina Costa, during a research visit to Milan in May 1990.
9. *Music on Record*, pp. 148–9.
10. ibid., p. 158.
11. *Musical Times*, 1 November, 1921.
12. *Christian Science Monitor*, 22 September, 1919.
13. EMI Archives, Hayes.
14. *My Life of Song*, p. 305.
15. EMI Archives, Hayes.
16. *Los Angeles Times*, 9 December, 1919, pt. 3, p. 4.
17. *The Spectator*, 'Town Talk', 13 December, 1919.
18. *San Francisco Examiner*, 8 December, 1919.
19. *My Life of Song*, p. 275.
20. Caruso, Dorothy (1946), *Enrico Caruso*, London: T. Werner Laurie, p. 161.

Chapter 19 – Conflict over Contracts

1. *North American*, 12 April, 1920. Other newspaper cuttings in the *San Francisco Chronicle* library archives unfortunately do not show names of newspapers from which taken. These have provided the information given in my account.
2. *New York Times*, 11 April, 1920.
3. *San Francisco Examiner*, 21 May, 1920.
4. *My Life of Song*, pp. 68–9.
5. This account of the negotiations over the recording contracts is based on the correspondence in the EMI Archives in the Tetrazzini folders.
6. *Music on Record*, pp. 102–3.

Chapter 20 – The First 'Farewell' Concert Tour

1. John Pitts Sanborn in the *Globe and Commercial Advertiser*, 6 December, 1920.
2. *San Francisco Examiner*, 25 March, 1921.
3. See Chapter 17, p. 179, where Tetrazzini mentions her collection of dolls kept in Lugano. Now she has brought most of them with her.
4. *San Francisco Chronicle*, 25 March, 1921.
5. ibid., 3 April, 1921.

6. Caruso, Enrico Jr. & Farkas, Andrew (1990), *Enrico Caruso: My Father and My Family*, Portland, Ore.: Amadeus Press, p. 389.
7. Newton, Ivor (1966), *At the Piano*, London: Hamish Hamilton, pp. 63–71.
8. *The Times*, 7 November, 1921.
9. *Musical Mirror*, February 1922, p. 35.

Chapter 21 – 'How to Sing'

1. *The Times*, 3 August, 1922.
2. Caruso, Enrico Jr. & Farkas, Andrew (1990), *My Father and My Family*, Portland, Ore.: Amadeus Press, p. 389; *Musical Mirror*, February 1930.
3. *The Times*, 10 December 1932.
4. *Musical Courier*, November 1922.
5. McCarthy, Desmond (1931), *Portraits*, London: Putnam, p. 266.
6. Newton, Ivor (1966), *At the Piano*, London: Hamish Hamilton, pp. 64–7.
7. EMI Archives, Hayes.
8. Hurok, Sol (1947), *Impresario*, London: Macdonald, p. 129.
9. Aspinall, Michael, *Luisa Tetrazzini: the voice and the records* – Notes accompanying EMI CLASSICS CDs CHS 7 63802 2.
10. Tetrazzini, Luisa (1923), *How to Sing*, C. Arthur Pearson, pp. 24–5.
11. ibid., Chapter 18.
12. ibid., p. 99.
13. ibid., pp. 34–5.
14. *Musical Times*, 1 September, 1924, p. 827.
15. Henderson, W. J. (1938), *The Art of Singing*, New York: Dial, pp. 90–1.
16. Caesari, Herbert (1958), *Tradition and Gigli*, London: Robert Hale, p. 125.

Chapter 22 – Tetrazzini Makes Broadcasting History

1. *Music on Record*, pp. 103, 148.
2. *Evening Standard*, 10 March, 1925.
3. *Daily Express*, 11 March, 1925.
4. *Evening Standard*, 11 March, 1925.
5. *Daily Mail*, 27 March, 1925.
6. ibid., 26 March, 1925.
7. *Daily Sketch*, 27 March, 1925.
8. *Evening Standard*, 27 March, 1925.
9. *Musical Times*, 1 May, 1925, p. 448.
10. *The Times*, 30 March, 1925; Ivor Newton, *At the Piano*, pp. 67–8.
11. *The Times*, 29 November, 1925.

Chapter 23 – A Second Marriage Fails

1. These contract negotiations are fully documented in the EMI Archives.
2. Moore, Gerald (1983), *Furthermore*, London: Hamish Hamilton, p. 46.
3. *San Francisco Chronicle*, 24 October, 1926.

4. *Musical Mirror*, 'Heard in the Interval', April 1929.
5. *San Francisco Chronicle*, 31 December, 1931.
6. *Musical Mirror*, February 1932, p. 32.
7. *San Francisco Chronicle*, 17 January, 1932.
8. Benoist, André (1938), *The Accompanist*, N.J.: Paganini Publications, Chapter X, last paragraph.
9. Lionel John Manning Powell had died on 23 December, 1931, aged 55.

Chapter 25 – The Last 'Farewell' Appearances

1. EMI Archives, Hayes.
2. *San Francisco Chronicle*, 27 June, 1933.
3. EMI Archives, Hayes.
4. *San Francisco Chronicle*, 21 August, 1933.
5. EMI Archives.
6. *San Francisco Chronicle*, 9 October, 1933.
7. EMI Archives.
8. Moore, Gerald (1983), *Furthermore*, London: Hamish Hamilton, pp. 30–1.
9. EMI Archives.
10. Quoted from Gaisberg's unpublished diaries by Jerrold Northrop Moore, *A Voice in Time* (1976), London: Hamish Hamilton, pp. 205–6.
11. EMI Archives.
12. Ivor Newton, *At the Piano*, pp. 66–7.
13. ibid., p. 70.
14. *Musical Opinion*, January 1934, p. 126.
15. *The Scotsman*, 4 December, 1933.
16. *Belfast Newsletter*, 12 December, 1934.
17. *Newcastle Daily Journal*, 15 December, 1933, p. 8, col. 4.
18. *Daily Independent*, 18 December, 1933.
19. *Yorkshire Telegraph and Star*, 19 December, 1933.
20. *A Voice in Time*, p. 206.
21. EMI Archives.
22. *San Francisco Examiner*, 5 November, 1934.
23. *San Francisco Examiner*, 2 December, 1934.
24. *San Francisco Chronicle*, 16 April, 1940.
25. *Nikitina by Herself* (1959), London: Allan Wingate, pp. 14–5, 120–1.

Chapter 26 – The Most Enduring of Memorials

1. *San Francisco Examiner*, 5 May, 1940.
2. Interviews with Millie Robbins, *San Francisco Chronicle*, 1 and 7 November, 1968.
3. Hurok, Sol (1947), *Impresario*, London: Macdonald, p. 129.
4. Rasponi, Lanfranco (1984), *The Last Prima Donna*, London: Gollancz, pp. 166–7.
5. Dawson, Peter (1951), *Fifty Years of Song*, London: Hutchinson, p. 92.
6. *Musical Times*, May 1940, p. 235.

Luisa Tetrazzini's Operatic Repertoire
by Charles Neilson Gattey and Thomas G. Kaufman

In Chronological Order by Assumption of Role

Opera and Composer	Role	City	Theatre	Date
L'Africana, Meyerbeer	Inez	Florence	Teatro Pagliano	21 Oct. 1890
Mirella, Gounod	Mirella	Rome	Teatro Argentina	28 Feb. 1891
Tutti in Maschera, Pedrotti	Vittoria	Rome	Teatro Nazionale	29 Mar. 1891
Le Nozze di Prigione, Usiglio	Tersicone	Rome	Teatro Nazionale	30 Apr. 1891
Crispino e la comare, Ricci	Annetta	Florence	Teatro Nicolini	19 June 1891
La Figlia del Reggimento, Donizetti	Maria	Buenos Aires	Teatro San Martin	22 Oct. 1892
Carmen, Bizet	Micaela	Buenos Aires	Teatro San Martin	3 Nov. 1892
Rigoletto, Verdi	Gilda	Buenos Aires	Teatro San Martin	18 Nov. 1892
Lucia di Lammermoor, Donizetti	Lucia	Buenos Aires	Teatro San Martin	3 Nov. 1892
Le Donne Curiose, Usiglio	Corallina	Rosario	Teatro Olimpo	Dec. 1892
La Sonnambula, Bellini	Amina	Rosario	Teatro Olimpo	Dec. 1892
Linda di Chamounix, Donizetti	Linda	São Paulo	Teatro San José	6 June 1893
Fra Diavolo, Auber	Zerlina	Rio de Janeiro	Teatro Lyrico Fluminense	3 Aug. 1893
La Traviata, Verdi	Violetta	Rio de Janeiro	Teatro Lyrico Fluminense	3 Sep. 1893
Il Barbiere di Siviglia	Rosina	Buenos Aires	Teatro San Martin	6 Mar. 1894
I Puritani, Bellini	Elvira	Buenos Aires	Teatro San Martin	9 Oct. 1894
Dinorah, Meyerbeer	Dinorah	Buenos Aires	Teatro San Martin	15 Nov. 1894
Faust, Gounod	Margherita	Cordoba	Teatro Rivera Indarre	24 June 1895
Mignon, Thomas	Philine	Buenos Aires	Teatro San Martin	17 Sep. 1895
Martha, Flotow	Lady Harriet	Buenos Aires	Teatro San Martin	18 Oct. 1895
Pagliacci, Leoncavallo	Nedda	Warsaw	Teatro Wielki	10 June 1896
Gli Ugonotti, Meyerbeer	Margherita di Valois	Warsaw	Teatro Wielki	12 June 1896

Amleto, Thomas	Ofelia	Madrid	Teatro Real	12 Nov.	1896
Un Ballo in Maschera, Verdi	Oscar	St Petersburg	Grande Salle du Conservatoire	31 Dec.	1896
L'Elisir d'Amore, Donizetti	Adina	St Petersburg	Grande Salle du Conservatoire	11 Jan.	1897
Il Profeta, Meyerbeer	Bertha	St Petersburg	Grande Salle du Conservatoire	25 Jan.	1897
I Pescatori di Perle, Bizet	Leila	St Petersburg	Grande Salle du Conservatoire	14 Mar.	1897
Il Demone, Rubinstein	Tamara	St Petersburg	Grande Salle du Conservatoire	17 Mar.	1897
Lenora, Capri	Molli	St Petersburg	Grande Salle du Conservatoire	2 Apr.	1897
La Bella Fanciulla di Perth	Caterina	Madrid	Teatro Principe Alfonso	5 May	1897
Guglielmo Tell, Rossini	Mathilde	Buenos Aires	Teatro de la Opéra	7 June	1898
Ruslan e Ludmilla, Glinka	Ludmilla	St Petersburg	Grande Salle du Conservatoire	15 Jan.	1899
La Bohème, Puccini	Musetta	St Petersburg	Grande Salle du Conservatoire	30 Jan.	1899
Roberto il Diavolo, Meyerbeer	Isabella	St Petersburg	Grande Salle du Conservatoire	28 Jan.	1902
Romeo e Giulietta, Gounod	Giulietta	St Petersburg	Grande Salle du Conservatoire	5 Mar.	1903
La Bohème, Puccini	Mimi	Havana	Teatro Nacional	3 Mar.	1904
Lakmé, Delibes	Lakmé	Mexico City	Teatro Arbeu	12 Nov.	1904

A Chronology of Tetrazzini's Appearances

Charles Neilson Gattey and Thomas G. Kaufman

Work on this chronology began independently ten years ago with the help of contacts in the countries where Tetrazzini performed. By the time forces were joined we had succeeded in overcoming many of the difficulties that made progress hard due to the fact that it took her much longer to achieve international stardom than it did singers like Caruso or Patti whose chronologies have been published in recent years. Thus, Tetrazzini's career, especially in its early stages, took her to many remote places in Latin America, Imperial Russia and Eastern Europe where she sang in opera houses and theatres for which there is no published document-ation and one has to rely on local newspapers for much information and these are often hard to find. Nevertheless, the listings that follow for both operatic performances and concerts are probably well over 90 per cent complete. A chronology on a singer like Tetrazzini can never be 100 per cent complete for there may always be additional information in a rare book on a locality where she sang or by someone with whom she toured, or in some obscure theatrical journal.

This chronology is arranged by season because the usual engagement in many of the capitals of Europe spanned the autumn of one year and the winter/early spring of the next. All seasons are listed as if they had been in the Northern Hemisphere. Thus a period from May to August in Buenos Aires uses the heading 'Spring and Summer' even though it was actually autumn and winter in the Southern Hemisphere. The operas are listed in chronological order except for side trips, which are indicated as having taken place concurrently with the main season. Principal singers are given when verified. To list full casts, frequently impossible, would have made this chronology unwieldy and over long. The same applies to showing the roles sung by every cast member. Singers are identified as to vocal register, but this is intended to serve only as a guide for in many cases it was difficult to determine whether a singer was a baritone or a bass (Pietro Cesari, for example, sang both such roles) or, for that matter, a soprano or mezzo-soprano. The symbols used are: 's.' – soprano; 'ms.' – mezzo-soprano or contralto; 't.' – tenor; 'b.' – baritone; 'bs.' – bass; 'cond.' – conductor.

It would have been ideal to have made these annals a complete, day-by-day listing, but again on account of the space that would have required this was not feasible. Therefore only the dates of the first performances of works during a season are provided. Since Tetrazzini created one role and took part in some local premières, these are indicated thus:

**world première   *confirmed local première

The absence of an asterisk should not be construed to mean that a given production was not a local première as this could not always be ascertained.

Concerts played an important role in Tetrazzini's career. 'Concert' in this Chronology indicates a performance in which she and possibly other soloists sang or played arias, instrumental solos and ensembles. The accompaniment could be either orchestra or piano. Usually reference in some detail has already been given in the text to the occasion. The programme for a 'Gala Concert' consisted of individual acts or extended scenes of one or more operas, almost always in costume.

As a season's end approached it was customary for each star singer, the conductor and sometimes others in key roles to give benefit performances. In most cases the singer decided on the opera (if the programme consisted primarily of a single work), sang one or more other selections, and other principals might also have taken part. On other occasions, such a benefit might consist of individual acts from operas, again chosen by the beneficiary. This would be listed as a Gala Concert.

When singing on the operatic stage, Tetrazzini did so in Italian. Sometimes, as in the case of *Faust*, a translation from the French would be used. But with other French or German works such as *Fra Diavolo*, *Martha*, *La figlia del reggimento*, and *Dinorah* the Italian versions were sanctioned by the composers with new recitatives or even arias added.

Finally, a question mark indicates that there is doubt about the preceding item of information. Thus, 'Jan.?' means that the month is in doubt, not that the date is unknown. (The latter would be expressed as just 'Jan.'). If the 12th of the month is the most likely date it would be expressed as 'Jan. 12?'

Acknowledgements

This chronology would not have been possible without assistance from many persons. Of these, Richard Bebb deserves special thanks. Eduardo Arnosi, Roberto di Nobile Terré, Miguel Ezquerro and Julio Goyen Aguado provided data on Tetrazzini's performances in the Argentine provinces, while Dr Susana Salgado did the same for Uruguay, Carlo Marinelli for Italy, Dr Jurgen Kindermann for Berlin, Professor Dr Octavian Lazăr Cosma for Bucharest, Dr Nóra Wellmann for Budapest, Dr Anna Rosa Gentilini for Faenza, the Sezione Musicale della Biblioteca Palatina for Parma, Dr Jaromir Pacit for Prague, and Mme Katarzyna Raozkowska for Warsaw. Lim Lai looked up dates and casts in his unique collection of books and programmes, while Charles Mintzer with his profound knowledge of singers' careers was always of help.

Thanks are also due to Dr Mario Moreau of Lisbon, Antonio Massissimo of Barcelona, François Nouvion, Dr Antonino Defraia, Andrew Farkas, Lewis Hall, and Richard Miller.

Equally important are the contributions made by Francesca Franchi, the Covent Garden Opera House Archivist; Barbara R. Geisler, Librarian of the San Francisco Performing Arts Library and Museum; the staff of the *San Francisco Chronicle* and that of the *Examiner*. Ms Janet Bone, Mrs Ruth Schultz and Mrs Susan Rowe of the Morris County Free Library, Mrs Josepha Cooke of the Drew University Library, and Ms Linda Naru of the Center for Research Libraries helped us to locate and borrow many of the books, newspapers and periodicals essential to research. Donald Wisdom and Frank Carroll of the Newspapers and Periodicals Division of the Library of Congress were most co-operative in providing ready access to countless old newspapers. Our thanks are due as well to the staffs of the Libraries at the Universities of Princeton, Illinois, Missouri, Minnesota, North Carolina; the Music Division of the Library of Performing Arts; the Rutgers University Library; the Ball State University Library; the Music Division of the Library of Congress; the New York Music Library at Lincoln Center; and the British Library including the Colindale Newspaper Library. Our thanks are also due to Richard Miller for valuable information regarding US concert tours. We apologise to anyone inadvertently omitted.

At the end of the Chronology which now follows is a list (in alphabetical order) of supporting singers and also conductors mentioned and giving their first names where known. This method has been adopted to save repetition and space.

AUTUMN 1890 FLORENCE–TEATRO PAGLIANO

Oct. 21   *L'africana* (as Inez)   R. Caligaris-Marti:s. (later
                                         T. Singer:s.) G. Sani:t.
                                         S. Carobbi:b.
                                         G. Notargiacomo:bs.
                                         E. Usiglio:cond.

Nov. 15   *I vespri Siciliani*[1]   R. Caligaris-Marti:s.   G. Sani:t.
                                         S. Carobbi:b.
                                         G. Notargiacomo:bs.
                                         E. Usiglio:cond.

CARNIVAL 1890–91 ROME–TEATRO ARGENTINA

Dec. 26   *L'africana*   R. Caligaris-Marti:s.   G. Sani:t.
                                         S. Carobbi:b.
                                         G. Notargiacomo:bs.
                                         E. Usiglio:cond.

Feb. 28   *Mirella*   G. Zeppilli-Villani:ms.
                                         E. Giannini-Grifoni:t.
                                         A. Scotti:b.   L. Broglio:bs.
                                         A. Vessella:cond.

Mar. 8   Concert[2]

SPRING 1891 ROME–TEATRO NAZIONALE

Mar. 29   *Tutti in maschera*   E. Manenti:ms.   C. Lanfredi:t.
                                         C. Buti:b.   P. Cesari:bs.
                                         R. Bracale:cond.

Apr 30   *Le nozze di prigione*   E. Manenti:ms.   O. Emiliani:t.
                                         C. Buti:b.   P. Cesari:bs.
                                         R. Bracale:cond.

SPRING 1891 ROME–TEATRO ARGENTINA

May 5   Concert

SPRING 1891 FLORENCE–TEATRO NICOLINI

June 10   *Tutti in maschera*   L. Parpagnoli:ms.
                                         S. Arrighetti:b.
                                         T. Paterna:bs.   P. Cesari:bs.

June 19   *Crispino e la*   L. Parpagnoli:ms.
             comare   S. Arrighetti:b.
                                         T. Paterna:bs.   P. Cesari:bs.

AUTUMN 1892 BUENOS AIRES–TEATRO SAN MARTIN

Oct. 8   *Crispino e la*   P. Cesari:b.
             comare

Oct. 17   Concert

Oct. 22	*La figlia del reggimento*	T. Ristorini:t. P. Cesari:b.
Nov. 3	*Carmen*	Paoli-Bonazzo:ms. P. Cesari:b.
Nov. 8	Concert	
Nov. 15	Concert	
Nov. 18	*Rigoletto*	
Nov. 21	*Lucia di Lammermoor*	

AUTUMN AND WINTER 1892–93 ROSARIO–TEATRO OLIMPO

Dec. 2	*Crispino e la comare*	P. Cesari:b.
Dec. 8	*La figlia del reggimento*	P. Cesari:b.
Dec.	*Carmen*	Paoli-Bonazzo:ms. F. Pagano:t. P. Cesari:b.
Dec.	*Le donne curiose* (Usiglio)	P. Cesari:b.
Dec.	*La sonnambula*	P. Cesari:b.

WINTER 1893 BUENOS AIRES–TEATRO SAN MARTIN

Feb. 8	*La sonnambula*	P. Cesari:b.
Feb. 9	*Carmen*	Paoli-Bonazzo:ms.
Feb. 14	*Le donne curiose*	P. Cesari:b.

WINTER AND SPRING 1893 SÃO PAULO–TEATRO SAN JOSÉ

Mar. 1	*Crispino e la comare*	A. Vergari-Marangoni:ms. T. Ristorini:t. C. Tosi:b. P. Cesari:b.
Mar. 17	*La figlia del reggimento*	T. Ristorini:t. P. Cesari:b.
Apr. 13	*Carmen*	Paoli-Bonazzo:ms. F. Pagano:t. P. Cesari:b.
Apr. 25	*La sonnambula*	T. Rinaldi:t. P. Cesari:b.
May 10	*Lucia di Lammermoor*	F. Pagano:t. P. Cesari:b. A. Lippi:bs.
June 6	*Linda di Chamounix*	A. Vergari-Marangoni:ms. F. Pagano:t. P. Cesari:b. A. Lippi:bs. E. Marangoni:bs.

SUMMER 1893 RIO DE JANEIRO–TEATRO LYRICO FLUMINENSE

| June 20 | *Crispino e la comare* | A. Vergari-Marangoni:ms. T. Ristorini:t.   C. Tosi:b. P. Cesari:b. |

June 28	*La figlia del reggimento*	T. Ristorini:t. P. Cesari:b.
July 5	*Lucia di Lammermoor*	F. Pagano:t. P. Cesari:b. Razzoli:bs.
July 20	*La sonnambula*	T. Rinaldi:t. P. Cesari:b.
Aug. 3	*Fra Diavolo*	Anselmi:ms. Prati:t. Razzoli:bs. P. Cesari:b.
Aug. 18	*Linda di Chamounix*	A. Vergari-Marangoni:ms. F. Pagano:t. P. Cesari:b. Casali:bs. E. Marangoni:bs.
Sep. 3	*La traviata*	F. Pagano:t. P. Cesari:b.

WINTER AND SPRING 1894 BUENOS AIRES–TEATRO SAN MARTIN

Jan. 5	*Lucia di Lammermoor*	C. Elias:t. P. Cesari:b.
Jan. 15	*Linda di Chamounix*	C. Elias:t. P. Cesari:b.
Jan. 24	*La figlia del reggimento*	P. Cesari:b.
Jan. 29	*Crispino e la comare*	P. Cesari:b.
Feb. 8	Concert	
Feb. 12	*La sonnambula*	C. Elias:t. P. Cesari:b.
Mar. 6	*Il barbiere di Siviglia*	C. Elias:t. P. Cesari:b.
Mar. 30	Gala Concert	

SPRING 1894 MONTEVIDEO–NUEVO POLITEAMA[3]

| Apr. 14 | *Lucia di Lammermoor* | G. Pini-Corsi:t.   Urbinato:b. Lombardi:bs. |
| Apr. 18 | *La sonnambula* | P. Cesari:b. |

SPRING 1894 MONTEVIDEO–NUEVO POLITEAMA

Apr. 26	*Il barbiere di Siviglia*	C. Elias:t. P. Cesari:b. Lombardi:bs. Conti:bs.
Apr. 28	*Linda di Chamounix*	C. Elias:t. P. Cesari:b. Lombardi:bs. Conti:bs.
Apr. 29	*Fra Diavolo*	C. Elias:t. P. Cesari:b.
May 5	*La traviata*	G. Pini-Corsi:t. P. Cesari:b.
May 6	*Crispino e la comare*	P. Cesari:bs.
May 8	*La figlia del reggimento*	G. Pini-Corsi:t. P. Cesari:bs.

| May 10 | *Lucia di Lammermoor* | C. Elias:t. Urbinati:b. Lombardi:bs. |

SPRING AND SUMMER 1894 MENDOZA

SUMMER 1894 MONTEVIDEO–NUEVO POLITEAMA

| July 10 | *Lucia di Lammermoor* | F. Pagano:t. P. Cesari:b. |
| July 12 | *La traviata* | E. Zerni:t. P. Cesari:b. |

SUMMER AND AUTUMN 1894 BUENOS AIRES–TEATRO SAN MARTIN

Sep. 4	*Lucia di Lammermoor*	F. Pagano:t. (later E. Ghilardini:t.) E. De Bernis:b. F. Fabbro:bs.
Sep. 7	*Il barbiere di Siviglia*	E. Zerni:t. P. Cesari:b. Capurro:bs.
Sep. 11	*La sonnambula*	E. Zerni:t. P. Cesari:b. F. Fabbro:bs.
Sep. 21	*Linda di Chamounix*	P. Cesari:b.
Sep. 25	*Rigoletto*	F. Pagano:t. E. Sivori:b.
Oct. 9	*I puritani*	E. Zerni:t. P. Cesari:b. F. Fabbro:bs.
Oct. 16	*La traviata*	E. Zerni:t. E. Sivori:b.
Oct. 22	*Crispino e la comare*	P. Cesari:b.
Nov. 15	*Dinorah*	P. Cesari:b.
Nov. 19	Concert	

AUTUMN AND WINTER 1894–95 ROSARIO–TEATRO OLIMPO

Dec. 9	*Lucia di Lammermoor*	P. Cesari:b.
Dec. 18	*La sonnambula*	P. Cesari:b.
Dec. 20	*Linda di Chamounix*	P. Cesari:b.
Jan. 8	*Crispino e la comare?*	
Jan. 11	*I puritani?*	
Jan. 14	*Rigoletto*	

WINTER AND SPRING 1895 TOUR OF ARGENTINA

SPRING 1895 SALTA

| May 2 | *Lucia di Lammermoor* | |

SPRING 1895 ROSARIO–TEATRO OLIMPO

May	*Il barbiere di Siviglia*
	La sonnambula
	Lucia di Lammermoor
	Fra Diavolo?
	Dinorah
	Rigoletto
	I puritani

SPRING 1895 CORDOBA–TEATRO RIVERA INDARTE

June 15	*Lucia di Lammermoor*	E. Zerni:t. B. Bellati:b. A. Zacaria:bs. M. La Mura:cond.
June 16	*Il barbiere di Siviglia*	Conti:t. P. Cesari:b. M. La Mura:cond.
June 18	*Linda di Chamounix*	
June 20	*I puritani*	
June 22	*Crispino e la comare*	
June 24	*Faust*	E. Zerni:t. A. Zacaria:bs.
June 26	*Rigoletto*	
July 4	*La sonnambula*	E. Zerni:t. P. Cesari:b.
July 7	*La traviata*	
July 9	Concert	
July 16	Concert	

SUMMER AND AUTUMN 1895 BUENOS AIRES–TEATRO SAN MARTIN

Aug. 16	*Linda di Chamounix*	G. Quiroli:t. R. Bracale:cond.
Aug. 23	*I puritani*	R. Bracale:cond.
Aug. 27	*La sonnambula*	R. Bracale:cond.
Aug. 31	*Rigoletto*	G. Quiroli:t. V. Brombara:b. R. Bracale:cond.
Sep. 3	*Dinorah*	R. Bracale:cond.
Sep. 13	*Lucia di Lammermoor*	R. Bracale:cond.
Sep. 17	*Mignon*	R. Bracale:cond.
Oct. 8	*Il barbiere di Siviglia*	G. Quiroli:t. (later F. De Lucia:t.) A. Lanzoni:bs. R. Bracale:cond.

Oct. 18	*Martha*	A. Zeppilli:ms. G. Quiroli:t.
		M. Wigley:b. Conti:bs.
		R. Bracale:cond.

AUTUMN 1895 BUENOS AIRES–TEATRO NACIONAL

Oct. 11	*Il barbiere di Siviglia*	F. De Lucia:t.

WINTER 1896 LISBON–TEATRO SAO CARLOS

Feb. 9	*Lucia di Lammermoor*	G. Moretti:t. (later G. Bayo:t.)
		A. Modesti:b. F. Dubois:bs.
Feb. 16	*Il barbiere di Siviglia*	G. Bayo:t. A. Modesti:b.
		A. Lanzoni:bs. P. Cesari:bs.
	Faust	C. Zawner:ms. G. Moretti:t.
		(later G. Bayo:t.)
		A. Modesti:b. A. Lanzoni:b.

LENT 1896 NAPLES–TEATRO SAN CARLO

Mar. 26	*Lucia di Lammermoor*	F. Giannini:t. M. De Padova:b.
		N. Serra:bs.
		V. Lombardi:cond.
Apr. 5	*Il barbiere di Siviglia*	F. Giannini:t. A. Magini-Coletti:b. N. Serra:bs.
		L. Lucenti:bs.
		V. Lombardi:cond.

SPRING 1896 WARSAW–TEATR WIELKI

May 22?	*Lucia di Lammermoor*	A. Stampanoni:t. A. Scotti:b.
May 25	*La traviata*	A. Stampanoni:t. A. Scotti:b.
May ?	*I puritani*	A. Stampanoni:t. A. Scotti:b.
		A. Sillich:bs.
June 2?	*Rigoletto*	A. Scotti:b.
June	*Il barbiere di Siviglia*	A. Stampanoni:t. A. Scotti:b.
June 10	*Pagliacci*	G. Piccaluga:t. A. Scotti:b.
June 12	*Gli ugonotti*	M. De Nunzio:s.
		G. Piccaluga:t. A. Scotti:b.
		A. Sillich:bs.

SUMMER 1896 VENICE–TEATRO MALIBRAN

Aug. 20	*Lucia di Lammermoor*	A. Mauri:t. (later
		L. Signoretti:t.) A. Pini-Corsi:b. L. Contini:bs.
		S. Boscarini:cond.

| Aug. 27 | *Il barbiere di Siviglia* | L. Signoretti:t. A. Pini-Corsi:b.
L. Contini:bs. P. Cesari:b.
S. Boscarini:cond. |

SUMMER 1896 PORDENONE

| Sep. 5? | *Lucia di Lammermoor* | E. Zerni:t. F. Fabbro:bs. |
| Sep. 12? | *Il barbiere di Siviglia* | E. Zerni:t. P. Cesari:b.
F. Fabbro:bs. Migliara:bs.
E. Galeazzi:cond. |

AUTUMN 1896 TREVISO–TEATRO GARIBALDI

| Sep. 26? | *Lucia di Lammermoor* | E. Zerni:t. P. Cesari:b.
F. Fabbro:bs. |

AUTUMN 1896 UDINE–TEATRO MINERVA

| Oct. 3 | *Lucia di Lammermoor* | L. Mazzoli:t. P. Cesari:b.
F. Fabbro:bs. |

AUTUMN 1896 MADRID–TEATRO REAL

Oct. 29	*Il barbiere di Siviglia*	A. Stampanoni:t. C. Buti:b. G. Rossi:bs. A. Baldelli:bs. J. Goula:cond.
Nov. 12	*Amleto*	R. Blanchart:b. C. Walter:bs. J. Goula:cond.
Nov. 14	*Gli ugonotti*	C. Bordalba:s. G. Russitano:t. R. Blanchart:b. later C. Buti:b. C. Walter:bs. F. Navarrini:bs. J. Goula:cond.
Dec. 1	*Dinorah*	A. Stampanoni:t. I. Tabuyo:b. M. Verdaguer:bs. P. Urrutia:cond.

WINTER 1896–97 ST PETERSBURG–GRANDE SALLE DU CONSERVATOIRE

Dec. 31	*Un ballo in maschera*	M. McIntyre:s. A. Brogi:t. M. Battistini:b.
Jan. 11	*L'Elisir d'amore*	A. Masini:t. V. Brombara:b. P. Cesari:b.
Jan. 25	*Il profeta*	R. Vidal:ms. F. Tamagno:t. V. Brombara:b. G. Rossi:bs. A. Silvestri:bs. V. Podesti:cond.
Feb.	*Rigoletto*	A. Masini:t. V. Brombara:bs.

		G. Rossi:bs.
Feb. 22	*Gli ugonotti*	M. McIntyre:s. T. Carotini:ms.
		A. Brogi:t. M. Battistini:b.
		G. Rossi:bs. A. Silvestri:bs.
		V. Podesti:cond.
Mar. 4	*Lucia di Lammermoor*	A. Brogi:t. V. Brombara:b.
		A. Silvestri:bs.

LENT 1897 ST PETERSBURG–GRANDE SALLE DU CONSERVATOIRE

Mar. 14	*I pescatori di perle*	A. Masini:t. V. Brombara:b.
Mar. 17	*Il Demone*	A. Masini:t. M. Battistini:b.
		G. Rossi:bs.
Apr. 2	*Lenora*** (Capri) (as Molli)	T. Carotini:ms. A. Brogi:t.
		V. Brombara:b.
Apr. 8	*Carmen*	C. Ferni:ms. A. Brogi:t.
		V. Brombara:b.
Apr. 10	*Rigoletto*	T. Carotini:ms. A. Masini:t.
		V. Brombara:b.
		A. Silvestri:bs.

SPRING 1897 MADRID–TEATRO PRINCIPE ALFONSO

May 2	*La sonnambula*	G. Ercilla:t. A. Calvo:bs.
		P. Urrutia:cond.
May 5	*La bella fanciulla di Perth**	G. Ercilla:t. G. Hernandez:b.
		M. Verdaguer:bs.
May 13	*Lucia di Lammermoor*	M. Sigaldi:t. G. Hernandez:b.
		P. Urrutia:cond.
May 19	*Gli ugonotti*	M. De Lerma:s. M. Sigaldi:t.
		G. Hernandez:b.
		L. Rossato:bs.

AUTUMN 1897 MILAN–TEATRO DEL VERME

Oct. 6	*Il barbiere di Siviglia*	A. Stampanoni:t. P. Cesari:b.
		L. Contini:bs. F. Galletti-Gianoli:bs.
		N. Guerrera:cond.

AUTUMN 1897 TURIN–TEATRO VITTORIO EMANUELE

Oct. 22?	*Lucia di Lammermoor*	S. Mastrobuono:t.
		V. Brombara:b. F. Fabro:bs.

AUTUMN 1897 TRIESTE–POLITEAMA ROSSETTI

Nov. 27	*Lucia di Lammermoor*	L. Mazzoli:t. Mentasti:b.
		L. Contini:bs.

WINTER 1897–98 ODESSA–TEATRO MUNICIPALE

Dec. 31?	*Il barbiere di Siviglia*	F. Daddi:t. G. Polese:b. A. Sabellico:bs. P. Cesari:bs.
Jan. 2?	*Lucia di Lammermoor*	A. Matassini:t. G. Polese:b. A. Nicolini:bs.
Jan. 3	*Fra Diavolo*	E. Longhi:ms. F. Daddi:t. M. Polli:b. P. Cesari:bs.
Jan. 8	*Rigoletto*	E. Longhi:ms. A. Matassini:t. G. M. Sammarco:b. S. Cirotto:bs.
Jan. 14	*Gli ugonotti*	R. Caligaris-Marti:s. I. Monti- Baldini:ms. F. Signorini:t. G. Polese:b. A. Sabellico:bs. S. Cirotto:bs. Pribik:cond.
Feb. 1	*Amleto*	A. Cucini:ms. G. M. Sammarco:b. A. Sabellico:bs.

LENT 1898 BOLOGNA–TEATRO BRUNETTI

Mar. 25?	*Lucia di Lammermoor*	G. Masin:t. G. Albinolo:b.

SPRING AND SUMMER 1898 BUENOS AIRES–TEATRO DE LA OPERA

May 24	*Lucia di Lammermoor*	G. Borgatti:t. E. Giraldoni:b. G. Di Grazia:bs. L. Mugnone:cond.
June 7	*Guglielmo Tell*	F. Tamagno:t. E. Giraldoni:b. R. Ercolani:bs. L. Mugnone:cond.
June 19	*Rigoletto*	L. Berlendi:ms. G. Borgatti:t. G. M. Sammarco:b. R. Ercolani:bs. L. Mugnone:cond.
July 7	*Amleto*	V. Guerrini:ms. G. M. Sammarco:b. G. De Grazia:bs. L. Mugnone:cond.
July 21	*Gli ugonotti*	L. Ehrenstein:s. L. Berlendi:ms. F. Tamagno:t. G. M. Sammarco:b. R. Ercolani:bs. G. De Grazia:bs. L. Mugnone:cond.

SUMMER 1898 LA PLATA–TEATRO ARGENTINO

Aug. 15	*Il barbiere di Siviglia*	P. Maini:t. P. Cesari:b. A. Resplendino:bs. J. Conti:bs. R. Bonicioli:cond.
Aug. 17	*Lucia di Lammermoor*	P. Maini:t. P. Cesari:b. A. Resplendino:bs. R. Bonicioli:cond.
Aug. 20	*Fra Diavolo*	F. Zucchi:t. P. Cesari:b.

SUMMER 1898 MONTEVIDEO–TEATRO SOLIS

Aug. 24	*Lucia di Lammermoor*	P. Maini:t. S. Athos:b. R. Bonicioli:cond.
Aug. 25	*Il barbiere di Siviglia*	C. Elias:t. S. Athos:b. R. Bonicioli:cond.
Aug. 27	*Rigoletto*	E. Ferrari:ms.C. Elias:t. S. Athos:b. A. Resplendino:bs. R. Bonicioli:cond.
Aug. 28	*Faust*	C. Elias:t. S. Athos:b. A. Resplendino:bs. R. Bonicioli:cond.
Aug. 31	*Fra Diavolo**	E. Ferrari:ms. P. Maini:t. F. Zucchi:t. P. Cesari:b. A. Resplendino:bs. R. Bonicioli:cond.
Sep 1	*I puritani*	C. Maini:t. S. Athos:b. R. Bonicioli:cond.
Sep. 3	*Dinorah**	F. Zucchi:t. P. Cesari:b. A. Resplendino:bs. R. Bonicioli:cond.
Sep. 8	*La traviata*	P. Maini:t. S. Athos:b. R. Bonicioli:cond.
Sep. 11	Gala Concert	

SUMMER AND AUTUMN 1898 CORDOBA–TEATRO RIVERA INDARTE

Sep. 15	*Il barbiere di Siviglia*	L. Maristani:t.
Sep. 17	*Fra Diavolo*	
Sep. 20	*Lucia di Lammermoor*	
Sep. 22	*Faust*	
Sep. 24	*La traviata*	

Sep. 27   *Rigoletto*
Sep. 29   *Linda di*
          Chamounix

AUTUMN 1898 ROSARIO–TEATRO OLIMPO

Oct. 1   *Il barbiere di*   L. Maristani:t.   C. Thos:b.
          Siviglia
Oct. 2   *Lucia di*   L. Maristani:t.
          Lammermoor
Oct. 4   *Rigoletto*
Oct. 6   *Faust*
Oct. 8   *La sonnambula*

AUTUMN 1898 ROSARIO–TEATRO OLIMPO

Nov. 12   *La sonnambula*
Nov. 13   *Lucia di*
          Lammermoor

WINTER 1899 ST PETERSBURG–GRANDE SALLE DU CONSERVATOIRE

Jan. 2   *Rigoletto*   T. Carotini:ms.   A. Masini:t.
                                 M. Battistini:b.
                                 V. Arimondi:bs.
                                 V. Podesti:cond.

Jan. 11   *Un ballo in*   A. Giacchetti:s.   T. Carotini:ms.
          maschera   F. Marconi:t.
                                 M. Battistini:b.
                                 V. Podesti:cond.

Jan. 15   *Ruslan e Ludmilla*   A. Giacchetti:s.   A. Masini:t.
                                 M. Battistini:b.
                                 V. Brombara:b.
                                 V. Arimondi:bs.
                                 V. Podesti:cond.

Jan. 30   *La bohème** (as   S. Arnoldson:s.   E. Caruso:t.
          Musetta)   V. Brombara:b.
                                 V. Arimondi:bs.
                                 V. Podesti:cond.

Feb. 1   *I puritani*   F. Marconi:t.   M. Battistini:b.
                                 V. Arimondi:bs.

Feb. 22   *Lucia di*   E. Caruso:t.   V. Brombara:b.
          Lammermoor   A. Silvestri:bs.
                                 V. Podesti:cond.

Feb. 23   *Mignon*   S. Arnoldson:s.   T. Carotini:ms.
                                 A. Masini:t.   A. Silvestri:bs.

Feb. 26 *Il barbiere di* A. Masini:t. M. Battistini:b.
         Siviglia V. Arimondi:bs. P. Cesari:bs.
Mar. 16 *Amleto* T. Carotini:ms. M. Battistini:b.
         V. Arimondi:bs.

SPRING 1899 ROVIGO-TEATRO SOCIALE

May 6 *Lucia di* F. Granados:t. V. Brombara:b.
        Lammermoor A. Silvestri:bs.
        E. Galeazzi:cond.
May 20 *I puritani* F. Granados:t. V. Brombara:b.
        A. Silvestri:bs.
        E. Galeazzi:cond.

SPRING 1899 TREVSIO–TEATRO GARIBALDI

May *I puritani* F. Granados:t. V. Brombara:b.
     A. Silvestri:bs.
     G. Abbate:cond.
June 1? *Lucia di* F. Granados:t. V. Brombara:b.
          Lammermoor A. Silvestri:bs.
          G. Abbate:cond.

SUMMER 1899 LIVORNO–POLITEAMA

July 20? *Il barbiere di* E. Cavara:t. A. Gnaccarini:b.
          Siviglia C. Fiegna:bs.

SUMMER 1899 FERMO–TEATRO DELL'AQUILA

Aug. 18? *Lucia di* F. Granados:t. L. Bellagamba:b.
          Lammermoor A. Venturini:bs.
          D. Acerbi:cond.

SUMMER 1899 TURIN–TEATRO REGIO

Sep. 5 *Lucia di* G.Apostolu:t. G. Boisson:b.
         Lammermoor G. Scolari:bs.
         A. Luzzatti:cond.

AUTUMN 1899 ROME–TEATRO ADRIANO

Oct. 11 *Dinorah* G. Pini-Corsi:t. (later
         O. Gennari:t.) A. Magini-
         Coletti:b. L. Rossato:bs.
         G. Golisciani:cond.
Nov. 9 *Il barbiere di* O. Gennari:t. A. Magini-
         Siviglia Coletti:b. L. Rossato:bs.
         P. Cesari:bs.
         G. Golisciani:cond.
Nov. 21 *La sonnambula* O. Gennari:t. A. Venturini:bs.
         G. Golisciani:cond.

AUTUMN 1899 ROME–TEATRO COSTANZI
(Concurrent with the season at the Teatro Adriano)

| Oct. 23 | Il barbiere di Siviglia | O. Gennari:t. P. Cesari:b. (later E. Moreo:b.) G. Balisardi:bs. E. Borelli:bs. T. De Angelis:cond. |
| Oct. 30 | Crispino e la comare | C. Verdi:ms. C. De Rossi:t. P. Cesari:b. G. Balisardi:bs. T. De Angelis:cond. |

WINTER 1900 ST PETERSBURG–GRANDE SALLE DU CONSERVATOIRE

Jan. 1	Mignon	S. Arnoldson:s. F. Granados:t. A. Silvestri:bs.
Jan. 11	Un ballo in maschera	S. Kruszelnicka:s. T. Carotini:ms. E. Caruso:t. V. Podesti:cond.
Jan. 15	Amleto	T. Carotini:ms. M. Battistini:b. V. Arimondi:bs.
Jan. 18	La bohème	S. Arnoldson:s. E. Caruso:t. V. Brombara:b. V. Arimondi:bs. V. Podesti:cond.
Jan. 31	Dinorah	M. Battistini:t. A. Silvestri:bs.
Feb. 2	Rigoletto	T. Carotini:ms. A. Masini:t. M. Battistini:b. V. Arimondi:bs.
Feb. 16	Il barbiere di Siviglia	A. Masini:t. M. Battistini:b. V. Arimondi:bs. P. Cesari:b.
Feb. 28	Lucia di Lammermoor	E. Caruso:t. V. Brombara:b. A. Silvestri:bs.

LENT 1900 MOSCOW–TEATRO BOLSHOI

Mar. 14	Dinorah	T. Carotini:ms. A. Rossetti:t. M. Battistini:b. A.Silvestri:bs.
Mar. 20	Un ballo in maschera	M. de Lerma:s. T. Carotini:ms. E. Caruso:t. M. Battistini:b. V. Podesti:cond.
Mar. 28	Lucia di Lammermoor	E. Caruso:t. V. Brombara:b. A. Silvestri:bs.

SPRING 1900 ROME–TEATRO ADRIANO

Apr. 14	*Dinorah*	C. Benvenuti:t. A. Magini- Coletti:b. L. Rossato:bs. G. Golisciani:cond.
Apr. 26	*I puritani*	G. Masin:t. A. Magini- Coletti:b. L. Rossato:bs. G. Golisciani:cond.
May 1	Concert	

SPRING 1900 WARSAW–TEATR WIELKI

May 7	*Dinorah*	Morlacchi:t. M. Battistini:b.
May 9	*Il barbiere di Siviglia*	M. Battistini:b.
May 16	*Amleto*	M. Battistini:b.

AUTUMN 1900 WARSAW–TEATR WIELKI

Oct. 1	*Rigoletto*	T. Carotini:ms. F. Constantino:t. V. Grobzewsky:b. A. Didur:bs.
Oct. 3	*Amleto*	D'Orio:ms. Morlacchi:t. R. Blanchart:b. A. Sillich:bs.
Oct.	*La traviata*	F. Constantino:t. R. Blanchart:b.
Oct. 11	*Lucia di Lammermoor*	F. Constantino:t. R. Blanchart:b. A. Sillich:bs.

SPRING 1901 TBILISI–IMPERIAL THEATRE

Mar. 28?	*Lucia di Lammermoor Il barbiere di Siviglia*	
Mar. 30?	*Dinorah*	
Apr.	*La sonnambula*	
Apr.	*La traviata*	
Apr.	*Rigoletto*	
Apr.	*Amleto*	

SPRING 1901 KHARKOV

Apr.	*Il barbiere di Siviglia*	Montevecchi:t.
Apr.	*La sonnambula*	Montevecchi:t.
Apr.	*Lucia di Lammermoor*	Montevecchi:t.
Apr. 29?	*Rigoletto*	

SPRING 1901 KIEV

May 5?	*La sonnambula*	Montevecchi:t.
May	*Lucia di Lammermoor*	
May	*Rigoletto*	
May	*Il barbiere di Siviglia*	
May	*La traviata*	
May	*Gli ugonotti*	

SUMMER 1901 LUGANO–TEATRO APOLLO

Sep. 10	*Lucia di Lammermoor*	L. Signoretti:t. R. Billi:b. M. Baldelli:bs. G. Puccetti:cond.

AUTUMN 1901 COMO–TEATRO CRESSONI

Oct. 5	*Lucia di Lammermoor*	A. Stampanoni:t. R. Billi:b. P. Cesari:bs. P. Duffau:cond.
Oct. 10	*Il barbiere di Siviglia*	A. Stampanoni:t. E. Sottolana:b. G. Rossi:bs. A. Rossi:bs. P. Duffau:cond.

AUTUMN 1901 ROME–TEATRO ADRIANO

Oct. 25	*Il barbiere di Siviglia*	F. Bravi:t. E. Sottolana:b. F. Navarrini:bs. E. Coletti:bs. A. Jacchia:cond.

WINTER 1902 ST PETERSBURG–GRANDE SALLE DU CONSERVATOIRE

Jan. 10	*I puritani*	F. Marconi:t. G. Pacini:b. V. Arimondi:bs.
Jan. 14	*Rigoletto*	C. Pagnoni:ms. F. Constantino:t. G. Pacini:b.
Jan. 19	*Carmen*	S. Kruszelnicka:s. F. Constantino:t. M. Battistini:b.
Jan. 22	*La bohème*	S. Arnoldson:s. F. Constantino:t. V. Brombara:b. G. Pacini:b. V. Arimondi:bs.
Jan. 23	*Un ballo in maschera*	S. Kruszelnicka:s. C. Pagnoni:ms. F. Marconi:t. M. Battistini:b. V. Arimondi:bs. C. Fiegna:bs.

Jan. 28	*Roberto il Diavolo*	S. Kruszelnicka:s. F. Marconi:t. V. Arimondi:bs.
Feb. 2	*Il barbiere di Siviglia*	F. Constantino:t. M. Battistini:b. V. Arimondi:bs. P. Cesari:bs.
Feb. 9	*Guglielmo Tell*	M. Mariacher:t. M. Battistini:b. V. Arimondi:bs.
Feb. 12	*Marta*	C. Pagnoni:ms. F.Marconi:t. G. Pacini:b. P. Cesari:bs.
Mar. 3	*Gli ugonotti*	S. Kruszelnicka:s. C. Pagnoni:ms. M. Mariacher:t. G. Pacini:b. V. Arimondi:bs. C. Fiegna:bs.

LENT AND SPRING 1902 TBILISI–IMPERIAL THEATRE

Mar.	*Lucia di Lammermoor*	
	Rigoletto	P. Ferrari:t. G. Pacini:b.
	Faust	
	La traviata	
	Il barbiere di Siviglia	P. Cesari:bs.
	Mignon	P. Cesari:bs.
	Linda di Chamounix	G. Pacini:b. P. Cesari:b.
	La figlia del reggimento	P. Cesari:bs.
	Gli ugonotti	

SPRING 1902 BERLIN–KROLLOPER

May 4	*Un ballo in maschera*	M. De Macchi:s. A. Kitzu:ms. E. De Marchi:t. V. Brombara:b. V. Arimondi:bs. A. Silvestri:bs. A. Vigna:cond.
May 11	*Rigoletto*	V. Guerrini:ms. E. De Marchi:t. G. M. Sammarco:b. V. Arimondi:bs. A. Vigna:cond.
May 18	*La traviata*	E. De Marchi:t. V. Brombara:b. A. Vigna:cond.

SPRING 1902 PRAGUE–NEUES DEUTSCHES THEATER

May 30	*Un ballo in maschera*	M. De Macchi:s. A. Kitzu:ms. E. De Marchi:t. G. M. Sammarco:b. V. Arimondi:bs. A. Vigna:cond.
May 31	*La traviata*	E. De Marchi:t. V. Brombara:b. A. Vigna:cond.

AUTUMN 1902 GENOA–POLITEAMA

Oct. 16	*Lucia di Lammermoor*	V. Bieletto:t. G. Polese:b. E. Ciccolini:bs. U. Zanetti:cond.
Oct. 26	*Il barbiere di Siviglia*	A. Parola:t. G. Polese:b. C. Tanzini:bs. P. Cesari:bs. U. Zanetti:cond.

AUTUMN 1902 FLORENCE–TEATRO NICOLINI

Nov. 17	*Il barbiere di Siviglia*	P. Bersellini:t. F. Federici:b. M. Baldelli:bs. Bianchi:bs. G. Falconi:cond.
Nov. 23	*I puritani*	R. Andreini:t. F. Federici:b. M. Baldelli:bs. G. Falconi:cond.
Dec. 3	*La sonnambula*	R. Andreini:t. G. Falconi:cond.

WINTER 1902–3 BUCHAREST–TEATRUL NACIONAL

Dec. 24?	*Lucia di Lammermoor*	V. Coppola:t. I. Bozzoli:b. A. Dadò:bs.
Dec. 26?	*Il barbiere di Siviglia* *La traviata?*	I. Bozzoli:b. A. Dadò:bs.
Dec. 31?	*Rigoletto* *Dinorah?*	A. Sarcoli:t. I. Bozzoli:b. P. Vallini:cond.

WINTER 1903 ST PETERSBURG–GRANDE SALLE DU CONSERVATOIRE

Jan. 23	*La bohème*	S. Arnoldson:s. A. Bassi:t. V. Brombara:b. V. Arimondi:bs.
Jan. 26	*Un ballo in maschera*	E. Bianchini-Cappelli:s. C. Marchesini:ms. A. Cecchi:b. E. Giraldoni:bs. V. Arimondi:bs. C. Fiegna:bs.

Jan. 28	*La traviata*	A. Masini:t. (later A. Bassi:t.) E. Giraldoni:b.
Jan. 29	*I pescatori di perle*	A. Masini:t. E. Giraldoni:b.
Jan. 30	*Rigoletto*	A. Masini:t. E. Giraldoni:b.
Feb. 1	*Mignon*	S. Arnoldson:s. A. Masini:t. (later L. Sobinoff:t.) V. Arimondi:bs.
Feb. 15	*Il barbiere di Siviglia*	A. Masini:t. E. Giraldoni:b. V. Arimondi:bs. P. Cesari:b.
Mar. 5	*Romeo e Giulietta*	L. Sobinoff:t. E. Giraldoni:b. V. Arimondi:bs.

WINTER AND SPRING 1903 CONCERT TOUR OF ROMANIA

SPRING 1903 FLORENCE–TEATRO VERDI

May 5	*Il barbiere di Siviglia*	P. Lara:t. F. Federici:b. R. Galli:bs. R. Tamanti:bs. P. Vallini:cond.
May 11	*Lucia di Lammermoor*	E. Colli:t. F. Federici:b. R. Galli:bs. P. Vallini:cond.
May 23	Gala Concert	

SPRING 1903 FAENZA–TEATRO COMUNALE

| June 6 | *I pescatori di perle* | A. Masini:t. O. Beltrami:b. A. Pomé:cond. |
| June 17 | *La traviata* | A. Masini:t. O. Beltrami:b. A. Pomé:cond. |

AUTUMN 1903 MEXICO CITY–TEATRO ARBEU

Oct. 22	*Lucia di Lammermoor*	E. Colli:t. V. Bellati:b. A. Mariani:bs. G. Polacco:cond.
Oct. 29	*Il barbiere di Siviglia*	E. Colli:t. V. Bellati:b. G. Caruson:b. G. Rossi:bs. P. Cesari:b. G. Polacco:cond.
Nov. 6	*La traviata*	E. Colli:t. G. Caruson:b. G. Polacco:cond.
Nov. 15	*Un ballo in maschera*	M. Grisi:s. M. Pozzi:ms. L. Longobardi:t. V. Bellati:b. G. Rossi:bs. G. Polacco:cond.
Nov. 19	*I puritani*	E. Colli:t. L. Mazzoleni:b. A. Mariani:bs. G. Polacco:cond.

Nov. 28	*Gli ugonotti*	A. De Roma:s. M. Pozzi:ms. L. Longobardi:t. G. Caruson:b. G. Rossi:bs. A. Mariani:bs.
Dec. 1	*Rigoletto*	A. Belloni:ms. E. Colli:t. V. Bellati:b. G. Rossi:bs. G. Polacco:cond.
Dec. 8	*La sonnambula*	E. Colli:t. G. Rossi:bs. G. Polacco:cond.
Dec. 19	*Dinorah*	A. Braglia:t. V. Bellati:b. G. Golisciani:cond. (later G. Polacco:cond.)

WINTER 1903–4 MEXICO CITY–SALA WAGNER
Dec. 22   Concert

AUTUMN AND WINTER 1903–4 GUADALAJARA–TEATRO DEGOLLADO

Dec. 25	*Lucia di Lammermoor*	E. Colli:t.
Dec. 27?	*Il barbiere di Siviglia*	E. Colli:t.
Dec. 30?	*Rigoletto*	E. Colli:t.
Jan. ?	*La traviata*	
Jan. 3?	*La sonnambula*	E. Colli:t.

WINTER 1904 PUEBLA–TEATRO PRINCIPAL

Jan. 8	*Lucia di Lammermoor*	
Jan. 10	*Il barbiere di Siviglia*	
Jan.	*La sonnambula?*	
Jan.	*Rigoletto?*	

WINTER 1904 HAVANA–TEATRO NACIONAL

Jan. 30	*Lucia di Lammermoor*	E. Colli:t. V. Bellati:b. A. Mariani:bs. G. Polacco:cond.
Feb. 2	*Il barbiere di Siviglia*	E. Colli:t. V. Bellati:b. G. Caruson:b. A. Mariani:bs. G. Rossi:bs.
Feb. 6	*La sonnambula*	E. Colli:t. G. Rossi:bs.
Feb. 9	*I puritani*	E. Colli:t. L. Mazzoleni:b. A. Mariani:bs.

Feb. 20	*Rigoletto*	M. Pozzi:ms. E. Colli:t.
		V. Bellati:b. G. Rossi:bs.
Feb. 23	*La traviata*	E. Colli:t. G. Caruson:b.
Feb. 25	*Gli ugonotti*	A. De Roma:s. M. Pozzi:ms.
		L. Longobardi:t.
		G. Caruson:b. G. Rossi:bs.
		A. Mariani:bs.
Mar. 1	*Dinorah*	E. Colli:t. V. Bellati:b.
		G. Golisciani:cond.
Mar. 3	*La bohème* (as	G. Maccari:s. V. Bellati:b.
	Mimi)	G. Polacco:cond.
Mar. 5	*Faust*	E. Bettini:ms. E. Colli:t.
		V. Bellati:b. A. Mariani:bs.

WINTER 1904 CARDENAS–TEATRO OTERO

Mar. 13	*Lucia di*	A. Braglia:t. O. Vertova:cond.
	Lammermoor	
Mar. 15	*La sonnambula*	A. Braglia:t. G. Rossi:bs.
		O. Vertova:cond.
Mar. 17	*Rigoletto*	
Mar. 20	*Il barbiere di*	
	Siviglia	
Mar. 22	*I puritani*	

SPRING 1904 CIENFUEGOS

| Mar. | *Lucia di* | |
| | *Lammermoor?* | |

SPRING 1904 SANTIAGO DE CUBA–TEATRO ORIENTE

Apr. 3	*Lucia di*	A. Braglia:t. L. Mazzoleni:b.
	Lammermoor	G. Rossi:bs.
		O. Vertova:cond.
Apr. 5	*La sonnambula*	A. Braglia:t. G. Rossi:bs.
		O. Vertova:cond.
Apr. 7	*I puritani*	A. Braglia:t. L. Mazzoleni:b.
		G. Rossi:bs.
		O. Vertova:cond.
Apr. 9	*Rigoletto*	A. Braglia:t. L. Mazzoleni:b.
		G. Rossi:bs.
		O. Vertova:cond.
Apr. 10	*La traviata*	A. Braglia:t. L. Ottoboni:b.
		O. Vertova:cond.

SPRING 1904 HAVANA–TEATRO ALBISU

Apr. 23	*La sonnambula*	A. Braglia:t. G. Rossi:bs. O. Vertova:cond.
Apr. 26	*Lucia di Lammermoor*	A. Braglia:t. L. Ottoboni:b. G. Rossi:bs. O. Vertova:cond.
Apr. 29	*Faust*	A. Braglia:t. L. Ottoboni:b. G. Rossi:bs. O. Vertova:cond.

AUTUMN 1904 MEXICO CITY–TEATRO ARBEU

Oct. 2	*I pescatori di perle*	G. Bazelli:t. G. La Puma:b. G. Golisciani:cond.
Oct. 9	*Lucia di Lammermoor*	C. Cartica:t. G. La Puma:b. S. Cirotto:bs. G. Polacco:cond.
Oct. 12	*Mignon*	L. Berlendi:s. G. Bazelli:t. S. Cirotto:bs. G. Golisciani:cond.
Oct. 22	*La sonnambula*	G. Bazelli:t. G. Polacco:cond.
Oct. 23	*Rigoletto*	G. Bazelli:t. A. Romboli:b. S. Cirotto:bs. G. Golisciani:cond.
Nov. 3	*Romeo e Giulietta*	G. Bazelli:t. G. La Puma:b.
Nov. 7	*La traviata*	E. Colli:t. A. Romboli:b.
Nov. 12	*Lakmé*	G.Bazelli:t. G. La Puma:b. G. Rossi:bs.
Nov. 20	*Faust*	G. Bazelli:t. A. Romboli:b. G. Rossi:bs. G. Polacco:cond.
Nov. 26	*Il barbiere di Siviglia*	G. Bazelli:t. A. Romboli:b. G. Rossi:bs. G. Polacco:bs.

AUTUMN 1904 MEXICO CITY–CIRCO ORRIN

Nov. 29	*Il barbiere di Siviglia*	G. Bazelli:t. A. Romboli:b. G. Rossi:bs. G. Polacco:cond.
Dec. 6	*Faust*	G. Bazelli:t. A. Romboli:b. G. Rossi:bs.
Dec. 7	Concert	
Dec. 8	*Lucia di Lammermoor*	E. Colli:t.

Dec. 10   *I pescatori di perle*   G. Bazelli:t.
Dec. 11   *Rigoletto*
Dec. 15   *La traviata*

AUTUMN 1904 SAN LUIS POTOSI–TEATRO LA PAZ
Dec. 17?   *Lucia di*   E. Colli:t.
             Lammermoor
             Rigoletto   G. Bazelli:t.   S. Cirotto:bs.
             I pescatori di perle
             Il barbiere di   G. Bazelli:t.
             Siviglia
             Romeo e Giulietta
             Mignon

WINTER 1904–5 GUADALAJARA–TEATRO DEGOLLADO
             Il barbiere di   G. Bazelli:t.   G. La Puma:b.
             Siviglia
             I pescatori di perle   G. La Puma:b.
             Romeo e Giulietta   G. La Puma:b.
             Rigoletto   S. Cirotto:bs.
             Mignon

WINTER 1905 SAN FRANCISCO–TIVOLI THEATRE
Jan. 11   *Rigoletto*   E. Bettini:ms.   G. Bazelli:t.
                                     A. Romboli:b.   S. Cirotto:bs.
                                     G. Polacco:cond.
Jan. 13   *Il barbiere di*   G. Bazelli:t.   G. La Puma:b.
             Siviglia   G. Rossi:bs.   N. Cervi:bs.
                                     G. Polacco:cond.
Jan. 17   *Lucia di*   E. Colli:t.   G. La Puma:b.
             Lammermoor   L. Munoz:bs.
                                     G. Golisciani:cond.
Jan. 19   *La traviata*   E. Colli:t.   (later G. Bazelli:t.)
                                     A. Romboli:b.
Jan. 24   *Faust*   G. Bazelli:t.   E. Baker:ms.
                                     A. Romboli:b.   G. Rossi:bs.
                                     G. Polacco:cond.
Feb. 9   *I pescatori di perle** G. Bazelli:t.   G. La Puma:b.
                                     N. Cervi:bs.
Feb. 14   *I puritani*   E. Colli:t.   (?)[4] A. Romboli:b.
                                     S. Cirotto:bs.
                                     G. Polacco:cond.
Feb. 24   *Mignon*   L. Berlendi:s.   G. Bazelli:t.
                                     S. Cirotto:bs.

SPRING 1905 CHIHUAHUA–TEATRO DE LOS HEROES[5]

May 4	*Lucia di Lammermoor*	G. Bazelli:t. D. Viglione Borghese:b.
May 6	*La traviata*	G. Bazelli:t. D. Viglione Borghese:b.
May 11	*Rigoletto*	G. Bazelli:t. B. Franco:ms. D. Viglione Borghese:b. G. Wanrell:bs.
May 13	*Faust*	G. Bazelli:t. B. Franco:ms. D. Viglione Borghese:b. G. Wanrell:bs.
May 16	*La sonnambula*	G. Bazelli:t. G. Wanrell:bs.
May 18	Gala Concert	

SPRING 1905 EL PASO–OPERA HOUSE

May 20?	*Lucia di Lammermoor?*
May 22?	*La traviata?*
May 24?	*Rigoletto?*

SPRING 1905 GOMEZ PALACIO–TEATRO UNION

May 26	*Lucia di Lammermoor*	G. Bazelli:t. D. Viglione Borghese:b.
May 28	*La traviata*	G. Bazelli:t. D. Viglione Borghese:b.

SPRING 1905 DURANGO

May	*Lucia di Lammermoor?*
June	*La traviata?*

SPRING 1905 TORREON

SPRING 1905 MONTERREY–TEATRO JUAREZ

June 15	*Lucia di Lammermoor*	G. Bazelli:t. D. Viglione-Borghese:b.
June 17	*La sonnambula*	G. Bazelli:t. G. Wanrell:bs.
June 18	Gala Concert	

SUMMER 1905 SALTILLO–ATENEO DE LA FUENTE

June 28	*Lucia di Lammermoor*	G. Bazelli:t. D. Viglione Borghese:b.
July 1	*Rigoletto*	G. Bazelli:t. D. Viglione Borghese:b.

SUMMER 1905 SAN LUIS POTOSI–TEATRO LA PAZ

| July 3 | *Lucia di Lammermoor* | G. Bazelli:t. D. Viglione Borghese:b. |

SUMMER AND AUTUMN 1905 SAN FRANCISCO–TIVOLI THEATRE

Sep. 12	*Rigoletto*	M. Grasse:ms. G. Bazelli:t. A. Gregoretti:b. J. Gravina:bs. G. Polacco:cond.
Sep. 19	*Lucia di Lammermoor*	V. Coppola:t. (later G. Bazelli:t.) A. Gregoretti:b. G. Polacco:cond. (also G. Longo:cond.)
Sep. 24	*La traviata*	G. Bazelli:t. A. Gregoretti:b. G. Polacco:cond.
Oct. 3	*Il barbiere di Siviglia*	G. Bazelli:t. A. Gregoretti:b. N. Cervi:bs. A. Dadò:bs. G. Polacco:cond.
Oct. 10	*La sonnambula*	G. Bazelli:t. J. Gravina:bs. G. Polacco:cond.
Oct. 24	*Dinorah*	G. Bazelli:t. A. Gregoretti:b. J. Gravina:bs. G. Polacco:cond.
Nov. 7	Concert	

AUTUMN AND WINTER 1905–6 MEXICO CITY–TEATRO ARBEU

Dec. 3	*Rigoletto*	A. Belloni:ms. G. Bazelli:t. R. Astillero:b. A. Dadò:bs. G. Longo:cond.
Dec. 8	*Lucia di Lammermoor*	G. Bazelli:t. G. Rebonato:b. A. Dadò:bs.
Dec. 10	*Il barbiere di Siviglia*	G. Bazelli:t. G. Rebonato:b. A. Dadò:bs. N. Cervi:bs. G. Longo:cond.
Dec. 12	*La traviata*	G. Bazelli:t. G. Rebonato:b. G. Longo:cond.
Dec. 14	*La sonnambula*	G. Bazelli:t. A. Dadò:bs.
Dec. 20	*Faust*	G. Bazelli:t. R. Astillero:b. J. Torres Ovando:bs.
Dec. 21	*Dinorah*	G. Fabbri:ms. G. Bazelli:t. G. Rebonato:b.
Dec. 28	Concert	

SPRING AND SUMMER 1907 BUENOS AIRES–TEATRO COLISEO

May 21	*Lucia di Lammermoor*	G. Zenatello:t. R. Tegani:b. J. Torres de Luna:bs. G. Barone:cond.
May 28	*La sonnambula*	C. Dani:t. G. Barone:cond.
May 30	*La traviata*	G. Armanini:t. (later C. Dani:t.) R. Tegani:b. G. Barone:cond.
June 8	*Rigoletto*	A. Torretta:ms. G. Armanini:t. P. Amato:b. G. Barone:cond.
June 14	*Il barbiere di Siviglia*	G. Armanini:t. (later C. Dani:t.) F. Corradetti:b. J. Torres de Luna:bs. G. Barone:cond.
July 3	*L'Elisir d'amore*	C. Dani:t. F. Corradetti:b. R. Ercolani:bs. G. Barone:cond.
July 25	*Dinorah*	G. La Puma:b. G. Barone:cond.

SUMMER 1907 MONTEVIDEO–TEATRO URQUIZA

Aug. 4	*Lucia di Lammermoor*	G. Armanini:t. R. Tegani:b. J. Torres de Luna:bs. G. Barone:cond.
Aug. 8	*Il barbiere di Siviglia*	G. Armanini:t. F. Corradetti:b. J. Torres de Luna:bs. G. Barone:cond.

SUMMER 1907 ROSARIO–TEATRO OLIMPO

Aug. 13	*Lucia di Lammermoor*	G. Armanini:t. R. Tegani:b. J. Torres de Luna:bs. G. Barone:cond.
Aug. 15	*Il barbiere di Siviglia*	C. Dani:t. G. La Puma:b. J. Torres de Luna:bs. R. Ercolani:bs. G. Barone:cond.
Aug. 18	*La traviata*	C. Dani:t. G. Barone:cond.
Aug. 22	*Rigoletto*	C. Dani:t. P. Amato:b. G. Barone:cond.

SUMMER 1907 SAO PAULO–POLITEAMA

Sep. 2	*La traviata*	C. Dani:t. R. Tegani:b. G. Barone:cond.

SUMMER 1907 RIO DE JANEIRO–TEATRO LYRICO

Sep. 11	*Rigoletto*	A. Torretta:ms. C. Dani:t.
		P. Amato:b. R. Ercolani:bs.
		G. Barone:cond.
Sep. 14	*La traviata*	G. Zenatello:t. P. Amato:b.
		G. Barone:cond.

AUTUMN 1907 LONDON–COVENT GARDEN

Nov. 2	*La traviata*	F. Carpi:t. G. M. Sammarco:b.
		(later A. Scandiani:b.).
		E. Panizza:cond.
Nov. 15	*Lucia di Lammermoor*	F. Carpi:t. (later F. Vignas:t.)
		G. De Luca:b. C. Thos:bs.
		E. Panizza:cond.
Nov. 23	*Rigoletto*	J. McCormack:t. (later
		F. Carpi:t.)
		G. M. Sammarco:b.
		O. Luppi:bs. E. Panizza:cond.
Dec. 3	Concert	
Dec. 7	Concert	
Dec. 10	Concert	
Dec. 12	Concert	

WINTER 1908 NEW YORK CITY–MANHATTAN OPERA

Jan. 15	*La traviata*	A. Bassi:t. (later
		G. Zenatello:t.) M. Ancona:b.
		C. Campanini:cond.
Jan. 20	*Lucia di Lammermoor*	G. Zenatello:t.
		G. M. Sammarco:b.
		V. Arimondi:bs.
		C. Campanini:cond.
Jan. 29	*Rigoletto*	E. De Cisneros:ms. (later
		G. Giaconia:ms.) A. Bassi:t.
		M. Renaud:b. (later
		G. M. Sammarco:b.)
		V. Arimondi:bs.
		C. Campanini:cond.
Feb. 26	*Dinorah*	E. Trentini:s. G. Giaconia:ms.
		F. Daddi:t. E. Venturini:t.
		M. Ancona:b. L. Mugnoz:bs.
		C. Campanini:cond.
Mar. 6	*Crispino e la comare*	E. Zaccaria:ms. E. Venturini:t.
		G.M. Sammarco:b.
		F. Gianoli-Galletti:bs.

                            V. Arimondi:bs.
                            C. Campanini:cond.
Mar. 28   Gala Concert

SPRING 1908 PHILADELPHIA–ACADEMY OF MUSIC

Mar. 19   *Lucia di*   G. Zenatello:t.
             Lammermoor   G. M. Sammarco:b.
                                 C. Campanini:cond.

SPRING 1908 LONDON–COVENT GARDEN

Apr. 30   *La traviata*   O. Mařák:t.
                                 G. M. Sammarco:b.
                                 C. Campanini:cond.
May 2   *Lucia di*   J. McCormack:t. (later
             Lammermoor   A. Bonci:t.)
                                 G. M. Sammarco:b.
                                 R. Radford:bs.
                                 C. Campanini:cond.
May 14   *Rigoletto*   E. Thornton:ms.
                                 J. McCormack:t. (later
                                 A. Bonci:t.)
                                 G. M. Sammarco:b. (later
                                 A. Scotti:b.) G. Vanni-
                                 Marcoux[6]:bs.
                                 C. Campanini:cond.
May 27   Gala Concert[7]
June 15   *Il barbiere di*   A. Bonci:t. G. M. Sammarco:b.
             Siviglia   F. Navarrini:bs.
                                 C. Gilibert:bs.
                                 C. Campanini:cond.
June 19   *I pescatori di perle*   A. Bonci:t. G. M. Sammarco:b.
                                 G. Vanni-Marcoux:bs.
                                 C. Campanini:cond.
July 11   *Gli ugonotti*   E. Destinn:s. F. Dereyne:ms.
                                 G. Zenatello:t. A. Scotti:b.
                                 G. Vanni-Marcoux:bs.
                                 J. Nivette:bs.
                                 C. Campanini:cond.

AUTUMN 1908 CONCERT TOUR

This concert tour covered twelve cities, including Cheltenham (Oct. 3),
Birmingham (Oct. 5) and Manchester (Oct. 20).

AUTUMN AND WINTER 1908–9 NEW YORK CITY–MANHATTAN OPERA

Nov. 14	*Il barbiere di Siviglia*	A. Parola:t. G. M. Sammarco:b. A. Perello de Segurola:bs. C. Gilibert:bs. C. Campanini:cond.
Nov. 18	*Lucia di Lammermoor*	G. Taccani:t. (later F. Constantino:t.) G. Polese:b. (later G. M. Sammarco:b.) G. De Grazia:bs. (later V. Arimondi:bs.) C. Campanini:cond. (later A. Parelli:cond.)
Dec. 5	*Rigoletto*	A. Ponzano:ms. F. Constantino:t. G. M. Sammarco:b. (later M. Renaud:b.) V. Arimondi:bs. (later A. Perello de Segurola:bs.) C. Campanini:cond.
Dec. 12	*La traviata*	F. Constantino:t. (later G. Taccani:t.) G. M. Sammarco:b. C. Campanini:cond.
Jan. 9	*Crispino e la comare*	G. Severina:ms. E. Venturini:t. G. M. Sammarco:b. F. Gianoli-Galletti:bs. V. Arimondi:bs. C. Campanini:cond.
Feb. 13	*La sonnambula*	A. Parola:t. A. Perello de Segurola:bs. A. Parelli:cond.
Feb. 26	*I puritani*	F. Constantino:t. G. Polese:b. A. Perello de Segurola:bs. C. Campanini:cond. (later A. Parelli:cond.)

AUTUMN AND WINTER 1908–9 PHILADELPHIA–OPERA HOUSE
(Concurrent with the New York season)

Nov. 21	*Il barbiere di Siviglia*	A. Parola:t. G. Polese:b. A. Perello de Segurola:bs.)

		C. Gilibert:bs. G. Sturani:cond.
Nov. 26	*Lucia di Lammermoor*	G. Taccani (later F. Constantino:t.) G. Polese:b. V. Arimondi (later G. De Grazia (and then M. Sampieri:bs.) G. Sturani:cond.
Dec. 1	*Rigoletto*	A. Ponzano (later M. Aldrich:ms.) F. Constantino:t. G. M. Sammarco (later M. Renaud:b.) V. Arimondi:bs. G. Sturani:cond.
Dec. 19	*La traviata*	G. Taccani:t. (later F. Constantino:t.) G. Polese:b. C. Campanini: (later G. Sturani:cond.)
Jan. 23	*Crispino e la comare*	G. Severina:ms. E. Venturini:t. G. M. Sammarco:b. F. Gianoli-Galletti:bs. V. Arimondi:bs. A. Parelli:cond.
Jan. 30	*La sonnambula*	A. Parola:t. V. Arimondi:bs. A. Parelli:cond.
Mar. 13	*I puritani*	F. Constantino:t. G. Polese:b. V. Arimondi:bs. A Parelli:cond.

WINTER 1909 BALTIMORE–LYRIC THEATRE

Jan. 4	*Lucia di Lammermoor*	F. Constantino:t. G. Polese:b. V. Arimondi:bs. G. Sturani:cond.
Jan. 11	*La traviata*	G. Taccani:t. G. Polese:b. G. Sturani:cond.

SPRING 1909 BOSTON–BOSTON THEATRE

Mar. 29	*Lucia di Lammermoor*	F. Constantino:t. G. Polese (later G. M. Sammarco:b.) G. De Grazia:b. C. Campanini:cond.
Mar. 31	*La traviata*	F. Constantino:t. (later G. Taccani:t.)

			G. M. Sammarco:b.
			C. Campanini:cond.
Apr.	6	*Rigoletto*	A. Ponzano:ms.
			F. Constantino:t.
			M. Renaud:b. A. Perello de
			Segurola:bs.
			C. Campanini:cond.

SPRING 1909 SHEFFIELD–ALBERT HALL
Apr. 28   Concert

SPRING AND SUMMER 1909 LONDON–COVENT GARDEN

May 1	*La traviata*	J. McCormack:t.
		G. M. Sammarco:b. (later
		A. Scotti:b., then
		A. Scandiani:b.)
		C. Campanini:cond.
May 3	*Lucia di Lammermoor*	J. McCormack (later
		G. Anselmi:t.)
		G. M. Sammarco:b.
		M. Davey:bs.
		C. Campanini:cond.
May 14	*Rigoletto*	J. Bourgeois:ms. J. McCormack
		(later G. Anselmi:t.)
		G. M. Sammarco:b.
		G. Vanni-Marcoux:bs. (later
		A. Huberty:bs.)
		C. Campanini:cond.
May 29	*La sonnambula*	J. McCormack:t.
		A. Scandiani:b.
		E. Panizza:cond.
May 31	*Il barbiere di Siviglia*	G. Anselmi:t.
		G. M. Sammarco:b.
		G. Vanni-Marcoux:bs.
		C. Gilibert:bs. (later
		F. Gianoli-Galletti:bs.)
		E. Panizza:cond.
June 21	*Gli ugonotti*	E. Destinn:s. A. O'Brien:ms.
		G. Zenatello:t. A. Scotti:b.
		M. Davey:bs. M. Journet:bs.
		C. Campanini:cond.

SPRING 1909 PARIS–TROCADERO
June 26   Concert

AUTUMN 1909 CONCERT TOUR
Cities visited include Sheffield (Sep. 28), Glasgow (Oct. 11), Dundee (Oct. 18) and Birmingham (Oct. 25).

AUTUMN AND WINTER 1909–10 NEW YORK CITY– MANHATTAN OPERA HOUSE

Nov. 10	*La traviata*	J. McCormack:t. G. M. Sammarco:b. O. Anselmi:cond.
Nov. 15	*Lucia di Lammermoor*	J. McCormack:t. G. M. Sammarco:b. G. De Grazia:bs. O. Anselmi:cond.
Nov. 22	*La figlia del reggimento*	M. Duchène:ms. J. McCormack:t. C. Gilibert:ms. O. Anselmi:cond.
Feb. 11	*Rigoletto*	A. Gentle:ms. J. McCormack:t. (later O.Harrold:t.) M. Renaud (later G. M. Sammarco:b.) J. Vallier:bs. (later H. Scott:bs.) O. Anselmi:cond.
Mar. 21	*Lakmé*	M. Duchène:ms. J. McCormack:t. A. Crabbé:b. G. Huberdeau:bs. C. Nicosia:cond.

AUTUMN AND WINTER 1909–10 PHILADELPHIA
(Concurrent with the New York season)

Nov. 13	*Lucia di Lammermoor*	J. McCormack:t. (later F. Carasa:t.) G. Polese:b. (later G. M. Sammarco:b.) H. Scott:bs. (later G. Malfatti:bs.) G. Sturani:cond. (later O. Anselmi:cond.)
Nov. 25	*La figlia del reggimento*	M. Duchène:ms. J. McCormack:t. C. Gilibert:bs. G. Sturani:cond.

Dec. 7	*La traviata*	J. McCormack:t.
		G. M. Sammarco:b. (later
		G. Polese:b.) G. Sturani:cond.
Jan. 8	*Rigoletto*	B. Soyer:ms. (later
		A. Gentle:ms.)
		J. McCormack:t. G. Polese:b.
		(later G. M. Sammarco:b.)
		G. Huberdeau:bs. (later
		H. Scott:bs.) G. Sturani:cond.
Mar. 24	*Lakmé*	M. Duchène:ms.
		J. McCormack:t.
		A. Crabbé:b.
		G. Huberdeau:bs.

AUTUMN 1909 CHICAGO–AUDITORIUM
Dec. 12   Concert

AUTUMN 1909 PITTSBURGH

Dec. 20	*Lucia di*	J. McCormack:t. G. Polese:b.
	Lammermoor	G.De Grazia:bs.
		O. Anselmi:cond.
Dec. 22	*La traviata*	J. McCormack:t. G. Polese:b.
		O. Anselmi:cond.

WINTER 1910 WASHINGTON–BELASCO THEATRE

Jan. 10	*Lucia di*	J. McCormack:t. G. Polese:b.
	Lammermoor	H. Scott:bs.
		G. Sturani:cond.
Jan. 12	*La traviata*	J. McCormack:t.
		G. M. Sammarco:b.
		O. Anselmi:cond.
Jan. 14	*La figlia del*	J. McCormack:t. C. Gilibert:bs.
	reggimento	G. Sturani:cond.

WINTER 1910 CONCERT TOUR
Cities visited include Cleveland (Jan. 24), Detroit (Jan. 26), Chicago
(Jan. 30), St Louis (Jan. 31), Kansas City (Feb. 2), Columbus (Feb. 4),
Buffalo (Feb. 6), Pittsburgh (Feb. 8?), Montreal (Mar. 14) and probably
Toronto.

WINTER 1910 PHILADELPHIA

| Feb. 11 | *Rigoletto* | J. McCormack:t. M. Renaud:b. |

SPRING 1910 BOSTON–BOSTON THEATRE

Mar. 29	*Lucia di*	J. McCormack:t. G. Polese:b.
	Lammermoor	G. De Grazia:bs.
		O. Anselmi:cond.

| Mar. 31 | *La figlia del reggimento* | J. McCormack:t.   C. Gilibert:bs. G. Sturani:cond. |
| Apr. 2 | *La traviata* | J. McCormack:t.   G. Polese:b. O. Anselmi:cond. |

SPRING AND SUMMER 1910 LONDON–COVENT GARDEN

Apr. 27	*Rigoletto*	N. Rostovsky:t. G. M. Sammarco:b. M. Davey:bs. (later G. Vanni-Marcoux:bs.) C. Campanini:cond.
Apr. 29	*La traviata*	J. McCormack:t. G. M. Sammarco:b. C. Campanini:cond.
May 13	*Il barbiere di Siviglia*	N. Rostovsky:t. G. M. Sammarco:b. G. Vanni-Marcoux:bs. P. Malatesta:bs. C. Campanini:cond.
May 26	*La sonnambula*	J. McCormack:t. E. Burke:bs. C. Campanini:cond.
June 18	*Lakmé*	J. McCormack:t. E. Burke:bs. C. Campanini:cond.
July 1	*Gli ugonotti*	E. Destinn:s. E. Di Lima:ms. N. Zerola:t. L. Lestelly:b. (later A. Scotti:b.) M. Davey:bs. E. Burke:bs. E. Panizza:cond. (later C. Campanini:cond.)

AUTUMN 1910 PARMA–TEATRO REGIO

Sep. 8	*Lucia di Lammermoor*	J. Palet:t. G. Polese:b. A. Riccieri:bs. C. Campanini:cond.
Sep. 13	*Il barbiere di Siviglia*	U. Macnez:t. G. M. Sammarco:b. G. Vanni-Marcoux:bs. P. Malatesta:bs. C. Campanini:cond.
Sep. 17	*La figlia del reggimento*	J. McCormack:t. E. De Cisneros:ms. G. Vanni-Marcoux:bs. C. Campanini:cond.

AUTUMN 1910 LONDON–CRYSTAL PALACE
Sep. 24   Concert   H. Wood:cond.

AUTUMN 1910 CONCERT TOUR
Cities visited include Cardiff (Sep. 27), Bristol (Sep. 29), Cheltenham
(Oct. 1), Birmingham (Oct. 3), Manchester (Oct. 5), Liverpool (Oct.
7), Blackpool (Oct. 9), Glasgow (Oct. 12), Edinburgh (Oct. 15),
Sunderland (Oct. 17), Newcastle (Oct. 19), Sheffield (Oct. 21), Dublin
(Oct. 25), Belfast (Oct. 27), and Dublin (Oct. 29).

AUTUMN AND WINTER 1910–11 CONCERT TOUR
Cities visited include San Francisco (Dec. 12, 17, 20, 24, and 26),
Oakland (Dec. 28), Portland (Dec. 30), Tacoma (Jan. 3), Victoria (Jan.
10), Vancouver (Jan. 12), Seattle (Jan. 16), Spokane, San Francisco
(Jan. 19), Pasadena (Jan. 21), Los Angeles (Jan. 24, 27 and ?) Denver
(Feb. 1), Kansas City (Feb. 6), St Paul (Feb. 9), Minneapolis (Feb. 11),
Cincinnati, Chicago (Feb. 23), Cleveland (Feb. 27), New York (Mar. 6
and 12), Boston (Mar. 9), Philadelphia (Mar. 14), Washington (Mar. 20),
Montreal (Mar. 24), Rochester (Mar. 27), New Haven (Mar. 29), and
New York (Apr. 2).

SPRING AND SUMMER 1911 LONDON–COVENT GARDEN

Apr. 22	*Lakmé*	J. McCormack:t. E. Burke:bs. E. Panizza:cond.
Apr. 25	*Rigoletto*	T. Di Angelo:ms. J. McCormack:t. G. M. Sammarco:b. (later D. Gilly:b.) G. Huberdeau:bs. E. Panizza: cond.
May 5	*La traviata*	J. McCormack (later G. Armanini:t.) G. M. Sammarco:b. (later D. Gilly:b) C. Campanini:cond.
May 31	*Il barbiere di Siviglia*	G. Armanini:t. G. M. Sammarco:b. G. Vanni-Marcoux:bs. P. Malatesta:bs. E. Panizza:cond.
June 16	*La sonnambula*	J. McCormack:t. E. Burke:bs. E. Panizza:cond.
June 26	Coronation Gala Concert	

June 29	*Gli ugonotti*	E. Destinn:s. A. Wilna:ms.
		F. Darmel:t.
		G. M. Sammarco:b.
		L. Sibiriakoff:bs.
		G. Huberdeau:bs.
		C. Campanini:cond.

AUTUMN 1911–CONCERT TOUR

Cities visited include Birmingham (Oct. 9), Liverpool (Oct. 11), Manchester (Oct. 13), Sheffield (Oct. 16), Glasgow (Oct. 18), Edinburgh (Oct. 21), Newcastle (Oct. 24), Nottingham (Oct. 26), and Bournemouth (Oct. 28).

AUTUMN 1911 PHILADELPHIA–METROPOLITAN OPERA HOUSE

Nov. 15	*Lucia di*	A. Bassi:t. G. M. Sammarco:b.
	Lammermoor	H. Scott:bs.
		C. Campanini:cond.
Nov. 18	*La traviata*	A. Bassi:t. G. M. Sammarco:b.
		C. Campanini:cond.

AUTUMN 1911 CLEVELAND

Nov. 21	*Lucia di*	A. Bassi:t. A. Costa:b.
	Lammermoor	H. Scott:bs.
		C. Campanini:cond.

AUTUMN 1911 CHICAGO–AUDITORIUM

Nov. 24	*Lucia di*	A. Bassi:t. G. M. Sammarco:b.
	Lammermoor	C. Campanini:cond.
Nov. 28	*La traviata*	A. Bassi:t. G. M. Sammarco:b.
		C. Campanini:cond.
Nov. 30	*Rigoletto*	G. Giaconia:ms. A. Bassi:t.
		G. M. Sammarco:b.
		G. Huberdeau:bs.
		C. Campanini:cond.
Dec. 4	*Il barbiere di*	L. Remella:t.
	Siviglia	G. M. Sammarco:b.
		B. Berardi:bs.
		P. Malatesta:bs.
		C. Campanini:cond.
Dec. 6	*Lakmé*	G. Giaconia:ms. A. Bassi:t.
		A. Crabbé:b.
		G. Huberdeau:bs.
		C. Campanini:cond.

AUTUMN 1911 CINCINNATI–MUSIC HALL

| Dec. 11 | *Lucia di Lammermoor* | A. Bassi:t.   G. M. Sammarco:b. |

AUTUMN 1911 BOSTON–BOSTON OPERA HOUSE

| Dec. 20 | *Lucia di Lammermoor* | F. Constantino:t.   G. Polese:b. A. Silli:bs. R. Moranzoni:cond. |
| Dec. 23 | *Mignon* | F. Dereyne:ms.   J. Swartz:ms. E. Clement:t.   L. Rothier:bs. W. Goodrich:cond. |

WINTER 1911–12 NEW YORK CITY–METROPOLITAN OPERA

Dec. 27	*Lucia di Lammermoor*	F. Constantino:t. P. Amato:b. (later G. Campanari:b.) H. Witherspoon:bs. G. Sturani:cond.
Jan. 6	*La traviata*	D. Smirnoff:t. G. Polese:b. (later P. Amato:b.) G. Sturani:cond.
Jan. 11	*Rigoletto*	J. Mauburg:ms. (later T. Orridge:ms.) D. Smirnoff:t. (later E. Caruso:t.) D. Gilly (later M. Renaud:b.) A. Perello de Segurola (later L. Rothier:bs.) G. Sturani:cond.

WINTER 1912 PROVIDENCE–INFANTRY HALL

| Jan. 16 | Concert | R. Blanchart:b.   J. Mardones:bs. |

WINTER 1912 BOSTON–BOSTON OPERA HOUSE
(Concurrent with the season at the Metropolitan Opera)

Jan. 12	*Lucia di Lammermoor*	F. Constantino:t. G. Polese:b. R. Moranzoni:cond.
Jan. 20	*La traviata*	G. Zenatello:t. G. Polese:b. A. Conti:cond.
Jan. 29	*Il barbiere di Siviglia*	F. Constantino:t. R. Angelini-Fornari:b. G. Vanni-Marcoux:bs. L. Tavecchia:bs. A. Conti:cond.

WINTER 1912 NEW HAVEN
  Feb. 1   *Rigoletto*   E. Leveroni:ms.
                                     F. Constantino:t.
                                     G. Polese:b. A. Conti:cond.

WINTER AND SPRING 1912 CONCERT TOUR
Cities visited include New York (Feb. 18), Baltimore (Feb.), Atlanta
  (Feb. 23), Houston, Los Angeles (Mar.) San Francisco (Mar. 11, 17),
  San José (Mar.), San Francisco (Mar. 22), Sacramento (Mar. 23),
  Portland (Mar. 30), Fresno (Apr.), Berkeley (Apr. 7), Denver (Apr.
  10), Chicago (Apr. 14), Toronto (Apr. 16) and New York (Apr. 21).

SPRING AND SUMMER 1912 LONDON–COVENT GARDEN
  May 27   *Rigoletto*   E. Leveroni:ms.
                                     J. McCormack:t. D. Gilly:b.
                                     (later V. Romano:b.)
                                     G. Huberdeau:bs.
                                     E. Panizza:cond.
  June 1   *Il barbiere di*   J. McCormack:t.
                Siviglia   G. M. Sammarco:b.
                                     G. Vanni-Marcoux:bs.
                                     P. Malatesta:bs.
                                     E. Panizza:cond.
  June 11   *Gli ugonotti*   E. Destinn:s. P. Donalda:s.
                                     P. Franz:t.
                                     G. M. Sammarco:b.
                                     G. Vanni-Marcoux:bs.
                                     V. Arimondi:bs.
                                     C. Campanini:cond.
  June 13   *La traviata*   J. McCormack:t. D. Gilly:b.
                                     E. Panizza:cond.

SUMMER 1912 LONDON–ROYAL ALBERT HALL
  June 16   Concert
  June 30   Concert

WINTER 1912–13 BOSTON–BOSTON OPERA HOUSE
  Dec. 21   *Lucia di*   G. Gaudenzi:t. (later
                Lammermoor   U. Sacchetti:t.) A. Rossi:b.
                                     (later G. Polese:b.)
                                     R. Moranzoni:cond.
  Dec. 25   *La traviata*   G. Gaudenzi:t. (later
                                     G. Zenatello:t.) A. Rossi:b.
                                     (later G. Polese:b.)
                                     R. Moranzoni:cond.

Jan. 12   Concert

WINTER 1913 HARTFORD–PARSON'S THEATRE
Jan.   9   Concert

WINTER 1913 CHICAGO–AUDITORIUM

Jan. 18	*La traviata*	A. Giorgini:t.
		G. M. Sammarco:b.
		C. Campanini:cond.
Jan. 21	*Rigoletto*	M. Keyes:ms. A. Giorgini:t.
		G. M. Sammarco:b.
		H. Scott:bs.
		C. Campanini:cond.
Jan. 23	*Lucia di Lammermoor*	A. Giorgini:t. G. Polese:b.
		(later G. M. Sammarco:b.)
		H. Scott:bs.
		C. Campanini:cond.
Jan. 24	Gala Concert	
Jan. 29	*Mignon*	M. Riegelman:s.
		L. Campagnola:t.
		H. Dufranne:b.
		M. Charlier:cond.

WINTER 1913 MILWAUKEE–ALHAMBRA THEATRE
(Concurrent with the Chicago season)

Jan. 31	*Lucia di Lammermoor*	A. Giorgini:t.
		G. M. Sammarco:b.
		H. Scott:bs. E. Perosio:cond.

WINTER 1913 PHILADELPHIA–METROPOLITAN OPERA HOUSE

Feb. 3	*Lucia di Lammermoor*	A. Giorgini:t.
		G. M. Sammarco:b.
		H. Scott:bs.
		C. Campanini:cond.
Feb. 12	*La traviata*	A. Giorgini:t. A. Rossi:b.
		C. Campanini:cond.
Feb. 20	*Crispino e la comare*	G. M. Sammarco:b.
		V. Trevisan:bs.
		C. Nicolay:bs.
		C. Campanini:cond.

WINTER 1913 BALTIMORE
(Concurrent with the Philadelphia season)

Feb. 7	*Lucia di Lammermoor*	A. Giorgini:t. A. Rossi:b.
		H. Scott:bs. E. Perosio:cond.

WINTER 1913 WASHINGTON
(Concurrent with the Philadelphia season)

Feb. 14	*Lucia di Lammermoor*	A. Giorgini:t. G. Mascal:b. H. Scott:bs. E. Perosio:cond.

WINTER 1913 DALLAS–COLISEUM

Mar. 1	*Lucia di Lammermoor*	A. Giorgini:t. G. Polese:b. H. Scott:bs.

WINTER 1913 LOS ANGELES–AUDITORIUM

Mar. 5	*Rigoletto*	M. Keyes:ms. A. Giorgini:t. G. M. Sammarco:b. G. Huberdeau:bs.
Mar. 8	*Lucia di Lammermoor*	A. Giorgini:t. G. Polese:b. G. Huberdeau:bs. C. Campanini:cond.

WINTER AND SPRING 1913 SAN FRANCISCO–NEW TIVOLI
THEATRE

Mar. 12	*Rigoletto*	M. Keyes:ms. A Giorgini:t. G. M. Sammarco:b. (later G. Polese:b.) G. Huberdeau:bs. C. Campanini:cond.
Mar. 15	*La traviata*	A. Giorgini:t. G. Polese:b. C. Campanini:cond.
Mar. 18	*Lucia di Lammermoor*	A. Giorgini:t. G. Polese:b. H. Scott:bs. C. Campanini:cond.
Mar. 20	*Crispino e la comare*	L. Bérat:ms. G. M. Sammarco:b. V. Trevisan:bs. C. Campanini:cond.

SPRING 1913 PORTLAND–ORPHEUM

Apr. 2	*Lucia di Lammermoor*	A. Giorgini:t. G. Polese:b. H. Scott:bs. C. Campanini:cond.

SPRING 1913 SEATTLE–MOORE THEATER

Apr. 5	*Lucia di Lammermoor*	A. Giorgini:t. G. Polese:b. H. Scott:bs. C. Campanini:cond.
Apr. 6	Concert	

SPRING 1913 DENVER–AUDITORIUM

Apr. 12	*Lucia di Lammermoor*	A. Giorgini:t. G. Polese:b. H. Scott:bs. C. Campanini:cond.
Apr. 13	Concert	

SPRING 1913 WICHITA

Apr. 14	*Lucia di Lammermoor*	A. Giorgini:t. G. Polese:b. H. Scott:bs. C. Campanini:cond.

SPRING 1913 KANSAS CITY–CONVENTION HALL

Apr. 16	*Lucia di Lammermoor*	G. Gaudenzi:t. G. Polese:b. H. Scott:bs. E. Perosio:cond.

SPRING 1913 ST LOUIS–ODEON THEATRE

Apr. 19	*Lucia di Lammermoor*	A. Giorgini:t. A. Crabbé:b. C. Campanini:cond.

SPRING 1913 CHICAGO–AUDITORIUM

Apr. 21	*Crispino e la comare*	

SPRING 1913 MINNEAPOLIS

Apr. 24	*Lucia di Lammermoor*	G. Gaudenzi:t. G. Polese:b. G. Huberdeau:bs. E. Perosio:cond.

SPRING 1913 CINCINNATI

Apr. 28	*Rigoletto*	A. Giorgini:t. G. Polese:b. G. Huberdeau:bs. E. Perosio:cond.

SPRING 1913 COLUMBUS

Apr. 30	*Lucia di Lammermoor*	G. Gaudenzi:t. C. Whitehill:b. C. Nicolay:bs. E. Perosio:cond.

SPRING 1913 NEW YORK CITY–METROPOLITAN OPERA

May 3	*Lucia di Lammermoor*	A. Giorgini:t. G. Polese:b. C. Nicolay:bs. E. Perosio:cond.

AUTUMN 1913 LONDON–ALBERT HALL

Sep. 18	Concert

AUTUMN 1913 CONCERT TOUR

This concert tour covered fourteen cities, including Plymouth,

Portsmouth, Middlesborough, Leicester, Manchester, Edinburgh, Glasgow and Dundee.

AUTUMN 1913 BUDAPEST–OPERAHAZ

Nov. 4	*La traviata*	G. Taccani:t. A. Szemere:b. E. Tango:cond.
Nov. 8	Concert	

AUTUMN 1913 VIENNA–KONZERTHAUS

Nov. 19	Concert

AUTUMN 1913 LONDON–QUEEN'S HALL

Dec. 5	Concert

AUTUMN AND WINTER 1913–14 BOSTON–OPERA HOUSE

Dec. 19	*La traviata*	V. Tanlongo:t. M. Ancona:b. R. Moranzoni:cond.
Dec. 24	*Lucia di Lammermoor*	V. Tanlongo:t. R. Angelini-Fornari:b. J. Mardones:bs. R. Moranzoni:cond.
Dec. 29	*Rigoletto*	E. Leveroni:ms. A. Giorgini:t. M. Ancona:b. J. Mardones:bs. R. Moranzoni:cond.

WINTER 1914 NEW YORK–HIPPODROME

Jan. 18	Concert

WINTER AND SPRING 1914 CONCERT TOUR

She was accompanied on the first part of this tour by T. Ruffo:b., who was replaced in Des Moines by R. Diaz:b. Cities visited include Cincinnati (Jan. 21), Minneapolis (Jan. 23), Toronto (Jan. 28), Buffalo (Jan. 30), Boston (Feb. 5), Philadelphia (Feb. 10), Milwaukee (Feb. 13), Chicago (Feb. 15), Des Moines (Feb. 17), Los Angeles (Feb. 20), Dallas (Feb. 23), San Francisco (Mar. 5 and 17), Los Angeles (Mar. 22), Pasadena, Santa Monica, New Orleans, Nashville (Apr. 3), Dayton (Apr. 7), Cleveland (Apr. 12), Canton (Apr. 14), Toledo (Apr. 17), Indianapolis (Apr. 21), Detroit (Apr. 24), Bridgeport (May 4), and Washington (May 8).

SPRING 1914 LONDON–ROYAL ALBERT HALL

June 4	Concert
June 23	Concert

LENT 1919 TRIESTE–TEATRO VERDI

Mar. 3	Concert	T. Ruffo:b. L. Mancinelli:cond.

AUTUMN 1919 CONCERT TOUR
Cities visited include London (Sep. 20) and Leeds (Sep. 27).

AUTUMN, WINTER AND SPRING 1919–20 CONCERT TOUR
Cities visited include Boston (Nov. 27), New York (Nov. 30), San
Francisco (Dec. 7), Los Angeles (Dec. 9 and 13), San Francisco (Dec.
16), Oakland (Dec. 19), Portland (Dec. 29), Seattle (Jan. 2), Spokane
(Jan. 5) Salt Lake City (Jan. 9), Denver (Jan. 15), Dallas (Jan. 20),
Tulsa (Jan. 26), Topeka (Jan. 29), Kansas City (Feb. 1), Muskogee (Feb.
3), St Louis (Feb. 6), Lincoln Ne. (Feb. 9), Chicago (Feb. 15), Cleveland
(Feb. 21), Detroit (Feb. 26), Erie (Feb. 29), Buffalo (Mar. 2), Rochester
(Mar. 5), Harrisburg (Mar. 8), Baltimore (Mar. 10), New York (Mar.
14), Washington (Mar. 17), Philadelphia (Mar. 20), Scranton (Mar. 22),
Richmond (Mar. 29), Norfolk (Mar. 31), Boston (Apr. 4), Grand Rapids
(Apr. 8), Cincinnati (Apr. 14), Galesburg (Apr. 16), Springfield (Apr. 21),
Providence (Apr. 25), Newark (Apr. 30), New York (May 2),
Spartansburg (May 6), and Macon (May 15).

SPRING 1920 NEW YORK CITY–LEXINGTON OPERA HOUSE
(Concurrent with concert tour)
  Mar. 28   Concert   E. Caruso:t. R. Stracciari:b.

AUTUMN 1920 LONDON–ROYAL ALBERT HALL
  Oct. 9   Concert

AUTUMN, WINTER AND SPRING 1920–21 CONCERT TOUR
Some of the cities visited include New York (Dec. 5), Boston, Toledo
(Jan. 13), St Louis (Feb. 6), San Diego, Los Angeles (Mar. 18), San
Francisco (Mar. 27) and Oakland (Apr. 4).

SPRING 1921 NEW YORK CITY–HIPPODROME
  Apr. 23   Concert   T. Ruffo:b.

SUMMER 1921 LONDON–ROYAL ALBERT HALL
  July 14   Concert

AUTUMN 1921 CONCERT TOUR
Cities visited include London (Sep. 25), Birmingham (Sep. 28), Liverpool
(Oct. 1), Glasgow (Oct. 5), Edinburgh (Oct. 8), Bradford (Oct. 11),
Manchester (Oct. 15), Hull (Oct. 18), Manchester (Oct. 22), Bristol (Oct.
26), Cardiff (Oct. 29), London (Nov. 6), Newcastle (Nov. 9), Nottingham
(Nov. 11), Leicester (Nov. 17), Sheffield (Nov. 21), Preston (Nov. 24),
Middlesborough (Nov. 28), London (Dec. 4), Hanley (Dec. 9), and
Halifax (Dec. 12).

AUTUMN 1922 CONCERT TOUR
Cities visited include London (Oct. 1), Reading (Oct. 4), Edinburgh (Oct.

7), Dundee (Oct. 10), Glasgow (Oct. 13), Belfast (Oct. 17), Dublin (Oct. 21), Liverpool (Oct. 25), London (Oct. 29), Preston (Nov. 1), Manchester (Nov. 4), Birmingham (Nov. 8), Sunderland (Nov. 10), Hull (Nov. 13), Sheffield (Nov. 17), Leeds (Nov. 21), London (Nov. 26). Nottingham (Nov. 29), Manchester (Dec. 2), Bristol (Dec. 13), and Cardiff (Dec. 16).

SPRING 1925 LONDON–BBC
Mar. 10   Radio Concert

SPRING 1925 LONDON–ROYAL ALBERT HALL
Mar. 25   Concert
AUTUMN 1925 CONCERT TOUR
Cities visited include Scarborough (Oct. 4), Halifax (Oct. 8), London (Alexandra Palace – Oct. 10), Hanley (Oct. 12), Manchester (Oct. 17), Plymouth (Oct. 22), Torquay (Oct. 24), Swindon (Nov. 3), Swansea (Nov. 5), Bristol (Nov. 10), Liverpool (Nov. 12), Dublin (Nov. 21), Belfast (Nov. 23), Glasgow (Nov. 25), Perth (Nov. 28), Edinburgh (Dec. 1), London (Dec. 6), and Cardiff (Dec. 13).

AUTUMN 1928 LONDON–ROYAL ALBERT HALL
Oct. 21   Concert

AUTUMN 1929 LONDON–ROYAL ALBERT HALL
Oct. 20   Concert

WINTER 1931 FLORENCE–TEATRO VERDI
Jan. 20   Concert

WINTER 1932 BOSTON–BOSTON CINEMA
Jan. 16   Variety show

WINTER 1932 NEW YORK CITY–PARAMOUNT CINEMA
Mar. 13   Vaudeville programme

AUTUMN 1932 LONDON–ROYAL ALBERT HALL
Dec. 8   Concert

AUTUMN 1933 CONCERT TOUR
Cities visited include Reading (Oct. 18), Bournemouth (Oct. 22), Doncaster (Oct. 25), Eastbourne (Oct. 28), Leeds (Oct. 31), Taunton (Nov. 2), Torquay (Nov. 4), Plymouth (Nov. 6), Folkestone (Nov. 9), London–Alexandra Palace (Nov. 12), Middlesborough (Nov. 14), Leicester (Nov. 16), Glasgow (Nov. 20), Dundee (Nov. 23), Manchester (Nov. 25), Bristol (Nov. 27), Liverpool (Nov. 30), Edinburgh (Dec. 2),

Birmingham (Dec. 5), Dublin (Dec. 9), Belfast (Dec. 11), Newcastle (Dec. 14), and Sheffield (Dec. 18).

WINTER 1934 LONDON–PALLADIUM
Mar. 11   Concert

Notes

1. The chorus for the barcarolle in Act II was augmented by some of the principal singers of the company who did not take part in the rest of the performance. In addition to Tetrazzini, they were E. Petri:s., E. Giannini-Griffoni:t., M. Ancona:b. and L. Broglio:bs.
2. This was Tetrazzini's benefit. According to Rinaldi's study of the Teatro Argentina (p. 1194) she sang the Liebestod from Tristan.
3. Tetrazzini sang a few performances with the company then active in Montevideo as a guest. Shortly after that, she was joined by some of the artists from Buenos Aires who participated in a new season with her as the star of the company (see next heading).
4. The *San Francisco Chronicle* cited the bass S. Cirotto as singing the role of Arturo. If so, it would have been a unique occurrence in the Annals of Opera.
5. This was the first stop in an extended tour of Mexico which lasted about 3–4 months. In addition to Chihuahua, Gomez Palacio, Monterrey and Saltillo, for which some details are available at this time, the touring company visited or planned to visit Zacatecas, Aguascalientes, San Miguel Allende, Guanajuato, Guadalajara, Toluca, and other centres.
6. The French bass-baritone Vanni-Marcoux was actually born in Turin of French parents. His original name was Giovanni (or 'Vanni') Marcoux, which was later used as a stage name. In the interest of consistency he will be listed as having a given name, while in the interest of recognisability, his last name will remain Vanni-Marcoux. Thus, he will be G. Vanni-Marcoux, although it is understood that his 'Christian' name also became part of his stage name.
7. In honour of the State Visit of President Armand Fallères of France.

Alphabetical List of Conductors and Singers with Their Given Names Where Known

Abbate, Gennaro, cond.
Albinolo, Giovanni, bar.
Aldrich, Mariska, ms.
Amato, Pasquale, bar.
Ancona, Mario, bar.
Andreini, Remo, ten.
Angelini-Fornari, Rodolfo, bar.
Anselmi, ?, ms.
Anselmi, Giuseppe, ten.
Anselmi, Oscar, cond.
Apostolu, Giovanni, ten.
Arimondi, Vittorio, bass
Armanini, Giuseppe, ten.
Arnoldson, Sigrid, sop.
Arrighetti, Silvio, bar.
Astillero, Rogeio, bar.
Athos, Sante, bar.

Baker, Elsie, ms.
Baldelli, Antonio, bass
Baldelli, Mariano, bass
Balisardi, Giovanni, bass
Barone, Giuseppe, cond.
Bassi, Amedeo, ten.
Battistini, Mattia, bar.
Bayo, Gioacchino, ten.
Bazelli, Giorgio, ten.

Bellagamba, Lorenzo, bar.
Bellati, B., bar.
Bellati, Virgilio, bass.
Belloni, Amalia, ms.
Beltrami, Ottorino, bar.
Benvenuti, Carlo, ten.
Berardi, Berardo, bass
Bérat, Louise, ms.
Berlendi, Livia, ms.
Bersellini, Pietro, ten.
Bettini, Ernestina, ms.
Bianchi, ?, bass
Bieletto, Vincenzo, ten.
Billi, Remo, bar.
Blanchart, Ramon, bar.
Boisson, Giuseppe, bar.
Bonci, Alessandro, ten.
Bonicioli, Riccardo, cond.
Bordalba, Concetta, sop.
Borelli, Ettore, bass
Borgatti, Giuseppe, ten.
Boscarini, Silvio, cond.
Bourgeois, Jane, ms.
Bozzoli, Ignazio, bar.
Bracale, Rodolfo, cond.
Braglia, Alfredo, ten.
Bravi, Francesco, ten.

Brogi, Augusto, ten.
Broglio, Luigi, bass
Brombara, Vittorio, bar.
Burke, Edmund, bass
Buti, Carlo, bar.

Caligaris-Marti, Rosa, sop.
Calvo, Agostino, bass
Campagnola, Leon, ten.
Campanari, Giuseppe, bar.
Campanini, Cleofonte, cond.
Carasa, Frederico, ten.
Carobbi, Silio, bar.
Carotini, Tilde, ms.
Carpi, Fernando, ten.
Caruso, Enrico, ten.
Caruson, Guglielmo, bar.
Casali, ?, bass
Cavara, Enea, ten.
Cervi, Natale, bass
Cesari, Pietro, bar./bass
Charlier, Marcel, cond.
Ciccolini, Ettore, bass
Cimini, Gaetano, cond.
Cirotto, Sebastiano, bass
Clement, Edmond, ten.
Coletti, E., bass
Colli, Ernesto, ten.
Constantino, Florencio, ten.
Conti, ?, bass
Conti, ?, ten.
Conti, Arnoldo, cond.
Conti, J., bass
Contini, Lodovico, bass
Coppola, Vincenzo, ten.
Corradetti, Feruccio, bar.
Costa, Alfredo, bar.
Crabbé, Armand, bar.
Cucini, Alice, ms.

D'Orio, ?, ms.
Daddi, Francesco, ten.
Dadò, Augusto, bass
Dani, Carlo, ten.

Darmel, Francois, ten.
Davey, Murray, bass
De Angelis, Teofilo, cond.
De Bernis, Emilio, bar.
De Cisneros, Eleanora, ms.
De Grazia, Giuseppe, bass
De Lerma, Matilde, sop.
De Lucia, Fernando, ten.
De Macchi, Maria, sop.
De Marchi, Emilio, ten.
De Nunzio, Maria, sop.
De Padova, Michele, bar.
De Roma, Amalia, sop.
De Rossi, Cesare, ten.
Dereyne, Fely, ms.
Destinn, Emmy, sop.
Di Angelo, Tina, ms.
Di Lima, Edna, ms.
Didur, Adamo, bass
Donalda, Pauline, sop.
Dubois, Francesco, bass
Duchène, Marie, ms.
Duffau, Pietro, cond.
Dufranne, Hector, bar.

Ehrenstein, Luisa, sop.
Elias, Candido, ten.
Emiliani, Oreste, ten.
Ercilla, G., ten.
Ercolani, Remo, bass

Fabro, Ferdinando, bass
Falconi, Giulio, cond.
Federici, Francesco, bar.
Ferni, Carolina, ms.
Ferrari, E., ms.
Fiegna, Camillo, bass
Franco, Beatriz, ms.
Franz, Paul, ten.

Galeazzi, Ettore, cond.
Galletti-Gianoli, Ferdinando, bass
Galli, Ruggero, bass
Gaudenzi, Giuseppe, ten.

Gennari, Oreste, ten.
Gentle, Alice, ms.
Ghilardini, Enzo, ten.
Giachetti, Ada, sop.
Giaconia, Giuseppina, ms.
Giannini, Francesco, ten.
Giannini-Grifoni, Enrico, ten.
Gilibert, Charles, bass
Gilly, Dinh, bar.
Giorgini, Aristodemo, ten.
Giraldoni, Eugenio, b.
Gnaccarini, Agostino, bar.
Golisciani, Gino, cond.
Goodrich, Wallace, cond.
Goula, Juan, cond.
Granados, Francesco, ten.
Grasse, Maria, ms.
Gravina, Juan, bass
Gregoretti, Adamo, bar.
Grisi, Maria, sop.
Grobzewsky, Victor, bar.
Guerrera, Nicolò, cond.
Guerrini, Vittoria, ms.

Harrold, Orville, ten.
Hernandez, Gabriele, bar.
Huberdeau, Gustave, bass
Huberty, Albert, bass

Jacchia, Agide, cond.
Journet, Marcel, bass

Keyes, Margaret, ms.
Kitziu, Aurelia, sop.
Kruszelnicka, Salomea, sop.

La Mura, M., cond.
La Puma, Giuseppe, bar.
Lanfredi, Carlo, ten.
Lanzoni, Agostino, bass
Lara, Pietro, ten.
Lestelly, Louis, bar.
Leveroni, Elvira, ms.
Lippi, A., bass
Lombardi, Emilio, bass

Lombardi, Vincenzo, cond.
Longhi, E., sop.
Longo, Giuseppe, cond.
Longobardi, Luigi, ten.
Lucenti, Luigi, bass
Luppi, Oreste, bass
Luzzatti, Arturo, cond.

McCormack, John, ten.
Macnez, Umberto, ten.
Magini-Coletti, Antonio, bar.
Maini, Primo, ten.
Malatesta, Pompilio, bass
Malfatti, Giorgio, bass
Mancinelli, Luigi, cond.
Manenti, E., ms.
Marak, Ottokar, ten.
Marconi, Francesco, ten.
Mardones, José, bass
Mariacher, Michele, ten.
Mariani, Alfonso, bass
Maristani, Luigi, ten.
Mascal, Georges, bar.
Masin, Gianni, ten.
Masini, Angelo, ten.
Mastrobuono, Stanislao, ten.
Matassini, Achille, ten.
Mauburg, Jeanne, ms.
Mauri, Aurelio, ten.
Mazzoleni, Luigi, bar.
Mazzoli, ?, ten.
Mazzoli, L., ten.
McIntyre, Margaret, sop.
Mentasti, ?, ten.
Migliara, Francesco, bass
Modesti, Alessandro, bar.
Montevecchi, ?, ten.
Monti-Bladini, Irma, ms.
Moranzoni, Roberto, cond.
Moreo, Enrico, bar.
Moretti, Giuseppe, ten.
Morlacchi, ?, ten.
Mugnone, Leopoldo, cond.

Munoz, Luigi, bass

Navarini, Francesco, bass
Nicolay, Constantin, bass
Nicolini, Alessandro, bass
Nicosia, Carlo, cond.
Nivette, Juste, bass
Notargiacomo, Gaetano, bass

O'Brien, Alice, ms.
Orridge, Theodora, ms.
Ottoboni, Libero, bar.

Pacini, Giuseppe, bar.
Pagano, F., ten.
Pagnoni, Cesira, ms.
Palet, José, ten.
Panizza, Ettore, cond.
Paoli-Bonazzo, ?, ms.
Parelli, Attilio, cond.
Parola, Angelo, ten.
Parpagnoli, Linda, ms.
Paterna, Tomasso, bass
Perello de Segurola, Andrès, bass
Perosio, Ettore, cond.
Petri, Elisa, sop.
Piccaluga, Girolamo, ten.
Pini-Corsi, Antonio, bar.
Pini-Corsi, Gaetano, ten.
Podesti, Vittorio, cond.
Polacco, Giorgio, cond.
Polese, Giovanni, bar.
Polli, Massimiliano, bar.
Pomé, Alessandro, cond.
Ponzano, Adele, ms.
Pozzi, Maria, ms.
Prati, ?, ten.
Pribik, ?, cond.
Puccetti, Gino, cond.

Quiroli, Giorgio, ten.

Radford, Robert, bass
Razzoli, ?, bass
Rebonato, Gaetano, bar.

Remella, Luigi, ten.
Renaud, Maurice, bar.
Resplendino, Adolfo, bass
Riccieri, Angelo, bass
Riegelman, Mabel, sop.
Rinaldi, T., ten.
Ristorini, T., ten.
Romano, Virgilio, bar.
Romboli, Arturo, bar.
Rossatto, Luigi, bass
Rossetti, Antonio, ten.
Rossi, Anafesto, bass
Rossi, Giulio, bass
Rostovsky, Nicolas, ten.
Rothier, Leon, bass
Ruffo, Titta, bar.
Russitano, Giuseppe, ten.

Sabellico, Antonio, bass
Sacchetti, Umberto, ten.
Sammarco, G. Mario, bar.
Sampieri, Michele, bass
Sani, Giovanni, ten.
Sarcoli, Adolfo, ten.
Scandiani, Angelo, bar.
Scolari, Giovanni, bass
Scott, Henri, bass
Scotti, Antonio, bar.
Serra, Narciso, bass
Severina, Gina, ms.
Sibiriakoff, Leon, bass
Sigaldi, Michele, ten.
Signoretti, Leopoldo, ten.
Signorini, Francesco, ten.
Silli, A., bass
Sillich, Aristedemo, bass
Silvestri, Alesandro, bass
Singer, Teresa, sop.
Sivori, Ernesto, bar.
Smirnoff, Dimitri, ten.
Sobinoff, Leonid, ten.
Sottolana, Eduardo, bar.
Soyer, Berthe, ms.

Stampanoni, Amerigo, ten.
Stracciari, Riccardo, bar.
Sturani, Giuseppe, cond.
Swartz, Jeska, ms.
Szemere, Árpád, bar.

Tabuyo, Ignazio, bar.
Taccani, Giuseppe, ten.
Tamagno, Francesco, ten.
Tamanti, Roberto, bass
Tango, Egisto, cond.
Tanlongo, Vincenzo, ten.
Tanzini, Giovanni, bass
Tavecchia, Luigi, bass
Tegani, Riccardo, bar.
Thornton, Edna, ms.
Thos, Costantino, bass
Torres de Luna, José, bass
Torretta, Annita, ms.
Tosi, C., bar.
Trentini, Emma, ms.
Trevisan, Vittorio, bass

Urbinati, ?, bar.
Urrutia, Pedro, cond.
Usiglio, Emilio, cond.

Vallier, Jean, bass
Vallini, Pietro, cond.

Vanni-Marcoux, Giovanni, bar./
  bass
Venturini, Alfredo, bass
Venturini, Emilio, ten.
Verdaguer, Martino, bass
Verdi, Clotilde, ms.
Vergari-Marangoni, Adelina, ms.
Vertova, Ottorino, cond.
Vessella, Alessandro, cond.
Vidal, Renée, ms.
Viglione-Borghese, Domenico, bar.
Vigna, Arturo, cond.
Vignas, Francesco, ten.

Walter, Carlo, bass
Wanrell, Gioacchino, bass
Whitehill, Clarence, bar.
Wigley, Michele, bar.
Wilna, Alice, ms.
Witherspoon, Herbert, bass
Wood, Sir Henry, cond.

Zacaria, Antonio, bass
Zaccaria, Emma, ms.
Zanetti, Ubaldo, cond.
Zawner, Carolina, ms.
Zenatello, Giovanni, ten.
Zeppilli, Alice, ms.
Zeppilli-Villani, Giuseppina, ms.
Zerni, E., ten.
Zerola, Nicola, ten.
Zucchi, Francesco, ten.

Discography
by Charles Neilson Gattey

All Luisa Tetrazzini's recordings were made for three firms – the Universal Talking Machine Company of New York labelled 'Zon-O-Phone' for sales in the United States, or 'Disco Zonofono' for sales in Latin America; the Gramophone and Typewriter Company, which in November 1907 sold the typewriter part of its business becoming the Gramophone Company of London; and the Victor Talking Machine Company of Camden, New Jersey. According to W. R. Moran, the American musicologist, the date he found in the Victor files for making her Zon-O-Phone masters is 8 September, 1904. Philip H. Wade in his Luisa Tetrazzini Discography published in 'The Record Collector' for August 1956, wrote that she at one time denied having made any recordings before 1908, but on being pressed by him admitted doing so 'a long time ago' with Cleofonte Campanini, her brother-in-law, at the piano. As stated in Chapter 4, it was on 10 September 1904 that she signed a contract with Heinrich Conried of the Metropolitan Opera Company in New York for her to commence singing there in late 1905. According to the account in the *New York World* for 29 December 1907, she spent some months during the summer of 1904 in that city and herself negotiated the terms with Conried. There is strong evidence therefore that these early recordings were made during her stay.

Each Zon-O-Phone has a matrix number and two catalogue numbers. Details (with disc sizes) are:

M. 3515 Cat. 2500 later 10000, *Lucia, Mad Scene* labelled 'Rondo'. (10⅝")
M. 3513   "   2501   "   10002, *Il Barbiere di Siviglia, Una voce...* (8⅞") IRCC 3091rr
M. 3511   "   2502   "   10001, *Rigoletto, Caro nome* (10⅝")
M. 3508   "   2503   "   10003, *Romeo e Guilietta, Nella calma* (8⅞")
M. 3516   "   2504   "   10004, *La Sonnambula, Ah, non giunge* (8⅞") IRCC 3091rr

These bear dark green labels and are brown or black. Speeds for all are 81.82 rpm according to Mr Moran's calculations. He states that 3510,

3512, 3514, and 3517 were by Giulio Rossi. It was with this bass that Tetrazzini eloped to the United States on deserting Pietro Cesari in Havana in May, 1904. Transfers from the first five of these Tetrazzini recordings were included in PEARL GEMM CD 9225, bands 17 to 21.

In the following pages the recording and other details have been taken from the EMI Archives at Hayes for Gramophone Company discs and obtained from W. R. Moran for the Victor ones in the USA. Matrix and take numbers are important in identifying records. The Gramophone Company used another matrix number if any later recordings of an aria or song were made, whereas with Victor the original basic matrix number was retained even though new recordings were later substituted. Tetrazzini's Gramophone Company recordings were at first also marketed by Victor in the USA and listed in their 92,000 series. Once she started recording for Victor in March 1911, the older lists were withdrawn except for five titles which were renumbered in their 88,000 series.

In England, the Gramophone Company initially gave Tetrazzini's records pink labels. When in 1909 the dog listening to a gramophone appeared for the first time on labels, the prefix 'HMV' for His Master's Voice came into use.

Key to record labels on some Tetrazzini reissues (LPs unless otherwise stated)

ASCO 109: American Sterophonic Corp., New York (2 discs set).
ATL 4079: Delta, London.
EJS 223: Golden Age of Opera, E. J. Smith, New York.
EMI CLASSICS: EMI Records Ltd.
GVC 17: Ember, Great Britain.
HER. & XIG: Heritage, London.
HMV COLH 136: HMV, London.
HMB 23: Historic Masters Ltd., Hove, England.
H.R.S.: Historic Record Society, USA.
I.R.C.C: International Record Collectors Club, USA (& 78s).
LCT: RCA VICTOR "Treasury of Immortal Performances"
ORL 210: Olympus Records, London.
PEARL GEM CDS 9221–5: Pavilion Records Ltd., Wadhurst, GB.
QALP 10336: Voce del Padrone, Italy.
ROCOCO 13 & 5361: Ross, Court & Co., Toronto.
U.O.R.C. 105: Unique Opera Record Corporation, USA.
VB: Gramophone Company, London (78s).
VOCE 13: Voce, USA.
WCT: RCA VICTOR (45 r.p.m.) "Treasury of Immortal Performances"

Nimbus Records included in their PRIMA VOCE series a compilation of 19 digital ambisonic Tetrazzini recordings taken from original 78 rpm discs – NI 7808. Pearl brought out a boxed set of 5 CDs (GEMM 9220) also available separately (GEMM 9221–5) entitled 'The Complete Recordings 1903 (sic) – 22'. This, however, does not include all her recordings as further research has revealed. The *Opera News* critic, Mr Innaurato claims that the smoothest transfers he has heard were on a Conductart cassette (CV–1002).

Last of all, EMI issued in 1992, 3 boxed CDs (CHS 7 63802) labelled 'The London Recordings, 1907–22' which therefore does not include Tetrazzini's 1904 Zon-O-Phone recordings, which are in the Pearl collection. J. B. Steane in his review appearing in *The Gramophone* for September that year wrote:

> For quality of recorded sound, I have no doubt that most listeners will get on best with the EMI. The Pearl transfers have their merits, but they are likely to appeal primarily to those who are already well-practised in listening to 78s and who have *a priori* views of what might be called a non-interventionist kind, in the matter of transfers.

According to Alan Blyth in *The Daily Telegraph*, to hear Tetrazzini in all her glory one needs to turn to the EMI three-disc issue.

> The transfers are arrestingly clear and trouble-free. Had Tetrazzini's contemporaries been able to listen to the diva in such wonderful sound they would have bought her discs in even greater numbers than was already the case. Here is a handsome glittering voice of appreciable power capable of technical feats few other singers would think feasible.

Playing Speeds

W. R. Moran contributed the excellent detailed discography to *Enrico Caruso: My Father and My Family* by Enrico Caruso Jr. and Andrew Farkas, published by Amadeus, in which he gives expert advice on how to calculate correct playing speeds. During the early days of gramophone recording those in charge of the studios omitted to note down the speeds at which the turntables were operated. A variation in speed of 4 revolutions per minute altered the pitch (and thus the key) by one-half tone. Not only is the pitch wrong when a record is not played at the speed when originally made, but – far more essential – the vocal tone and quality is distorted. (In a letter to me, Mr Moran stressed that speeds must be calculated from the Tetrazzini original pressings, as those listed by the Gramophone Company were wrong).

When there is no written evidence of the speeds then employed, these must be calculated by using an instrument correctly tuned. Moran says that an organ is best for this purpose. Otherwise the most convenient way of finding out the speed of a revolving turntable is through placing a stroboscopic card on the playing record. These cards bear designs with varying bands of patterns or lines for particular speeds, which will appear to remain stationary when the turntable is revolving at the speed indicated for each band.

> The numbers shown for suggested playing speeds are equivalent to those on certain standard stroboscopes or are an arithmetical average of speeds falling between two record bands which will appear to be revolving in opposite directions at the same rate. If the listener, using whatever method at his or her disposal, will attempt to adjust the turntable speed as closely as possible to those indicated, the records should be reproduced almost at the original recording speeds.

W. R. Moran, who is regarded as the expert on Victor recordings, has provided me with what his meticulous calculations indicate to be the correct playing speeds for Tetrazzini's Victor discs. Another authority, Richard Bebb, has done the same for the Gramophone Company's published ones.

The recording venue for the Gramophone Company was at 21 City Road, Finsbury Square, London, until July 1912. From then onwards all Tetrazzini's recordings were made at the new studios situated at 1/3 Uxbridge Road, Hayes, Middlesex. The engineer in charge from the commencement of her association with the Company until November 1910 was Will Gaisberg. After that time the work was shared with his brother Fred, W. Hancox, George Dillnutt and Edward Pearce.

The following tables are in chronological order. Gramophone Company details come from the EMI Archives at Hayes and I am most deeply grateful to Ruth Edge and her staff for all their help and guidance during my lengthy visits there, followed by careful replies to my letters and many phone calls. Further assistance came from Richard Bebb, Keith Hardwick, Alan Kelly (whose admirably researched *His Master's Voice* was often consulted), and Tom Peel of the *Recorded Vocal Arts Society*. As regards the Victor recordings, here I am much indebted to W. R. Moran who corrected and added to the draft tables I sent him.

Key

An asterisk * before a Discography number indicates that a NOTE will be found at the end, giving additional information.
All recordings were made by Tetrazzini in Italian unless otherwise indicated – (E) in English; (F) French; (S) Spanish; (Neap.) Neapolitan.
Orchestra (or.) Pianoforte (pf.) Conductor's name shown where employed.

When there are more than one take, the one used is underlined.

When there are two catalogue numbers for a single-faced issue, these are placed one above the other. A parenthesis around a number signifies one assigned but not used. rr = dubbings. (Nos. 48 and 76 at 45 r.p.m).

Dashes in a column indicate that no record bearing that title was issued in that category. If there is a line of dashes under every catalogue number column the record was not published as a 78. This treatment enables it to be shown further along the entry that a recording never issued as a 78 did come out later on LP – as with the 1922 Gramophone Company recordings and Victor's 1920 *Come le rose* and *Gli' angui d'inferno* from *Il Flauto Magico* (the last two issued only on UORC 105).

THE GRAMOPHONE COMPANY, LONDON

Dis. No.	Matrix No. / Date	G&T/HMV Single Face No.	G&T/HMV Double Face No.	Victor Single Face No.	Victor Double Face No.	'78' rpm Reissues	Re-recordings on Long-Playing Discs	Speed of Original Issue
1. *Rigoletto*: Caro nome, che il mio cor – Verdi (or. Percy Pitt)								
	2170f Dec.'07	053141	—	92014	—	—	GEMM CD 9221 ASCO 109 EMI CHS 7 63802 2 ROCOCO R–13	78
2. *Mignon*: Io son Titania (Polonaise) – Thomas (or. P. Pitt)								
	2171f Dec.'07	053142		92015	15–1001	—	GEMM CD 9221 ASCO 109 EMI CHS 7 63802 2	78
3. *Lakmé*: Dov' è l'indiana bruna? (Bell Song) – Delibes (or. P. Pitt)								
	2172f Dec.'07	053150		92016	—	—	GEMM CD 9221 ROCOCO R–13 EMI CHS 7 63802 2	78
4. *Dinorah*: Ombra leggiera (Shadow Song) – Meyérbeer (or. P. Pitt)								
	2175f Dec.'07	053143		92017 88298	—	—	GEMM CD 9221 ASCO 109 EMI CHS 7 63802 2	78
5. *Lucia di Lammermoor*: Splendon le sacre faci – Donizetti (or. P. Pitt)								
	2176f Dec.'07	053144		92018	—	—	GEMM CD 9221 ASCO 109 EMI CHS 7 63802 2	78
6. *Le Nozze di Figaro*: Voi che sapete – Mozart (or. P. Pitt)								
	2177f Dec.'07	053145		92019 88300	15–1001	—	GEMM CD 9221 ASCO 109 EMI CHS 7 63802 2	78
7. *Il Barbiere di Siviglia*: Una voce poco fa – Rossini (or. P. Pitt)								
	2178f Dec.'07	053146		92020	—	—	GEMM CD 9221 ASCO 109 EMI CHS 7 63802 2 ROCOCO R–13	78

#	Title	Matrix	Date					Reissues	Year
8.	*La Traviata*: Follie! ... Sempre libera – Verdi (or. P. Pitt)	2179f	Dec.'07	053147	92021	—	—	GEMM CD 9221 / ASCO 109 / EMI CHS 7 63802 2	78
9.	*Don Giovanni*: Batti, batti, o bel Masetto – Mozart (or. P. Pitt)	2180f	Dec.'07	053148	92022	—	—	GEMM CD 9221 / EMI CHS 7 63802 2	78
10.	*Romeo e Giulietta*: Nella calma (Waltz) – Gounod (or. P. Pitt)	2524f	13 Jul.'08	053195 / DB 542	92061 / 88302	6345	—	GEMM CD 9221 / ASCO 109 / EMI CHS 7 63802 2	78
11.	*La Traviata*: E strano! ... Ah, fors' è lui – Verdi (or.)	2573f	Aug.'08	053196	92060	—	—	GEMM CD 9221 / ASCO 109 / EMI CHS 7 63802 2	78
12.	*Mignon*: Io son Titania (Polonaise) – Thomas (or. P. Pitt)	2574f	Aug.'08	—	—	—	—	EMI CHS 7 63802 2	78
13.	*Il Flauto Magico*: Gli angui d'inferno – Mozart (or. P. Pitt)	2585f	Sep.'08	—	—	—	—	EMI CHS 7 63802 2	78
14.	Voci di Primavera – J. Strauss, op. 410 (pf. P. Pitt)	2586f	Sep.'08	053197	—	—	IRCC 148	GEMM CD 9221 / ROCOCO R–13 / EMI CHS 7 63802 2	77
15.	*Un Ballo in Maschera*: Saper vorreste – Verdi (or. P. Pitt)	3076f	25 May '09	053222	92068	—	—	GEMM CD 9221 / ROCOCO R–13 / EMI CHS 7 63802 2	80
16.	*Lucia di Lammermoor*: Regnava nel silenzio – Donizetti (or. P. Pitt)	3077f	25 May '09	053223 / DB 528	92067 / 88303	6396	—	GVC 17 / GEMM CD 9221 / ROCOCO R–13 / NI 7808 / EMI CHS 7 63802 2	80

Dis. No.	Matrix No. Date	G&T/HMV Single Face No.	G&T/HMV Double Face No.	Victor Single Face No.	Victor Double Face No.	'78' rpm Reissues	Re-recordings on Long-Playing Discs	Speed of Original Issue
17.	*Lucia di Lammermoor:* Quando rapito in estasi – Donizetti (or. P. Pitt)							
	3078f 25 May '09	053224	DB 528	—	—	—	GVC 17 / GEMM CD 9221 / EMI CHS 7 63802 2	80
18.	*Il carnevale di Venezia* Part 1 – Benedict (or. P. Pitt)							
	3079f 25 May '09	053225	—	—	—	—	GEMM CD 9221 / EMI CHS 7 63802 2	80
19.	*Il carnevale di Venezia* Part 2 – Benedict (or. P. Pitt)							
	3080f 25 May '09	053226	—	—	—	—	GEMM CD 9221 / EMI CHS 7 63802 2	80
20.	*La Sonnambula:* Ah, non credea mirarti – Bellini (or. P. Pitt)							
	3101f 2 Jun.'09	053227	—	92069	—	—	GVC 17 R–13 / GEMM CD 9221 / EMI CHS 7 63802 2	80
21.	*I Pescatori di Perle:* Siccome un dì – Bizet (or. P. Pitt)							
	3102f 2 Jun.'09	053228	DB 544	—	—	—	GEMM CD 9221 R–13 / EMI CHS 7 63802 2	80
22.	*Aprile* – Tosti (pf. P. Pitt)							
	3103f 2 Jun.'09	053229	DB 538	92070 88306	6336	—	GEMM CD 9221 / EMI CHS 7 63802 2	80
23.	*La Serenata* – Tosti (pf. P. Pitt)							
	3104f 2 Jun.'09	053230	—	(92063)	—	—	GEMM CD 9222 R–13 / EMI CHS 7 63802 2	80
24.	*I Pescatori di Perle:* Brahma, gran Dio! – Bizet (or. P. Pitt)							
	3423f-1,–2 5 Jul.'09	2–053012	DB 544	—	—	—	GEMM CD 9222 R–13 / EMI CHS 7 63802 2	79

25. *Romeo e Giulietta*: Nella calma (Waltz) – Gounod (or. P. Pitt)
    3424f   5 Jul.'09   —   —   —
    3425f   5 Jul.'09   —   —   —

26. *Mirella*: Oh d'amor messaggera (Waltz) – Gounod (or. P. Pitt)
    3426f-1,–2   5 Jul.'09   2–053013   DB 703   —   GEMM CD 9222 / EMI CHS 7 63802 2   79

27. *Las Hijas Del Zebedeo*: Al pensar en el dueño – Carceleras (Chapi) (S) (or. P. Pitt)
    3551f   28 Jul.'09   2–063001   —   GEMM CD 9222 / R–13 / EMI CHS 7 63802 2   80

28. *Linda di Chamounix*: O, luce di quest' anima – Donizetti (or. P. Pitt)
    4576f   2 Nov.'10   2–053035   —   ROC 5361 / GEMM CD 9222 / EMI CHS 7 63802 2   80

29. *I Vespri Siciliani*: Mercè, dilette amiche (Bolero) – Verdi (or. P. Pitt)
    4577f   2 Nov.'10   2–053033   —   GEMM CD 9222 / R–13 / EMI CHS 7 63802 2   80

30. *Semiramide*: Bel raggio lusinghier – Rossini (or. P. Pitt)
    4578f   2 Nov.'10   2–053034   DB 537 / VB 15   —   ROC 5361   GVC 17 / GEMM CD 63802 2 / EMI CHS 7 63802 2   80

31. *L'Eco* – Eckert (pf. P. Pitt)
    4579f   2 Nov.'10   (2–053030)   —   —

32. *Peer Gynt*: Solveig's Song, Op. 23 No. 1 (pf. P. Pitt)
    4580f   2 Nov.'10   2–053031   —   GEMM CD 9222 / EMI CHS 7 63802 2   80

33. *Pur dicesti* – Lotti (pf. P. Pitt)
    4581f   2 Nov.'10   (2–053032)   —   —

VICTOR TALKING MACHINE COMPANY, CAMDEN, N.J., USA

Dis. No.	Matrix No. / Date (B = 10", C = 12")	G/HMV Single Face No.	G/HMV Double Face No.	Victor Single Face No.	Victor Double Face No.	'78' rpm Reissues	Re-recordings on Long-Playing Discs	Speed of Original Issue
34.	*Las Hijas Del Zebedeo*: Al pensar en el dueño – Carceleras (Chapi) (S) (or. W. Rogers)							
	C10057-1 15 Mar.'11	—		—				
	-2 17 Mar.'11	—	—	—	—			
	-3 18 Mar.'11	2-063004	DB 523	88294	—	HRS 1015	GEMM CD 9223	76.00
35.	The Last Rose of Summer – Moore (E) (or. W. Rogers)							
	C10058-1 15 Mar.'11	—		—				
	-2 15 Mar.'11	03241	DB 527	88308	6343		GEMM CD 9223	76.00
36.	*Un Ballo in Maschera*: Saper vorreste – Verdi (or. W. Rogers)							
	C10059-1 15 Mar.'11	2-053048	DB 539	88304	6341		RHA 6008 NI 7808 / GEMM CD 9223	76.00
37.	*La Sonnambula*: Ah non credea – Bellini (or. W. Rogers)							
	C10064-1 16 Mar.'11	2-053049	DB 533	88305	6396		GEMM 9223	76.00
38.	*La Traviata*: Ah, fors' è lui . . . Sempre libera – Verdi (or. W. Rogers)							
	C10065-1 16 Mar.'11	2-053038	—	88293	6344		GEMM CD 9223	76.00
39.	Il carnevale di Venezia Part 1 – Benedict (or. W. Rogers)							
	C10066-1 16 Mar.'11	2-053043	DB 689	88291	6339		GEMM CD 9223	76.00
40.	Il carnevale di Venezia Part 2 – Benedict (or. W. Rogers)							
	C10067-1 16 Mar.'11	2-053044	DB 689	88292	6339		GEMM CD 9223	76.00

41. *Lucia di Lammermoor:* Splendon le sacre faci – Donizetti (or. W. Rogers; flute Walter Oesterreicher)
    C10068–1   16 Mar.'11   2–053047   DB 535   88299   6337   —   NI 7808   GVC 17 / GEMM CD 9223   76.00

42. *L'Eco* – Eckert (or. W. Rogers)
    C10070–1   17 Mar.'11   —   —   —   —
    C10070–2   18 Mar.'11   2–053040   DB 530   88311   6342   NI 7808   GVC 17 / GEMM CD 9224   76.00

*43. *Il Barbiere di Siviglia:* Una voce poco fa – Rossini (or. W. Rogers)
    C10071–1   17 Mar.'11   2–053046   DB 690 / DB 1979   88301   6337 / 7883   NI 7808   GVC 17 / GEMM CD 9224   76.00

44. *La Perle du Brésil:* Charmant oiseau – David (F) (or. W. Rogers; flute Walter Oesterreicher)
    C10072–1   17 Mar.'11   (2–033026)   —   88318   6343   —   GEMM CD 9224   76.00

45. *Mignon:* Io son Titania (Polonaise) – Thomas (or. W. Rogers)
    C10073–1   17 Mar.'11   2–053042   —   88296   6342   —   NI 7808   GEMM CD 9224   76.00

*46. *Rigoletto:* Caro nome che il mio cor – Verdi (or. W. Rogers)
    C10074–1   18 Mar.'11   2–053050   DB 536 / DB 1979   88295   6344 / 7883   NI 7808   GEMM CD 9224   76.00

*47. *Lakmé:* Dov'è l'indiana bruna? (Bell Song) – Delibes (or. W. Rogers)
    C10075–1   18 Mar.'11   (2–053039)   —   88297   —   NI 7808   GEMM CD 9224   76.00
       –2   18 Feb.'13   —   —   88297(R)   6340   GEMM CD 9224   76.60(R)

48. *La Sonnambula:* Ah non giunge – Bellini (or. W. Rogers; flute C. Barone)
    C10076–1   18 Mar.'11   2–053041   DB 533   88313   6345 / 17–0045rr   NI 7808: WCTIO: LCT 1006 / GEMM CD 9224   76.00

49. *Variazioni* – Proch (or. W. Rogers; flute C. Barone)
    C10077–1   18 Mar.'11   2–053045   DB 523   88307   6336   —   NI 7808   GEMM CD 9224   76.00

THE GRAMOPHONE COMPANY, LONDON

Dis. No.	Matrix No.	Date	G/HMV Single Face No.	G/HMV Double Face No.	Victor Single Face No.	Victor Double Face No.	'78' rpm Reissues	Re-recordings on Long-Playing Discs	Speed of Original Issue
50. The Last Rose of Summer – Moore (pf. P. Pitt)									
	ac5160f	11 Jul.'11	—		—	—	—	—	—
51. *La Perle du Brésil*: Charmant oiseau – David (F) (or.)									
	ac5161f	11 Jul.'11	2–033027	—	—	—	—	GEMM CD 9222 / EMI CHS 63802 2	82
52. Variazioni – Proch (pf. P. Pitt)									
	ac5162f	11 Jul.'11	—		—	—	—	—	—
53. *Carmen*: Io dico, no non, son paurosa – Bizet (or.)									
	ac5163f	11 Jul.'11	2–053060	—	—	—	—	GEMM CD 9222 / EMI CHS 63802	82
54. *La Traviata*: Ah, fors' è lui … Follie! – Verdi (or.)									
	ac5164f	11 Jul.'11	2–053059	DB 531	—	—	—	GEMM CD 9222 / EMI CHS 7 63802 2	82
	ac5165f	11 Jul.'11	—		—	—	—	—	—
55. *Lakmé*: Candida Durga (Preghiera) – Delibes (chorus & or.)									
	ac5166f	11 Jul.'11	2–053055	DB 532	—	—	IRCC 27	GEMM CD 9222 / EMI CHS 7 63802 2	82
56. *Lakmé*: Dov' è l'indiana bruna? (Bell Song) – Delibes (or.)									
	ac5167f	11 Jul.'11	2–053056	DB 532	—	—	—	GEMM CD 9222 / EMI CHS 7 63802 2	82
57. *Don Giovanni*: Batti, batti o bel Masetto – Mozart (or.)									
	ac5168f	11 Jul.'11	2–053057	DB 537	—	—	—	GEMM CD 9222 / EMI CHS 7 63802 2	82
58. *La Traviata*: Sempre libera – Verdi (or.)									
	ac5169f	11 Jul.'11	2–053062	DB 531	—	—	—	GEMM CD 9222 / EMI CHS 7 63802 2	82

59. *Aida:* L'insana parola ... I sacri nomi – Verdi (or.)
    ac5170f   11 Jul.'11   2–053064   DB 529 | IRCC 27 | GEMM CD 9222 / EMI CHS 7 63802 2 | 82

60. *Linda di Chamounix:* O, luce di quest' anima – Donizetti (or.)
    ai5179f   14 Jul.'11   2–053061   — | — | GVC 17 / GEMM CD 9222 / EMI CHS 7 63802 2 | 82

61. *Amleto:* Ed ora a voi (Mad Scene) – Thomas (or.)
    ai5180f   14 Jul.'11   2–053063   DB 543 | — | GEMM CD 9222 / EMI CHS 7 63802 2 | 82

62. *Mignon:* Io son Titania (Polonaise) – Thomas (or.)
    ai5181f   14 Jul.'11   2–053058   DB 540 | — | GEMM CD 9222 / EMI CHS 7 63802 2 | 82

63. Deh, torno mio bene (Air and variations) – Proch (or. with flute obbligato by C. Barone)
    ai5182f   14 Jul.'11   2–053065   DB 523 | — | GEMM CD 9222 / EMI CHS 7 63802 2 | 82

THE VICTOR TALKING MACHINE COMPANY, CAMDEN, N.J., USA

64. *Lucia di Lammermoor:* Chi mi frena (w. Caruso, Amato, Journet, Jacoby & Bada; or. W. Rogers)
    C11446–1,–2   10 Jan.'12   —   96201 | — | GVC 17 / GEMM CD 9224 | 76.00
    –3,–4   19 Jan.'12   2–054034   16–5000

65. *Rigoletto:* Bella figlia dell' amore – Verdi (w. Caruso, Amato, Jacoby; or. W. Rogers)
    C11447–1,   10 Jan.'12   —
    –2,   19 Jan.'12   —
    –3,–4   13 Feb.'12   2–054038   15–1019 | IRCC–36 | NI 7808 / GEMM CD 9224 | — / 77.43

66. The Swallows – Cowen (E) (or. W. Rogers)
    C11589–1   13 Feb.'12   03280   88349   6338   DB 526 | — | GEMM CD 9224 | 77.43

THE GRAMOPHONE COMPANY, HAYES, MIDDLESEX

No. / Title / Matrix	Date	Cat.		Reissue	Reissue	
67. *Il Trovatore*: Tacea la notte – Verdi (or.)						
HO187ac	9 Jul.'12	—	—	—	—	—
68. *La Sonnambula*: Come per me sereno … Sovra il sen – Bellini (or.)						
HO188ac	9 Jul.'12	2-053070	—	IRCC 148	GVC 17 / GEMM CD 9223 / EMI CHS 7 63802 2	79
HO189ac	9 Jul.'12	—	—	—	—	—
69. O che assorta (Grande Valse) – Venzano (or.)						
HO190ac	9 Jul.'12	—	—	—	—	—
70. *Gli Ugonotti*: O vago suol – Meyerbeer (or.)						
HO191ac	9 Jul.'12	2-053071	VB 41	HRS 1015	ROC 5361 / GEMM CD 9223 / EMI CHS 7 63882 2	79
71. *I Puritani*: Vien diletto – Bellini (or.)						
HO192ac	10 Jul.'12	—	—	—	—	—
HO193ac	10 Jul.'12	2-053072	—	IRCC 116	GEMM CD 9223 / EMI CHS 7 63802 2 / GVC 17	79
72. Home, sweet home – Bishop (or.)						
HO194ac	10 Jul.'12	—	—	—	—	—
HO195ac	10 Jul.'12	03286	DB 527		GEMM CD 9223 / EMI CHS 7 63802 2	79
73. O che assorta (Grande Valse) – Venzano (or.)						
HO196ac	10 Jul.'12	2-053073	—	—	GEMM CD 9223 / EMI CHS 7 63802 2	79
HO197ac	10 Jul.'12	—	—	—	—	—
74. The Swallows – Cowen (E) (or. P. Pitt)						
HO 198ac	10 Jul.'12	—	—	—	—	—

THE VICTOR TALKING MACHINE COMPANY, CAMDEN, N.J., USA

Dis. No.	Matrix No.	Date	G/HMV Single Face No.	G/HMV Double Face No.	Victor Single Face No.	Victor Double Face No.	'78' rpm Reissues	Re-recordings on Long-Playing Discs	Speed of Original Issue
75. Rhapsody (Reginald De Koven) (E) (Vlc. R. Bourdon; or. W. Rogers)									
	8–12916–1	18 Feb.'13	—			—	—	—	—
76. *Rosalinda*: Meco varrai su quella (Pastorale) – Veracini (or. W. Rogers)									
	C12917–1	18 Feb.'13	—						
	–2	21 Feb.'13	2–053092	DB 690	88432	17–0363 rr	—	WCT–62: LCT 1039 / GEMM CD 9224	76.60
77. *Il Trovatore*: Tacea la notte placida – Verdi (or. W. Rogers)									
	C12918–1	18 Feb.'13	2–053084	DB 540	88420	6346	—	GEMM CD 9224 / NI 7808	77.42
78. *Il Trovatore*: D'amor sull'ali rosee – Verdi (or. W. Rogers)									
	C12928–1	19 Feb.'13	2–053085	DB 536	88426	6346	—	GEMM CD 9224	77.42
79. (a) Rhapsody (De Koven) (E); (b) Serenata inutile (Brahms, Op. 84 No. 4) (I) (Vlc. Bourdon; or. W. Rogers)									
	C12929–1	19 Feb.'13	2–053086	—	88427	—	—	ROC 5361 / GEMM CD 9224 / NI 7808	77.42
80. O che assorta (Grande Valse) – Venzano, Op. 10 (or. W. Rogers)									
	C12930–1	19 Feb.'13	2–053087	DB 530	88423	6341	—	GEMM CD 9224 / NI 7808	77.42
81. *Dinorah*: Ombra leggiera – Meyerbeer (or. W. Rogers)									
	C12931–1	19 Feb.'13	2–053207	DB 534	88298 R	6340	—	GEMM CD 9224	77.42
82. Bonnie Sweet Bessie – Gilbert (E) (or. W. Rogers)									
	C12944–1	21 Feb.'13	03336	DB 526	88428	6338	—	GEMM CD 9224	76.60

THE GRAMOPHONE COMPANY, HAYES, MIDDLESEX

Dis. No.	Matrix No. C = 12"	Date	G/HMV Single Face No.	G/HMV Double Face No.	Victor Single Face No.	Victor Double Face No.	'78' rpm Reissues	Re-recordings on Long-Playing Discs	Speed of Original Issue
83. *La Traviata*: Addio del passato – Verdi (or.)									
	HO519af	26 Sep.'13	2–053096	DB 539	—	—	IRCC 116 rr	GEMM CD 9223 / NI 7808 / EMI CHS 7 63802 2	77
84. *Crispino e la comare*: Io non sono – Ricci (or.)									
	HO520af	26 Sep.'13	2–053093	DB 535 / VB 41	—	—	—	ROC 5361 / GEMM CD 9223 / EMI CHS 7 63802 2	77
85. *La Stella Del Nord*: La, la, la (Grand Air) – Meyerbeer (or. flutes Gilbert Barton, Robert Murchie)									
	HO521af	26 Sep.'13		DB 542	—	—	IRCC 3091	GEMM CD 9225 / EMI CHS 7 63802 2	77
	HO522af	26 Sep.'13	2–053094	VB 15	—	—	rr		
86. *La Serenata*: Leggenda valacca (Angel's Serenade) – Braga (violin, harp and piano)									
	HO526af	26 Sep.'13	(2–053095)	—	—	—	—	—	—

THE VICTOR TALKING MACHINE COMPANY, CAMDEN, N.J., USA

87. Tre giorni son che Nina – Ciampi, arr. F. Dulcken (or. W. Rogers)
C14815-1, –2 11 May '14 2–053117 — 88505 | GEMM CD 9225 NI 7808 | 76.60

88. Somewhere a voice is calling – Tate (or. W. Rogers)
C14816-1, –2, 11 May '14 (88501) | VOCE 88 | 76.60
–3 2 Nov.'20

89. *Linda di Chamounix:* Ah! tardai troppe... O luce di quest' anima – Donizetti (or. W. Rogers)
C14817-1 11 May '14 DB 543 | —
–2 13 May '14 2–053115 88506 | GEMM CD 9225 | 76.60

90. *Semiramide:* Bel raggio lusinghier – Rossini (or. W. Rogers)
C14818-1 11 May '14 | —

91. *Carmen:* Io dico no non son paurosa – Bizet (or. W. Rogers)
C14819-1, –2 11 May '14 2–053113 DB 703 88503 | 6397 | GEMM CD 9225 | 76.60

92. *Peer Gynt:* Canzone di Solveig – Grieg, Op. 23, No. 1 (or. W. Rogers)
C14820-1 12 May '14 88508 | —
–2 13 May '14 2–053116 DB 534 | GEMM CD 9225 | 76.60

93. *La Forza Del Destino:* Pace, pace mio Dio – Verdi (or. W. Rogers)
C14821-1 12 May '14 2–053114 DB 538 88502 | 6397 | GEMM CD 9225 | 76.60

94. *Vespri Siciliani:* Mercè diletti amici – Verdi (V) (or. W. Rogers)
C14822-1 12 May '14 2–053118 DB 529 88504 | GEMM CD 9225 NI 7808 | 76.60

95. *Amleto:* Mad Scene – Thomas (or. W. Rogers)
C14823-1 13 May '14 | —

THE GRAMOPHONE COMPANY, HAYES, MIDDLESEX

Dis. No.	Matrix No. Date	G/HMV Single Face No.	G/HMV Double Face No.	Victor Single Face No.	Victor Double Face No.	'78' rpm/ Reissues	Re-recordings on Long-Playing Discs	Speed of Original Issue
96.	*La Forza del Destino:* Creda sventura – Verdi: Opening 'Pace, mio Dio' omitted. (or.) HO547c 20 Jun.'14	(2-053106)	—	—	—	HMB 23	EMI CHS 7 63802 2	80
97.	Somewhere a voice is calling – Tate (E) (or.) HO548c 20 Jun.'14	(03389)	—	—	—	—	EMI CHS 7 63802 2	80
98.	*Rosalinda:* Meco verrai su quella (Pastorale) – Veracini (or.) HO550c 20 Jun.'14	(2-053107)	—	—	—	—	ROC 5361 EJS 23 NI 7808 GEMM CD 9223 EMI CHS 7 63802 2	80
99.	*Fra Diavolo:* Or son sole – Auber (or.) HO551c 20 Jun.'14	—	—	—	—	—	—	—
100.	*Faust:* Ah! è strano (Jewel Song) – Gounod (or.) HO552c 20 Jun.'14	(2-053108)	—	—	—	HMB 23	ROC 5361 EJS 23 GEMM CD 9223 EMI CHS 7 63802	80
101.	La Serenata: Leggenda valacca (Angel's Serenade) – Braga (violin, harp and piano) HO553c 20 Jun.'14	—	—	—	—	—	—	—
102.	La Serenata: Leggenda valacca (Angel's Serenade) – Braga (violin, harp and piano) HO554c 20 Jun.'14	(2-053109)	—	—	—	—	ROC 5361 EJS 23 GEMM CD 9223 EMI CHS 7 63802 2	80
103.	Tre giorni son che Nina – song attrib. Ciampi (or.) HO1020b 13 Jul.'14	(7-53013)	—	—	—	—	ROC 5361 EMI CHS 7 63802 2	—

Dis. No.	Matrix No. Date	G/HMV Single Face No.	G/HMV Double Face No.	Victor Single Face No.	Victor Double Face No.	'78' rpm Reissues	Re-recordings on Long-Playing Discs	Speed of Original Issue
THE VICTOR TALKING MACHINE COMPANY, CAMDEN, N.J., USA								
104.	Come le rose – Lama (or. Joseph Pasternack) B24675-1,-2 2 Nov.'20	—		—		—	UORC 105	—
105.	Il Flauto Magico: Gl'angui d'inferno – Mozart (or. J. Pasternack) B24676-1,-2 2 Nov.'20	—		—		—	UORC 105	—
THE GRAMOPHONE COMPANY, HAYES, MIDDLESEX								
*106.	Viens près de moi – Daniderff (F) (with Toto Amici, guitar) Bb1807-1,-2 11 Sep.'22	—		—		—	—	—
*107.	Vous dansez, Marquise – Lemaire (F) (with Toto Amici, guitar) Bb1808-1,-2 11 Sep.'22	—		—		—	ROC 5361 GEMM CD 9225 EMI CHS 7 63802	—
*108.	Piccolo amore – Lama (with Attilio Baggiore, tenor, Toto Amici, guitar) Bb1809-1,-2 11 Sep.'22	—		—		—	ROC 5361 GEMM CD 9225 EMI CHS 7 63802 2 EMI CHS 7 63802 2	—
*109.	Voce e notte – De Curtis (with Toto Amici, guitar) Bb1811-1,-2 11 Sep.'22	—		—		—	—	—
*110.	Cara piccina – Lama (with Toto Amici, guitar) Bb1818-1,-2 13 Sep.'22	—		—		—	ROC 5361 GEMM CD 9225 EMI CHS 7 63802 2	—

*111. Nuttata napulitana – Valente: Neap. (with Toto Amici, guitar)
Bb1819-1,-2 13 Sep.'22 — | ROC 5361 GEMM CD 9225 EMI CHS 7 63802 2

*112. *Madame Sherry*: Je n'sais comment – Hoschna (F) (with Toto Amici, guitar)
Bb1820-1,-2 13 Sep.'22 — ROC 5361 GEMM CD 9225 EMI CHS 7 63802 2

*113. So' nnammurata 'e te! – De Curtis: Neap. (with Toto Amici, guitar)
Bb1821-1,-2 13 Sep.'22 — ROC 5361 GEMM 9225 EMI CHS 7 63802 2

*114. O mare canta! – Lama: Neap. (with Toto Amici, guitar)
Bb1824-1,-2 13 Sep.'22 — ROC 5361 GEMM 9225 EMI CHS 7 63802 2

*115 I Milioni d'Arlecchino Serenata – Drigo (or. P. Pitt)
Bb1835-1,-2 15 Sep.'22 — EMI CHS 7 63802 2

*116. Come le rose – Lama (or. P. Pitt)
Bb1836-1,-2 15 Sep.'22 — GEMM CD 9225 EMI CHS 7 63802 2

*117. Parla valse – Arditi (or. P. Pitt)
Cc1837-1,-2 15 Sep.'22 — |

*118. Serenata – Toselli (or. P. Pitt)
Bb1883-1   23 Sep.'22 — |

*119. *I Puritani:* Son vergin vezzosa in ve stadi sposa (Rondo) – Bellini (or. P. Pitt)
Bb1884-1,-2 23 Sep.'22 — |

*120. *Rigoletto:* È il sol dell'anima – Verdi (w. Attilio Baggiore; or. P. Pitt)
Cc1885-1   23 Sep.'22 — |

Notes

*43 Re-recorded electrically with added new orchestra and numbered under each category: 2 B–5032–1 DB 1979 V 7883 New Speed 78.26.

*46 Re-recorded electrically with added new orchestra and numbered under each category: 2 B–5033–1 DB 1979 V 7883 New Speed 78.26.

*47 2 (R) – a notation advising dealers that the original recording issued under this catalog number had been replaced by a new version. In this case there was a remake in 1913 at a different speed, 76.60.

*81 The original issue of catalog number 88298 had been a renumbering of 92017 (2175f). The symbol (R) advised dealers that a new version had been substituted.

*106–20 All these 1922 recordings made at Hayes have 'Rejected' written across each entry on the recording sheets preserved in the EMI Archives. Nos 115 to 120 were made there on behalf of the Victor Talking Machine Co. All the matrixes were then destroyed. White label sample pressings given to Tetrazzini were retained by her and passed into the possession of her husband Pietro Vernati who sold them to people in Rome. A. G. Ross of Rococo Records, Toronto, on a visit there bought the samples for Nos 107–8, 110–14 and they were published on Side 2 of ROCOCO 5361. The samples for Nos 115–6 were bought by Luciano di Cave of Rome who lent them to EMI and they were transferred by Keith Hardwick to CHS 7 63802 2 together with recordings on Canadian tapes taken from the Rococo white label samples, obtained from Professor Stratton in Toronto.

Elvira Tetrazzini

Luisa Tetrazzini's second sister made a number of records. Roberto Bauer in *The New Catalogue of Historical Records*, gives the following details:

Black & Silver Columbia, Milano, 1904.

10298	*Manon Lescaut*: In quelle trine morbide (7″)	Puccini
10295	*Zazà*: Non so capir perchè (w. Baldassare) (7″)	Leoncavallo
10296	*Don Giovanni*: Là ci darem la mano (w. Baldassare)	Mozart
10328	*Educande di Sorrento*: Un bacio rendimi (w. Baldassare)	Usiglio

July 1904.

10392	*Traviata*: Un dì felice (w. Santini)	Verdi
10393	*Lucia di Lammermoor*: Verranno a te (w. Santini)	Donizetti
10394	*Rigoletto*: È il sol dell'anima (w. Santini)	Verdi
10395	*Amico Fritz*: Quei fiori son per me (w. Santini)	Mascagni
10396	*Amico Fritz*: Tutto tace (w. Santini) (7″)	Mascagni
10397	*Adriana Lecouvreur*: Tu sei la mia corona (w. Santini) (7″)	Cilea

Fonodisc, Milano, 1906–07.

97	*Don Giovanni*: Là ci darem la mano (w. Baldassare)	Mozart
133	*Bohème*: Dite ben (w. Baldassare)	Puccini
141	*Traviata*: Addio del passato	Verdi
148	*Il libro santo*	Pinsuti
165	*Rigoletto*: Quartetto (w. Del Lungo, Acerbi & Baldassare) 1st part	Verdi
166	*Rigoletto*: Quartetto (w. Del Lungo, Acerbi & Baldassare) 2nd part	Verdi
189	*Rigoletto*: V'ho ingannato (w. Baldassare)	Verdi
250	*Nuvole bianche*	Roessinger
251	*Ave Maria*	Cherubini
298	*Lucia di Lammermoor*: Sestetto (w. Braglia, Zuffo & Galli)	Donizetti
305	*Don Pasquale*: Tornami dir che m'ami (w. Acerbi)	Donizetti
307	*Bohème*: Mi chiamano Mimi	Puccini
357	*Rigoletto*: Giovanna ho dei rimorsi (w. Acerbi)	Verdi
358	*Rigoletto*: È il sol dell'anima (w. Acerbi)	Verdi
373	*Traviata*: Un dì felice (w. Acerbi)	Verdi
462	*Ernani*: O sommo Carlo (w. Martinez-Patti & Baldassare)	Verdi
465	*Forza del destino*: La vergine degli angeli	Verdi
475	*Traviata*: Brindisi (w. Martinez-Patti)	Verdi

Fonografia Nazionale's catalogue dated December 1924 still listed Nos 165 – 166 – 305 – 307 – 357 – 373 – 465 – 475 as on sale, whilst Artiphon in their 1929 one offered Nos 165 – 166 – 307 – 357 – and 373, so these acoustic discs must have sold or Artiphon would not have retained them.
NOTE: *Eva Tetrazzini made no records as far as is known.*

Some Critics' Assessments of Tetrazzini's Records

J. B. Steane wrote in his book *The Grand Tradition* on the subject of vocal art on records, that Tetrazzini's singing in *La Traviata* is genuinely dramatic and that in *Una voce poco fa* she gives:

> not only a glorious display of virtuosity but also a vivid characterisation, snapping out a crisp 'ma', singing her 'amorosa' with nice suggestiveness, and 'prima di cedere' with cunning.[1]

He found that she varied from one recording session to another. *Io son Titania* was better in 1908 than in 1911 – *O luce di quest' anima* superior in 1910 to 1911's version. Listening to the Zonophone recordings made in 1904, Steane had noticed 'some delightful embellishments in the Mad Scene from *Lucia di Lammermoor* omitted in later renderings. *Ah, non credea mirarti* from *La Sonnambula* recorded for Victor in 1911 (2–053049) preserved for posterity her 'immensely exciting decorations'. This disc had 'many marvels'. The phrase *Potri novel vigore* provided an instance. 'After taking a fair-size breath she interpolates a stunning top C and a descending scale from it.' *Ah, non giunge* (2–053041) from the same opera showed Tetrazzini at her best.

> Here is this shining brilliantly projected tone in its sprightliest form, taking the runs, trills and staccatos in sheer joy, singing with just that easy vitality that the spring of the music requires.

Steane adds that she had 'the bright tone of a Bach trumpet'.

Caro nome was the first aria recorded by Tetrazzini for the Gramophone Company in December 1907. Of the recording she made for Victor in 1911 (DB 536), Richard Osborne wrote in *Opera on Record 1*:[2]

> Here is a most magical version and a most winning personality in spite of everything – and everything includes no rests in the opening phrases, fudged low Es and F sharps and a bird-like brilliance in the cadenza. Yet with what

heart-rending innocence the voice can soar: one goes back to the record for
that alone.

In the same volume,[3] he points out that in *Il Barbiere di Siviglia* Rosina
must sing *Una voce* in its original key, E major, if it is to make its full
effect.

> After E major, a key rich in promise, full of splendour but capable of conveying,
> too, an arcane suggestion, F major (the key of the soprano Rosinas) is altogether
> more innocuous, vapid and watery.

While Tetrazzini made a Victor recording in the higher key in 1911 (DB
690), her 1907 Gramophone Company recording (053146) is in E.

> Perhaps the low tessitura at the start does produce a strained discoloured
> quality, but when the music begins to soar, the voice and the personality behind
> it seems limpid and sweet. The magical upward elision in 'e cento trapole', the
> lightening 'ma', the seductively limpid descent on the word 'amorosa' convey
> a sense of play, a silken inventiveness, which no other soprano quite matches.

In *Opera on Record 2*,[4] John T. Hughes recommends Tetrazzini's 14 July
1911 recording of *Io son Titania* for the Gramophone Company
(2–053058), saying that she sounds full of extrovert sparkle that suits
Philine's character. He finds one or two trills not as well formed as they
ought to be and her singing of that third 'ah!' staccato spoiling the desired
effect. 'That, however, is a relatively minor detail in view of the fine
performance with some shimmering descents in semitones.'

In the same volume,[5] Lord Harewood considers the best performance
on record of *Brahma, gran Dio* from *I pescatori di perle* to be that made
by Tetrazzini for the Gramophone Company in July 1909 (2–053012), in
which she 'exhibits a fullness of tone and brilliance of execution without
serious rival'. One of the two early recordings of *Siccome un dì* that he
liked best was the 'uncharacteristically gentle singing' of this, 'as if Leila
were already under the spell of Nadir's obsessive love' (2 June 1909;
053228).

In *Opera on Record 3*,[6] Lord Harewood wrote that having listened to
24 versions of the bolero *Mercè dilette amiche*, from *I vespri siciliani*, he
regards those by Tetrazzini – the one recorded for the Gramophone Company in 1910 (2–053033) and the other for Victor in 1914 (2–053118)
as the best. He comments:

> She was the Horowitz of vocalists and there is an exemplary clarity and firmness
> about all her singing. The London version (1910) unlike the American (1914)
> ends with a top E and each contains some extraordinary singing.

Charles Osborne in the first volume[7] described as 'a vivid example of her
brilliant vocalisation' Tetrazzini's recording not only of the opening section
of the *Lucia di Lammermoor* Mad Scene twice, but also Lucia's Act I

cavatina complete in two parts. This was for the Gramophone Company on 25 May 1909 (053223–4; DB 528).

Michael Scott in his biography of Maria Callas compares her recordings of *Io son Titania* and Proch's *Air and Variations* with those of Tetrazzini.[8] He describes them as 'both sonically primitive'. In the latter's case he finds that one is at once aware of 'facile execution, faultless attack, self assurance and splendidly firm rhythm' which effect is mostly achieved by her taking the florid music 'at what to present day listeners appears a stupendous pace compared with Callas's more expansive tempo'. In his opinion, far from Tetrazzini's speed having a trivializing effect, her command of rhythm proved her to have been an accomplished musician.

Scott continues that even in a piece without any fioritura, like Violetta's *Addio del passato*, Tetrazzini's rendering is musically impressive. 'Her tone is so limpid that she lets the registration of her voice itself freely colour the rise and fall of the vocal line.' He comments that Rossini's Rosina often sounds nothing more than a shrew, but if we listen to Tetrazzini's classic rendering of *Una voce poco fa* (December 1907: 053146) we hear that 'it is possible not only to dazzle but charm too. By so doing she adds another dimension to the characterization: the buffo style'. As I have myself pointed out earlier on in this book, Tetrazzini must have learnt much at the start of her career from the fourteen years' long partnership with Pietro Cesari who excelled in buffo roles.

Scott believes that records show Tetrazzini to have been the last coloratura in the grand tradition to sing florid music 'with the accuracy, brilliance and sweep that Callas was to bring back to this music' But her voice lacked Callas's exceptional range and power.

In his booklet accompanying her London recordings on CD, Michael Aspinall points out that Tetrazzini regarded the Bell Song from *Lakmé* as the most difficult in her repertoire, and of the four records she made of it he selects the first (053150; London, December 1907) as the best. He comments:

> The forward recording catches the beauty of the voice; in the hauntingly oriental opening section she floats up to a soft, sustained high B like a radiant star. Then she becomes dramatic as she describes the young man's plight when attacked by the tiger, and finally off she goes into a brilliant series of staccati as Lakmé imitates the bells.

Aspinall maintains that Callas is the only singer who has ever come within challenging distance of Tetrazzini's imaginative conception and execution of this aria. His sole criticism is that towards the end Tetrazzini is careless about the difficult passage of rapid legato scales 'for which others have substituted some easy staccati – but she does not disappoint with the final trill and high E natural'.

Of Tetrazzini's August 1908 recordings Aspinall considers her *Ah, fors'
è lui* as perhaps the most touching record ever made of this (053196).
Her phrasing is 'exquisitely musical and elegant' – 'all the ornaments in
keeping and adding to the beauty of the aria' – 'the high C in the cadenza,
attacked slowly, swelled to forte and back to piano, is a great *tour de
force*'.

The English recordings of May, June and July 1909 capture the beauty
of Tetrazzini's voice as never before or after in Aspinall's estimation. *Saper
vorreste* is 'a polished and dazzling performance, in which she even
changes words in order to achieve more audacious "bridge-overs" in phrasing'. A string of staccato high Ds is followed by a chromatic scale of two
octaves, 'a "teasing" cadenza musically and dramatically appropriate'. But
Aspinall wishes the repeated 'La la la' were not so open and metallic,
contrasting 'rather grotesquely with the covered primadonna-ish notes on
the upper F sharp and G'. In *Regnava nel silenzio* (053223) she was trying
perhaps too obviously to be dramatic and baby talk intrudes in the passage
of trills where Lucia describes blood reddening the fountain, but 'there
are some very lovely moments ... especially the reprise of the melody at
E l'onda pria'. *Quando rapito* (053224) is

> a wonderful display of full-throated florid singing with a happy lilt, but it ends
> rather suddenly after an unfamiliar ornament (a staccato scale up to high E).

Aspinall wonders whether this was a studio cut or whether she always
sang it that way.

Siccome un dì from *I pescatori di perle* (053228) Aspinall calls 'a model
of lyric soprano singing' with an inimitable, 'quietly unobtrusive final
cadenza'. Her rendering of the 'Carnival of Venice' variations (053225–6)
showed her to be

> a vocal virtuoso without a peer for her staccati, chromatic runs, echo effects,
> swelling and diminishing of a tone, and the ravishing curve of her portamento.

The records made on 2 November 1910 include 'a hauntingly beautiful
Solveig's Song which she sings like a true Leider singer' (2–053031).
Charmant oiseau recorded the following July (2–033027) is 'a blueblooded performance', and her *Io dico, no non, son paurosa* as Micaela
(2–053060) from the same session is sung 'with impeccable legato and
portamento and effective carrying over of phrases'. Aspinall rates it one
of her best. That same year on 14 July Tetrazzini recorded *Ed ora a voi*
from Ophelia's Mad Scene in Thomas's *Hamlet* (2–053063) – which was
to become one of her great numbers at concerts in her later years. Aspinall
writes:

> The performance is effective, and if she is slipshod about details – there is a
> rare musical slip and she does not differentiate between the sobs and the

laughter of poor Ophelia – there is nothing wrong with the chromatic scale up to E natural. . . . She even interpolates some of the flute's part into her own.

Two years later, on 26 September 1913 Tetrazzini was in superb voice when she recorded *Io son sono* from *Crispino e la Comare* (2–053093). The waltz tempo put her on her mettle, and 'the brilliant variations take her up to several sustained high Ds and a fleeting E'. Also that day she recorded the Grand Air from Act II of Meyerbeer's *L'Étoile du nord* (2–053094) and used baby talk to express Catherine's madness affectingly. Aspinall calls this 'one of her most bewilderingly ornate records' which demonstrates her unrivalled precision and brilliance and panache in this remarkable Mad Scene sung here with flautists Gilbert Barton and Robert Murchie on either side of her.

Till now unpublished records include some made in 1914 – possibly overlooked on account of the war. Aspinall praises 'the sparkling, caressing and dainty way' in which Tetrazzini sings the 18th century music of the pastorale from Veracini's *Rosalinda* (2–053107). He describes as one of her most touching successes the singing to harp and violin accompaniment of Braga's *Serenata* in which she gives her violinist lessons in portamento and phrasing (2–053109).

The music critic Herman Klein, who knew Tetrazzini published comments on her records in *The Gramophone* comparing her singing of certain arias with that of other sopranos. These can be found in *Herman Klein and The Gramophone* edited by William R. Moran and published by Amadeus Press in 1990.

Notes

1. Steane, J. B. (1974), *The Grand Tradition*, London: Duckworth, p. 72.
2. *Opera on Record 1* (1982) (ed. Alan Blyth), London: Hutchinson, p. 217.
3. ibid., p. 149.
4. *Opera on Record 2* (1983) (ed. Alan Blyth), London: Hutchinson, p. 145.
5. ibid., p. 190.
6. *Opera on Record 3* (1984) (ed. Alan Blyth), London: Hutchinson, p. 107.
7. *Opera on Record 1*, p. 188.
8. Scott, Michael (1991), *Maria Callas*, London: Simon & Schuster, pp. 71, 73, 134.
9. Aspinall, Michael (1992), Booklet accompanying Luisa Tetrazzini, *The London Recordings*, EMI Classics, CHS 7 63802 2.

Bibliography

Agliati, Mario (1967), *Il Teatro Apollo di Lugano*, Istituto Editoriale Ticinese.

Alcari, C. (1929), *Il Teatro Regio di Parma nella sua storia dal 1883 al 1929*, Officina Grafica Fresching, Parma.

Aldrich, Richard (1941), *Concert Life in New York, 1902–1925*, New York: Putnam.

Aldrich, Richard (1928), *Musical Discourses from The New York Times*, London: Humphrey Mitford.

Bauer, Roberto (1947), *The New Catalogue of Historical Records*, 1898–1908/1909. London: Sidgwick & Jackson Ltd.

Benoist, André (1938), *The Accompanist*, New Jersey: Paganini Publications.

Benson, E. F. (1987), *Final Edition*, London: Hogarth Press.

Blyth, Alan (ed.) (1979), *Opera on Record*, London: Hutchinson.

Blyth, Alan (ed.) (1983), *Opera on Record 2*, London: Hutchinson.

Blyth, Alan (ed.) (1984), *Opera on Record 3*, London: Hutchinson.

Bosch, Mariano G. (1910), *Historia del Teatro in Buenos Aires*, Establecimiento Tipografico El Commercial, Buenos Aires.

Caesari, Edgar Herbert (1965), *The Alchemy of Voice*, London: Robert Hale.

Caruso, Dorothy (1946), *Enrico Caruso, His Life and Death*, London: T. Werner Laurie.

Caruso, Enrico Jr., and Farkas, Andrew (1990), *Enrico Caruso: My Father & My Family*, Portland, Oregon: Amadeus Press.

Celletti, Rodolfo (ed.) (1964), *Le Grandi Voci*, Roma: Istituto per la Collaborazione Culturale.

Cervetti, Valerio & Claudio Dal Monte (1980), *Cronologia degli Spettacoli Lirici 1879–1929*, Parma.

Colson, Percy (1932), *Melba*, London: Grayson & Grayson.

Cone, John Frederick (1966), *Oscar Hammerstein's Manhattan Opera Company*, Oklahoma: University of Oklahoma Press.

Davis, Ronald L. (1965), *A History of Opera in the American West*, Englewood Cliffs, New Jersey: Prentice Hall.

Davis, Ronald L. (1966), *Opera in Chicago*, New York: Appleton-Century.

De Oliveiro Castro Cerquera, Paulo (1954), *Um Seculo de Opera em Sao Paulo*, Sao Paulo.

Dickson, Samuel (1955), *The Streets of San Francisco*, Stanford University Press.

Dizionario la Musica (1968), Unione Tipografico Editrice Torinese.

Duey, Philip A. (1951), *Bel Canto in Its Golden Age*, New York: King's Crown Press.

Eaton, Quaintance (1957), *Opera Caravan*, New York: Farrar, Strauss & Cudahy.

Eaton, Quaintance (1965), *The Boston Opera Company*, New York: Appleton-Century.

Farkas, Andrew (1984), *Titta Ruffo*, Westport, Conn.: Greenwood Press.

Ferrarini, Maria (1978), *Parma Teatrale Ottocentesca*, Parma.

Fonseca y Benevides Francisco (1902), *O Real Teatro di S. Carlos de Lisbona-Memorias, 1883–1902*, Lisbon.

Forster, E. M. (1924), *Where Angels Fear to Tread*, London: Edward Arnold.

Frajese, Vittorio (1978), *Dal Costanzi all'Opera*, Rome: Capitolium.

Frassoni, Edilio (1980), *Due Secoli di Lirica a Genova*, Cassa di Risparmia di Genova e Imperia.

Gaisberg, Fred W. (1946), *Music on Record*, London: Robert Hale.

Gesualdo, Vicente (1961), *Historia de la musica en la Argentina*, Buenos Aires: Editorial Beta.

Gonzalez Maestre, Francesco (1901), *Teatro Real, Historia Viva, 1878–1901*, S.A. Madrid: Mundimusica.

Gualerzi, Valeria, Giorgio Gualerzi and Giorgio Rampone (1990), *Momenti di Gloria, Il Regio Teatro di Torino 1740–1936*, Turin: Daniela Piazza Editore.

Hurok, Sol (1947), *Impresario*, London: Macdonald.

Hurst, P. G. (1963), *The Golden Age Recorded*, Lingfield: Oakwood Press.

Klein, Herman (1909) *Unmusical New York*, London and New York: John Lane.

Kolodin, Irving (1953), *The Story of the Metropolitan Opera 1883–1950*, New York: Knopf.

Krehbiel, Henry Edward (1908), *Chapters of Opera*, New York: Henry Holt.

Lahee, Henry C. (1912), *Grand Opera Singers of Today*, Boston: Page.

Lancellotti, Arturo (1958), *Le Voci d'Oro*, Rome: Editori Fratelli Palombi.

Marinelli-Roscioni, Carlo (1987), *Il Teatro di San Carlo*, Naples: Cronologie.

Maxwell, Elsa (1954), *I Married the World*, London: Wm. Heinemann.

Moore, Edward C. (1930), *Forty Years of Opera in Chicago*, New York: Horace Liveright.

Moore, Gerald (1983), *Furthermore*, London: Hamish Hamilton.

Moore, Jerrold Northrop (1976), *A Voice in Time: The Gramophone of Fred Gaisberg, 1873–1951*, London: Hamish Hamilton.

Moran, William R. (1985), *Nellie Melba: A Contemporary Review*, Westport and London: Greenwood Press.

Moran, William R., ed. (1990), *Herman Klein and The Gramophone*, Portland, Ore.: Amadeus Press.

Moses, Montrose J. (1916), *Heinrich Conried*, New York: Thos. J. Crowell.

Newton, Ivor (1966), *At the Piano*, London: Hamish Hamilton.

Nichols, John Beverley (1949), *All I Could Never Be*, London: Cape.

Olavarria y Ferrari, Enrique (1961), *Reseña historica del teatro en Mexico*, Mexico City: Biblioteca Porrua.

Parker, H. T. (1922), *Eighth Notes*, New York: Dodd Mead.

Pleasants, Henry (1967), *The Great Singers*, London: Gollancz.

Pound, Reginald (1969), *Sir Henry Wood*, London: Cassell.

Radic, Thérèse (1986), *Melba the Voice of Australia*, Melbourne: Macmillan.

Rasponi, Lanfranco (1982), *The Last Prima Donnas*, New York: Alfred A. Knopf.

Rinaldi, Mario (1978), *Due Secoli Di Musica Al Teatro Argentina*, Firenze: Leo S. Olschki Editore.

Rosenthal, Harold D. (1958), *Two Centuries of Opera at Covent Garden*, London: Putnam.

Scott, Michael (1977), *The Record of Singing: To 1914*, London: Duckworth.

Scott, Michael (1988), *The Great Caruso*, London: Hamish Hamilton.

Shaw, Bernard (1932), *Music in London 1890–94*, London: Constable.

Shawe-Taylor, Desmond, 'A Gallery of Great Singers: 13 – Luisa Tetrazzini', *Opera*, Sept. 1963, pp. 596–8.

Sheean, Vincent (1956), *The Amazing Oscar Hammerstein*, London: Weidenfeld & Nicolson.

Steane, J. B. (1974), *The Grand Tradition*, London: Duckworth.

Strong, L. A. G. (1947), *John McCormack: The Story of a Singer*, London: Methuen.

Subira, José (1949), *Historia y anécdotario del teatro Real*, Madrid.

Tetrazzini, Luisa (1921), *My Life of Song*, London: Cassell.

Tetrazzini, Luisa (1923), *How to Sing*, London: C. Arthur Pearson.

Tetrazzini, Luisa (1909), *Caruso and Tetrazzini on the Art of Singing*, New York: The Metropolitan Company (Dover reprint 1975).

Verdi, Fortunino Giuseppe (1942), *Verdi: The Man in His Letters*, New York: L. B. Fischer.

Viglione Borghese, Domenico (1939), *Due Ore Di Buon Umore*, Milan: Edizione Grafiche Alba.

Wood, Henry J. (1938), *My Life of Music*, London: Gollancz.

Ybarra, Thomas R. (1954), *Caruso*, London: Cresset Press.

Sources

Sources for information about performances given in the main text and in the Chronology are also as follows:

DAILY NEWSPAPERS

Belfast Newsletter
Berliner Lokalanzeiger
Birmingham Post
Bohemia, Prague
Boston Evening Telegraph
Boston Evening Transcript
Boston Globe
Boston Herald
Boston Post
Brooklyn Eagle
Chicago Daily Tribune
Chicago Evening Post
Christian Science Monitor
Cincinnati Enquirer
Cleveland Plain Dealer
Colonia Svizzera
Corriere della Sera, Milan
Daily Express, London
Daily Graphic, London
Daily Mail, London
Daily News, London
Daily Sketch, London
Daily Telegraph, London
El Dia, Montevideo
Diario della Marina, Havana

Epoca, Bucharest
La Epoca, Madrid
Evening Mail, Dublin
Evening Standard, London
Freeman's Journal, Dublin
Glasgow Herald
Globe & Commercial Advertiser, New York
El Imparcial, Mexico City
L'Indépendance Roumaine, Bucharest
Irish Independent
Irish Times, Dublin
Jornal de Commercio, Rio de Janeiro
Kurser Warszawski, Warsaw
La Nación, Buenos Aires
Leicester Mercury
Liverpool Daily Post
Los Angeles Times
Manchester Guardian
Neue Preussische Zeitung, Berlin
New York Telegraph
New York Times
New York Tribune

Novoe Vremia, St Petersburg
O Estado de Sao Paulo
Pietersburgskiia Viedomostim
Philadelphia Inquirer
Philadelphia Record
Pittsburgh Post
La Prensa, Buenos Aires
La Riforma, Rome
Russkaia Viedomosti, Moscow
St Louis Globe Democrat
San Francisco Bulletin
San Francisco Call
San Francisco Chronicle
San Francisco Examiner
Sanktpeteraburgskiia Viedomosti, St Petersburg
Scotsman, Edinburgh
The Spectator, London
The Standard, Buenos Aires
The Times, London
The Washington Daily Post
Western Mail, Cardiff
Westminster Gazette, London

THEATRICAL, LITERARY AND MUSICAL NEWSPAPERS AND PERIODICALS

Cosmorama Pittorico, Milan
Era, London
Gazzetta Musicale di Milano
Il Mondo Artistico, Milan
Musical America, New York
Musical Courier, New York
Musical Standard, London
Musical Times, London

Musical World, London
Rassegna Melodrammatica, Milan
The Record Collector, England
Rivista Teatrale Melodrammatica, Milan
Il Trovatore, Milan
The Voice, London

Index